Parental Overprotection

Parental Overprotection
A Risk Factor in Psychosocial Development

Gordon Parker, M.D., F.R.A.N.Z.C.P.

Professor of Psychiatry
School of Psychiatry
University of New South Wales
Sydney, Australia

GRUNE & STRATTON

A Subsidiary of Harcourt Brace Jovanovich, Publishers
New York   London
Paris   San Diego   San Francisco   São Paulo
Sydney   Tokyo   Toronto

© 1983 by Grune & Stratton, Inc.

All rights reserved. No part of this publication may be reproduced or transmitted in any form or by any means, electronic or mechanical, including photocopy, recording, or any information storage and retrieval system, without permission in writing from the publisher.

Grune & Stratton, Inc.
111 Fifth Avenue
New York, New York 10003

Distributed in the United Kingdom by
Grune & Stratton, Inc. (London) Ltd.
24/28 Oval Road, London NW 1

Library of Congress Catalog Number 83-48653
International Standard Book Number 0-8089-1557-6
Printed in the United States of America

*No cord nor cable can
so forcibly draw, or hold
so fast, as love can do
with a twined thread.*

—Robert Burton, *Anatomy of Melancholy*

Contents

Preface	ix
Acknowledgments	xv

PART I.	GENERAL CONSIDERATIONS AND OVERVIEW OF PARENTAL OVERPROTECTION	1
1.	Clinical Examples of Parental Overprotection	3
2.	Fictional Descriptions of Parental Overprotection	9
3.	Commentaries and General Studies	14
4.	Consequences of Parental Overprotection	31
5.	The Mother–Child Tie: Its Nature and Factors Influencing Its Evolution	41

PART II.	MEASUREMENT OF PARENTAL OVERPROTECTION	85
6.	Studies Attempting to Define and Calibrate Parental Overprotection	87
7.	Development of the Parental Bonding Instrument and the Parent Opinion Form	95

PART III.	RESEARCH STUDIES	127
8.	Schizophrenia	131

9.	Depression	152
10.	Anxiety	174
11.	Phobic States	185
12.	Asthma	195
13.	Transsexualism	203
14.	Dependency, Hypochondriasis, and Utilization of Primary Physicians	210
15.	Cross-cultural Studies of Parental Overprotection: Jewish and Greek Families in Australia	222
16.	Influences on Maternal Overprotection	233
17.	Conclusion	268

Appendices	287
References	297
Index	317

Preface

> *"Hence it is that men come to resent, of all things, protection, because it so often means restriction of their liberty."*
> —*Bernard Shaw*

Parental overprotection is a subject that has almost entirely escaped close attention by psychiatrists. Apart from the careful clinical observations made by Levy (1943) of a small group of overprotective mothers some 40 years ago, subsequent considerations have generally been derivative or simplistic. This book is offered as a comprehensive review; as a research analysis of the determinants of maternal overprotection and its relevance to abnormal development; as a report of a new and efficient research method to measure high-risk overprotective parenting; and as a stimulus to encourage interest in the potential of the inquiry. Observations on the origins of overprotection may well evoke from the reader a response similar to the comment Dr. Johnson made about Lord Lyttelton—that the author has merely ended up telling "the world what the world had all his life been telling him"—but let that be.

Clinical work with a number of patients suffering from situational depressive disorders stimulated my interest in parental overprotection. Such patients described their parents in two broad ways: one parental style is distinguished by an insufficiency of care and the other by overprotection and control. In a clinically based book (Parker, 1977), I suggested that such broad distortions in parental style could be termed "underbonding" and "overbonding," respectively, as if the two were categorically distinct. Subsequent research suggested that such a polarization is somewhat misleading: "overbonded" depressives are also likely to report an insufficiency in parental care. The present research suggests that there are two broad types of overprotection: a caring form labeled "affectionate constraint," which is not clearly associated with psychiatric disorder; and a form in which there is an associated decrement in care, labeled "affectionless control," which appears to be strongly associated with several psychiatric disorders and with several anomalies in psychosocial development.

While research reports investigating the parental cradle to neurosis frequently implicate maternal overprotection, a paternal overprotective contribution is rarely noted or investigated. That children also have fathers may be the aphorism for child development researchers in the 1980s, but it is a salient point nevertheless. As Greenburg (1964) noted: "You don't have to be either Jewish or a mother to be a Jewish mother." Along with Jewish mothers, the research assesses the relevance of paternal overprotection.

Reference to the literature reveals that maternal overprotection has been defined in a variety of ways and that it has been incriminated as a causal influence in virtually all psychiatric disorders known to classificatory systems; it has been proposed as a contributing factor to psychosomatic disorders ranging from asthma to rheumatoid arthritis; and it has been promoted as a marked deleterious influence on personality development—although such propositions have rarely been subjected to critical analyses. In this book an attempt is made to define, via clinical, literary, and statistical analyses, the key constructs of parental overprotection. Detailed reviews and research studies are then used to evaluate the relevance of parental overprotection to a number of psychiatric and other disorders.

Community concerns about sequelae of maternal overprotection appear to be timeless and institutionalized in the myths and legends of many cultures. Anthony (1974) draws attention to the messages in the tales of Achilles and Balder. Achilles' mother, Thetis, hearing of his destiny, tried to protect him by immersion in the river Styx and later disguised him as a girl to prevent his induction into the army. In the Teutonic myth, Frigg had a premonition of danger concerning her beautiful son Balder. She sought a vow from all on earth not to harm him, but overlooked the mistletoe, which was subsequently used by an envious god to kill Balder. Anthony (1974) argues that such myths offer a warning to mothers: despite manipulation of the external environment, any attempt by a mother to foster invulnerability in a child can never be complete, and "the incomplete immunity is always purchased at high psychological cost to both parent and child." Parents and children are directed by myths and legends to set their sights on Hercules and other heroic figures instead. In such stories, as Anthony (1974) notes, "Rather than being overprotected from risk, the hero is constantly exposed to it and seems to gain in both confidence and competence from each encounter." By such endeavors the child achieves a "truer invulnerability, one that is self-generated and enduring, in spite of overwhelming hazards." Myths and legends thus serve as a constant warning to parents about the pointlessness of their being overprotective.

The endurance and popularity of such polarized myths suggest an awareness of the salience of parental overprotection and its sequelae over time. It is nevertheless likely that the issue is of varying relevance in differing cultures and at different times. It is my impression that concerns about overprotection attracted the interest of parents and observers rather extremely in the 1940s, at least in North America. Psychiatrists also appeared to be preoccupied with a nuance of overprotection at that time, and everything was Oedipal in its own way. Perhaps one should not be too disparaging about the Oedipal complex when, as Woody Allen said in another context, it is, after all, "sex with someone you love," but I suspect that a preoccupation with Oedipal issues held back psychiatric theorizing and research on the possibility that more central constructs of the overprotective maternal system exist. There are few Oedipal references to be found in this book and even fewer apologies for such an omission.

There is some journalistic support to suggest that community concern about and interest in maternal overprotection are undergoing a resurgence. In one report, examining the extreme interest in Nancy Friday's book, *My Mother/My Self,* which was titled "Remembering Mother Too Much" (*Time,* February 26th, 1979), the writer suggests that the "maternostra theme" had been described as "the great unwritten theme" (by one poet), as "the last liberation" (by the femininist movement), and as "the last taboo" by author Friday. It is journalistic license to suggest that such a love has dared not speak its name when literature is riddled with attempts to describe and dissect the nature of Mrs. Portnoy's complaint.

If it can be accepted, however, that parental overprotection has evoked considerable attention in the past few decades, then it is reasonable to ask why. Apart from changes in family structure, a more general reason may be discerned in statements made by Grigson (1963) in his contemplation of modern world literature. Grigson suggests that the recurrent experience, and therefore the recurrent artistic theme of the 20th century, has been the capacity of society to triumph over man. Noting that literature is essentially a liberal endeavor, preoccupied with the freedom of man, Grigson comments, "Surely what some of the differing works of our time . . . have in common is the sense that it is hard enough for the respecter of individual virtue to protect even his own individuality." Thus, if 20th century Anglo-American literature seeks to preserve a liberal tradition, attempts to describe oppression, and promotes the freedom of the individual, then it is hardly surprising that many of its representatives take up the theme of parental overprotection, with the recipient's struggles toward freedom and self-fulfillment as a powerful theme.

At this point I would like to provide a brief overview of the structure of the book. Part I is largely, but not entirely, theoretical, considering the imputed characteristics, possible origins and course, and nominated consequences of parental overprotection. Specifically, in Chapter 1, parental overprotection is defined within a clinical context, and an evocative description by one recipient is provided. In Chapter 2, representative literary descriptions of maternal overprotection are noted, and in the following chapter several general commentaries and notations are provided. Levy's comprehensive clinical study is considered in some depth. There is a general review of the wide range of described sequelae of parental overprotection in Chapter 4. The fifth chapter is ambitious in design: presuming that maternal overprotection is likely to reflect a quantitative and/or qualitative disturbance of the evolving mother–child tie, I attempt to review currently postulated processes by which a child is said to attach and then detach from a mother figure, to review other relevant influences on that process, and to draw attention to likely ways by which an overprotective mother might promote anomalous "attachment" and hinder the "detachment" process. While that review implicitly generates a large number of testable hypotheses, only a few are examined in the subsequent research chapters.

The material in Part I may well suggest that parental overprotection has been defined more by the subjective eyes of the recipient or observer, and rarely by refined and presumably more objective measures. In Part II, previous attempts to measure overprotection are reviewed (Chapter 6), and two attempts to determine the underlying structures of significance and to measure overprotection with some accuracy are considered (Chapter 7). Since one measure, the Parental Bonding Instrument (PBI), was designed as a self-report of recipients' views of fundamental parental characteristics, and since it is the measure used throughout the research chapters, it is important that its relevant properties (including its validity as a measure of *actual* and not merely *perceived* parental characteristics) are examined and reported in some detail. It is reassuring that the PBI, which is an experiential measure assessing perception of parental characteristics and their meaning to the recipient, appears also to provide an acceptable picture of actual parental characteristics. An attempt to provide a complementary questionnaire, a self-report of a mother's judgment of her own degree of overprotectiveness, was not successful.

Part III of the book seeks to clarify, by means of a series of research studies, issues raised in Part I. A principle aim of the studies is to evaluate whether parental overprotectiveness is overrepresented in a number of

Preface

disorders. The reasons for adopting case-control comparisons and for using the concept of "relative risk" are outlined. The several ways that PBI scores may be used to measure "overprotection" are considered, and it is argued that the flexible strategy of adopting more than one technique in the exploration is more likely to promote the goal of epidemiology—the identification of an efficient cause. In the next eight chapters (8–15), the relevance of parental overprotection to psychiatric and other disorders, to several personality characteristics, and to a so-called psychosomatic disorder is investigated, as are cultural influences on overprotection.

In the final research chapter (Chapter 16), possible determinants of maternal overprotection are investigated within a nonclinical group. The study implicates a maternal contribution, effected principally through levels of anxiety, as the major influence, but suggests also that a child's characteristics and his or her cultural influences may make a contribution. The proposal that some women are destined to be overprotective of their children, as a consequence of high levels of anxiety and associated personality characteristics, and that such women may be predicted even before they have their first child, raises important implications for primary prevention. Results from that study and from several others reported in this book suggest that anxious mothers are overprotective mothers and that the association is a strong one. Moliere's warning that "if all the evidence as you receive it leads to but one conclusion . . . don't believe it," should perhaps be invoked until confirmatory evidence is obtained from other studies of both clinical and nonclinical groups.

In Chapter 17, several key issues are addressed. It is suggested that two types of parental overprotection can be defined quite readily by use of the PBI. It is argued that the PBI delineates a parental style of "affectionless control" that resembles the overprotective parental style incriminated in clinical reports as a causal influence on anomalous childhood development. Relative risk estimates suggest that exposure to such a parental style is distinctly more likely for patients with neurotic disorders. While it does not appear to be significantly overrepresented in people who develop psychotic disorders, such a parental style may influence the onset and course of the disorder. The risk estimates also suggest that "affectionless control" may be one of the strongest risk factors for neurosis yet described. These findings, along with others showing that PBI scores are highly discriminating in predicting schizophrenic relapse, suggest that the PBI is a useful and efficient (perhaps first-stage) measure in delineating exposure to a pathogenic environment—and thus is a predictor of psychosocial vulnerability. The view that parental overprotection is a nonspecific risk to psychosocial development, as suggested in the literature reviews, is clarified with a pathogenic style of overprotection, and its clearest consequences, defined. As the identification of a risk factor is as important in psychiatry as it is in epidemiology, the further development and investigation of such a simple research tool as the PBI would appear to be warranted.

Gordon Parker

Acknowledgments

I am indebted to Professor Leslie Kiloh (School of Psychiatry) and Professor Laurie Brown (School of Psychology) of the University of New South Wales for their encouragement during the lengthy period required for the research for this volume, and for their critical reading of an earlier draft. The present research was assisted by the appointment of an extremely competent psychologist, Penny Lipscombe, to a position perceptively funded by the Australian National Health and Medical Research Council for one year. Dr. Kevin Bird and Dr. Megan Neilson ably resolved a number of statistical problems. Jan Cunningham, from the Child Study Center library, Yale University, and Mrs. Jacquelyn Ristau and the late Mrs. Nan Friend, at the Rozelle Hospital library, Sydney, assisted considerably in tracking elusive reference material. Several of the studies were conducted while I was on leave, and I thank Professor Michael Gelder at the Department of Psychiatry, University of Oxford, for his guidance in the study of the phobic patients, and Myrna Weissman at the Depression Research Unit, Yale University, for several research techniques and ideas that have been incorporated in this book.

A number of psychiatrists (Ron Barr, Gordon Johnson, Michael Fairley, Stephen Jurd, Jim Greenwood, Jonathan Phillips, the late Phyllis Shaw, Derrick Silove, and Kay Wilhelm), general practitioners (Barry Abeshouse, Earle Connolly, Hugh Hazard, Richard Herlihy, and Vivian Pleshivtseff), and psychologists (Marsha Leeman and Hilary Tupling) assisted considerably in the data collection.

Psychiatrists Bryanne Barnett and Robert Finlay-Jones read and made constructive comments on the final draft—a formidable task.

The following publishers kindly gave permission for copyrighted material to be published: Angus and Robertson (Sydney), Elsevier Biomedical Press B.V. (Amsterdam), Plenum Publishing Corporation (New York), and William & Wilkins (Baltimore).

The editors of the following journals graciously allowed previously published material to be included in this volume: Professor E. Strömgren, *Acta Psychiatrica Scandinavica* (Chapter 10); Dr. R. Green, *Archives of Sexual Behavior* (Chapter 13); Professor J. Watson, *British Journal of Medical Psychology* (Chapters 7, 9, 10, and 14); Dr. J. Crammer, *British Journal of Psychiatry* (Chapters 8–11, and 16); Professor E. Paykel, *Journal of Affective Disorders* (Chapter 7); Professor E. Brody, *Journal of Nervous and Mental Disease* (Chapter 8); and Professor C. Aitken, *Journal of Psychosomatic Research* (Chapters 9 and 12).

The association with my publisher has been a pleasure. I am extremely grateful to all these people and institutions for their ready and constructive assistance. Two others deserve special mention. My secretary, Barbara Bucknor (of Rozelle Hospital), tackled the preparation of this book with care, expertise, and vigor, against the usual background of a life event score that would shatter mere mortals. My wife, Heather, has always understood and allowed me the liberty to write and assisted in the preparation of this book in so many ways. Thank you.

Parental Overprotection

PART I

General Considerations and Overview of Parental Overprotection

Part I presents a wide range of definitions and observations of parental overprotection, including clinical and fictional accounts and commentaries and research studies. This section also documents the extraordinary broad range of disorders in which parental overprotection has been incriminated as a pathogenic influence, as well as reviews the nature and ontogenesis of the normal mother–child tie in order to assist in the consideration of possible origins, determinants, and early expressions of overprotection.

1
Clinical Examples of Parental Overprotection

The research presented later in this book (Chapters 7–16) was stimulated by clinical work with a number of patients who had described one or both of their parents as being overprotective. Four of those clinical examples are discussed since they demonstrate a number of the key components of "overprotection" (e.g., control, intrusion, encouragement of dependence, and exclusion of outside influences). They illustrate a number of the common problems that recipients of overprotection describe and that are often considered to be consequences of that experience (e.g., socialization difficulties, anxiety, depression, retributive aggression). They suggest that considerations of overprotection should not be limited to its expression in mothers, since fathers, grandparents, and even nonfamily members (e.g., family physicians) are often reported as joining together with parents and extending the overprotective umbrella. These four patients will be described briefly following some general comments about research based on clinical observations.

One of the chief tasks of a clinical psychiatrist is to search for meaning in each individual patient, an interpretative approach aimed at understanding that single person, and a complex process when the nuances and richness of human existence are conceded. However, as Slater and Roth (1969) noted, an excessive preoccupation with individuals is heuristically sterile, and progress in the field of psychopathology depends on the recognition of similarities in phenomena so that general causes may be deduced. The researcher is obliged to avoid any undue preoccupation with individual cases and, instead, study distilled generalizations. But as general themes are taken from their clinical context and are conceptualized, or even "operationalized," they often assume a different identity, and contact with the original phenomena may be progressively tenuous.

In subsequent chapters a number of studies are reported examining aspects of parental overprotection, including its possible determinants and sequelae. Such studies need a reference point so that the degree to which the clinical and research phenomena correspond can be assessed. The following clinical examples are presented to provide that reference point.

Example 1

A 22-year-old librarian presented with marked symptoms of anxiety that dated back to early childhood. Although she had liked school, as a child she was unable to socialize with the other children. When she was 8 years old she stayed at home for 3 months and was prescribed sedatives by her local doctor; she believed that that episode had reflected "delayed shock" following a dog attack a year before. Similar episodes had occurred throughout her schooling, and her academic performance deteriorated in secondary school. At the age of 19 years, while attending university, she had her first panic attack after a friend made sexual advances. Subsequently, moderate agoraphobic symptoms (feeling panicky in crowds and shops, and avoiding such situations) and social phobic symptoms (anxiety upon speaking to people, especially men) developed. At the time of her presentation she described diffuse anxiety symptoms that had been present for some months. She had consulted a counselor 3 years previously for similar symptoms and described moderate relief in response to relaxation training and a desensitization program.

She lived with her mother and maternal grandparents, her parents having been divorced when she was 11 years old. Her parents had been separated on numerous occasions during the marriage, and at those times the mother had returned with her only child to her own parents. The patient described her father as an aggressive alcoholic but noted that she had never been hit by him. Her mother claimed to have had no social life since the break-up of her marriage; however, the patient had been surprised and resentful to learn a year earlier that her mother had been having an intermittent affair.

The maternal grandmother was described as "dominating and possessive . . . making up illness to make people feel guilty if they left her." She dominated her husband, a submissive "hen-pecked hypochondriac" who had no interest apart from obeying his wife's orders. Both the patient and her mother were only children. The mother had stated that she had wanted no more children as childbirth had "nearly torn her insides out."

The patient was not allowed as a child to play with local children and was unable to socialize with the other girls at school. In primary school she was taken by a family member to and from school. In secondary school a hired car was employed by the family for her transport.

As a component of therapy the patient was encouraged to attempt a more independent existence. This move was resisted by all members of the family, most particularly the grandmother. When the patient spoke of leaving home to join another girl in an apartment, the grandmother made a number of threats including disinheritance. On the day she left, the grandmother claimed that the patient had caused her to have a heart attack (not confirmed at a general hospital). The patient was visited in her apartment every day by her mother, was phoned several times a day by the grandmother, and was asked to return for the evening meal each day. The patient persisted for some 6 months in her relatively independent living and then returned home "temporarily" to find her room had been preserved as a shrine.

Although the patient's mother and two grandparents were overprotective, in this instance the overprotection was effected most by the grandmother, and it was the grandmother whom the patient described as the family member most difficult to leave. A family with two generations of matriarchal figures has been called the "dominant matriarch syndrome" (Clarke, 1967) and will be considered in Chapter 4.

Example 2

A 29-year-old receptionist was admitted to hospital following a suicide attempt. She described an ephemeral depression following a marital argument about her 1-year-old child. Interviews with the patient and her family members suggested that she had little ability to mother the child but was extremely sensitive to any implication of parental incompetency.

She described a distant relationship with her mother but an extremely close one with her father who had adored her from birth. At that time he had taken night employment so that he could look after her during the day. The patient remembered her father as the parent who bought her clothes and washed and dressed her. From adolescence on he accompanied her to parties, and they went on holidays together without her mother. When she was 24 years old, after an argument with her father, she impulsively married a serviceman, whom she had met 1 week before. He resembled her father physically and had the same given name. Her father, who had always intensely disliked her boyfriends, assaulted her for the first time. On the first night of the honeymoon she had wanted to return home following an argument with her husband. She called her father and begged him to take her home. He refused: "You made your bed and now you've got to lie in it." She responded by taking an overdose of sleeping tablets.

A developmental history revealed the picture of a socially isolated girl who had no friends during childhood and who had episodic periods of depression and anxiety during adolescence, handled by reckless behaviors (e.g., indiscriminate drug taking, excessive alcohol intake, violent breaking of household furniture), and short periods of employment. There were marked histrionic personality traits.

During her admission, her husband visited briefly on two occasions, while her father spent most of the day and the evening in the ward, desperately clutching her when she made herself available and appearing lonely and worried at other times. At follow-up 3 years later she was still married, although the turbulence of the marriage severely tested the patience of her husband.

Example 3

A 19-year-old student was referred as an outpatient with feelings of dejection, sadness, and pessimism, intermittent but increasing in severity since his 13th birthday. He had made a serious attempt at suicide shortly after his 16th birthday and on three subsequent occasions.

He said that his mother had sought an intense and deeply emotional relationship in marriage but that her husband only was able to provide her with a physical relationship. She became indifferent to her husband and turned to her children for an emotional relationship. At the time of his birth, her marriage was disintegrating and he became the "center of my mother's universe." He had been described as a beautiful baby, and between his mother and himself "an abnormal relationship developed; an overprotective relationship, a rather interdependent one." School had meant facing the outside world but he was "unprepared for this cutting of the umbilical cord." There he found teachers and other boys to be strange, insensitive, and incomprehensible. While he wished for some company he feared ridicule and fell back to an introverted existence. "Although I obtained a certain independence from my mother . . . paradoxically my emotional dependence intensified." Whereas the relationship was happy and close prior to adolescence, he subsequently experienced aggressive thoughts toward her and had dreams of killing her. These thoughts accompanied the pessimistic preoccupation that he could never successfully break away, and they increased after the death of his mother's father. Following that death the mother had clung more tightly to him, took him with her to live in another part of the city away from the remainder of the family, and appeared less able to allow him minimal freedom.

He established a working relationship with the psychiatrist but maintained his initial restraint and distance. In the relationship he expressed his fears about being engulfed in relationships and noted that "my interest in the outside world is negligible. The fact that I am relating more to you . . . suggests a transfusion to an already dead man." He wrote down his dilemma: "To continue? What else can one do! Death—uncertain; life—unpleasant, but nevertheless all the certainty one has."

Three years later, and 2 years after the completion of therapy, he was a lonely young man who lived by himself and had great difficulties in forming friendships, but he received pleasure and some success in the literary field. He denied depression and expressed surprise that his earlier episode had caused him to make several suicide attempts.

Example 4

A 26-year-old pharmacist, unmarried and living in a country town with both parents, presented with a history of recent depression and marked social anxiety since adolescence. At a party or when shopping he would blush and develop palpitations and a panicky feeling. As a consequence he was never able to invite out a woman. He spent his evenings rowing on the town lake or going alone to the cinema. In his shop he managed to talk to only a few of the customers and usually sent his assistant to deal with them. He described episodes of deep suicidal depression, which began when he was 15 years old. The worst episode had occurred on an overseas trip, which he had taken impulsively as a defiant gesture of independence—only to return to the family, cowed, frightened, and still depressed. He considered that he and his mother were one person, that he could be

Clinical Examples of Parental Overprotection

safe only with her, and that he was in danger whenever he was away from her. The following excerpt of a more complete report (Parker, 1978, pp. 119–121, by permission of Angus & Robertson Publishers, Sydney) reveals a poignant description of an overprotective parental system and its perceived consequences.

> There was a time when I regarded life as an avalanche of fears. It was impossible to get through a day without experiencing panic. The panic would be triggered by everyday occurrences. For examples, someone calling my name in the school ground, or the ringing of the school bell. The school boy calling my name might want me to accept a responsibility for him, and I knew I would be too timid to say no. If I failed to fulfill that responsibility adequately then I placed myself in a position where I would be rejected. The school bell meant the possibility of a confrontation with my teacher who would ask me a question which I could not answer and then criticise me for my failure. But the fear I experienced was all out of proportion with the criticism or rejection. It was as if I had been sentenced to death in the gas chambers of Auschwitz.
>
> So why this terror of life? Where did it start? I guess I got the impression that life was very dangerous from my parents. They always seemed apprehensive about anything and everything. Whenever anything was discussed a very large warning would be attached.
>
> My father was a farmer and because of marketing difficulties it was necessary to sell on the blackmarket, as all the other farmers did in that area. If a farmer was caught this would result in a substantial fine. But that was all. They didn't cart you off to a concentration camp. After all we weren't living in Stalin's Russia. But the prospect of being caught by an inspector put the fear of God into my parents.
>
> So my illogical panics are partly tied up to the example set by my parents. But there was something else which probably played a far bigger role in creating these panics.
>
> My parents overprotected me.
>
> Why did they overprotect me? Because a country doctor, who had served with distinction at Gallipoli, and had not read a medical journal since, told my mother that I would have to be protected from head injuries after I had taken several convulsions. Convulsions triggered by a temperature of 40°C, not brought on by physical trauma.
>
> If I got the opportunity to ride a children's pony that had been raised especially for the purpose, my mother would insist on holding the reins just in case the damn thing broke into a murderous gallop. I came to the conclusion that I was different, more fragile, less capable of fending for myself than others. So I had to play tennis with the asthma sufferers, epileptics and those who stuttered. Obviously their parents had come to the same conclusion as mine.
>
> At the beginning I resisted their overprotectiveness. But as time went by I was worn down to a state where I just gave up and did whatever my parents wanted me to do. The more dependent I became on my mother the more frightened I became of using my own initiative. The few times I did

use my initiative I fell flat on my face and so resolved never to try anything again without my mother's advice and support. This lead to a situation where I was afraid and unable to make even the smallest decisions without first going to my mother and asking her advice. I became 100 percent dependent upon her.

My school work suffered because I couldn't make sense of anything unless my mother explained it to me. It got to a stage where I wouldn't even pay attention to the teacher because my mother would explain it all when I got home. My initiative dropped to zero. I was unable to formulate an original idea because I was afraid to do it without first going to my mother. If my mother was not available I'd copy someone else's work, even if that student was hopeless. I would rather copy his work than risk using my own intelligence to solve a problem.

Every now and again I would break away and do something I considered reckless and even dangerous. First a trip to Tasmania and then six months in Palestine, hoping that these experiences would somehow bring about a magical change in my personality. But the fears remained and I found myself substituting others for my mother.

It is only recently that I've started to say no when asked to do a favour. I'm afraid of alienating myself from people who have to some degree taken the place of my mother and adviser. If I offend them then they won't be around when I need them to lean on. I guess that's no different than saying I must not offend my mother otherwise she will abandon me and I'll have no crutch to lean on!

At this stage there will be no attempt at interpretation of these clinical cases. They serve as an initial reference point, to be joined in the next section by several novelists' descriptions of maternal overprotection.

2
Fictional Descriptions of Parental Overprotection

Parental overprotection is an issue that is commonly explored in fiction. Several selected examples are presented to illustrated variations in both expression and degree of subtlety.

An American Example

The Jewish American writer Philip Roth often deals with the theme of parental overprotection, perhaps most distinctly in *Portnoy's Complaint* (1969) and *My Life as a Man* (1974).

In *Portnoy's Complaint* the parents and their displays of overprotection are drawn with such emphasis and with such bitter humor that they appear grotesque and, at times, seem to be little more than caricatures. In this book Roth not only describes components of overprotection but draws causal inferences about their immediate and subsequent effects. Control is an important component of overprotection that constricts and supresses the child's tendencies toward independence. Patience, concentration, and a dedicated and self-sacrificing parent are the necessary requirements to inhibit a hard-working attentive child so that he or she becomes a "really constrained and tight ass human being" (p. 79). Parental control is an attempt to protect the child against danger. The parent constantly intrudes into the world of the child, seemingly to ensure the offspring's safety.

Control *per se* and the attendent inability to trust the child to others outside the parent–child dyad have the effect of binding the child to that parent. Portnoy observes that his mother was so deeply imbedded in his consciousness that during his first year at school he believed that each of his teachers was his "mother in disguise" (p. 3). In Roth's novels, parental control may resemble what R. D. Laing (1967) has called a "protection racket." When the child obeys or achieves the parents' implicit or explicit wishes, the rewards are disproportionately great; when the child fails to observe the desired standards or criteria, the fall from grace is disproportionately severe. For example, when Portnoy was not being punished, he was being carried around "like the Pope through the streets of Rome" (p. 89). As a result of such experiences the child becomes preoccupied with doing "the right thing."* Furthermore, a mother who blindly adores her child and nourishes a boundless belief in the ability to achieve makes the child "less than fortified against the realities of setback and frustration" (*My Life as a Man,* 1974, pp. 213–215), and leaves the child with ambitions dissonant with the realities of the social world.

Portnoy's Complaint poignantly describes a process by which the overprotective parent promotes anxiety in the child. Mrs. Portnoy constantly checks her son Alex for the slightest sore throat, bowel change, headache, or stiff neck, always forewarning him with the "watch-its" and the "be-carefuls." Alex reflects on the intrusive vigilance of his parents, wondering as to what in their world was "not charged with danger, dripping with germs, fraught with peril?" (p. 35). He recounts his palpitations, flushes, and sweats to his psychiatrist before demanding: "Make me brave! Make me strong! Make me whole!" (p. 37). Furthermore, as seen in Roth's *My Life as a Man,* an overprotective parent can fail to provide the child with an appropriate perspective on life.

An Australian Example

Patrick White is Australia's most distinguished novelist and received the Nobel Prize for Literature in 1973. The literary critic, Beatson (1977), notes in his novels the preoccupation with several impediments to family love, including lust, jealousy, possessiveness, and hatred. He notes that in most of White's novels the family comprises a father, a mother, and two children, of whom one or both may be scarred by the imprints of certain parental attitudes during the formative years: "The daughter often experiences rejection . . . while the son may be the victim of over-protectiveness." (Beatson, 1977, p. 113). The mother, while intelligent and beautiful is also, according to Beatson, dominating and selfish, and simultaneously greedy and frigid. A portrait is drawn at two stages in her career—at the zenith of her beauty and power, and then in drawn-out old age marked by spiritual bankruptcy. Sometimes, says Beatson, her coldness and ruth-

---

*Such a consequence is explored in great depth and with great perspicacity by the Australian author Hal Porter in *The Right Thing* (1971), a novel that describes a landed family dominated by the grandmother.

lessness are emphasized, while on other occasions the "venom is withdrawn," and she is left only with her inability to love and her "etiolated old age" (Beatson, 1977, pp. 114–115). In the typical White family the father is a shadowy figure who is too innocent, decent, or weak to counterbalance the "dominance of the mother" (Beatson, 1977, p. 114). The father generally dies years before his wife, and his death clears the way for a protracted confrontation between the children and the mother. The themes of murder, particularly matricide and incest, appear repeatedly in White's novels and appear to arise, Beatson believes, from a desire for freedom, a sense of revenge, or an instinctive impulse.

Beatson points out that the oedipus complex is not a driving power in White's novels since the key components of the classical Freudian approach—the son's desire to kill the father and sleep with the mother—seem absent and the current of antagonism toward the mother and the affection or compassion for the father seem genuine.

Beatson notes that the children in White's families are estranged from the outside world, have an inability to form genuine human attachments, and are emotionally cold. The children have a "hole in the centre where the core should be" and bitterly resent the mother for causing the original rift of "the self from the self" (Beatson, 1977, p. 117).

Beatson suggests that *The Eye of the Storm* gives the most complete portrait of the mother who dominates the family group, and that this book is a consummation of White's art since it seems to have finally "pierced the heart of a lifetime's antagonist" to find "an unsuspected grace." *The Eye of the Storm* was first published in 1973 and was dubbed "King Lear Down Under" by the *Observer* critic, Paul Baily (*Observer*, September 9, 1973). Maternal overprotection and its sequelae are the theme of the novel. From the commencement of the book Elizabeth Hunter is described vitriolically, graphically, and clearly as the archetypal, predatory matriarch. Despite being in her 80s and being frail following a stroke, she rules all those around her with an iron hand, including private nurses, a housekeeper, and a solicitor, as she awaits the visit of her daughter, Dorothy (a French princess by marriage), and her son, Basil (a London actor-knight).

References to Mrs. Hunter as a devouring, engulfing, maternal figure abound. Sister Manhood (sic), one of the private nurses, observes how Mrs. Hunter had "sucked the living daylights" (p. 106) out of her family, including her husband and daughter. The daughter, Dorothy, notes to the family solicitor that "mother specialized in slaves" (p. 257). Even Mrs. Hunter is aware of her reputation. In response to accusations of devouring people, she suggests that "you couldn't help it if they practically stuck their heads in your jaws" (p. 90).

Even at her great age and when blind and frail, she rejoices in restricting the independence of her three nurses and the housekeeper. When one of the nurses protests to the housekeeper that she need not have put out the flowers as Mrs. Hunter would not be able to see them, the housekeeper observes that Mrs. Hunter will see through a wall if so determined. When the housekeeper muses as to why Anglo-Saxons reject the warmth of a family, the nursing sister replies: "They're afraid of being consumed. Families can eat you." (p. 22).

As Dutton (1971) has observed, White's novels are a barometer of the destructive process. White rages and condemns humans for their cruelty and indifference. In particular, the children in White's novels direct retributive anger towards the mother figure for her lack of sensitivity, and attention to their needs, and for rejecting them and consuming and sucking dry their initiative and independence when they were children.

A British Example

Sons and Lovers by D. H. Lawrence (1913) is another example of parental overprotection in literature. The Penguin edition (1948) describes Mrs. Morel as the dominant personality of the novel, "a woman of character and refinement, married to a virile but coarse-grained miner." Her favorite child is the third one, Paul, "Whose sensitive mind and artistic gifts become to her both a compensation and an incentive. Between Paul and his mother, then, there develops one of those delicate relationships in which love has to contend with possessiveness" (p. 19). Paul is born some time after Mrs. Morel had become embittered and disillusioned toward her husband; he is initially unloved by Mrs. Morel, since she never expected him to live. "Mrs. Morel's life now rooted itself in Paul" (p. 19), following her bitter disillusionment with her husband, the death of her son William from pneumonia, and Paul's near death from pneumonia. A close dyad develops between Paul and his mother. There are several components to Mrs. Morel's possessiveness and need for closeness to Paul. Clearly, with a coarse husband and a similarly developing younger son, Arthur, the softer, artistic, and sensitive Paul is attractive to the sensitive nature of Mrs. Morel. Mrs. Morel seeks and achieves vicarious gratification through Paul's successes. "She was to see herself fulfilled. Not for nothing had been her struggle" (p. 227).

Incestuous components are prominent. When Paul states that he did not love his girlfriend Miriam, his mother responds in a voice "trembling with passionate love" (p. 262) so that without knowing why, Paul gently strokes her face.

To Paul, Mrs. Morel is demonstrably possessive, intrusive, and demanding. The dyad develops into bondage. While his mother is the pivot of his existence, he cannot escape from her, cannot relate successfully to other women, and cannot achieve any real independence. At times he hates his mother, pulling at her "bondage" (p. 420) aware that with his love "turned back" to his mother he can never be free to go forward with his own life and "really love another woman" (p. 420).

He perceives Miriam as wanting to possess him as his mother has done and cannot help shrinking back from her: "I want a woman to keep me, but not in her pocket" (p. 339). Earlier, however, and presumably defensively, he refuses to listen to Miriam's explicit description of his mother's possessiveness and its effects on him.

After his mother's death Paul lives in a void aware that "his soul could not leave her." Tempted to join his mother, he muses that she was "the only thing that held him up" (p. 510).

Common Themes

Clearly, these books share common themes. First, the marital dyad is distinguished by a powerful woman and her weak husband who is drawn as an appendage and is quite clearly an ineffective father figure to the relevant children. Second, the mothers are dominant figures who overwhelm, control, and intrude into the lives of selected children. They offer a conditional love, dependent on the child's obedience to their wants and desires; they restrict the child's independence; they become imbedded in the child's consciousness. Third, the child is unable (as a consequence, it is suggested) to form deep human attachments. Parental overprotection is not an uncommon preoccupation of 20th century Anglo-American writers, and probably emerges from an interest in preserving the liberal tradition and, in describing bondage in interpersonal relationships, evidences an attempt to promote the freedom of the individual. Thus, it is hardly surprising that authors see parental overprotection, with the recipient's struggles toward freedom and self-fulfillment, as a powerful theme.

3
Commentaries and General Studies

In the previous chapter several literary examples of parental overprotection were provided. The artistic licence granted to fictional writers is a privilege capable of promoting great insights, but their observations should be compared with more objectively derived views. In the present chapter several commentaries and observations on maternal overprotection by nonfictional writers are examined, although the degree to which some reports can be regarded as "objective" is debatable. Commentaries about momism precede observational studies made by a sociologist and several psychiatrists.

Momism

Several American nonfiction commentators have considered maternal overprotection under the more generic term "momism," a term which, according to Sebald (1976), was introduced by Wylie in 1942 in the first edition of a book entitled *Generation of Vipers* (annotated version, 1955). Wylie vituperatively attacks a number of American institutions including momism, which he holds to be an American creation: "Our land, subjectively mapped, would have more silver cords and apron strings crisscrossing it than railroads and telephone wires" (p. 198).

Wylie is equally colorful in defining the characteristics of a "mom" as "a middle-aged puffin with an eye like a hawk that has just seen a rabbit twitch far below. "She cushions and protects her boy against any major step in his progress towards maturity" (p. 208). In a final abusive salute, he compares mom with the "black widow who is poisonous and eats her mate" (pp. 215–216).

Strecker (1946), a former chairman of the psychiatry department at the University of Pennsylvania and an adviser to the Secretary of War, also uses the term "mom" in describing a particular parental style. He studied men rejected from military service on psychiatric grounds and men who decompensated with symptoms of emotional stress during the Second World War, and judged that in the vast majority of case histories, a "Mom" was at fault (p. 23). In his book he defines a "mom" as a woman who has failed in "the elementary mother function of weening her offspring emotionally as well as physically" (p. 13).

He argues that there is no one distinctive mom—that they can be sweet, doting, self-sacrificing, stern, or domineering—but that they do have one thing in common: an emotional satisfaction or repletion in keeping their children "paddling about in a kind of psychological amniotic fluid rather than letting them swim away with bold and decisive strokes" (p. 30).

Apart from a "protective mom," Strecker describes five other types: a "common garden variety" (who supervises the children and their activities and is soft, persuasive, and somewhat devious); a "self-sacrificing mom;" an "ailing mom" (who is pitifully frail despite no evidence of organic disease); a "Polyanna mom" (with artificial expressions of love, harmony, and happiness); a "pretty-addlepated Mom" (who is narcissistic and, while uncaring of her children, allows them to regard her as a cult of beauty and as a shrine at which to worship); and finally, a "pseudo-intellectual mom" (who fascinates her children by her knowledge).

What he argues to be common to all those moms, although varying in degree, is their practice of holding on to their children and seldom being willing to relinquish their grasp. Strecker notes that fathers, grandmothers, mothers-in-law, teachers, and even governesses may have "Momish proclivities."

Moms, according to Strecker, are largely the result of having had a "mom" themselves, although lack of interest by their husbands, sexual frustration, defects or handicaps in the child, and even aspects of the social system, such as progressive education, foster momism.

Strecker's book is largely anecdotal and impressionistic, although his observations were based on a large sample. His book does provide a questionnaire, which he considers differentiates a "mom" from other mothers, although no properties of the questionnaire are reported. The 40 items require "yes" or "no" answers and include items such as:

Do you consider children of eight or nine years of age too young to spend their vacations away from home in summer camp? (Q2)

Do you comfort, pet, and reward a child after it has been justly punished? (Q17)

Sebald, a sociologist, published a book entitled, *Momism: The Silent Disease of America* (1976). He suggests that momism is a relatively new phenomenon on the American scene, and that in the more nuclear family of the past two generations the child has become "trapped" in a small and relatively isolated family unit, with rather exclusive person–to–person relationships with the mother, who is freed from traditional time-consuming responsibilities. Sebald proposes that the contemporary mother uses her child to resume a faltering sense of meaningfulness and to establish a stable identity, with the child providing a means to obtaining solutions to such anxieties. In taking part in such a "manufacturing process" and evidencing such features as "exclusive supervision," "scientific" approach, and "psychological manipulation," the mother establishes herself as an achiever, satisfies her success drive, and ultimately gains a sense of identity.

Sebald proposes that momism is most prevalent in the middle class and then offers a number of explanations for that predilection.

1. Middle-class women have experienced the greatest emancipation pressures (e. g., through the women's liberation movement), and the partially emancipated woman, as a consequence of resulting anxiety and insecurity, turns the wife–mother role into a career.
2. Momism is promoted by remote father involvement; the career demands of middle-class fathers result in child-rearing being a mother-dominated process.
3. Middle-class parents have smaller sized families, and "momistic practices" are usually found only in small families because the presence of siblings tends to insulate against momism.
4. The middle-class practice of maternal love is made conditional upon certain child behaviors that promote a child's insecurity and dependence.
5. Middle-class families accept incentives of competition and are achievement orientated so that they have a greater desire to control and shape their children.
6. The high divorce rate in the middle class promotes greater dependency of children on mothers.
7. There is an absence of appropriate rites of passage in the middle class.

Sebald notes that in more primitive cultures any strong social influence is balanced and neutralized by another social influence. For instance, in cultures where a child is breast-fed, sleeps with the mother and depends on her exclusively, there are marked rites of passage in which the youth (usually male and usually adolescent) undergoes seemingly harsh and demarcated extrusions. However, according to Sebald (1976), middle-class American children have a long and tedious adolescence, and the absence of such a rite together with other conditions prevents a child from "escaping a mother-imposed, continual childhood" (p. 82).

Sebald speculates further on the observation that boys appear to be more susceptible to momism than girls. He suggests that boys need an effective father-figure to develop appropriate behavior and that moms, in line with their particular needs and attitudes, tend to marry extremely submissive men whose influence they exclude from the child-rearing process. In the absence of an effective father-figure a boy's concerns and anxieties about sex-role behaviors are accentuated, while the Mom does not allow the son to liberate himself from her influence. Sebald makes the interesting suggestion that there might be a curvilinear relationship between maternal domination and resistance by boys: as maternal domination increases, the son's resistance increases; but, above a certain level of maternal domination, resistance decreases or is absent and reflects a sense of futility.

Sebald also concedes that the suggested preponderance of mother–son domination may be an artifact reflecting saliency. A daughter, in response to a dominant mom, may identify and imitate the mother and become momistic herself. Again, the consequences of momism (e. g. , insecurity, passivity) might be interpreted within the norms of feminine passivity and not perceived as distinctive or noteworthy.

Sebald acknowledges that momism is not restricted to mothers. Suggested parallels between dadism and momism include: the child not necessarily identifying with the major socializer; the spouse being weak and passive, and the relevant parent manipulating the child's desire for love. Sebald suggests that in both situations the children grow up seeking Mom and Dad surrogates for protection, suffering from overdependency and neurotic anxiety, and constantly seeking assurance of their self-worth.

Sebald (1976) describes several types of moms:

1. *The overprotective Mom* prevents the child from confronting hurdles in life and so reduces the child's urge toward independence. Thus the child cannot become autonomous but remains severely dependent instead. He states that only a few who experience the consequences of an overprotective mother and a passive father recover successfully and that the rest stay "crippled for the rest of their lives" (p. 141).
2. *The overindulgent Mom* craves the child's love and loyalty. The child, exposed to such maternal characteristics, grows up with "a gorged id" and is unable to give to others or take up adult responsibilities.
3. *The martyr Mom* manipulates (by disease, loneliness, feelings of ingratitude, etc.) her child's guilt, shame, and compassion, to retain the child's loyalty and keep the child tied to her.

4. *The domineering Mom* is more hostile than the overprotective mom and makes constant and excessive demands on the child. Such mothers are basically rejecting of the child, are highly judgmental and punitive, and use a technique of conditional love.

Other and less common variants are said to be the "star" Mom, the "pseudointellectual" Mom and the "child-worshipping" Mom.

Sebald describes a number of consequences of momism. He states that the recipients's personality is characterized by anxious self-tailoring to social expectations, and a search for security. The victim can remain a slave to the mom or gravitate toward some other to seek deliverance from anxiety. Homosexuality and transsexualism are more likely, according to Sebald, as are problems of dependence upon drugs and alcohol. Sebald (1976) suggests that psychological scars range from relatively mild neurosis to "withdrawal into schizophrenia" (p. 204). According to Sebald, recipients of momism have four key afflictions: insecurity, guilt, anxiety, and disorientation, and several telling characteristics (p. 233):

1. Inability to make decisions
2. Chronic feelings of inferiority
3. Frequently aroused anxiety
4. Irresponsible actions
5. Unchecked narcissism and immature "ego eccentrism"

Apart from the broad social factors considered earlier, Sebald suggests that the origin of momism lies in imitation of the subject's own mother, in hostility against males (the subjects adopt the model of their domineering and overbearing mother against a weak and submissive father) and in compensation against childhood powerlessness. Momism becomes a reaction against the experience of emotional neglect in childhood, a substitute for a nonresponsive husband, and a "cause," with motherhood being flaunted as a noble devotion and a safe island in an otherwise empty existence.

To prevent and cure momism Sebald suggests that mothers should freely choose motherhood, have their self-concept developed so that they do not resort to meeting needs in parasitic relationships, and give their children unconditional, not conditional love. Fathers, married to moms, should act as checks and balances against their wives' tendencies and interact as much as possible with the children. He suggests that family relationships need to be restructured to expand the narrow, confining boundaries of the small modern family. In addition, he considers the possible relevance of child care centers, maternal employment, alternative family groupings, modification of the educational system, provision of rites of passage for adolescents, and possible legislative changes to prevent exclusive supervision and domination by mothers.

Sebald states that his data came principally from close observation of, and contact with, the victims of momism in a teaching situation. Nevertheless, he did draw on the relevant literature (particularly suggesting associations between parental characteristics and several psychosocial anomalies in their children) to substantiate his argument.

The material by Wylie, Strecker, and Sebald would appear linked in that these authors have considered the concepts of momism within American society.

In a revised version of his book *Childhood and Society,* Erikson (1965) published a lengthy essay, "Reflections on the American Identity," which examines the issue of Mom and momism. He makes a number of indirect references to the descriptions of Mom by Wylie and Strekker and responds with considerable scepticism. Erikson suggests that momism is a too simple and too ready explanation by psychiatrists of psychological problems, who imply that the patient was "not made to feel at home in this world except under the condition that he behave himself in certain definite ways, which were inconsistent with the timetable of an infant's needs and potentialities and contradicitions in themselves" (p. 280). Furthermore, he suggests that the judgment is given perhaps "as if a villain had been spotted and cornered" (p. 281).

Another possible reason for neurotic soldiers reporting overprotective mothering (i.e., to Strecker), according to Erikson, is that those who were inadequately prepared for life tend to blame their mothers and the expert feels compelled to agree. If, however, Mom is a distinct type, Erikson suggests that she reflects a "steroyped caricature of existing contradictions which have emerged from intense, rapid, and as yet unintegrated changes in American history" (p. 283). He suggests that, "in the pursuit of the adjustment to and mastery over the machine, American mothers . . . found themselves standardizing and overadjusting children" (p. 287).

CHARACTERISTICS OF MATERNAL OVERPROTECTIVENESS: STUDY OF 20 CASES

In 1943, Levy, a child psychiatrist, published a monograph entitled *Maternal Overprotection,* and this work has become a classic reference. His study was designed to discover how a mother becomes overprotective; how her child is affected by living with that type of mother; and how to treat actual difficulties and prevent potential ones from resulting. Levy held from clinical study and common observation that the maternal overprotective attitude is a very common one, and very likely to be universal. He considered that he could best study overprotection by selecting mothers with a pronounced overprotective attitude, arguing that the intensive study of a few unusually clear cases yields more knowledge that a statistical study of several thousand cases. He sought instances where overprotection was clear at the time of the study and was judged with fair unanimity (at least by one lay observer beside staff members of the hospital). He sought only those cases where overprotection was directed toward a wanted child, arguing from experience that such a selection favors those cases in which the overprotecting factors are the most consistent. Cases where the father was clearly the overprotective parent were excluded as relatively few cases were found. Also excluded were cases where overprotection was a response to maternal guilt, where overprotection varied significantly at different stages of child development, and where severe illness, accidents, or deformities in children elicited overprotection.

Among 526 files at the Institute for Child Guidance in New York City, Levy and his staff found 20 cases of "true" overprotection: 19 of the 20 children were male, and the median age was 10 years. Intelligence testing classified 2 as dull, 5 as being of adequate intelligence, and 13 as superior to very superior. Compared with other cases seen at the Institute, the study group was rated as being younger and more intelligent and as having higher economic status and less delinquency.

According to Levy, there are four major manifestations of maternal overprotection, with maternal anxiety or oversolicitude being always manifested in one or more of the first three: (1) *excessive contact* ("the mother is always there"); (2) *infantilization* ("she still treats him like a baby"); (3) *prevention of independent behavior* ("she won't let him grow up," "she won't take any risks");. (4) a *lack or excess of maternal control,* with the former indicating a breakdown in the mother's ability to modify her child's behavior and the latter indicating excessive maternal domination of the child.

Levy suggests that excessive contact is manifested by continuous companionship of mother and child, prolonged nursing care, excessive fondling, or sleeping with the child long past infancy. He notes that 6 boys (ages 8–13 years) still slept with their mothers and that 8 had received prolonged nursing care because of illness. The overprotected group had more than twice as many illnesses, three times as many operations, and fewer accidents than "nonoverprotected" Institute cases. He interprets these findings as refleting the more accurate developmental histories of children given by overprotective mothers, the mothers' greater likelihood to seek medical care for their children and their inhibition of risk-taking in their children as reducing accidents, rather than that illness *per se* produces maternal overprotection, although he suggests that all conditions requiring nursing care act so as to reinforce overprotection. Thus he regards childhood illness as an added stimulus *strengthening* rather than *determining* overprotection.

Levy states that the overprotective mothers gave evidence of three types of infantilizing activities. Commonest was an extended period of breast feeding. Infantilization was indicated secondly by dressing and feeding, and thirdly by "waiting on" the child for services he could perform himself. In the overprotected group, breast feeding beyond 12 months of age occurred in 50 percent of cases, compared to 17 percent of the nonoverprotected cases in the Institute series. Cessation of breast feeding clearly reflected a difficulty in the mother separating from the child (e.g., Case 6: "You know he was all I had." Case 7: "You feel that they are taken away from you."). On the basis of his clinical observations, Levy held that, in general, all factors favoring rejection of the child tend to shorten, while all factors favoring overprotection tend to lengthen breast-feeding.

The third characteristic of maternal overprotection is the active prevention of the child's growth in the direction of self-reliance; Levy observed this in 18 of the 20 mothers in the study. He interprets such maternal behavior as reinforcing closeness and infantilization, as well as preventing growth into more independent behavior. The mother effectively prevents the child from developing responsibility by fighting his battles, by guarding him from social contacts outside the home, and by trying to overcome any possible hardship for him.

Levy notes several key responses to specific developmental stages of progressive independence for children. He considers that, for the most part, the overprotective mothers accepted their child's going to school but demonstrated overprotection in arranging extra coaching, discipline, and precaution against accidents on the way to, and at school. They were hostile in their attitudes to teachers and accompanied their child to and from school. Close association of the mother with her child resulted in the study children having high reading abilities and an extended vocabulary. The majority of the mothers directly or indirectly prevented or discouraged the formation of friendships by their children, and all 20 of the children were rated as having special problems in this.

Levy suggests that the fourth criterion, lack or excess of maternal control, may best be assessed by observation of the child. In 11 cases there was a lack of maternal control, with the mother being submissive to the child. In 8 cases there was an excess of control, with the child having a submissive, obedient, and dependent maternal relationship. Mothers of the dominating children were indulgent to such a degree that infantile power expanded into "a monstrous growth that tends to subjugate the parents" (p. 39). Mothers of the submissive children were dominating, and they constricted any growth of aggressive tendencies in their children. Levy suggests that the child's share in relation to whether the mother is dominating or indulgent is clearer than with the other criteria. It is important to emphasize that Levy equates maternal overprotection with excessive maternal care.

Levy speculates on the origins of maternal overprotection. He is impressed that 13 of the overprotective mothers had had a more prolonged period of anticipation before the birth of the index child (due to periods of relative sterility, spontaneous miscarriages, stillbirths, or other factors), and that such episodes made the mothers more apprehensive and protective in their attitude toward their offspring. He raises the possibility that all maternal overprotection could be regarded as compensatory to unconscious hostility and might even represent a type of neurosis with guilt producing exaggerated maternal care. Such a neurosis, he argues, resembles obsessional neurosis more than any other in its compulsive quality, the stubborn resistance to therapy, and the high degree of responsibility characterizing the overprotecting mother.

Levy considers that poor sexual relationships (16 of the 20 mothers) promote maternal overprotection. He found the mothers had a low rate of mutual social activities with their husbands and reduced social activities in general. Infrequent socialization had been an ongoing characteristic in 4 of the mothers and all socialization had been curtailed after marriage by 12, the child being given as the reason for withdrawing from established relationships in 8 cases.

Levy observed that 16 mothers had experienced severe deprivation of parental love, due to the early death of a parent or lack of an affectionate parent. He suggests that this created an "affect hunger" and exaggerated need for love. The mother sees the child as a solution to affect hunger; the poor sexual and interpersonal relationship between the parents offering no offsetting influence to the exaggerated maternal behavior.

Levy rated all 20 mothers as "responsible," by which he meant there was evidence that they helped to an unusual degree with the housework and care of siblings in their own childhood; before marriage they showed evidence of being stable, competent, reliable, and supportive of their family and themselves, and were stable in their work as employees. The mothers showed much evidence of thwarted ambitions in their own life and sought to fulfill these ambitions vicariously through their children.

Levy, on theoretical grounds, suggests that aggressive behavior is part of normal maternal behavior. He argues that aggression is manifested in protecting functions, as well as in dominating and training activities. He emphasizes its biological origins, citing a number of animal experiments demonstrating hormonal influences on maternal behavior, but notes that such a view does not preclude social and psychic factors. He sees the preponderance of the male children in the sample and the aggressive behavior of the mothers (the latter largely unsupported by clear documentation) as support for Freud's theory of penis envy in females, with sons being used as a means of satisfying unfulfilled ambitions and aggressions.

Levy provides a descriptive picture of the husbands of the overprotective mothers. He suggests that they could be characterized as submissive and stable, playing little or no authoritative role in the life of the child and, as their early attempts to discipline the child had been resented by the mothers, they offered little counteracting influence to the overprotection. Levy interprets the paternal role in the families as being either nullified or used to strengthen the overprotection. Interviews of the fathers revealed them to be stable and responsible workers who in their own childhood generally had been a favorite child or exposed to a dominating parent. He suggests their own early parental experience caused them to select dominating and maternal women as wives.

Bringing together material from the case notes Levy proposes a theory of maternal overprotection. "True" maternal overprotection occurs in "naturally maternal women" (women who have a "strong maternal drive" and who have shown evidence of maternal behavior in childhood) whose behavior as mothers is intensified by certain psychic and cultural influences. The psychic forces include "affect hunger," a prolonged period of anticipation before having their first child, death-threatening illnesses in the child, and marital sexual incompatibility. The cultural forces include early experience of the harsh realities of life (e.g., through death of parents or poverty) necessitating a substitution of work for childhood play and the taking up of responsibility permanently. In regard to the preference for the male child, Levy assumes penis envy as a primary determinant.

Levy accepts that such a generalization is based on a small number of cases and a largely uncontrolled study, but believes it likely to be valid, as only a "pure" sample was selected and the findings had been confirmed by other investigators. However, although he makes occasional reference to other work offering support for several of the specific findings, there is no confirmation of his general conclusions.

Levy's work is deservedly regarded as a classic study as it considers the manifestations, origins, and sequelae of maternal overprotection, and it provides information on the relevance of several interventions. It reveals all the strengths of the clinical approach—extensive documentation of historical information, illustration of key concepts by case studies and clinical vignettes, and the proposal of numerous hypotheses. It can well be argued that such an approach is the most appropriate one for any consideration of a largely uncharted field of human behavior. Weaknesses of the study are noted and accepted by Levy. The sample was small, selected on the basis of subjective ratings made by those in the clinic, selective (in that certain cases of "overprotection" were rejected), largely uncontrolled and with little use of objective rating measures.

Rutter (1977), in considering possible determinants of overprotection, reports Levy's insights extensively but does propose another factor. He suggests that overprotection might arise directly from "some forms of emotional disturbance in the parent which give rise, as it were, to an abnormal 'need' for the child's dependency."

Barker (1976) emphasizes several issues concerning parental overprotection that reflect Levy's views: First, that overprotection might be compensatory to parental rejection. Second, that while nonrejecting overprotection is less harmful than parental rejection, both can "retard a child's emotional growth." Third, that there is "usually excessive parental anxiety arising from factors in the parent's personality, often combined with the circumstances of the child's birth or health."

THE ISSUE OF THE CONTROLLING PERSONALITY

Although control would appear to be a component of overprotection, it is unlikely that overprotection should be equated with control. Baumrind (1966) provides a typology of parental control that has a different emphasis. She describes an *authoritarian* mother as one who attempts to "shape, control and evaluate the behavior and attitudes of the child in accordance with a set standard of conduct" which, she suggests, is usually theologically motivated and formulated by a higher authority. Such a mother "values obedience as a virtue and favors punitive, forceful measures to curb self-will . . . believes in keeping the child in his place, in restricting his autonomy" and regards the preservation of order as an end in itself. The *authoritative* mother, by contrast, attempts to direct the child in a "rational, issue-oriented manner." Such a mother values "disciplined conformity" as well as "autonomous self-will" so she "exerts firm control at points of parent–child divergence, but does not hem the child in with constrictions." The permissive mother behaves in a nonpunitive, accepting, and affirming manner toward her child and the child's actions. She allows the child to regulate his or her own activities as much as possible and attempts to use reason, rather than overt power, when attempting to shape her children. Other components of overprotection—intrusion, encouragement of dependency, etc.—are not apparent in these descriptions.

FAMILY SYSTEMS THEORIES

The family therapy literature reveals extensive consideration of the dynamics and determinants of "maternal overprotection," although that actual term is used only rarely. Before considering some representative views, it may be appropriate to note some basic concepts and constructs underlying the approach by family theorists and therapists. Of most importance is their reliance on what they variably describe as "systems theory" or "general systems theory." Either of these terms is appropriate, according to Skynner (1981), when living organisms can be fairly readily classified as part of a sequence of larger systems (e.g., family, groups, community, nation, etc.). Each system has a measure of independence from the *suprasystem* of which it is a part (e.g., the individual from the family), and the individuality of each system is maintained by its *boundary*, with communications across the boundary being controlled by *decider subsystems* (e.g., the parents of the family). The model assumes that the system can be activated at any number of points and that feedback mechanisms are operative at many points, so that every part of the system is seen as organizing and being organized by other parts. Skynner argues that if the family is to exist as an integrated system some hierarchy is essential (e.g., between parents, between parents and children), boundaries across systems need to be clearly defined, and interactions should be affiliative (based on trust and friendliness) rather than oppositional.

There is some consistency in the family therapy literature in that parental overprotection is viewed generally within the context of a more general failure of family members to differentiate from each other. For instance, Stierlin (1974) notes that Bowen described an "undifferentiated ego mass," Minuchin the "enmeshed family," and Roszormenyi-Nagy the "intersubjective fusion." Skynner (1981) suggests a maturational dimension to considerations of a family's capacity to differentiate. He suggests that optimal families are "well differentiated" with members having a number of capacities, including highly defined identities and the capacity to share intimacy and responsibility. According to Skynner, "the lower down the scale of differentiation one goes" the less the value placed on separateness, individuality, difference, and growth. He holds that there is a tendency for dysfunctional individuals and families to "cling to the known, to fear loss and change" and to order their lives in such a way that projected expectations are never contradicted or threatened with change. For example, the choosing of a spouse and friends and the embracing of political and ethical codes are influenced by a necessity to avoid new experiences that might demand growth and change. Skynner suggests that such maneuvers can be seen as proximity-seeking behaviors and a need to cling to security.

Stierlin (1974) conceptualizes family disturbances as "transactional mode disturbances" that reflect the "interplay and/or relative dominance of pushes and pulls into and out of families throughout all stages of the individuation and separation processes." He argues that such modes are transitive (in that they denote the parents' active molding of an immature, dependent, and captive child) and reciprocal (in the sense that there is always a two-way exchange, with the child and the parent molding and influencing each other). The first of the three modes ("binding," "expelling" and "delegating") would appear of most direct relevance to a consideration of parental overprotection, but it will emerge that the third is also of clear relevance. "Binding," according to Stierlin, occurs when "parents interact with their offspring in ways that seem designed to keep the latter tied to the parental orbit." He suggests that it may occur when the binding parent exploits a child's dependency needs at a cognitive level and mystifies the child about his needs, feelings, and wants, so that the parent "misdefines the child to himself," or when the parent exploits and fosters loyalty and guilt, so that separation (or even the thought of it) is experienced as a crime. The second mode, "expelling," involves an enduring neglect or rejection of the child by the parents. The third mode, "delegating," is a blend of binding and expelling. The child is allowed and encouraged to move out of the parental orbit but only to a certain point. The child may be encouraged to differentiate to the extent required for a specific mission—for instance, to become a famous artist to fulfill the parents' ego or ideals—but no further without incurring negative injunctions. Stierlin suggests that when the child is principally bound or delegated he or she must turn into a "specialist in symbiotic survival," specializing his or her skills and talents for "detoxifying" and yet retaining, as much as possible, the dangerous, overdemanding, and intrusive parent. In so doing this the child must sacrifice or leave undeveloped other skills and capacities needed for progressive individuation and separation.

Bowen (1971, 1976a; 1976b; Kerr, 1981) has developed a family systems theory that suggests a number of possible etiological factors for maternal overprotection. The theory posits two key variables—the degree of anxiety, and the degree of integration of self. Bowen regards the latter as the "cornerstone of the theory" (Bowen, 1976a) and suggests that people can be allocated along a continuum reflecting the degree of *fusion* or *differentiation* between emotional and intellectual functioning. At one end are people whose emotions and intellect are sufficiently fused that their lives are dominated by the emotional system so that they tend to be low on flexibility and adaptability, and emotionally dependent on others. They are said to live in a "feeling-dominated world" and are totally relationship orientated, seeking love and approval. If they fail to win that approval they spend their lives in withdrawal or fighting the other from whom they fail to win approval." They grow as "dependent appendages of their parents" seeking other equally dependent relationships (Bowen, 1976a). Their "pseudoself" (a self-concept fabricated by a vast assortment of principles, beliefs, and knowledge that one acquires to conform to the environment) is more prominent than their "solid self"—which is made up of definite beliefs, opinions and convictions, and incorporated by intellectual reasoning, life experiences, and careful consideration or relevant alternatives. Such people contrast with those at the other end of the dimension who are said to have a more developed solid self that is less a prisoner of the emotional-feeling world. Bowen (1976a) goes on to state that the more differentiated parent can permit their children to grow and to develop their own autonomous selfs without undue anxiety or without trying to fashion their children.

Bowen conceives that there is one brain region controlling emotions and another controlling intellectual functions and that in poorly functioning people, the two centers are fused, with the emotional center dominating the intellectual center. The greater the "separateness" between the two the more the intellectual center is able to resist or censor stimuli from the emotional center, and to function autonomously. "The screen process, which might be biochemical, operates best when anxiety is low" (Bowen, 1976a).

Bowen argues that when acute or chronic tension builds up in a marital couple, one or more of four options in response may occur:

1. Emotional distance between the members of the couple (although compensation may be sought or focused elsewhere—such as in a transference situation in psychotherapy or in an extra marital affair)
2. Marital conflict
3. Spouse dysfunction, with physical or mental illness, or social "acting out" behavior, in the partner whose "self" has been most eroded in the relationship
4. Impairment of children—which is the commonest pattern according to Bowen.

It is worth examining Bowen's observations on the fourth process. He suggests that a two-person relationship, in this instance the marital relationship, is an unstable one with a low tolerance for anxiety or tension. When tension increases an attempt is made to draw in a vulnerable third person to form a triangle and bring about a decrease in individual anxiety. For instance, in one dysfunctional form of marriage, tension may cause the partner in the "dependent-inadequate" position to become more dependent and less confident. The partner in the "strong-overadequate" position may become more authoritarian and critical but, at the same time, be trapped by the neediness and dependency, of the mate. One or both partners may experience a feeling of erosion of individuality. One, for example, the mother, being more uncomfortable, may move toward relationship fusion with a third person, leaving the partner an outsider. The father, in this instance, may feel relief in not having to deal with his wife's anxiety and the emotional issues but may feel neglected and rejected. In such a resulting "triangle" there are always two "insiders" and one "outsider." Triangles are evidence of failure in a two-person relationship. In the most commonly observed triangle the father takes the outside position—and is often described as being passive, weak, and distant—leaving the conflict between the mother and the child. The mother is often judged as "aggressive, dominating, and castrating." According to Bowen, triangles are driven by emotionality.

Bowen further describes a "family projection process" by which parental emotionality is able to define characteristics of the child. For instance, an insecure mother may focus on any sign of insecurity in her child, then see insecurity as a fact and so relate increasingly to the child as if the child were insecure; she thereby molds the child to her anxious focus, whether it be positive or negative in quality. Bowen suggests that the child may be "selected" from the siblings for such focusing by being first born, by being a particular sex, by being born at a time of family turmoil, by being the youngest, or by having a congenital defect. He emphasizes that such characteristics should be regarded as attracting but not determining the process.

The process begins with anxiety in the mother. . . . The anxious parental effort goes into sympathetic, solicitous, overprotective energy, which is directed more by the mother's anxiety than any reality needs of the child . . . Once such process of infantilizing has started, it can be motivated either by anxiety in the mother or anxiety in the child. (Bowen, 1976b)

Bowen further emphasizes that such a family style is inevitably a "multigenerational transmission process" with dysfunction developing in the family over many generations to create the end problem. He suggests that schizophrenia can be the product of several generations of increasing symptomatic impairment, with progressively lower levels of differentiation until there is a generation that "produces schizophrenia" (Bowen, 1976b). Bowen does not express any reservation about his theory being rather too embracing, arguing that neurosis and schizophrenia, and all other variations in human adaptation, may be placed on the same continuum (Bowen, 1976b).

A number of points made by Bowen are worthy of emphasis and closer consideration. He conceptualizes anxiety as having a central role in the development of fusion in the marital dyad and subsequently between one parent (usually the mother) and a selected child. Incidentally, this theory provides another explanation for associations linking the reporting of deficient social bonds (both quantitatively and qualitatively) with neurosis (Henderson et al. 1981), i.e., that the association may be brought about by an increase in neurotic symptomatology increasing togetherness forces (and fusion) in the marital dyad at the expense of other social bonds. In describing a "family projection process" Bowen suggests a mechanism by which insecurity and anxiety in an overprotective parent might be "transmitted" to a child. There are clear conceptual and therapeutic implications to Bowen's suggestion that family dysfunction develops over a number of generations. For instance, Skynner (1981) argues that unless there is extra family assistance, failures by the family to provide a sequence of social challenges to their children will be perpetuated over generations. Furthermore, a number of family therapists consider that optimal family therapy involves the treatment of grandparents as well as parents and children.

Finally, Bowen describes mechanisms by which triangulation develops in families. Most family theorists and therapists have stressed the relevance of the triangle or triad in conceptualizing family psychological problems, with Haley (1971) going so far as to suggest that most child problems include a triangle consisting of an overinvolved parent—child dyad and a peripheral parent. However, other family theorists have equated triangulation with the severity of family dysfunction. Thus, Lewis et al. (1976) suggest that parent–child coalitions (usually between the mother and the patient, with the father being ineffective and excluded) are seen most clearly in families in which the patient has a severe disorder, such as schizophrenia, or a sociopathic personality disorder. As such a family pattern is suggested commonly as relevant to maternal overprotection, Bowen's observations on the structure and determinants of triangulation is worthy of research attention.

While the degree to which "child-centeredness" corresponds to parental overprotection cannot be suggested with any certainty, it is perhaps useful to examine factors suggested by Barragan (1976) as leading to a child-centered family. He suggests that it is influenced by the cultural traditions and idiosyncrasies of the parents' own families and the degree to which boundaries are allowed between those parents and their children. The temperament of the parents and their lowered proficiency in interpersonal relationships is another contributing factor. Furthermore, child-centredness is more likely if parents fail to resolve issues of power, intimacy, and inclusion–exclusion of others into the marital system before the arrival of children. Barragan observes that parents in such families appear preoccupied with the child and invest a lot of time and money in the child while socializing minimally and showing little evidence of outside interests. The marriages are generally either "conflict-habituated" or conflict-free but devoid of zest. Dissatisfaction with the spouse is compensated for by the parent seeking the company and support of the child, by attempting to raise a perfect child, and by justifying deficiencies with the spouse with the excuse that one is sacrificing oneself for the future happiness of the children. Barragan suggests that such a parental style invariably results in symptomatic children, marked principally by impaired independence and autonomy. He suggests tha symptoms might be regarded as a protest against being focused on as a target for the maintainance of the dysfunctional pattern. If the parents ally with the child, anxiety or its equivalents (e.g., hypochondriasis, phobias) result, while if the couple unite against the child, behavior disorders and delinquency are likely outcomes. If the couple unite in overprotecting the child, then shyness, insecurity, and psychosomatic symptoms are likely sequelae.

4
Consequences of Parental Overprotection

In the previous chapters reference has been made to a number of proposed consequences of parental overprotection. Suggested short-term and, in particular, long-term consequences included neurotic anxiety, passivity, over dependency, self-esteem anomalies (e.g., feelings of inferiority and poorly developed concepts of individuality), difficulties in taking up an autonomous existence, and problems in socialization. There is some consistency in the conjecture and clinical notations, as will be demonstrated in this chapter, but the weight of such evidence does not establish that overprotection is a necessary cause of the many so-called consequences.

In many textbooks of psychiatry parental overprotection is implicated as relevant to a number of psychological disorders and psychiatric conditions. For instance, in the fourth edition of Kanner's (1972) textbook *Child Psychiatry*, it is stated that maternal overprotection "creates profound emotional difficulties in the infant." Parental oversolicitude is said in *Modern Clinical Psychiatry* (Kolb, 1973) to be more frequent than neglect but similarly pernicious in its results in causing children to be dependent, infantile, and frequently hostile.

In the *Comprehensive Textbook of Psychiatry* (Kaplan et al., 1980), several authorities describe parental overprotection in association with a wide range of disorders, including schizophrenia (Weiner, p. 1135); the so-called psychosomatic disorders such as bronchial asthma, ulcerative colitis, and rheumatoid arthritis (Weiner, p. 1136); manic-depressive psychosis (Wolpert, pp. 1322–1323); dependent personality disorder (Vaillant and Perry, p. 1585); drug dependence (Freedman, p. 1595); transsexualism (Stoller, p. 1700), and homosexuality (Green, pp. 1763–1765).

Anxiety and depression in a child are linked with overprotective parenting. Werkman observes, "Some parents teach their children to be anxious by overprotecting them from expectable dangers or by exaggerating the dangers of the present and the future" (p. 2624). Cytryn and McKnew suggest, in regard to depression, that overprotection would appear to induce depreciation in a child by emphasizing the "child's inadequacy and worthlessness" (p. 2802).

In the same textbook Call (1980) considers three types of attachment disorders. The third type, "attachment disorder of infancy, symbiotic type" is of relevance. Essentially, infants with this disorder show an exaggeration of the attachment behaviors noted in 18-month-old infants and fail to progress to independence and separation from the mother. The primary symptoms are said to include extreme distress on separating from the mother, excessive clinging to the mother, talk selectively concentrated on the mother, protest when the mother leaves, and severe regression in the absence of the mother. Call suggests that such a disorder is predisposed to by (1) those who are oversolicitous as parents, who failed in differentiating from their own parents, and who are dependent on others, and by (2) illness or handicap in the child. He states that such children have an affect dominated by anxiety, that they show anxiety in new situations and rage with both actual and threatened separation, that their "self" is slow to develop, and that there is a severe impairment of their overall psychosocial development. He notes that later sequelae include an immature personality, a predisposition to anxiety and depression, school phobia, and borderline personality state, while the high anxiety often leads to psychosomatic symptoms and manifestations of hypochondriasis. If the infant problem is moderate or severe there is said to be an increased risk of psychosis in adolescence and early life.

Support for such a disorder comes from individual case reports (e.g., Alpert and Krown, 1953) and clinical research studies. Jenkins (1973), for instance, selected 287 case notes from 1500 cases that allowed a diagnosis of "overanxious reaction." The children were generally described as chronically anxious, fearful, shy, submissive, and reluctant to attend school. Case notes, recorded by social workers, characterized the mothers as "infantilizing overprotective." Jenkins notes that the "whole picture is one of the timid child who has been taught to rely on the strength of others in a dependent relationship and has learned this lesson too well."

It would be useful to consider some other papers and studies that have suggested that parental overprotection may be a cause of psychological disorder and psychiatric disturbance. The following broad review briefly covers the published material. More specific reviews are presented later in the appropriate research chapters (Chapters 8–14).

DISORDERS IN CHILDHOOD

As previously suggested, parental overprotection is commonly implicated in children with *anxiety and depression,* and it is likely that anxiety is central to a number of the other disorders considered. For example, excessive *dependency* is commonly observed in children with high levels of anxiety. Barker (1976) comments that children subject to nonrejecting overprotection tend to remain overdependent on their parents. Herbert (1974) also suggests that a pattern of parental warmth and overprotection could lead to dependency. Several empirical studies support that view. Kagan and Moss (1962), in a longitudinal study of children from birth to early adulthood, noted that a judgment of maternal protectiveness during the first 3 years predicted passive and dependent behavior in boys for the first 10 years. On the basis of teacher ratings, Stedler (1954) compared overdependent children with control children and found some evidence to suggest that maternal overprotection was one of several factors associated with excessive dependency in 6-year-old children. Howe and Madgett (1975) examined the case notes of referrals from the child psychiatry clinic of London hospital, and found that children described as "submissive" were more likely to have mothers described as "overprotective."

In cases of *school phobia* and *school refusal* Barker (1976) notes that "the combination of an anxious and overprotective mother with a weak, ineffectual or absent father, is common." Rutter (1975) states that the "pattern of overprotection and an unusual degree of mutual dependence between mother and child has been particularly described in relation to the problem of school refusal."

Clarke (1967), in describing a "dominant matriarchal syndrome," delineates a three-generational family system that he suggests is commonly associated with school phobia. He describes the complex as being made up principally of three female generations within one family—the maternal grandmother, the mother, and the girl-child. The grandmother is the dominant figure and is married to a steady, dependable husband. While sex is distasteful to her, she produces a daughter who grows up markedly overprotected, heavily mother-oriented and hypochondriacal. The daughter marries a man with characteristics similar to her father, and they live with her parents even after having their daughter. The granddaughter suffers a number of ailments during childhood and, most commonly, develops school phobia in early adolescence.

Support for such a syndrome has come from a number of case report studies (e.g., Crumley, 1974). In a study of children persistently refusing to go to school, Hersov (1960) rated 50 percent of the mothers as overindulgent, and 25 percent as demanding and controlling. Coolidge and Brodie (1974) followed up 49 children who had been treated for school phobia some 10 years earlier. While the actual phobia had a good prognosis, the parents still showed clear anxiety about their child's separation–individuation, and communicated the "safety" of psychological symbiosis to their children. According to the authors, "autonomy was discouraged and dependency reinforced."

In regard to *hypochondriasis,* Shaw and Lucas (1970) express the opinion that the "hypochondriacal child, the neurotic child complaining of somatic symptoms, has probably been overprotected." Koupernik (1973) suggests that hypochondriasis in children is often associated with a rejecting mother who compensates for these feelings by showing an increased concern for the child's health. In such situations the child learns to mobilize the mother's attention by illness or by the pretence of illness.

A similar pattern is suggested by Jenkins (1973) as relevant to an *overinhibited personality structure* in children, "the mother compensating for some rejection by overprotection and overrestriction." Wergeland (1979) studied 11 children who had been admitted to a psychiatric clinic some 8–18 years earlier for *elective mutism.* Most were described as coming from families with a milieu of shyness, reservation, and social isolation, while "six were particularly overprotected." Wright (1971) observes that *delinquents with neurotic overinhibited patterns* (usually evidencing their delinquency in compulsive and solitary stealing) often have a family pattern where the mother is "overprotective and over-anxious, where there is some emotional instability in either or both of the parents, and where the parents set austere or uncompromising standards for their children." *Referral for psychiatric help* has, in itself, been interpreted by some (e.g., Howe and Madgett, 1975) as likely to be overrepresented in situations of parental overprotectiveness.

Minuchin et al. (1978) have argued for the relevance of enmeshment and overprotectiveness in the parents of *diabetics, asthmatics,* and those with *anorexia nervosa.* Christodoulou et al. (1977), in a case–control study, rated children with *peptic ulcer* as more likely to have overprotective parents. Kanner (1972) suggests that childhood *obesity* may reflect fundamental rejection of the child compensated for by overprotection and excessive feeding.

Ananthamurthy and Parameswaran (1978) argue that parental overprotection might be a causal factor in a number of speech disorders such as *delayed speech* and *stuttering.* Parental overprotection as a psychogenic cause of *learning disabilities* in children is suggested by Gardner (1977), although Wetter (1971) found evidence of greater maternal overindulgence and rejection, but not of overprotection, in a case–control study of children diagnosed as having a learning disorder.

Parental overprotection has been linked with several rarely considered situations. For instance in a review of the psychiatric literature,

Mack et al. (1973) suggest that *matricide* frequently occurs against a background of maternal overprotection, emerging out of a "pattern of enforced exclusive intimacy between the mother and the son," with the father absent, or effectively so, and with puberty intensifying the conflicts over the child's independence. Empirical support for this suggestion has emerged recently in a study of 58 males who had committed matricide (Green, 1981). Many years earlier Wertham (1941) suggested the term "Orestes complex" to describe a sexually immature yet homosexually orientated son who was locked in a hostile and dependent relationship with a possessive and overprotective mother.

Overprotection has been described as a *parental response to survival* following a massive stress. Trossman, a psychiatrist at the student mental health clinic at McGill University in Montreal, Canada, is quoted by Epstein (1979) in her study of the Jewish survivors of Hitler's concentration camps: "the first and perhaps most innocuous [feature] is that those parents are excessively overprotective, constantly warning their children of impending danger . . . . Consequently, many of the children have become moderately phobic, others locked in combat with their parents as they try to throw off the smothering yoke."

OVERPROTECTION OF CHRONICALLY ILL OR HANDICAPPED CHILDREN

Access to the computer listing of bibliographic citations to "parental overprotection" held by the National Institute for Mental Health, Bethesda, Maryland, revealed that the largest number of citations were in reference to *chronic childhood illness*. As it is often suggested that characteristics in the child may elicit parental overprotection, it is appropriate to review a number of the relevant papers. For the purposes of this review, chronic childhood illness refers to disorders that have a protracted course, may be progressive and fatal or may be associated with a normal life span, and are further defined by the impairment of physical and/or mental functioning.

Mattson (1972), Bentovim (1972a), and Fox (1977) state that a repeated finding by observers of the family environment of handicapped children is that the satisfactory emotional development of the child depends more on the way in which the parents and the family relate to the child than the extent of the handicap itself: "Long-term rejection or anxious overprotection masking ambivalent hostility shown to a child over the years markedly affects his degree of self-regard and self-confidence." (Bentovim, 1972a).

There is a high degree of consistency in the views of those describing the genesis, the existence, and the sequelae of parental overprotection of the handicapped child. Mattson (1972) states that parents who "remain highly anxious and guilt-laden about their ill child tend to cope with their emotional distress by overprotection and pampering him, and by limiting his activities with other children." He suggests that the child may develop a sense of vulnerability and a sense of likely premature death in response to these parental characteristics and may become passive-dependent or rebel and be daring and reckless. Those mothers who are described as constantly "worried and overprotective" usually have children who are fearful and inactive, and they show a lack of outside interests and a marked dependency on their families and on their mother in particular. Pinkerton (1970) suggests that parental overprotection is one of a number of patterns of "nonacceptance" of a child's handicap, and that overprotection involves "emotional smothering of the child, with denial of the chance to adapt realistically and so make optimal use of what potential he may still retain." He states that parental overprotection may mask "more sinister psychopathology," and may reflect a compensatory guilt response to early attitudes of rejection, may be an unconscious attempt to evade marital responsibilities, or may be an unconscious attempt to live through the child to compensate for emotional aridity in the marriage. Bentovim (1972b) emphasizes the dangers of overprotection: the child who is overcontrolled becomes overdependent and infantile and unable to respond to the stress inherent in development. In this "too perfect adaptation" or "too good mothering" there is a failure to appreciate that "some degree of frustration is essential for a child to feel it necessary to communicate through speech and to extend his social contact." Kasper (1978) suggests that parental overprotection enhances the self-doubts and insecurities that the disabled already possess.

An empirical study by Schaffer (1964) provides a clearer picture of the nature of overprotective parenting of handicapped children. Schaffer selected 13 families for study, on the basis of the family spending an excessive period of time together, from a total sample of 30 families having a preschool child with cerebral palsy. He describes how the mothers were unable to relinquish the hold on their child for even the briefest period (e.g., remaining by a window to watch their child playing in the garden, rarely leaving the child in the company of others, usually refusing to visit friends, and the majority having the child share the parental bed). The mothers expressed a constant theme—that harm might come to the child if left alone or in the company of others. As a consequence of this excessive cohesion (the fathers showed similar characteristics in most families), the mothers had little time to do housework, to care for their other children, or to participate in social activities. Schaffer found no evidence that the sex of the child, the presence or absence of siblings, or external pressures, such as family or community ostracism, influenced the excessive cohesion. Instead, he suggests that the handicapped child provides a challenge to parental capacities, which is met with annoyance, rejection, and hostility. Failure to resolve these emotions leads to an intense guilt, which is repressed and then promotes an overcompensation at an overt level.

He notes that all 13 mothers agreed that they were under considerable strain (e.g., "suffering from nerves," "depressed," "on edge,"), and described clear developmental and social lags in the children when they were compared with the remaining 17 children in the sample. For instance, children in the highly cohesive families were weaned and toilet trained at a later age, and most were being fed, washed, and dressed by parents when they were at an age appropriate for self-mastery of those tasks. Furthermore, there was evidence that they received little parental encouragement in locomotive tasks, speech, or formal learning. The affected children, when rated by their own therapists, presented a picture of "considerable social immaturity." Most exhibited an unnecessary "degree of helplessness," were emotionally dependent, clung to parents, and were reluctant to make extrafamily contacts. While they were not socially maladjusted in the family (presumably as interrelationships were balanced) they were quite egocentric and uncooperative in group and social situations.

Bell (1964) located five case–control studies in which scores on the PARI (a parental attitude scale) for parents of children with congenital disorders were compared against scores for parents with normal children. In all 5 studies (2 of congenitally blind children, 1 each of children with mongolism, congenital heart defects, and cerebral palsy) the mean scores on the intrusiveness scale were higher for the cases. He suggests that intrusiveness may be defined "as an effort on the part of the mother to enter the private world of the child" and that "it seems logically to be a key element in maternal overprotection." Bell interprets intrusiveness as being induced in mothers by stimulus properties of the child, particularly perceived or actual limitations in the child's coping ability.

Corrigan (1977) studied the organization of families whose children had inflammatory bowel disease. In a controlled study he found evidence of greater enmeshment and overprotection in the families with the ill child, but no evidence that the degree of those characteristics related to severity of symptoms in the children.

Schaffer suggests that maternal overprotection is often due to maternal overcompensation for feelings of rejection of the child, based on evidence of indifference to or rejection of the handicapped baby by some mothers who later became overprotective. Certainly an association between maternal rejection and overprotection has been shown in families with handicapped children. For instance, Jillings et al. (1976) had 56 mothers of handicapped children (13 with infantile autism, 23 with mongolism, and 20 with hearing disorders) complete a maternal attitude scale (Roth, 1961) measuring "acceptance," "rejection," "overprotection," and "overindulgence." Overprotection scores correlated negatively with acceptance (-0.57), and positively with rejection ($+0.32$) and overindulgence ($+0.62$) scores, the correlations being in the same direction and in the same order as those found in a middle-class, nonclinical group of mothers. While these findings support the view that maternal overprotection is associated with maternal rejection and less acceptance, they do not suggest that maternal rejection leads to overprotection. This issue will be addressed in more detail in Chapter 17.

As noted earlier, the nature of the specific illness or handicap, as opposed to its existence, does not seem to be an important variable, and a number of disorders for which maternal overprotection has been noted as a common accompaniment will be noted briefly. An overprotective parent is prevalent in families with a mentally retarded child (Molony, 1971; Carter, 1973; Krynski, 1975; Kantor et al., 1979), with mothers and fathers being equally susceptible (Staten, 1972) and with the parental style likely to exaggerate the degree of retardation and to further reduce the child's social capacities (Galazan, 1966). Parental overprotection is commonly noted for epileptic children (Breger, 1977; Mulder, 1977; Ross, 1977; Gordon, 1980), as it is for prematurely born children (Arajarvi et al., 1973), cerebral palsy children (Shere, 1955; Sharma and Koshy, 1972), children with chronic renal disease (Klein, 1976; Sigal et al., 1971) or children receiving a renal transplant (Hickey, 1972), and children with haemophilia (Agle, 1975; Steinhausen, 1976; Markova, 1979).

While a number of writers suggest that parental overprotection may be prevented or relieved to some degree by adequate counseling (e.g., Markova, 1979), such observations remain largely untested. Pinkerton (1970) suggests that exhortations or direct advice to a parent to "stop smothering usually falls on deaf ears." Fife (1978), noting two studies suggesting that overprotection is a common parental response to childhood leukemia, designed a study to see if such problems could be reduced by interventions. Eight parents of children ages 3–12 years with acute leukemia (in remission but requiring maintenance therapy) received "client-centered therapy" while a similar number received behavioral therapy. The former intervention was supportive and had the goals of improving function and coping while decreasing anxiety through self-learning and increasing self-understanding. The latter intervention was directed at changing specific coping behaviors that were assessed as impeding personal growth and family relationships. The same therapist was used for both groups. The primary goal was reduction in parental overprotection, as measured on an 8-item check list. Fife does not note whether parental overprotection altered for the whole group, but states that no significant difference emerged between the two groups, although those in the behavioral therapy group did begin to conceptualize family problems.

Hackett (1976) compared the effects of two sessions of counseling versus no counseling on mothers of children receiving heart surgery. Correlations revealed a significant clustering of maternal variables of anxiety, overprotection, restrictiveness, and special treatment with a significant level of maladjustment in the children. Counseling was associated with a change toward greater discipline, but with no change on measures of psychological adjustment, maternal anxiety or maternal overprotectiveness.

This review of the literature suggests that parental overprotection is a common concomitant of chronic illness, while several studies (comparing parental responses to unaffected siblings) suggest strongly that childhood illness acts to elicit overprotection. However, as overprotection is not elicited in all parents as a response to childhood illness, parent variables are clearly of importance. Two views suggesting mechanisms linking parental characteristics with overprotection are commonly offered by clinical commentators. First, parental overprotection is a response to a more basic and earlier feeling of wishing to reject the child or of hostility to the child's condition. Second, parental overprotection is a feature of parents who are anxious or who are evidencing psychological dysfunction. A consistent view by the commentators is that overprotection has deleterious effects on the chronically ill child—distorting the child's view of his or her illness, reducing the child's self-confidence and self-esteem, and slowing and restricting the child's social development. Only a few studies have been performed, and no study has demonstrated that intervention reduces maternal overprotectiveness in chronically ill children. It is of interest that no assessment has been made of the most commonly employed devices—exhortations and direct advice.

DISORDERS IN ADULTHOOD

As suggested earlier in this chapter, and as might be expected from the consideration of disorders in childhood, parental overprotection has been incriminated as a relevant causal influence on the development of a number of psychiatric disorders, including the so-called functional psychoses (schizophrenia and manic-depressive psychosis), certain neuroses (anxiety neurosis, depressive neurosis, hypochondriasis, and agoraphobia, in particular), certain personality disorders (e.g., dependent and borderline), certain sexual disorders (e.g., homosexuality and transsexualism), and several "psychosomatic," disorders (asthma, in particular). In addition, the experience of parental overprotection is often linked with personality characteristics of dependency, low self-esteem, socialization difficulties and excessive utilization of medical services. The suggested relevance of parental overprotection to the development of these disorders will be reviewed in the appropriate chapters in Part III (Chapters 8–16).

GENERAL CONSIDERATIONS

Parental overprotection has been incriminated as a factor in a wide range of psychiatric, psychological and psychosomatic disorders. While many authors have suggested that parental overprotection is a cause of such disorders, no attempt has been made to review the strengths or weaknesses of those claims in this chapter. A sophisticated research methodology is required before a disorder can be claimed to be a consequence of a particular environment. The wide range of disorders in which parental overprotection has been incriminated might suggest that parental overprotection is a nonspecific factor, a possibility suggesting a need to exclude its more direct association with a general variable such as psychiatric patient status. Such issues will be addressed in Part III but there is a need to raise them as caveats since parental overprotection has been offered so frequently (and some might argue, indiscriminately) as a cause of psychological and psychiatric disorder.

5
The Mother–Child Tie: Its Nature and Factors Influencing Its Evolution

In previous chapters an attempt was made to document the commonly cited characteristics of an overprotective maternal tie to a child and to consider some observations and speculations on the evolution of such a tie. Clearly, there has been an implicit assumption that maternal overprotection is pathological, first, because it is deviant from optimal mothering (quantitatively and/or qualitatively), and, second, because it has been incriminated as causing numerous psychosocial disorders. At this stage it is useful to consider the nature of the normal tie linking the child with its mother. Not only might this assist consideration of distinctions between optimal and overprotective mothering, but it also might assist speculation on the nature and genesis of the overprotective mother.

The evolution of the mother—child tie has attracted much theoretical and research interest, although more attention has been directed to considering those processes determining attachment than to those processes influencing the subsequent detachment of the child from the mother. Both processes are clearly of relevance to this inquiry; maternal overprotection may reflect quantitative or qualitative disturbances in either attachment and/or detachment processes.

As is true of child developmental research in general, several clear trends in mother–child attachment research are apparent. There is a trend toward reporting direct observations rather than accepting at face value retrospectively generated observations from adult psychiatric patients. There is also a trend toward describing development in a largely atheoretical way. Rutter (1980a) suggests that, while many of the theories of mother–child attachment are historically important, some no longer warrant serious attention in view of the mass of findings inconsistent with those theories. For instance, he notes that Lorenz's original view of imprinting has had to be considerably modified, while Freud's notion that object relations develop on the basis of feeding and Dollard and Miller's view that attachment is the result of secondary reinforcement are both inconsistent with findings suggesting the irrelevance of feeding and physical caretaking.

The following review is neither comprehensive in considering all the theoretical propositions that have been offered nor critical in examining the individual strengths and weaknesses of the various clinical and research observations. Numerous reviews of both types have been published, and many are referenced in this chapter. The principal intent of the present review is to consider preferentially those observations and interpretations that seem most relevant to the general inquiry. Some agreement between the descriptions of those representing psychoanalytic, psychosocial, and ethological views reflect a selective presentation with the aim of emphasizing convergence, rather than divergence, of views.

This review is also consistent with other contemporary trends in child developmental research. The traditional concept of the infant as a passive creature has given way to a greater appreciation of the infant's active interest in, and attempt to operate actively on, its environment. Transactional models, whereby the child is acknowledged as playing an active role in molding and shaping features of the environment, and vice versa, are now generally accepted. Extending that view more broadly, it has been gradually accepted that the behavioral organization of the child is the property of a wider system (perhaps involving the family and the culture) rather than merely being the property of the individual. Such a view is linked with the trend to define development as the outcome of an interaction between genetically determined patterns of biological growth and environmental experience (Call, 1979). Attention to interactions is important in considering the ways in which deviations from normal development may occur, as well as in explaining why it is so difficult to predict normal and abnormal development successfully given a number of independent risk factors. For instance, Sameroff and Chandler (1975) point out how individual differences in the constitutional matrix determining temperament may lead to differences in response to stress, play an important part in shaping life experience, influence the child's perception of the environment, influence what is an affective environment for him, and structure how other people respond to him. For those reasons evidence is reviewed suggesting that factors external to the mother–child tie (e.g., fathers, peers, culture) have the capacity to influence the tie. The difficulties inherent in analyzing interactional processes are noted where appropriate.

THEORIES OF PARENT–CHILD ATTACHMENT AND DETACHMENT PROCESSES

Psychoanalytic Views

Ainsworth (1973) notes that it was Freud who first directed attention to the significance of the infant–mother attachment (although he preferred the term "object relations") and to its origins and developmental course. Freud's instinctual theory supposed that excitation in specific regions of the body gives rise to tension, which is discharged through one of several bodily channels, and is directed at an object (most usually a specific person). The infant is said to have certain primary drives (e.g., to be fed) which are most usually responded to by the mother, and the infant's attachment to the mother evolves from the mother's responses to the infant's primary drives. Thus, according to this *secondary drive theory,* the infant's attachment to the mother is based on her gratification of his basic drives and physiological needs.

Freud believed that most important developments in personality occur in the first 6 years of life, and described development within a psychosexual context, with one erotogenic region after another becoming predominant. A number of shifts in parent–child attachment occur. Freud considered that the first 18 months of life comprise the *oral phase,* in which oral tensions and their satisfaction allow dependence on a mother figure to be established.

In the second, or *anal phase,* lasting from 2 to 4 years of age, conflicts with parents over anal control and appropriate toilet habits are preeminent. Freud considered that in this phase the child is attempting to achieve some independence of, and autonomy from, the parents, and that failure might lead to excessive shame, self-doubt, or a sense of defeat.

In the third, or *phallic phase,* lasting from 4 to 6 years of age, Oedipal and Electral conflicts occur. The child is strongly attracted to the parent of the opposite sex and has feelings of hostility to, and competition with, the parent of the same sex. If normal development is to occur, then a positive identification with the parent of the same sex is required.

Following the interruption of the latency period, roughly between the ages of 6 and 12 years, when affiliations are primarily isosexual, the adolescent begins to be attracted to members of the opposite sex with the biological aim of reproduction. In this genital phase, Oedipal or Electral impulses emerge again but this threat is avoided by the adolescent moving away from the family and selecting an external sexual partner.

Ainsworth (1973) provides a useful review of the modifications to Freud's views introduced by the "ego psychologists." As a general proposition, they hold that the development of object relations are "inextricably intertwined with ego development." (Ainsworth, 1973). They consider the newborn to be wholly undifferentiated: the infant can neither distinguish separate objects in its environment, nor self from the external world. As a consequence the infant experiences everything as part of itself and is aware, due to a stimulus barrier to the external world, of little but the ebb and flow of its own tensions. The infant is, in their terms, "undifferentiated," "objectless," or "narcissistic," and its responses are tied to visceral, autonomic, and emotional organizations rather than being based on perceptual discrimination of the environment.

Need gratification, particularly the feeding relationship, is said to be the origin of object relationships, with the infant attaching libidinal energy to the experience of satisfaction and relief rather than to the person who has gratified it. At a later stage the food, rather than the experience of need satisfaction, becomes the source of pleasure. The infant's libidinal tie to the mother comes and goes in accordance with its need state, being extended when she gratifies its needs and withdrawn when she is either absent, or present and frustrating its needs. Only later in infancy does the child develop a tie to her irrespective of its need state, and whether she is gratifying or frustrating, present or absent. Ainsworth notes that Anna Freud called this the stage of *object constancy,* in which the infant perceives the mother as a person separate from itself. The mother is discriminated perceptually from all others, an internalized representation of her can be held for a short period, and the infant is distressed by her leaving.

Bowlby (1969) criticizes a number of ego psychologists (e.g., Anna Freud, Melanie Klein, Margaret Ribble, Therese Benedek, and Rene Spitz), who, having made empirical observations of nonoral social interaction between mothers and infants (i.e., suggesting social bonds), then showed "a compulsion to give primacy to needs for food and warmth and to suppose that social interaction develops only secondarily and as a result of instrumental learning."

While psychoanalytic views on the nature and origin of mother–infant attachment appear less able to explain observable phenomena than Bowlby's own theory (to be discussed shortly), observations by psychoanalysts on the process of "detachment" have contributed to the data base.

Mahler and Gosliner (1955) introduced the term *separation-individuation* to describe a process occurring in early childhood—although it has subsequently been used rather loosely by other writers to refer to a more general process extending across childhood and adolescence. In a later publication the theory and its development are considered in some detail (Mahler et al., 1975). There the authors report an analysis of data obtained from a nonclinical group of 38 children and 22 mothers whose interaction in a reasonably natural setting was observed over time.

The authors refer to the "psychological birth of the individual" as "the separation-individuation process: the establishment of a sense of separateness from, and relation to, a world of reality," particularly in regard to the infant's own body and primary parent-figure. They use the term *separation* to refer to the intrapsychic achievement of a sense of separateness from the mother and, through that, the world at large. They define *identity* as the awareness of a sense of being—"not a sense of *who* I am but *that* I am." While they hold that such a process is always active, they limit the separation-individuation process principally to a period lasting from the fourth or fifth month to the beginning or middle of the third year. Such a process involves the child's achievement of separate functioning in the presence of, and with the emotional availability of the mother, and takes place in a setting of a developmental readiness for independent functioning. Separation, the child's emergence from a symbiotic fusion with the mother, and individuation, the achievement of identity and the child's assumption of its own individual characteristics, are not identical, and, while intertwined, may proceed divergently. Mahler et al. (1975) provide a relevant example of how divergence may occur, when "an omnipresent infantilizing mother who interferes with the child's innate strivings for individuation . . . may retard the development of the child's full awareness of self-other differentiation."

They suggest that for the first few weeks of life the infant is in a *normal autistic phase;* while the infant may show some responsivity to external stimuli, the phase is marked by the infant's lack of awareness of a mothering agent. In the second month a *symbiotic phase* commences, in which the infant behaves and functions as though the infant and the mother were an omnipotent system. Inner sensations form the "core of the self" around which a sense of identity will become established.

At 4–5 months of age and at the peak of the symbiosis the first phase of the separation-individuation process—*differentiation*—appears; it is indicated by a preferential smiling response (in contrast to the earlier nonspecific social smile) to the mother. At 6 months of age tentative experimentation at separation-individuation begins (and is demonstrated, for example, by the infant exploring the mother's face visually and by touch). The authors comment that optimal development is associated in this phase with "curiosity and wonderment" when inspecting strangers, but if basic trust is less than optimal there may be an abrupt change to anxiety toward strangers.

The timing of differentiation within the symbiotic phase is influenced by a number of factors, such as the mother's enjoyment of the phase, the absence of conflict, and the infant being either "saturated" or "oversaturated" with the mother. Differentiation may be delayed or premature, the latter resulting in the infant subsequently being overwhelmed by anxiety because autonomous ego capacities are precocious and vulnerable. Anomalies in differentiation occur if the mother is ambivalent, intrusive, or "smothering." The authors describe a group of mothers who could not endure disengagement of the infant at the beginning of the separation-individuation phase.

Subsequently, but overlapping with the differentiation subphase, is a *practicing* subphase when the toddler concentrates on practicing and mastering its own skills and autonomous capacities. Mahler et al. suggest that there are two separate stages of this subphase. The early stage is evidenced by motor activities such as crawling and climbing, interest in inanimate objects (some of which become transitional objects), and exploring away from the mother but returning to her intermittently as a "home base" for physical contact. In the later stage, lasting approximately from 10 to 18 months of age, there is a rapid increase in practicing motor skills and in exploring the environment, both animate and inanimate. It is a period marked by a "love affair with the world," according to Greenacre (1957). Mahler et al. note that exhilaration in the practicing subphase was lacking in those children whose symbiotic relationship had been unduly prolonged or disturbed by an excessively close or parasitic symbiosis with the mother, and diminished or irregular in children when the mother was unpredictable and impulsive, or partly engulfing and partly rejecting.

Following the practicing subphase, there is a *rapprochement* subphase, lasting approximately from 15 to 24 months of age. During this period there is a seemingly constant concern with the mother's whereabouts. The toddler shadows its mother (by incessantly watching or following her). The authors comment that excessive shadowing is evidence that a child is finding its awareness of separation a stress. The child's usual pattern of alternate shadowing and running away from its mother is said to show both a wish for reunion with the love object and a fear of reengulfment by it. The authors suggest that the child fears a loss of love but does not want to surrender the recently achieved autonomy, which is evidenced, in part, by the frequent use of "no" statements. In this phase individuation is proceeding very rapidly, and the infant is aware of its separateness from the mother, which it seeks to resist and revoke.

The authors distinguish three stages in the rapprochement subphase. In the first stage, commencing at about 15 months, the child realizes that it and its mother do not always have similar views and wishes. The child wishes to share its discoveries of the world with her, its social relationships expand (shown in distinct attachment to its father and in relating to substitute adults), and its play (specifically involving the disappearance and reappearance of things) shows an attempt to deal symbolically with the absence of the mother. The end of that stage is marked by the appearance of temper tantrums behaviors suggesting rage and helplessness, and the reappearance of reactions to strangers. A second stage, commencing at approximately 18 months, consists of rapid switches in pushing the mother away and in clinging to her, together with a tendency to use the mother as an extension of self. The child is said to often appear to "lose" the mother, seeming to forget about her presence even when she is in the same room. The third stage, at approximately 21 months, reveals a lessening in the rapprochement struggle. There is a reduction in the struggle for omnipotent control, in the anxiety for separation and in the alternate demands for closeness and autonomy, each child finds optimal distance from the mother.

Mahler et al. suggest that the optimal maternal attitude in this phase is represented by quiet availability, sharing of exploits, reciprocity, and giving a gentle push or encouragement to independence. Of particular relevance, is their observation that some mothers "by their protracted doting and intrusiveness rooted in their own anxiety" becomes themselves "shadowers" of the child.

Following the rapprochement subphase, and in the third year of life, there is a *consolidation of individuality* and the beginning of "emotional object constancy" (a gradual internalization of a constant, positively cathected maternal image with fusion of "good" and "bad" objects into one whole representation). This achievement allows both a lengthening in, and a better toleration of, temporary separations, so that the child can commence school and cope with other periods of separation. This subphase is marked by the unfolding of complex cognitive functions (e.g., verbal communication, fantasy, reality testing), and as mental representations of the self become established the way to self-identity formation is paved. The more intrusive, or the less predictably reliable, the mother-figure is, the more likely it is for a "bad" introject to form, and for aggression in the child to be promoted.

The authors distinguish their term "object constancy" from Piaget's term "object permanence," suggesting that Piaget (1954) referred to the infant developing the concept that objects in his environment are permanent (and do not cease to exist when out of his reach of view), while they are referring to the development of a constant, inner image of the mother.

In their description of individual study cases the authors make a number of interesting observations, including the suggestion that infants may develop quasiphysical precursors of defense mechanisms (e.g. pushing away) in response to overprotective parenting.

As psychoanalysts have traditionally shown little interest in the middle years of childhood, their considerations of the processes underlying parent–child detachment have attended principally to the first few years of childhood and to adolescence. A representative psychoanalytic view of detachment during the latter period is expressed by Blos (1967). Blos views adolescence as a period for a second individuation process. By the shredding of family dependencies disengagement occurs. Unless there is a successful disengagement from "infantile internalized objects," the finding of extrafamilial love objects in the outside world is likely to be precluded, hindered, or remain restricted. Blos suggests that the peer group allows "role try outs" without any permanent obligations, and experimentation with interaction, but if the peer group simply replaces childhood dependencies then the adolescent proces is effectively short-circuited.

Blos argues that successful passage through adolescence can only be accomplished by a return to earlier phases of development, with reanimation of infantile emotional involvements so that disengagement from "internal objects" can be achieved. This regressive task is required in adolescence to promote the individuation process. Failure in individuation may be indicated in "acting out" behaviors, learning disorders, a lack of purpose, procrastination, moodiness, and negativism.

Clearly, the present overview of psychoanalytic views is highly selective. Psychoanalytic theories of object relations subscribe to a secondary drive theory of mother–infant attachment, an emphasis on dependency, and a view of the newborn infant as "undifferentiated" or unable perceptually to discriminate objects in the social world for some period of time. According to Rutter (1980a), such views do not warrant serious consideration as there is a mass of findings inconsistent with the central components of the analytic view. However, in the rush to dismiss psychoanalytic theorizing it is possible that much useful observational data may be ignored. This applies, in particular, to the description of demarcated phases in a child's moves to greater independence and autonomy. The data reported by Mahler and colleagues seems to be worthy of keen attention, particularly because they are in broad synchrony with, and complementary to, observations made by those supporting an ethological–evolutionary view.

Psychosocial Views

A psychosocial view, according to Newman and Newman (1975), is based on four organizing concepts: (1) there are separate stages of development, (2) there are separate developmental tasks at each stage, (3) each stage may provide a "psychosocial crisis" for the individal, and (4) the individual makes active efforts to resolve stresses emerging at each developmental stage which require integration of his or her own needs and skills with the demands of the culture. Erik Erikson provided one of the earliest and also a relatively enduring, psychosocial framework for conceptualizing child and adult development. According to Kaplan et al. (1975), Erikson brought Freud's psychoanalytic theory out of the bounds of the nuclear family.

Erikson (1968) considers development to be epigenetic or layered, whereby certain potentialities require environmental stimulation for their appearance and/or modification. The individual develops biologically in a sequence of steps that influence psychological and social development at those times. Five of the eight steps, and their associated tasks, are relevant to this chapter:

1. *Oral-sensory stage.* This stage corresponds to Freud's oral stage and extends through the first year of life, with oral incorporation and sensory discriminatory activities being dominant. If progress is optimal the infant develops a mutually satisfying relationship with the mother-figure and develops a sense of basic trust in itself. In exploring the environment, in adjusting instinctual needs to social realities, and in the relationship with the mother-figure, the infant progressively develops an awareness of itself as an individual, and so lays the basis for later interpersonal relationships.
2. *Musculo-anal stage.* This stage is akin to Freud's anal stage, and extends through the second and third years of life. Optimally, basic internal controls are established, the child finds pleasure in the discovery and mastery of tasks, and some separation from the mother-figure occurs.
3. *Locomotor stage.* This stage lasts through the fifth year. The child initiates more activities and has the capacity to develop initiative. In its drive toward intimate contact with its mother, in seeking parental affections, and in its explorations outside the home, the child meets restrictions that help to define the social world. Erikson suggests that if this stage is not mastered adequately, perhaps because parents crush the child's explorations, then the child may develop an overly harsh or punitive conscience and be left with a sense of disappointment and guilt.
4. *Latency stage.* This stage lasts until puberty. There is less reliance on the family as socialization continues. Kaplan et al. (1975) point out that Erikson emphasizes that social institutions (such as schools) may counteract the malignant influences of nonsupportive parents, or produce deleterious effects on the child's self-esteem despite supportive parents.
5. *Puberty and adolescence.* The task in this stage is the development of a mature sense of identity, which is a crucial issue in the second or third decade. "Identity formation emerges as an evolving configuration . . . gradually integrating constitutional givens, idiosyncratic libidinal

needs, favored capacities, significant identifications, effective defences, successful sublimations, and consistent roles" (Erikson 1965).

Newman and Newman (1975) differ from Erikson in distinguishing an "early adolescence" period from a "later adolescence" period. They suggest that *early adolescence* begins with the onset of puberty and ends at the time of graduation from high school. This period is characterized by rapid physical changes (bringing adolescents closer to an image of themselves as adults, strengthening sex-role identification, and creating ambivalence), rapid conceptual maturation (thinking becomes more abstract so that hypotheses can be generated about events not perceived and an extended sense of the future develops) and a heightened sensitivity to peer approval (when the rewards and limitations of an extensive group identification become apparent). It has been suggested (e.g., Goodman, 1969) that the peer group serves as a transitional world between dependency and autonomy. During this period the adolescent has to continue to be, and meet obligations as, a son or daughter and, at the same time, abandon the role of a dependent child and become an independent, autonomous adult. Signs of independence may be glaringly overt (and perhaps suggested in the style of dress or staying out late), but an emotional attachment to the family is usually apparent. Newman and Newman review several studies (e.g., Douvan and Gold, 1966) suggesting that independence is promoted more by democratic-style families than by authoritarian families.

Later adolescence is a period beginning at approximately 18 years of age and lasts 3–4 years. It is characterized by the attainment of independence from family and the development of a sense of personal autonomy. Optimally, the individual is sufficiently physically mature, has mastered the skills, and has the information base for independent living. Newman and Newman suggest that the adolescent may have to leave the parents abruptly or reveal evidence of seeming "alienation" to achieve independence. Such a period of alienation follows the earlier period of dependence and is followed, perhaps years later, by a period of psychological closeness to parents, as an approximation of values and other issues occurs and is perhaps realized. While it would be useful to relate the psychological processes involved in adolescence to the psychological processes of puberty, such attempts are restricted by problems of definition overlap and a lack of research data.

Adolescence is usually said to commence with puberty, that period of physiological development when a number of biological changes occur. These changes are triggered by mechanisms in the hypothalamus and other brain centers, and are mediated in part by hormonal changes that have resisted precise clarification (Katchadourian, 1979). The assumption of adult status most usefully defines the termination of adolescence. However, as Muus (1975) notes, the relation between puberty and adolescence is complicated if cross-cultural comparisons are made. In some cultures puberty rites are associated with a transition from childhood to adulthood without any intervening period of adolescence. Whereas the duration of pubescence is determined more by biological factors, the duration of adolescence is influenced more by social institutions and cultural factors. Muus suggests that the termination of adolescence is related more to age and status definitions (e.g., reaching voting age) than to the time when social, personal, sexual, and religious adjustments are made, and emotional and financial independence of parents is achieved.

Any relationship between pubertal maturation and psychological development in adolescence can theoretically be linked by a *direct effects model,* with psychological changes being attributed directly to physiological processes, or by a *mediated effects model,* which assumes that a number of variables (e.g., culture) mediate the process. Peterson and Taylor (1980) suggest that the latter model is more accurate; although studies have not been conducted in pubescent subjects, the evidence linking a direct effect of hormones on behavior is generally weak.

Erikson's emphasis on identity formation as the primary task of adolescence is now considered in greater detail. According to his epigenetic view of development, failures at earlier stages influence identity formation in adolescence. For instance, failure to develop trust in infancy recurs as identity confusion in adolescence; failure to achieve autonomy in the second and third years of life promotes battles for autonomy and dependency, or a self-conscious vulnerability in adolescence; failure to develop a sense of initiative in the fifth year may contribute to a negative identity in adolescence by engendering guilt and fear; and failure to develop a sense of industry in the latency period may lead to a sense of futility and a lack of mastery in adolescence (Erikson, 1968).

Marcia (1967) has extended Erikson's formulations by suggesting that the attainment of a mature identity requires both a "crisis" (exposure to, and deliberation about, a range of options) and "commitment" (an investment in an occupation or belief). Muus (1975) applies Marcia's criteria of crisis and commitment to provide a typology of, and possibly a developmental sequence involved in, adolescence:

1. *Foreclosed adolescents* have not experienced crisis but have made commitments that have been "handed" to them ready made by others, most frequently by their parents. They appear committed to parental values, show undue respect for authority, and are often dependent on others (according to three, essentially correlational studies cited by Marcia, 1980).

2. *Identity diffusion* or *identity confusion* precedes crisis and commitment. These adolescents are in a state of "psychological fluidity" according to Muus (1975), and therefore are receptive to all kinds of influence. According to Marcia (1980), the research studies suggest that adolescents in this phase tend to report their parents as detached and rejecting.
3. In the *moratorium phase,* adolescents are in an acute stage of crisis; they have not made a real commitment (Erikson, 1968), and therefore tend to experiment with varying roles, beliefs, and occupations. Muus (1975) states that "Moratorium really is an essential prerequisite for identity achievement." Marcia (1980) suggests that these adolescents perceive their parents in rather ambivalent terms and that some, in particular, are trying "to struggle free" from their parents.
4. The *identity achieved* adolescent has experienced crises, resolved them on his own terms, made personal commitments to an occupation and belief system, and resolved issues such as sexuality. Research studies, according to Marcia (1980), find such adolescents to have "balanced views" of their parents.

Cross-cultural observations of adolescence have produced a wealth of information. Two broad findings are of particular relevance. First, Benedict (1950) reports that development in a number of primitive societies is gradual; children are gradually expected to assume adult responsibilities from an early age. In such societies, the emotional and social turbulence seen so commonly in Western adolescents is less obvious or not seen at all. Second, puberty rites vary from nonexistent to extreme; their existence and complexity depend on the judged change of status for the individual in that culture. Kessler (1976) notes that while some cultures have distinct puberty rites for girls only, others for boys only, and others for both sexes, overall such rites are more prevalent for boys. She suggests that such a sex difference might reflect a perceived need to separate boys from feminine associations, or the greater change in status and responsibilities faced by boys.

Clearly, sex differences reflect the orientation of the particular culture. For instance, Sarpong (1977) notes that the Ashanti people of West Africa—who have a matrilineal family organization and value daughters more than sons—have no initiation rites for boys (apart from the presentation of a gun, tool, or instrument to the son by the father) but have lengthy and complex initiation rites for their daughters at some time after first menstruation. In contrast, Whiting (1941) describes the extensive initiation rites for boys, compared to minor ones for girls, in the Kwoma tribe in the Sepik area of New Guinea. The boy initiates have their tongues and penises cut by an unrelated man, are given decorative combs by their ceremonial fathers, engage in hunting competitions, and live secluded from their family. It is interesting that their mothers are told that the initiates have been killed, suggesting an institutionalized symbolic message signifying that the maternal tie has been broken.

This overview of psychosocial views suggests several conclusions. These theories attend little to the possible processes involved in the development of mother–infant bonds. In contrast, they attend extensively to processes possibly involved in parent–child detachment, the development of independence, and the structuring of an identity. The psychological approach is an eclectic one and necessarily broad. Identity formation in adolescence is seen to be influenced by a large number of factors: earlier experiences in handling life stages, parental attitudes and behaviors, extrafamilial influences (e.g., school peers), experiential issues, cultural mores, and the defining aspects of the society. Personality development in childhood and adolescence is generally linked in an unidirectional way (with causality implicit or explicit) to certain parental characteristics; and other possible explanations are rarely conceded.

Ethological–Evolutionary Views

Implicit to the ethological–evolutionary views is that attachment and detachment processes are biologically mediated and can be comprehended within the context of evolutionary theory. Clearly, it is plausible to suggest that it would be of evolutionary importance for the human infant, being helpless at birth, to be equipped with age-specific mechanisms that would initially promote its attachment to a caregiver and protector, and later promote its progressive detachment from that caregiver, so that when mature it would be more likely to seek a mate from outside its own kinship system or tribe to ensure genetic heterogeneity. Furthermore, it would be important for mechanisms to exist that would promote the progressive socialization of the infant within the tribe, so that there would accrue the biological advantages of band assembly as summarized by Henderson (1980)—e.g., protection and upbringing of offspring, hunting in groups, collaboration in defense. Among those subscribing to the ethological–evolutionary view, the concept of attachment to parents has generated more interest and knowledge than the concept of detachment.

Attachment Processes

The ethological–evolutionary view of attachment states that "the young of most animal species are born with certain instinctive tendencies which promote the development of attachment to the primary adult caretaker and, thus, the development of the interactive relationship" (Osofsky & Connors, 1979). While a number of researchers have developed this view, the works of John Bowlby (1969, 1973, 1980) have perhaps provided the greatest impetus to an ethological consideration.

Bowlby (1969) argues that instincts are specific and sterotyped movements or behaviors that aid survival in many environments. He states that an instinctive behavior has the following four characteristics: (1) It is recognizable in almost all members of the species. (2) It is a sequence of behaviors, rather than a simple response, that usually runs a predictable course. (3) It is of evolutionary importance in that it aids survival. (4) It may be observed even when the ordinary opportunities for learning it are minimal or absent.

He suggests that the development and maintenance of attachment between the child and its mother is a result of a number of behavioral systems within the child that serve to ensure proximity to the mother and thus aid the child's survival. The behavioral systems are products of gene action and environment with certain stimuli, perhaps internal ones (such as hormones) and external environmental ones, acting so as to elicit, initiate, orient, or terminate behavior. Bowlby (1969) describes four, somewhat overlapping, phases in the development of attachment behavior in the human infant:

1. *Orientation and signals without discrimination of figure.* For the first 2–3 months the infant is unable to discriminate among those within his vicinity. It shows certain behaviors when people are close: following with its eyes, grasping, clinging, reaching, smiling, and babbling. Some of these behaviors would appear to serve to initiate contact, others to maintain it—but a general effect is that they increase the amount of time a person remains with the infant.
2. *Orientation and signals directed toward one (or more) discriminated figure(s).* During this period the infant begins to differentiate the mother-figure from others by voice (after 4 weeks) and by sight (after 10 weeks). Signals such as crying and smiling, which initially appeared endogenously based with rhythmic and rather automatic properties, now acquire a social context.
3. *Maintenance of proximity to a discriminated figure by means of locomotion as well as signals.* At 6 months or so, indiscriminate friendly responses to all but the mother-figure wane and the infant is able to recognize the mother-figure but cannot recall her, so that it does not appear to miss her when she is absent. The infant shows fear of strangers, reacting to them with caution or even marked alarm and withdrawal. The mother-figure is used as a base from which to explore. On return the infant will burrow into her and to no other, and if alarmed will move quickly to her.
4. *Formation of a goal-corrected partnership.* In this phase the infant is

more independent of the mother-figure. By 1 year the mother-figure is recognized and remembered. The child may be content to relinquish the mother-figure if given a transitional object, so that attachment has begun to diffuse. The child may vary its behavior to elicit certain responses from the mother and will explore away from her.

Whereas Bowlby (1969) argues that the infant is born with a biological propensity to seek attachment to a mother-figure, effected by environmentally stable and environmentally labile behaviors, more recently authors have preferred to describe the process of "attachment" rather than consider or impute underlying mechanisms (Cantwell & Tarjan, 1979; Osofsky & Connors, 1979; Rutter, 1980b).

Studies reviewed by these authors have established that at the age of 1 week infants prefer patterned to plain surfaces, that by 2 months they select three-dimensional in preference to flat objects, that they prefer moving to stationary objects at all ages, and that they develop a preference for the human face over other types of visual stimuli. In regard to auditory stimuli, infants respond best to speech sounds. By the fifth week the mother's voice is more effective than others in eliciting vocalization, and as early as 2 months of age infants can direct conversation with their mother. By the age of 3 months an infant can differentiate its mother-figure from others, as evidenced by studies measuring heart rate, pupillary dilatation, smiling, visual attention, and changes in behavior. In a series of studies Carpenter (1974) showed that infants, in the first few weeks of life, gave more attention to a mother's stationary face than to a live stranger's stationary face, and attended even longer when the mother's voice was combined with the mother's face. Babies vocalize more to their mothers than to strangers from the second month, and have several types of cry (hunger, anger, and pain) that serve to elicit differential parental responses.

An infant will smile from the time of birth without the need for any external stimulus—and this undifferentiated smile can be elicited by a variety of voices in the first week. The human voice is the best elicitor of such a smile in the third week, while eye-to-eye contact is the best elicitor in the fourth week. At 7 months a smile is elicited only by the faces of certain familiar people—and is now termed a "social smile." This heightened sensitivity continues for about 10 weeks until the onset of fear responses to unfamiliar objects. Smiling, states Rutter (1980b) is "a social reciprocal action which serves to prolong and develop any kind of personal interaction." In infant development, there is "a regular progression from spontaneous and reflex smiling to unselective social smiling . . . to increasingly discriminating social smiling."

Research evidence of this type supports the view that the infant is equipped with a number of evolving repertoires that serve to promote attachment to a caregiver and that the subsequent bond is progressively more interactive.

If there is a critical period for the establishment of attachment it is likely to be after the first 6 months since before then it is unlikely that the infant has sufficiently complex cognitive processes to allow it to differentiate its parent from self and other adults (Newman & Newman, 1975). Yarrow (1964) suggests that any critical period for the development of primary attachment may end when the infant is 2 years of age.

Since psychoanalysts and others describe the initial tie as a "dependent" one and the evolution of mother–infant interaction in terms of shifts in "dependency," it is important to emphasize that attachment theory rejects the term "dependency" in its formulations. Ainsworth (1972) distinguishes "attachment" and "dependency," the latter being a generalized, nonfocused response characteristic, whereas an attachment tie links two individuals. Attachments are said to be enduring (but not necessarily irreversible), with the implication that over long periods of time they have a pervasive effect, while dependency may be entirely transient. Attachments are regarded as characteristic of all ages, while dependency implies immaturity. Attachment is considered to suggest a strong affect, while dependency has no affective implication. Finally, attachment implies proximity-seeking to a discriminated figure, together with contact-maintaining behaviors, while dependency is not directed at a specific person.

Attachment, defined by Rutter (1980b) as proximity-seeking behaviors to parents or other specific individuals by the young, is a phenomenon observable in widely varying cultures and in a wide range of animal species. Rutter proposes four main features differentiating attachment from other forms of social interaction. First, anxiety in the infant or child intensifies attachment, resulting in following and proximity-seeking and, at least in infant monkeys (Rosenblum & Harlow, 1963), anxiety increases attachment regardless of the response of the attachment system. Second, the presence of an attachment object (animate or inanimate) promotes exploration and other adaptive responses—the so-called "secure base" effect. Third, the mere presence of an attachment figure reduces anxiety and distress. Fourth, separation from an attachment figure is associated, during a defined age period in the infant, with a "protest" phase in the infant.

The number and nature of different attachment objects have been studied, by Schaffer and Emerson (1964) and Ainsworth (1967) in particular. Rutter (1980b) summarizes the relevant studies to suggest that an infant is most likely to attach primarily to its mother, but that the mother is not invariably differentiated as the primary attachment figure; multiple attachments and attachments to inanimate objects do occur (and are more likely if there is optimal bonding with the mother). There is a hierarchy in attachments that has a tendency to endure over time; and attachments to the primary figure and to other discriminated figures are similar in kind.

Although attachment behaviors can be and have been defined with a high degree of consensus, "attachment" has resisted clear conceptualization. It has been operationally defined in terms of frequencies of discrete behaviors independent of any assumed meaning (Feldman & Ingham, 1975), as referring to the general interaction between the infant and the caregiver (Cairns, 1972), and as an enduring affective tie between infant and caregiver (Bowlby, 1969). Rutter (1980b) suggests that there is a difference between the general tendency to seek attachments and the formation of selective bonds that are personal, social, and reciprocal. For instance, in experiments by Harlow and Harlow, (1969) monkeys attached to inanimate objects but later were not capable of normal social relationships. Rutter suggests that the processes underlying attachment and selective bonding may differ, or (and he held the second to be more likely) the quality of the bond is determined in part by the attachment figure's response to the infant.

While discrete indices of attachment show little consistency across groups, situation, and time, and reveal little stability (Masters & Wellman, 1974), the quality of the attachment "can be reliably assessed and does yield stability" according to Sroufe (1979) and is supported by two studies (Ainsworth et al., 1971; Waters et al., 1979).

As noted earlier, secure attachment appears to be associated with, and perhaps promotes, exploration by the child. Empirical studies suggest that secure attachment assists exploratory play in unfamiliar situations and the infant's engagement with unfamiliar people (see Sroufe, 1979).

On theoretical grounds, a number of variables might influence the development of parent–child attachment; recent reviews indicate the large number of variables that have been nominated. In regard to child variables, Cantwell and Tarjan (1979) report a series of studies demonstrating that newborn infants show great differences in terms of sucking behaviors, startle responses, and responses to stress; even monozygotic twins can show very different constitutional capabilities. Osofsky and Connors (1979) found studies suggesting the relevance of infant temperament, sex, birth order, and responsiveness to tactile, visual, and auditory stimuli to the mother–infant relationship. Some of the developmental sex differences have a clear relevance to the present inquiry and should be considered in somewhat greater detail. Macoby and Jacklin (1980) note that there is little support for the stereotype that girls are more "dependent" than boys. In one study of young children the two sexes were very similar in respect to several attachment behaviors to parents (e.g., separation protest, proximity-seeking, smiling). In a cross-cultural review it was observed that boys generally make more dependency demands than girls. Studies measuring young children's response to strangers indicate it is unusual to find sex difference in the responses.

Rutter (1980b) lists a number of infant state variables that may influence attachment behavior. For instance, attachment behavior is increased when a child is tired, hungry, in pain, or unwell; it is also increased by fear, anxiety, and rejection by the attachment figure. Situational characteristics influence attachment behaviors. For example, attachment behaviors are usually increased if separation is enforced rather than voluntary, or in unexpected rather than familiar circumstances. Although attachment behaviors are usually terminated by contact with the mother, they may continue at high intensity if the mother is responsible for their activation.

The various reports and reviews considered above provide support for Bowlby's view that the child is equipped with a number of behavioral systems that serve, from its earliest days of life, to promote proximity to a mother-figure. The possibility that adults are equipped similarly with complementary behavioral caregiving systems has been studied less intensely. However, some comparative studies of maternal behaviors in nonhuman mammals have been conducted that allow human maternal behaviors to be viewed in an evolutionary context.

Trause et al. (1976) summarize observations of maternal care in a number of mammalian species. They state that all mammals prepare for the birth of their young by establishing a birth site and engaging in a number of preparatory activities. After the birth they ensure the warmth of the infant; they protect it by maintaining control over visitors, warding off intruders, and, in some species, retrieving young that stray. Licking and grooming the infant occurs in most mammalian species. The authors review a number of adoption studies in which infants were introduced to nonparturient females, and conclude that there appears to be a sensitive period after birth when females will adopt alien young; however, environmental conditions and unusual behavior on the part of the infant may interfere with successful adoption. The authors also review several studies designed to determine whether maternal behavior is triggered by hormonal changes within the mothers or elicited by characteristics of the infant. Those studies suggest that biological mechanisms (with the hormone estradiol being incriminated most clearly) are responsible for the mother's receptivity to an infant at the time of birth, but that such processes are time limited (i.e., there is a sensitive period). Subsequently, nonhormonal mechanisms appear to regulate maternal behaviors, with the mother responding to cues in the infant, the infant responding to maternal behaviors, and interactive patterns being established.

The possibility that a maternal sensitive period may exist in humans has been suggested by Klaus and Kennell (1976). Kennell et al. (1979) review results from a number of similar studies and suggest that "the sooner a mother is allowed to interact with her infant, the firmer the resulting bond." They speculate on possible mechanisms. Noting that the infant is in a state of high responsiveness for about 1 hour after birth, before falling deeply asleep for some 4 hours, they conjecture that such a degree of "responsiveness to his environment to interact with his parents makes this period optimal for the formation of affectional bonds." In their earlier report (Klaus & Kennell, 1976) they suggest that the infant triggers an initial maternal response which, in optimal circumstances, is species specific (although the speed of the sequence is modified by environmental conditions) and is quite characteristic. The mother, when allowed to hold the baby, gazes into its eyes, and physical contact and inspection proceed from fingertip touching of the extremities to palmar contact with the trunk. The mother speaks to the baby in a high-pitched voice. By the time the infant is 2 weeks of age the mother has developed maternal characteristics that are somewhat persistent over time.

Lozoff (1976) has evaluated such maternal attachment behaviors in terms of their survival value or evolutionary significance. He suggests that it is unclear whether many of the "affectionate" maternal behaviors described by Klaus and Kennell are crucial to infant and species survival. He notes that they are not specific to the mother–infant relationship and suggests that they are not consistent across cultures. The accurate detection of a sensitive period for maternal attachment would require better determination of relevant maternal behaviors, and particularly those specifically necessary for survival.

Such observations suggest (but have been disputed) that a mother is equipped biologically with a capacity to be "attached" to her baby, and that there may be a critical period for the optimal development of the maternal contribution to the dyad. Any further consideration of possible mechanisms underlying such a process would be speculative; as Parke (1979) notes: "almost no information at the human level is available concerning the role of hormonal or physiologic factors in mediating reactions to infants or to the readiness to undertake caretaking and nurturant activities."

A number of observers (Brazelton and Young, 1964; Richards, 1971; Lewis, 1972; Wertheim, 1975a; Osofsky and Connors, 1979) have considered the suggestion that the infant and the mother have the immediate potential after the birth process to elicit in each other certain behaviors that are complementary and that can bond the two in a "sustained reciprocal rhythm" (Kennell et al., 1979).

Several observational studies have helped to define the nature and evolution of synchrony in parent–infant interaction. Greenberg (1971) observes that infants initiate stimulation from their mothers in a number of ways, and after receiving stimulation for a period will turn their heads away before allowing further interaction to take place. Although the rules of the interaction change constantly, mothers soon develop a sensitivity to the components of the interaction. Osofsky and Connors (1979) suggest that in optimal development the infant regulates the interaction and that, at least for some rhythms, synchrony should be established within the first 10 days after birth, the mother responding appropriately at that time to the infant's oscillation between states of alertness and unavailability.

Stechler and Carpenter (1967) suggest that early regulation by the infant can be divided into two types. First, an "alloplastic" mode of regulation, when social communication with the caretaker produces changes in the infant's environment. Second, an "autoplastic" regulation, which takes over when alloplastic regulation fails (i.e., when social communication from the infant produces no change in the environment), and when the infant attempts to control input by altering its perception of the stimulus field. Autoplastic regulation is said to be used defensively against purely physical stimuli and against human stimuli; in the latter situation, it has an "unmistakeable message of interpersonal avoidance or withdrawal" (Wertheim, 1975a). Typical responses that have been described include turning away, lowering of the eyelids, extended closing of the eyes and the eyelids, and directing the eyes to the periphery of the target. Wertheim (1975a) suggests that evidence of alloplastic regulation indicates an appropriate balance of autonomy in the infant–caretaker system, while autoplastic regulation points to an unfavorable balance and the emergence of defensive strategies in the infant who is seeking to make an active contribution to interpersonal regulation. Thus, she argues that the earliest roots of autonomy are to be sought in the structural and functional synchrony of the reciprocal infant–caretaker system.

Sander (1976), on the basis of longitudinal observations of primiparous mothers and their infants, suggests that in optimal development a mother is required to adjust to her infant's behavioral cues in the first 2 months and to take part in a reciprocal interchange with the infant between 2 and 5 months of ages. From 5 to 9 months of age the infant makes efforts to establish areas of reciprocity with the mother; for the next 6 months the infant behaves in a way that monopolizes the mother. Sander (1969) suggests that, irrespective of the developmental level of the infant, there is reciprocal regulation of development.

Although not directly researching that issue, Ainsworth's work helps to define the nature of a synchronous mother–infant relationship. Ainsworth et al. (1971) designed a standardized separation–reunion sequence for 12-month-old infants and their mothers. Maternal behaviors were rated on four empirically differentiated scales assessing sensitivity (versus insensitivity), acceptance (versus rejection), cooperation (versus interference), and accessibility (versus ignoring). Further analysis suggested that the sensitivity measure was the central one: sensitivity correlated highly with acceptance, cooperation, and accessibility. A sensitive mother was "able to see things from her child's point of view" and responded to her baby's signals promptly and appropriately, taking up a reciprocal role to her baby. In contrast, an insensitive mother geared her interactions and initiated interactions almost exclusively in terms of her own style and needs.

Although a number of variables associated with mother–infant interaction have been described, possible influences on, and determinants of maternal sensitivity have not been clearly delineated. Indirect studies suggest a range of possible variables. In their review of several studies Osofsky and Connors (1979) found that certain infant characteristics (e.g., helplessness) facilitate the initiation of parental caregiving, and that certain infant physical characteristics and temperamental traits may elicit differential maternal responses. Male infants have been described as more irritable and difficult to soothe than female infants, perhaps making it more difficult for a mother to develop reciprocity with sons than with daughters. The authors suggest that high maternal anxiety and low maternal self-confidence may affect the interaction deleteriously. They also suggest a possible social class variable, in that middle-class mothers appear to be more responsive to their infant's behavior, talk more to the infant, and encourage more reciprocity between the infant and themselves, in contrast with lower social class mothers, who are more physically stimulating of their infant and believe that they have less control over their child's development.

Detachment Processes

There is, as yet, no developed theory of detachment. As suggested earlier, the most likely explanation is that aspects of child development can be (and have been) just as well described as "parent–child attachment" processes as they can be described as "parent–child detachment" processes. Rutter (1980b) notes that there has been a great deal of research on the development of attachment in infancy, but considerably less attention has been given to the course of social development during childhood. Clearly, children become less closely tied to parents as they grow older and they are more capable of tolerating separation. Schaffer (1971), who described the progressive socialization of the child in some detail, suggests that the process is one of weakening of parent–child bonds and the development of detachment. Rutter suggests that this may be misleading, and that children, as they grow older, may maintain bonds to parents without the requirement for physical continuity. The likely reality is that both attachment and detachment processes exist, are interdependent, and, as Rheingold and Eckerman (1971) observe, the "preoccupation with the attachment of the young to its mother has obscured the importance and considerations of detachment processes."

It is likely that detachment processes evolve throughout the period of childhood and adolescence, altough it is traditional to suggest that such processes are most active in early childhood and at adolescence. Those two periods are considered selectively in this section. Early childhood is considered first.

Wertheim (1975a) argues that the human mother and her offspring are genetically programmed to lengthen the distance between them as the infant becomes capable of moving progressively further away from the mother-figure. She reviews studies showing that as motor skills improve, the infant finds certain physical objects in its environment attractive and moves toward them; an infant becomes bored (i.e., frets) in a monotonous environment. The evidence that infants initiate social interaction has been considered earlier. An appropriate balance between physical stimualtion and active communication with the caretaker may increase motivation to attend to external stimuli, promote the focused attention of the infant, encourage active sensory exploration of the environment, and aid the building of cognitive schemas (Wertheim, 1975c).

The view that "attachment" and "detachment" are interdependent processes has been strongly supported by Ainsworth. Ainsworth et al. (1971) introduced the term *attachment-exploration* to describe a causal connection between a secure base provision from the mother and the infant venturing into the world to explore it. Attachment is said to have the capacity to promote, rather than restrict, the detachment process.

Wertheim (1975a) suggests that infants seek autonomy for their own sake (primary autonomy) and transact it within the infant–caretaker system (instrumental autonomy). Infants are equipped at birth or soon after with prelinguistic signaling action systems (and later with linguistic systems) that are primed for social communication (i.e., autonomy) and have "specific, biologically determined roots" (Wertheim, 1975b).

Wertheim (1975b) speculates that during detachment a child develops interpersonal regulation. Fretting on separation is more prominent in children with a satisfactory mother–child relationship; Wertheim interprets this as a reaction by the young child to a profound failure of interpersonal regulation, rather than distress at the actual physical loss of the mother.

In her review Wertheim considers evidence supporting an epigenetic course of autonomy, at least early in development, and suggests modifications to the epigenetic sequences in infant–caretaker adaptations identified and defined by Sander (1974), who observed 22 children during the first 3 years of life. Sander argues that adaptations occur in a specific temporal order, that each have to be successfully negotiated before further optimal development can proceed, and that each interaction between the infant and the caretaker can be analyzed in terms of three features: initiation, reciprocation, and regulation. While both Sander and Wertheim consider these stages in terms of shifts in autonomy, Wertheim suggests that each stage involves a key developmental task of competence for the infant as well.

Sander proposes that the first 3 months of infancy represents a period of *initial regulation,* when the mother seeks to establish basic routines of feeding and sleeping in the infant. He notes that one of the features most idiosyncratic during that period is the extent to which the infant is facilitated or compromised in its attempts to determine aspects of its own regulation, an issue considered above in the discussion on mother–infant synchrony. Wertheim (1975a) relabels this first phase *mutual synchronization.* In Sander's second phase *reciprocal exchange,* lasting from 4 to 6 months of age, patterns of reciprocal behavior (such as those involved in feeding) are established; Wertheim relabels this phase *practice of reciprocity.* Sander terms the third phase, lasting from 7 to 9 months of age, *infant initiative,* as the infant expresses increasingly clear intentions to explore the world as his motor apparatus develops and activities such as crawling are possible. Sander suggests that this is an important stage for a bifurcation in maternal response to the infant's initiative, and that there is a rather precise sensitivity of the infant to inhibition by the mother. Wertheim relabels this phase *shared interpersonal regulation,* as she judges the infant as now capable of taking over some of the intrasystemic regulation from the caretaker. A fourth phase, from 10 to 13 months of age, is termed *focalization* by Sander, who describes a further development in the capacity of the infant to direct his own activities. Wertheim judges that the infant's activities in this phase show repeated experimentation in assuming control over the caretaker, and relabels the phase *regulatory role reversal.* The fifth period is designated *self-assertion* by Sander who describes it as lasting from 14 to 20 months of age. He suggests that the infant has the capacity to organize its world, assert itself, and widen any initiative to activity. While clearly involved in reciprocal activities with its mother, the infant often appears to seek initiative for its own sake. Wertheim argues that this phase corresponds to the first true attempts at self-direction by the infant, at times in opposition to the caretaker, and prefers the term *bipolar regulation.*

The ethologic explanation of these progressive shifts in favor of independence and autonomy is that, by the infant acquainting itself with the physical environment, the chances of survival are improved (Rheingold & Eckerman, 1971).

Summary

As Ainsworth (1973) points out, in proposing a new psychological theory to explain the origin of the child's attachment to the mother, Bowlby has freed considerations from an allegiance to the concept of dependency and borrowed much from ethology. He proposes that an infant's attachment to its mother originates in a number of biologically determined species-characteristic behavior patterns, initially relatively independent of each other, which mature at different times, and serve to bind the mother and the child to each other, and function to protect the child from danger. Bowlby's delineation of attachment behaviors and his formulations have stimulated much research, which has both supported and suggested revisions to his original theory.

Data from a number of studies have shown that the infant is equipped with a perceptual capacity to discriminate a human face and voice from an early developmental age and to respond in a way that is likely to attract a caregiver. Both processes promote an initial attachment (therefore aiding the infant's survival), and the progressive development of a selective and affectional bond that is personal, social, and reciprocal; this bond is presumed to provide the basis for the development of later social bonds (Rutter, 1980a). Secure attachment would appear to have one other signal advantage of considerable relevance to the present inquiry—it appears to assist exploratory play and attempts at socialization.

Also relevant to the inquiry is the possibility that mothers may be equipped with behavioral systems that promote optimal maternal responses, and which can be activated during a certain critical period. The view that optimal development is assisted if the infant and the caregiver bond in a "sustained reciprocal rhythm" is clearly important to the present inquiry.

Although an attempt is made to consider "attachment" and "detachment" processes separately, the division is likely to be artificial and possibly misleading. As yet it remains unclear whether "detachment" involves processes separate to those involved in "attachment," the former merely represents an evolution of the latter (or even a difference in labeling), or if separate (but possibly interdependent) processes exist. In suggesting that infants are primed for and seek autonomy at an early stage in development, Wertheim reinterprets what many would view as developments in attachment as evidence of progressive developments in autonomy and competence. In contrast, Ainsworth suggests that attachment and detachment are interdependent and concurrent processes, with secure attachment promoting exploration, competence, and independence. At this time perhaps all that can be concluded is that there is strong evidence from numerous research studies to suggest that the infant is equipped with mechanisms that promote its progressive attachment to one or more caregivers, and its progressive development of autonomy and social competence; as Rutter (1980a) oberves, "theoretical closure is not yet possible."

RELEVANCE OF FATHERS

Since the beginning of the Industrial Revolution, child care in Western societies has been assigned almost exclusively to the mother. Twentieth century theorizing, which held that the feeding context was a key influence on social development, further reinforced that practice despite the circularity of the argument. In 1951 Bowlby stated that infants and young children require warm, intimate, and continuous relationships with their biological mother. Those suggested requirements, which reified the view of a mandatory mother–infant relationship, served as a stimulus for considerable research, reviewed comprehensively by Rutter (1972). Of most relevance to this discussion are two congruent findings. First, the infant is less passive than had been previously judged, and it seeks to attach to both parents if they are available. Second, others besides the biological mother may serve adequately and appropriately as primary attachment figures—as demonstrated initially by Schaffer and Emerson (1964).

Largely because infants spend most of their time with the mother, it was held that mothers were of unique importance. That view lost ground when research evidence (reviewed by Lamb, 1980) showed that duration of maternal contact is a poor predictor of the quality of a mother–child relationship. Furthermore, an exclusive mother–infant bond can hardly be supported as biologically destined. Numerous anthropological studies (Parke, 1979) indicate that the father is not assigned a secondary role to the mother in all cultures. Animal studies (usually with primates) suggest that, while males are generally involved minimally in the nurturance of infants, appropriate caring paternal behaviors can be elicited (Redican, 1976). As suggested by Parke (1979), the increasing adoption of caretaking functions by a number of fathers in Western society (sometimes by desire, sometimes by default following marital separation) supports the view that paternal caretaking is sensitive to cultural pressures, norms, and changes. Finally, while home-based studies have shown that infants are responsive to both their parents, responsiveness to a father is strongly related to his involvement in routine caretaking activities with the infant (Parke, 1979).

While such observations and findings suggest that fathers may influence the course of child development, they have also complicated the traditional research model (i.e., a unidirectional one with the mother influencing the child's development). The current model is infinitely more difficult to research, not only because another parent (the father) has been introduced into the analysis, but also because there is a greater recognition that parents and infants bring certain constitutional qualities to the interaction and development is influenced by reciprocal and dyadic interactions as well.

Parke (1979) reviews a number of studies describing similarities and differences in the contribution to the interaction made by mothers and fathers. For instance, numerous studies have shown that fathers and mothers engage in similar behaviors when in contact with their newborn infant; however, fathers tend to hold the baby longer than the mother, while mothers engage in more smiling at the infant than fathers. While fathers appear less likely to feed infants than mothers, fathers are equally successful in feeding the baby and equally sensitive to cues from the baby. Vocalization by the infant in the feeding situation is more likely to produce a tactile response by mothers and a vocal response by fathers. Although fathers appear to be the more active stimulators of the newborn infant, mothers take up a more active role within a few weeks. A few weeks after birth mothers are more likely to engage in soft, repetitive, imitative talking with the infant, while fathers are more likely to touch the infant with a rhythmic, tapping pattern. Such differences in the parental contribution to interaction with the infant continue, although necessarily evolve, throughout infancy. Late in infancy fathers engage in much more rough-and-tumble play with the infants than mothers. Lamb (1980) summarizes the view that there are functional differences between mothers and fathers with infants by stating that mothers are more involved in caretaking while fathers are more involved in play. He concludes that mothers tend to inhibit exploration by the child, while fathers are more likely to encourage an infant's curiosity and sense of mastery over the environment.

The sex of the infant appears to have an effect on father–infant interaction. Studies suggest that fathers prefer sons to daughters, and show sex-typing concepts and socialization patterns from the time of the birth of the child (Parke, 1979). Specifically, fathers vocalize more to newborn sons than to daughters and provide more visual and tactile stimulation if playing with, or feeding, a son. In general, parents tend to stimulate the same-sex infant more than the opposite-sex infant. The nature of these sex differences has been considered by a number of researchers. Parke suggests that sex-role attitudes are likely to be more important than biological difference, and two studies support that view.

Bem et al. (1976) examined interactions between college students (who provided self-ratings on their perceived degree of masculinity and femininity) and infants. Students scoring as androgynous or feminine showed more nurturant behaviors than those who scored as masculine, regardless of the biological sex of the student. Field (1978) compared mothers and fathers who were primary caretakers with fathers who were secondary caretakers, and found that the primary caretaker fathers were closer to the mothers in several of their interactional qualities than to the secondary caretaker fathers.

In his review of a number of studies considering the influence of the father on child development, Lamb (1980) first notes the numerous methodological issues and confounding variables hindering clarification. Nevertheless, he suggests that an affectionate father–child relationship facilities sex-role development (father absence being associated with reduced masculinity or compensatory masculinity in boys, and with heterosexual interaction difficulties in adolescence in girls), academic performance at school, self-esteem (especially in boys), and optimal personality adjustment. Lamb's speculation about the distinct role of fathers, based on his review of relevant studies, is of considerable interest to the present inquiry. He suggests that the infant perceives interaction with the father as pleasurable and stimulating—and that these qualities enhance the child's desire to have commerce with the world in which the father immerses himself, and to explore the wider social system of which the father is the most accessible representation.

In summary, cultural factors appear to influence strongly the degree to which fathers take an active or indifferent role in parenting. It is now accepted that infants seek to attach to others as well as the biological mother, including the father, and that the caretaking capacities of the father influence qualitative aspects of the bond and perhaps personality development and socialization. Fathers seem to differ from mothers in their relationship to the child in ways that assist the child's progressive socialization and independence.

PEER AND OTHER FAMILY INFLUENCES

One of the most comprehensive reviews of peer interaction is that by Hartup (1980), who observes that "an appreciation of the role of peer interaction in the growth of social competence has emerged only recently." His description of several contextual and developmental characteristics of peer relationships helps to elucidate the possible functional significance of peers in child development.

The proportion of time spent with peers in social activities increases throughout childhood, and in most cultures the child is exposed mostly to older children. As with other expressions of socialization, peer interactions proceed from simple organizations (e.g., 1-year-old infants are attracted to other "responsive" infants) to discriminative interactions in adolescence, when a clear empathic component emerges. It appears that aggressive interaction and sociable interactions are more common in same-age peer relations, while mixed-age relations are often marked by dominance behaviors in the older child and dependency behaviors in the younger child. Hartup suggests that correlational studies provide presumptive evidence that peer interaction assists sociability, socialization, and the development of moral values. Furthermore, he cites several studies suggesting that poor peer relations in childhood are predictive of adult psychopathology.

Hartup describes a number of differences between child–child and adult–child relationships. In young children, child–child interaction is said to be more intrinsically "social" and to involve more play interactions, while stress-elicited proximity seeking, clinging, and intense physical contact directed toward a familiar adult is characteristic of adult–young child interactions. In older children, adult–child interaction is distinguished by nurturance/dependency and domiance/submission complementarities; these are infrequent in peer interaction, where prosocial, sociable, and aggressive interactions predominate.

Hartup suggests that there are two principal models linking socialization within the family and within the peer culture: *Single-process theories* presume that social competence is determined fundamentally by family interactions, with peer interactions serving only to elaborate or extend competence. Psychoanalysts and social learning theorists, who hold that the initial attachment to the mother determines the nature and quality of secondary attachments, would support a single-process theory. *Dual-process theories* hold that social competency may be influenced independently by family and peer interactions.

One classic study (Harlow, 1969) is often presented as support for the dual-process view. In that study of rhesus monkeys, it was observed that those raised without contact with their mother but with peer contact subsequently showed strong peer attachment and appropriate social contact with other monkeys. In contrast, rhesus monkeys raised by their mothers but without peer contact later showed clear social anomalies and disturbances in affective development. However, the author's conclusion that peer–peer interaction is more important for normal social development than mother–infant interaction has been criticized by a number of workers. For instance, Hartup (1980) suggests that as the mothers and infants were caged together, confinement could have made the mothers irritable with their infants, thereby distorting the socialization process.

Hinde (1974) suggests that infants without peer access attempt to play with the mother and that such overtures elicit negative reactions from the mother. Hinde (1980) also criticizes the study design of examining dyads rather than examining the compexities of triadic relationships.

Hartup (1980) notes several other experimental studies and results suggesting that family and peers seem to "interact as a complementary synergism." While a number of studies (e.g., Easterbrooks & Lamb, 1979; Lieberman, 1977; Waters et al., 1979) have shown that a secure attachment to the mother is associated with effective engagement and development of peer relationships, the nature of that association has not been clearly established.

In his review Hartup (1980) concludes that parental relations and peer relations are different social systems. The former, with the mother–child relationship being the most influential, provide a secure base from which the child can explore the wider social world without distress and may influence self-esteem, language, and certain skills. Exploratory activity promotes contact with peers, and such interactions (which differ in type from parent–child interactions) extend competencies and result in the acquisition of attitudes and affects that are integral to social adaptation.

In comparison to peer relationships, family relationships are more difficult to describe systematically in terms of their structure and function. According to Fleck (1975), the family is "the universal primary social unit" providing offspring with "biological and cultural heritages." He suggests that the family is both a "link between generations that ensures the stability of the culture and also a crucial element in culture change." Fleck, like most writers describing family relationships, holds that they may be described best in terms of general systems theory. Thus he suggests that the family is an open system with many subsystems, including the marriage as such, the marriage as a parental coalition, triads of parents and each child, sibling coalitions, and possible subsystems of grandparents, other kin, and friends. Each family has a boundary (enabling it to be a distinct unit) and an organization (e.g., sharing affection, and tending to the nurturance, rearing, education, and enculturation of the children). Shared rituals connect the family with the larger culture. Families may have widely differing tasks ranging, for example, from subsistence to the less tangible tasks of guiding the younger generation into adulthood. Similarly, marital roles may vary widely, from complementary sex-linked roles to task-sharing ones. It is generally accepted that in most societies the position of the father determines the status of the family and that the father serves as the children's model of societal tasks and roles. Mothers are more likely to be concerned with the affective lief of the family, and to tend to its biological needs in health and sickness.

As a social system (with each member interdependent with others in dyadic reciprocal bonds), the family has boundaries delimiting expected or proscribed attitudes and behaviors in its family members. These may be regulated overtly or covertly, and usually emerge from a mythology initially shared between the parents, which is then taken up by the children through a process of observation and imitation. Lewis (1979) emphasizes the parental relationship as being the cornerstone of family structure to which much that occurs in the life of the family is directly related. The functional significance of having a family mythology is to maintain stability, to self-perpetuate the system, and to resist change that runs counter to or threatens the emotional balance of the family (Andrews, 1974). Beyond the family's function in helping its members to survive, Lewis (1979) suggests that there are other purposes, influenced by cultural and historical factors. He states that the family in the Western world has two central purposes: "the stabilization of adult family members' personalities and the production of autonomous children."

Numerous studies have been conducted (see Bowlby, 1969) in an attempt to define family characteristics associated with the development of optimally functioning children. Most are of limited value because samples have generally been drawn from unrepresentative groups, because of the difficulties inherent in defining "optimal functioning" in children, and because in most studies only correlational data have been reported (correlations do not, of necessity, imply causality). Nevertheless, the general consistency in results does argue for the possible importance of certain family styles as "negative risk" factors to the development of psychopathology in children. The study by Lewis et al. (1976) provides a list of characteristics that are representative of much of this research. They are, in order of their apparent importance,

1. An "affiliative attitude" to human encounter (i.e., open and trusting)
2. A high respect for individuality, autonomy, and privacy in members
3. Open, clear communication
4. Firm parental coalitions, with authority being shared between parents
5. Flexible and negotiable discipline and control of children, but with a clear parent–child hierarchial boundary
6. Highly spontaneous interaction with evidence of considerable humor and wit
7. High levels of initiative
8. Encouragement of uniqueness and difference rather than encouragement of conformity.

Cross-cultural examinations reveal considerable variations in family structure. Queen and Habenstein (1974) suggest that the "adaptive urban matricentric black family" emerges for several reasons: living in a ghetto, economic insecurity, and a growing disparity between male and female occupational chances, the male having fallen behind the female in that regard. They describe the female in such families as being the pivotal figure, with the male parent-figure present occasionally, itinerant, or permanently absent and thus having a weak or incidental role. They state that such a genus of family structure is found wherever there are poverty-stricken people—a point made by Lewis (1959), who notes that the culture of poverty defines a relatively constant family structure.

Lewis drew attention to several common characteristics in lower class settlements in London, Glasgow, Paris, Harlem, and Mexico City: mother-centered families, abandonment of wives and children by the fathers, and frequent use of physical violence in the training of children. A typical description of family structure and functioning in such a situation is provided by Hippler (1974), who describes life in a black ghetto in San Francisco. If breast-fed (which is common), the babies are weaned abruptly at about 4 months of age. At approximately 1 year of age (and usually when another child is born) emotional nurturance from the mother is replaced by a marked switch to seemingly rejecting attitudes. The child becomes the almost exclusive recipient of the mother's negative attitudes. From the age of 3 years the children are locked out of the house, except for meals, during the day. Hippler interprets this change not as an attempt by the mother to create independence but rather the opposite, with the mother abandoning the child because it refuses to remain gratifyingly tied to her.

Another contemporary family structure that is clearly distinguishable from a pattern commonly described for Western society is that found in the kibbutz. First established in Israel in 1909, the establishment of kibbutizim commenced as a group protest by Jewish intellectuals against the mores of the traditional Jewish village; they had an important underlying principal of "individual liberty and the limitations of personal power" (Queen & Habenstein, 1974). Parents did not see their children for more than a couple of hours a day, while the children were cared for by attendants in nurseries and special schools until high school graduation. A recent report (Beit-Hallahmi & Rabin, 1977) suggests that a long-term consequence of this experiment was that the children, when young adults, were highly independent but had difficulty in establishing interpersonal relationships. If correct, this could be the consequence of any number of factors—including the intent of the kibbutz to foster individual growth, creative self-expression and personal freedom, or the allocation of several parent-figure in the nurseries and schools.

While there is considerable variation in the practices, rules, and sentiments in the domestic institutions of different people, there are some strong constants, according to Queen and Habenstein (1974) including a strong tie, at least in the early years, between the mother and the child.

While these observations on family structure and function are useful in that they reveal contrasts in the promotion of independence in the child, they fail to illustrate the almost insurmountable difficulties inherent in studying family influences on infant and child development. This difficulty has been addressed extensively by Hinde (1980), who concludes that the delineation of a family influence as a predictor variable is only likely to occur if the family is robust, if it is not subject to marked interactional effects, and if other factors can be held constant; failure to confirm a variable as a predictor cannot be interpreted with any clarity.

In summary, peer interaction increases with age, in terms of both time and complexity. While such changes may merely be correlates of evolving social systems and a maturational process in the child, it has also been suggested that peers may promote socializaton and placement within the social hierarchy independent of any contribution made by the child or the parents. Cultural factors appear to influence both family structure and family functioning. While family structure should be considered in studies of child development, complex issues of analysis need to be conceded.

CULTURAL INFLUENCES

Comparative studies of child development within different cultures have the potential to assist considerations of normal development. They may allow delineation of invariable and variable patterns in child-raising and in the evolution of attachment and detachment processes, and thereby clarify the relative contribution of biological and cultural influences. Such studies range from broad comparative approaches (e.g., Leiderman et al., 1977) to narrow ones considering individual attachment behaviors. As an example of the latter approach, Ainsworth (1967) noted differences in the organization of attachment behaviors between children in Uganda and the United States, but found that the maternal characteristics encouraging secure attachment are similar in the two cultures.

There are difficulties inherent in the interpretation of such studies, according to Quinton (1980). Ainsworth's finding of varying patterns in protest at separation from the mother might suggest a cultural difference, but could instead merely reflect a nutritional difference. Furthermore, asks Quinton, if differences exist, how can the more optimal pattern be defined, when effects may take a long time to emerge? May not the same developmental end be achieved along different paths?

Comparative examinations across differing cultures have a second theoretical advantage. It is rarely feasible or ethical for researchers to alter predictor variables (e.g., parental styles, family structure) to examine the effect on child development. Naturally occurring cross-cultural variations often allow consideration of how variations in child-rearing patterns may determine the developmental course of the child. In *Childhood and Society* (1965) Erikson reports a classic study and analysis suggesting that cultural experiences are powerful determinants of later personality. He compares the Sioux (a group of militant wanderers forced, at the time of the study, to occupy reservations and land they did not desire) with the Yurok (who had a secluded and steadfast life along a river, dependent for their livelihood upon the salmon coming "home" once a year.) The Sioux were treated indulgently by their parents in childhood; they were given considerable early freedom and urged to discharge aggressive and social impulses, so that they were encouraged to independence and an adult life of militant wandering. By comparison, the Yurok regulated themselves and their children in ways of cleanliness, supplication, control, and cautious hoarding, so that their cautiousnes and meticulousness prepared them well for a steadfast existence in adulthood. Thus, Erikson concludes, the mothers in those societies were endowed with "an instinctual power of adaptation which permitted them to develop child-training methods appropriate for the production of hunters and hunters' wives in a nomadic society, and of fisherman and acorn gatherers in a sedentary valley society."

Quinton (1980) draws attention to a number of problems in the conducting and interpretation of such studies. In particular, he notes that differences are usually interpreted as reflecting cultural adaptation to particular environmental exigencies and constraints, and that it is usually suggested that such differences have developed to fit the future adult into the particular social system. He suggests that the evidence drawn from such studies is limited, as data vary widely in quality and character, and are usually deficient in detailed information on child development. A particular difficulty arises in interpreting the influence of parental characteristics on child development when it is not clear whether parental characteristics reflect the personality of the parent or are a reflection of the culture. Thus personality and child-rearing may both be expressions of general cultural preferences or themes.

For these reasons there is little point in reviewing the many studies that have attempted to analyze the nature of relationships among culture, parental rearing styles, and childhood development. Instead, two short analyses are reviewed that consider two distinct cultural subgroups within the wider American culture and suggest varying expressions of, and concerns about, parent–child interdependence.

Noshpitz (1979) speculates on the relationships between parental style, culture, and development of the Jewish child in an elegant and penetrating essay. He suggests that there is a very powerful and pressing sense of family and community togetherness in the Jewish family that has been determined by external cultural tensions and menace, and by components of Judaism (including a formal religion, a sense of an historical origin, the conviction of an ultimate historical destiny, a number of traditional in-group languages, and a set of personal and social attitudes). These factors have led to a "style of child rearing which strongly emphasized dependency as contrasted to autonomy, and attachment rather than independence."

Noshpitz considers the nuances, evolution and implications of such a child-rearing style. He suggests that, in the early development of the Jewish child, much emphasis is placed on holding and comforting the baby and, in particular, on his protection, for the world tends to be seen by the parents as a dangerous place." Parental discipline involves a great deal of verbalization, varying from continuous nagging to endless moralizing, which is intended to appeal to the child's better nature. Taught "survival techniques" from infancy, the children are "hovered over and worried over" and are not allowed out of the mother's sight lest "catastrophe befall." This overprotection promotes narcissism, and a greater likelihood that the children will be infantile and demanding. Such a pattern of rearing leads the child to all the derivatives of separation anxiety, expecially anxiety reaction, narcissistic disorders, and character problems. Either the Jewish child develops a strong superego, which promotes neurotic self-criticism, pessimism, and a tendency toward depression, or employs certain defenses (e.g., manipulation, evasion, defiance of existing authority structures). Nosphitz suggests that two aspects of the Jewish parental style have clear advantages in the long term: the strong emphasis on closeness and dependency during early childhood protects the recipient from later addiction, and the strong verbal flavor to child-rearing decreases any later tendency to act out in violent ways.

In contrast, the white Anglo-Saxon Protestant (WASP) child is exposed to different religious (Christian Protestantism), ethnic, and linguistic and cultural (Anglo-Saxon) influences. According to Adams (1979), the key elements of the Protestant ethos are individualism, lay control as opposed to clerical control, an emphasis on personal salvation and an awareness of self, and an appeal to the Bible or to individual conscience. As a developmental consequence, a WASP child has the sense of a cherished family heritage, of not being rootless, and of being individually accountable and responsible; the child is encouraged to be willing to change and to take risks. Adams states that "Familism joins forces with individualism." While the child has the sense of being in a vital network of "loving care" there is the later requirement to break away from incestuous family bonds. Adams suggests that economic (or class) differences have a telling effect on the development of a WASP child. Middle-class WASP households have a family style of great intensity, and stress the growth and actualization of the individual. Blue-collar WASP households have more familism at the expense of individualism, while lower class families in America resemble lower class blacks or Chicanos more than whites in the sense that the family is matrilocal (it is female centered and adult males, if present, are marginal and clearly devalued by all the women in the family).

According to Adams, the WASP child learns that he is "immersed in a sea of caring, loving interdependence" as an infant and young child. During development, if "not held in bondage to symbiotic infantile patterns," he grows to have a resourceful self-esteem. Adams considers the risk of maternal overprotection (although in different terms) to the WASP child. He suggests that "mother-fixated immaturity," as described by a number of writers (e.g., Tennesseee Williams, Carson McCullers, Flannery O'Connor), is one outcome in a WASP culture when parents show ambivalence about their child's freedom, so that they wish to have individuality unfold and, at the same time, wish to civilize by extracting obedience.

Until more detailed cross-cultural studies are performed, it is too early to speculate on the constancy and variability of patterns of attachment and caretaking behaviors across cultures. The degree to which they may be genetically determined does not require the demonstration of invariant patterns, as genetic determinism means only the *capacity* to develop a certain array of traits or behavioral repertoires. Erikson suggests that cultural experiences may be strong determinants of later personality, but a more general factor may determine both components of the culture and personality characteristics of the individual. It may be more circumspect to conclude that culture factors act principally to stabilize and define, rather than dictate, the interplay between individuals in groups. The possibility that parental overprotection may be of particular relevance in certain cultures is often suggested anecdotally and in theoretical considerations. The common sterotype of differences in the degree of overprotection experienced by Jewish and WASP children is superficially supported by the analyses by the Noshpitz (1979) and Adams (1979), but it is also apparent that concerns about individuality and dependency on parents are relevant to members of both subcultures.

SUBHUMAN PRIMATE STUDIES

Studies of attachment and detachment processes in primates are of interest because of "the greater simplicity and invariance of their expression in monkeys" (Harlow & Harlow, 1966). Harlow and Harlow (1965, 1966) suggest that there are five relatively separate affectional systems (infant–mother; mother–infant; father–infant; peer; sexual and heterosexual) in the primate order, and that these systems evolve and interact in an orderly, sequential manner. Their observations are largely based on data from rhesus macaques living in small laboratory cages with restricted access to social companions, but their observations can be integrated with (and largely supported by) observations made by other researchers who have studied other species of macaques as well as free-ranging species.

Harlow and Harlow (1965) suggest that the infant's attachment to its mother may be divided into four stages, although the nature of that attachment is a function of many variables in the mother, infant, and species. The first is a *reflex stage,* with reflexes promoting nursing (e.g., rooting and forced upward climbing that assist the infant to obtain the mother's nipple) and intimate physical contact (e.g., clinging reflexes that result in the infant being attached to the ventral surface of the mother and orally to her breast). After 2–3 weeks the reflex pattern of dependence subsides and is supplanted by voluntary activities and actual breaks in contact. Rosenblum (1971) suggests that breaks in contact with the mother are initiated as early as the second day, and may be observed regularly by the second week in captured and free-ranging rhesus macaques. He describes a clear pattern in the two parameters of contact time and distance between the infant and the mother, although the pattern varies considerably between different species. The second stage, according to Harlow and Harlow, is one of *comfort and attachment,* during which the infant is the recipient of maternal attention to body needs, contact, warmth and proprioceptive stimulation, and protection. The infant stays in close proximity to the "highly protective mother." The finding by Harlow and Harlow that the infant keeps in similarly close contact with a cloth surrogate mother emphasizes the strong infant contribution at this stage.

The third stage is a *security stage.* The infant shows a fear response to a strange environment by reacting in a characteristic way—rushing to the mother or cloth surrogate and clinging to her/it tenaciously, only later relaxing and moving away to explore. In the absence of the mother, emotional distress increases in the infant (indicated by behaviors such as vocalization, rocking, smiling, etc.). The studies by Harlow and Harlow suggest that actual mothers are superior to cloth surrogate mothers, and that both are much more effective than wire surrogate mothers, in imparting security to infants. A *separation stage* comes next, in which the "outer-world lives of exploration and play are powerful forces acting to produce part-time maternal separation" (Harlow & Harlow, 1965). Harlow and Harlow suggest that the affectional bond is never broken, but is merely attenuated or changed in its characteristics.

Harlow and Harlow (1965) also divide the maternal affectional system into several developmental stages. There is an initial stage of *maternal attachment and protection* that commences at the time of birth or shortly afterwards. Maternal responses to the neonate (e.g., cradling, nursing, restraining) are almost entirely protective. Later in this stage there is a change to a looser attachment, with the mother cradling rather than holding the infant tightly to her. This step in detachment is clearly initiated by the mother, since, if two neonates are placed together they will cling tenaciously and lengthily to each other in ventral–ventral contact. The authors propose that the mother's initiation of detachment promotes the infant's interaction with age and peer groups, and the mother gradually gives the choice of leaving to the infant, interfering only if she is disturbed by some fear-evoking stimulus. Long after control of the attachment has shifted mainly to the infant, the mother will rally to protect the infant against real or imagined danger, suggesting that maternal protective responses persist longer and with more intensity than maternal attachment responses.

Rosenblum (1971) makes some interesting observations on aspects of maternal protection in macaques. Protection appears to commence at birth and be somewhat undirected, in that mothers will zealously guard the uneaten placenta or the body of a stillborn infant. While it serves to bring the dyad together, it may also be interpreted in terms of regulatory behavior. It may occur in the presence of a social threat or danger, but it is often observed when no external provocation exists. "In such instances it would appear only that an observable but difficult to define increase in maternal agitation instigated the protective behavior." Rosenblum proposes several substages in the developmental course of maternal protectiveness. Initially, there are behaviours that clearly restrain the infant from breaking contact with the mother. Subsequently, the protectiveness changes to allow some infant autonomy. Now the mother may guard by moving along next to the infant, stretching a hand out toward the infant's side, stretching herself over the infant to produce a "kind of canopy," or making frequent and rapid manual retrievals. Later, protection changes to prolonged watching and attentiveness to vocalization.

According to the Harlow and Harlow (1965), the second stage in the maternal affectional system is a *transitional or ambivalence stage,* when the mother shows ever-increasing indifference to, and at times will punish, her infant. The third stage is one of *maternal separation or rejection,* when the mother unequivocally and forcefully rejects attempts by the infant to attach to her. Rosenblum (1971) suggests that maternal rejection of the infant may be demonstrated by the mother removing the infant from her body or preventing contact, by weaning the infant, and by quite primitive methods of deterrence—biting, mouthing, and clasp pulling.

Kaufman and Rosenblum (1969) describe clear species differences between bonnet and pigtail macaques in the maternal–infant systems, particularly during this rejection phase. Bonnet mothers restrain, guard, and retrieve their infants less than do pigtail mothers, and they are less likely to withdraw the nipple from the infant or actually punish the infant, and they allow other adult females to interact with the infant. This appears to be a reflection of more diffuse differences in social organization, as bonnets have more placid interindividual relations than pigtails. Hinde (1971) suggests that temperamental differences in the mothers account for the differences in mother–infant interactions.

These differences have caused some researchers to challenge the "rejection" concept of the rejection phase proposed by the Harlows. Hinde (1971) states that bonnets are rejected less than pigtails by their mothers, yet are more independent of their mothers, so that rejection cannot be the determinant of growing independence. Furthermore, while harsh or abrupt rejection in a "rich" environment tends to promote separation, such rejection in a "deprived" environment tends to result in increased clinging by the infant. Rosenblum (1971) suggests that a "complex" or dangerous environment causes contraction of the mother–infant dyad even during this stage. Rosenblum also notes the striking differences between rejection patterns of pigtails and bonnet monkeys, without concomitant differences in the ontogeny of contact and separation patterns in those species. Rosenblum and Hinde therefore throw some doubt on the interpretation that rejecting behaviors by the mothers are as relevant to the promotion of independence in the infant as has been suggested.

Maternal behaviors have been shown to be influenced by external stimuli (e.g., clinging and nursing by the infant), experiential variables (e.g., multiparous mothers exhibit rejecting behaviors earlier and more strongly than primiparous mothers), and hormonal regulation (Harlow & Harlow, 1965). While the male of the species is generally more independent than the female infant, the male is more sensitive to the deleterious effects of being raised in partial or total social isolation Hinde (1971).

Harlow and Harlow (1965) describe several stages in the development of age-mate or peer affectional systems. In a *reflex stage* infant rhesus macaques act as an integrated social group; if one of a small group leaves the group, the others will follow or it will return to the group. In an *exploratory stage* there is a brief, gross bodily contact, and oral and tactile contact with animate objects. The infant appears to seek maximal interactive responsiveness with age-mates until they respond with aggressive behaviors creating aversive stimulation. Next there is a stage of *interactive play*, which may be broadly divided into rough-and-tumble play and approach–withdrawal play. The next stage is *aggressive play,* when dominance patterns are established, social status develops, and status relations are formed. Finally, there is a *mature interaction stage* (Harlow & Harlow, 1966), with play decreasing during adolescence and adult life; but the ties that develop in play continue in affectional relationships, while new affectional ties develop without the necessity for play. Harlow and Harlow (1965) argue that such systems are of vast importance to normal adolescent and adult social development.

Harlow and Harlow (1965) similarly describe four stages in the development of heterosexual affectional systems, commencing with a *reflex stage*, when infants of both sexes demonstrate pelvic thrusting to a soft stimulus, progressing through an *infant heterosexual stage* (changing from polymorphous elicitation to relatively discrete intersex elicitation), to a *preadolescent heterosexual stage* (with clear diferences between the sexes in expression), and finally, to an *adult heterosexual* system. Finally, Harlow and Harlow (1965) describe a paternal affectional system noting that primates show varying degrees of care and protection of females and their offspring, and frequently become involved in intimate relations with their own or substitute children. Mitchell and Brandt (1972) consider paternal behavior in primates more extensively, and suggest that it may range from not being evident at all to tolerance, friendly interaction, caring for, and even adopting an infant. In some species the male parent may do more for the infant than the female parent: in the titi monkey the male will hold and carry the infant all the time except when it is being nursed. Mitchell and Brandt examine the relevance of infant characteristics on such a process and suggest that paternal interest is more evident toward female than male infants, and toward younger, orphaned, and defective infants.

In arguing that human social behavior rests on a genetic foundation, Wilson (1978) points out that the "more stereotyped forms of human behavior are mammalian and even more specifically primate in character." The argument that certain affectional systems in humans are genetically determined is clearly strengthened by such evidence as presented in this section; the similarities between attachment behaviors (and perhaps peer affectional systems) in macaques and those described in human infants can be clearly seen. Similarities in the ontogenesis of maternal affectional systems in macques and humans are not so clearly evident; therefore, it might not be prudent to suggest that protective behaviors are influenced by similar mechanisms in the differing species. Two findings, however, are highlighted for further consideration: first, in macques, the mother clearly makes a contribution to the infant–mother detachment process; second, maternal protective behaviors in macaques are increased in association with maternal agitation, whether or not an external threat is apparent.

OVERVIEW

In this chapter several theories of the origin and development of an infant's attachment to a caregiver have been examined. Bowlby's theory and its subsequent developments have been emphasized. This theory suggests that an infant is disposed to seek attachment initially as a consequence of a number of species-characteristic behavior patterns, which are largely if not entirely instinctive. Later the attachment systems are less sterotyped and fulfill the characteristics of goal-corrected systems—being influenced and perhaps modified by feedback and experience, but still having the predictable outcome of keeping the infant and caregiver in physical proximity to each other. Other, and later, characteristics of attachment bonds are that they are affectional, discriminating and specific, associated with affects (principally positive ones), and endure over time. Several factors increase, or are associated with increased or excessive attachment behavior. Reciprocal maternal care systems in humans and infrahuman primates, also promote attachment and keep the two partners in proximity. Ainsworth suggests that mother–child interaction can be viewed as a result of several classes of behavior: the child's attachment behavior, the child's behavior antithetic to attachment (especially exploration and play), the mother's parental care behavior, and her behavior antithetic to parental care. There is a resulting dynamic equilibrium among behaviors in each of the four classes, which vary in intensity from time to time.

It is likely that overprotective mothering reflects a quantitative disturbance in the equilibrium between behavioral systems that subserve an infant's attachment and a mother's caretaking. This might occur as a consequence of excessive attachment requirements by the infant or child, excessive caregiving behaviors (e.g., pronounced proximity and retrieval-type behaviors) by the mother during the process of attachment, or the mother–child interaction itself. There must be some suspicion that if maternal overprotection is effected early it prohibits or otherwise limits the capacity for "sensitive responsiveness."

Ainsworth (1973) suggests that sensitive responsiveness appears to be the key quality in any parent–child interaction, and that it fosters secure personal bonding. As Rutter (1980a) notes, the concept of sensitive responsiveness reflects a general shift of view from "parenting as doing things to the baby to parenting as a process of reciprocal interaction." The possibility that infant and mother have an immediate potential to bond in a sustained reciprocal rhythm was considered earlier. Optimal development seems to require the early development of what has been termed "synchrony," "reciprocal interaction," or "mother–infant equilibrium." Observational studies suggest that infants are sensitive to the degree of stimulation and that they seek to regulate the mother–infant interaction soon after birth. Clearly, some mothers are able to perceive accurately their infant's behavioral cues and respond appropriately to oscillating needs for stimulation. This maternal capacity is important with older infants as well, throughout the first year. Rutter (1980a) observes that there is general agreement that parenting involves reciprocity and sensitivity to the baby's cues and signals but that "we have some way to go before we have either adequate concepts or adequate measures of what is meant by sensitive responsiveness." Rutter suggests that it is likely that it involves discrimination of cues provided by the baby, the giving of appropriate differentiating responses, the initiation of interactions, and the ability to get pleasure from the baby's reciprocity.

The possibility that maternal overprotection may reflect an inability by the mother to develop a synchronous relationship with her infant, that it may be associated with excessive and inappropriate stimulation of the infant, and that it may result in qualitative and quantitative disturbances in mother–infant attachment are issues that need to be considered in any attempt to understand the pathogenesis of maternal overprotection.

While "traces of any relationship significant enough to be termed an attachment are never altogether lost" (Ainsworth, 1973), detachment processes evolve just as do mother–infant attachment bonds. Clearly, we know less at this stage about detachment than about attachment processes. There is some evidence suggesting that an infant seeks autonomy from the caregiver for its own sake, and that it seeks to gain interpersonal regulation and social competence. There is evidence that a mother and her offspring are programed genetically to lengthen the spatial distance betweeen them. The degree to which such changes reflect evolution in attachment or detachment processes is an arguable point. If we can accept Ainsworth's view that attachment and detachment processes are interdependent, and that the provision of a secure base encourages the infant to explore away from that base, then attempts to distinguish strictly between functionally related and interdependent processes would seem to be relatively unimportant.

An important issue is the probability that detachment processes exist that are relatively independent of mother–child dyadic factors. There is much to suggest that fathers and peers (and perhaps other family members) have the capacity to promote mother–child detachment, and appear principally to do so by assisting the child's broader socialization. Cultural factors may also promote the detachment process. Subhuman primate studies appear to confirm the universality of many of these processes. Studies of macaques illustrate the early contribution made by infants to the detachment process. While observational data suggest that both the infant and the mother can initiate components of the detachment processes, the relative contribution made by each partner and the degree to which contributions may be interdependent remain to be explained. A striking component of "detachment" in maternal "rejection" was noted in the macaque studies. The resemblance of such component behaviors to those observed in human mothers in a matrilocal ghetto community is apparent. Such behaviors may reflect an instinctual mechanism (unmodified by cultural constraints) to detach a child abruptly and forcefully. It could certainly be argued that it would be adaptive for a mother to reject a child as soon as it is capable of surviving, so that she could prepare to nurse her next infant. The rejecting nature of such behaviors has been challenged because they generally result in increased clinging by the infant macaque, just as a human infant's attachment behaviors may increase in the face of maltreatment and severe punishment (Rutter, 1980a). Such an argument does not, by itself, however, necessarily make the rejection component invalid. The nature of the rejection and the factors associated with its presence or absence in human and infrahuman primates, require elucidation.

In any attempt to consider the nature and determinants of maternal overprotection some consideration must be given to the mother's incapacity to allow a child's progressive detachment. It could reflect maternal characteristics, infant characteristics, or mother–infant and environmental interactions; the main observational data appear to implicate the maternal contribution. For instance, Mahler et al. (1975) suggest that a child's strivings for individuation may be interfered with by an "omnipresent infantilizing mother"; difficulty in the differentiation phase may occur if the infant is oversaturated with the mother or if the mother is intrusive or smothering. They describe a group of mothers who "could not endure the gradual disengagement of the infant at the beginning of the separation-individuation phase." They found that anxious mothers with symbiotic-parasitic needs were doting and intrusive and were shadowers of their child late in the separation-individuation process of childhood. However, possible infant characteristics (e.g., sex, temperament) and mother–infant interaction factors (e.g., environmental danger) have also been suggested as relevant to delayed or restricted detachment.

The review presented in this chapter allows testable hypotheses to be generated about correlates and determinants of maternal overprotection. For instance, at an extremely simple level, overprotection might be predicted by demographic data. It might be predicted that greater evidence of maternal overprotection would be found when a father is absent, or effectively absent, than if he is an involved caregiver—irrespective of whether this reflects a primarily overprotective mother who excluded him from parenting, a defensive strategy by an unsupported mother, a failure in his capacity to act as the socializer of the child, or some other factor. Similarly, we might expect overprotected children to have few companions—either because a primarily overprotective mother elected to restrict her child's socialization or because the absence of companions interferes with the usual process of detachment from the mother. This review of the processes influencing a child's tie to its mother suggests possible determinants (ranging from immediate parental influences to wider cultural influences) for research consideration. The research reported in Part III will attend principally to the parental contribution, and factors influencing a mother's capacity to be overprotective but also will make some examination of child variables and cultural influences.

PART II

Measurement of Parental Overprotection

Measurement is fundamental to any research endeavor, but a rigorous approach is of particular relevance in this instance when parental overprotection has been defined variably, and most commonly, subjectively. To some observers overprotection is a benign parental style of caring indulgence, while to others it is a malignant dimension associated with parental rejection, the dissonance in definition promoting further conceptual confusion and incongruities between studies. Parental overprotection first should be defined, and then measured with an instrument of demonstrable reliability and validity. Only then may the relevance of parental overprotection to psychiatric and other disorders be assessed and possible determinants of parental overprotection studied.

6
Studies Attempting to Define and Calibrate Parental Overprotection

In earlier chapters it is suggested that there is some agreement in commentators' definitions of maternal overprotection, despite widely differing approaches and viewpoints. Definition has also been provided by the use of factor-analytic techniques. Such procedures have been employed frequently on checklists of parental attitudes and behaviors; they allow, in effect, the gross anatomy of parental characteristics and the interrelationships of the component constructs to be delineated. Such procedures assist data reduction; more specifically, if the goal is to design a measure of parental overprotection, these procedures can be used to suggest appropriate items for inclusion and to indicate whether one or several subscales may be appropriate.

It is important to note one reservation about factor-analytic techniques. Any set of variables obtained in a factor analysis is derived only from those variables entered initially. If the original variables are limited in scope or are idiosyncratic, then the final factors or components will reflect those limitations. A researcher wishing to examine the relationship of parental overprotection to other parental characteristics would need to ensure that variables assessing those other characteristics were well represented in the item pool.

Ad hoc questionnaires developed intuitively and unevaluated (e.g., the 40-item measure of "momistic tendencies" described by Strecker in 1946) are not reviewed.

The first standardized rating scales to measure parental behaviors were designed by Champney (1941). Developed at the Fels Institute in Ohio, the Fels Scales were designed to allow a trained rater to assess parent–child relationships in the home, and take some 4 hours to administer. Scores are assigned on 30 scales, including "child-centeredness of home," "restrictiveness of regulations," "general babying," and "general protectiveness," which might be regarded as encompassing some of the general constructs underlying overprotection. Independent assessment of the scales (Buros, 1970) has shown that they are of acceptable (test–retest) reliability. Their validity was assessed by comparing the evaluations of independent raters, and generally acceptable correlations were obtained; however, it would be unwise to conclude that such a procedure is adequate to assess their validity. Buros emphasizes that the scales are useful only in the hands of a skilled interviewer. Data from these scales were later factor analyzed by Roff (1949), who extracted seven major factors. The first factor measured Concern for the Child. The second and third factors (Democratic Guidance, and Permissiveness) could be held to reflect positive and negative expressions of overprotection.

Becker (1964; Becker et al., 1959; Becker et al., 1962) subsequently used a number of items from the Fels Scales together with other (clinic) interview ratings of parents and children, largely to find and measure variables in parent behavior which were critical to the development of the child. In one study (Becker et al., 1962), the sample comprised volunteers drawn from kindergartens as well as families with kindergarten children that had sought professional help for behavioral problems with their children. Sixteen items from the Fels Scales were included, along with "most" of the rating scales used by Sears et al. (1955) and "a few specially devised scales." Variables were deleted if their interrater reliability coefficients were less than 0.50. Separate factor analyses were performed of the maternal interview data (71 variables) and of the paternal interview data (64 variables). Five factors, including one labeled "permissiveness versus restrictiveness" appeared similar across both samples. A "restrictive" parent emphasized care of the house and furniture, pressured the child to neatness and orderliness, was strict, demanded high-level table manners, and used overt rewards frequently. A factor termed "child-rearing anxiety versus unsolicitousness" had items suggesting a parent who was anxious about child-rearing, was solicitous of the child's welfare, was highly maladjusted and had a low self-esteem, experienced noteworthy disciplinary friction, and was dissatisfied with the "current situation." The authors note that that "factor is not at all unlike the constellation of behaviors which Levy (1943) called *maternal overprotection.*"

In a review Becker (1964) attempts to draw together his earlier studies and those of several other workers. He states that the results of the factor analyses suggest that parental behaviors might best be represented by a three-dimensional model with dimensions of warmth versus hostility, restrictiveness versus permissiveness, and anxious–emotional in-

Studies Attempting to Define and Calibrate Parental Overprotection

volvement versus calm detachment. He argues that an overprotective parent is high on both warmth and restrictiveness. It is perhaps worth noting at this stage that his model further suggests a negative relationship between an "overprotective" and an "anxious, neurotic" parent. Thus Becker was less interested in developing a measure of parental characteristics than in attempting to isolate critical parental characteristics and their interrelationships.

Roth (1961) selected 48 items that he held reflected parental attitudes of rejection, overindulgence, overprotection, and acceptance, to create the Mother–Child Relationship Evaluation. Subjects agree or disagree with the statements on a 5-point scale; the scores are said to provide "an objective assessment of a mother's relationship to her child." Test–retest reliability coefficients of $r = +0.53$ (on the overprotection scale) and $r = +0.41$ (on the overindulgence scale) were obtained. Validity was considered only in terms of construct validity. In a personal communication to an independent assessor (Buros, 1970), Roth reported zero-order correlations between mothers' responses to the measure and their college-age children's perceptions of how the mothers would score themselves; these findings fail to support the validity of the measure.

Roe and Siegelman (1963) asked members of two groups (college students and professionals) to score their parents (on a 4-point scale) on the Parent–Child Relations Questionnaire (PCR), assessing remembered parental behaviors in childhood. The PCR contained 15 items culled or adapted from the literature to fit 10 categories which were considered to reflect broad parental responses.

Properties of the measure (i.e., reliability and validity) were not assessed. Scores on the 10 subscales were factor analyzed and a 3-factor solution and varimax rotation were imposed. The first factor was bipolar and termed "loving–rejecting." The second factor, also bipolar, was termed "casual–demanding." High scorers at one pole of this factor were perceived as "demanding" (e.g., setting high standards, imposing strict regulations, imposing obedience, being highly punitive), as evidencing "symbolic-love punishment" (e.g., shaming the child in front of others, isolating the child, withdrawing love from the child), and as using "direct-object punishment" (e.g., punishing physically, reducing allowances, denying promised trips). High scorers at the "casual" pole were perceived as easygoing, having few rules, which were not enforced, and usually responding in a mildly affectionate way to the child. Their third factor was a unipolar one termed "overt concern for the child." High scorers were "protective" (e.g., had the child's interest as a first priority, were affectionate, selected the child's friends, protected the child from experiences in which he might suffer hurt, were highly intrusive, and rewarded dependency) and used "direct-object" rewards. The authors do not state why they factor analyzed subscale scores instead of the scores for each individual item. The interrelationship between the suggested dimensions cannot be clearly assessed in their report.

Pitfield and Oppenheim (1964) developed an attitude inventory (52 questions covering 10 areas) to assess child-rearing practices. The test is self-administered, with a parent selecting 1 of 5 responses reflecting degree of agreement or disagreement. The authors do not state how the items were generated. Dimensions were again derived from factor-analytic studies. The first factor is a "strictness" factor, and the second is an "acceptance–rejection" dimension on which attitude areas of "acceptance," "overprotection," and "objectivity" load. "Overprotection" is subdivided into "submissive" and "dominant" forms. A copy of the questionnaire obtained from the second author showed that "dominant" overprotection was assessed by items including the following: "It is all right for a mother to bath her child regularly even though he can do it himself"; and "A child should never be allowed to take the slightest risk." "Submissive" overprotection was assessed by items including the following: "It is difficult to deny children things if they ask for them"; and "Parents should be ready to sacrifice almost everything for their children." The view that overprotection may be associated with both domineering and indulging behaviors is consistent with Levy's (1943) theoretical view. The authors state that their inventory has a "reliability of 0.79" but do not note what aspect of reliability was assessed.

Schaefer and Bell (1958) developed the Parental Attitude Research Instrument (PARI), a self-report questionnaire with 80 items assessing maternal attitudes. Mothers are asked to indicate their opinion of each item on a 4-point scale. The items were collected into three sets by the researchers (principally on theoretical grounds) that were labeled "democracy–domination," "acceptance–rejection," and "indulgence–autonomy." None of the 14 subscales define a dimension of overprotection, although several possible components of overprotection ("excluding outside influence," "intrusiveness," and "fostering dependency") are collected in separate subscales.

Schaefer then proceeded to develop models of parental behavior from psychologists' ratings and from children's reports, and determine the degree to which the models resembled each other structurally. In the first study Schaefer (1959) reports a factor-analytic study of psychologists' ratings suggesting two orthogonal dimensions underlying parental behaviors ("love versus hostility," and "autonomy versus control"). Schaefer also proposes a "circumplex" model, i.e., a "circular order of neighboring constructs," for parental behavior developed from a "generalization of empirical data."

Subsequently, Schaefer (1965) developed the Children's Reports of

Parental Behavior Inventory (CRPBI) by having 3 psychologists generate 10 items for each of 26 concepts derived from the circumplex model conceptualized earlier. Questionnaires were completed by several clinical and nonclinical groups, with respondents scoring both their mothers and their fathers on state characteristics if they were children, or as the parents were remembered in adolescence if the respondents were adults. A principal components analysis of scores on the 26 scales was performed, a varimax rotation employed, and the first three factors were capable of clear interpretation. The first factor was a bipolar one termed "acceptance–rejection." The second factor, also bipolar, was termed "psychological control–psychological autonomy," and appeared to describe an overprotection dimension. Schaefer suggests that the defining scales "describe covert, psychological methods of controlling the child's activities and behaviors that would not permit the child to develop as an individual apart from the parent." The third factor was termed "firm control versus lax control," with the items at the former pole suggesting a parent who makes rules and regulations, sets limits to a child's activities, and enforces those rules and limits. Separate factor analyses of scores by the children and by the adults, and of scores returned for mothers and fathers, showed similar factor loadings, suggesting the general relevance of the proposed configurational model of parental behaviors. Despite a goal of developing "reliable scales," the authors assessed only the internal consistency reliability, obtaining correlation coefficients ranging from $+0.66$ to $+0.84$. The validity of the inventory was not examined.

A revised version of the questionnaire was completed by 182 French schoolchildren (Renson et al., 1968). As the factor structure was highly similar to that in the American sample, Renson et al. conclude that the validity of their three-dimensional model is supported.

Schvaneveldt (1968a, 1968b) sought to develop a film test to measure perceptions of maternal overprotection. Viewers are required to complete a checklist concerning several filmed episodes of parent–child interaction. The test–retest reliability scores were highly significant but no adequate test of validity was conducted.

Raskin et al. (1971) used a shortened form of Schaefer's questionnaire (the CRPBI) in a combined sample of 254 nonclinical adults and 548 depressed patients. In contrast to several of the earlier studies, test item scores rather than the composite scale scores were factor analyzed. In the factor analyses of the data from the different groups no more than three principal components were capable of clear interpretation and accounted for a significant amount of the variance. The first factor was unipolar, labeled "positive involvement," and described an accepting and affectionate interest in the child or in his activities. Items loading on the second unipolar factor, termed "negative control," reflected parental efforts to control their children's behavior in "negative and psychologically harmful ways," and comprised items defined by Schaefer as reflecting "psychological control." Factor three, again unipolar, and termed "lax discipline," comprised items suggesting allowance of child autonomy and lax discipline. The same items had comparable loadings on the maternal and paternal scales. Schaefer's work had suggested three dimensions of parental behaviors in studies of schoolchildren and college students. Although they used a shorter questionnaire and analyzed individual item scores rather than scale scores, Raskin et al. interpret the finding of similar dimensions in normal adults and depressed adults as suggesting some stability in these dimensions.

Solyom et al. (1976) devised a 50-item Maternal Overprotection Questionnaire (MOQ), largely using items based on Levy's (1943) criteria. Validity of the form was assessed by having 10 overprotective and 10 nonoverprotective mothers (as judged by psychiatrists) complete the form. Those in the first group scored significantly higher than those in the second group. The questionnaire has not, as yet, been published.

The Parental Bonding Instrument (PBI) was designed (Parker et al., 1979) to define the important parental dimensions more closely and to determine how accurately they might be measured. Its development is examined more closely in Chapter 7. It was developed in nonclinical groups. Subjects are asked to score parents as they remember them in the first 16 years. There are 13 items in the final "protection" scale, and 12 items in the "care" scale; scores on these two scales consistently correlated negatively in subsequent research studies, suggesting that overprotection is linked with insufficiency of care. The protection factor had one pole defined by control ("tried to control everything I did"), overprotection ("was overprotective of me"), intrusion ("felt I could not look after myself unless he/she was around"; "invaded my privacy"), infantilization ("tended to baby me"; "did not want me to grow up"), and encouragement of dependency ("tried to make me dependent on him/her"); the negative pole was defined by items suggesting the encouragement of autonomy and independence. Close agreement was found between the comparable mother and father factor loadings for both the care and protection factors. The reliability and validity of the PBI protection and care scales have been examined in clinical and nonclinical groups;' the findings, suggesting that the PBI has adequate properties, are presented in Chapter 7.

More recently, Perris et al. (1980) developed an inventory, the EMBU ("own memories of child-rearing experiences"). The initial inventory comprised items suggested by Jacobson et al. (1975) as reflecting child-rearing practices, along with qualities noted by other authors, and items reflecting Swedish rearing practices. The final form comprises 81 questions grouped into 15 subscales. A principal components analysis was carried out using the total scores for the subscales returned by a nonclinical group of 152 subjects. The first factor for mothers described controlling, performance-oriented, overinvolved, and guilt-engendering behaviors, while "overprotective behaviors" was the only subscale to load on the fourth factor. For fathers, "overprotective behaviors" loaded on the first factor, which was otherwise comparable with the first factor obtained for mothers.

Clearly, a number of reservations could be expressed about these factor-analytic studies. Item pools of parental behaviors and attitudes appear at times limited, at times idiosyncratic, and at times merely derivative. In most studies the rather limiting procedure of factor analyzing scale scores (with the collection of items into scales being decided on arbitrary, personal, or unstated grounds) has been employed rather than factor analyzing responses to individual items. Despite these and other limitations (e.g., wide variations in approach in using parents, recipients of parenting, or observers, and in studying nonclinical and clinical groups), the factor-analytic studies do allow some synthesis. The most important dimension underlying parental behaviors and attitudes is a "care" one, with parents being rated along a dimension ranging from "care" to "indifference or rejection." An "overprotection" dimension is most commonly the next suggested dimension. It may be unipolar, with another unipolar factor reflecting the "encouragement of independence or autonomy," or those two characteristics may align themselves as one bipolar factor.

"Overprotection" (as defined by such statistical procedures) would appear to be a term comprising a number of components. Excessive psychological control over a child is clearly an important construct. Other constructs commonly described are intrusion, infantilization, and encouragement of dependency. Less common are excessive contact, prevention of independent behavior, strictness, and parental obsessiveness. At least one study has suggested that overprotection may be associated with either domineering or indulging parental characteristics. The relationship between parental overprotection and parental care is unclear—some studies suggest that the two dimensions are orthogonal or independent, others that overprotection and care are positively related, and others that they are negatively related.

There are then a number of questionnaires that may be used to calibrate the degree of parental overprotection. Some (e.g., the PARI) are completed by mothers about themselves, some (e.g., the Fels Scales) are completed by trained raters, and some (e.g., the CRPBI and the PBI) are completed by respondents as they remember or perceived their parents. Rarely have the properties of these measures been assessed with any rigor.

Perhaps of most concern is the validity of such measures. Certainly scores by recipients of certain parental behaviors and attitudes have been shown to correlate with other measures of child and adult adjustment (see Schaefer, 1965), which might suggest some predictive validity—but there are other explanations of these associations. For instance, it is possible that such associations may be brought about by a plaintive set or other response bias in subjects, the bias causing the subject both to score high on measures of maladjustment and to score parents in a negative way, thereby creating a statistical association in the absence of any causal link between parental style and recipient maladjustment. It is important that the validity of any self-report measure be assessed in terms of its capacity to measure both *perceived* and *actual* parental characteristics.

The reason it is important to assess both aspects should be considered further. Let us assume that a causal link exists between the *perception* of a mother as overprotective and increased levels of anxiety in adult life. In such a situation the strength of the causal association is likely to be most accurately revealed by a valid measure of *perceived* overprotection. If, however, a causal link exists between *actual* maternal overprotection and recipient anxiety, then the association will be more accurately shown by a valid measure of *actual* overprotection. It is unlikely that the perception and actuality of parental characteristics correspond very closely, and therefore it is unlikely that a parental measure can be entirely valid on both counts. The researcher is obliged to consider the implications and limitations of each type of measure in choosing a measure of parental overprotection.

The MOQ and the PBI are the only measures of parental overprotection that have been subjected to validity assessment. Data on the PBI's concurrent validity and on its split-half reliability (analogous to convergent validity) support it as a measure of perceived parental characteristics. Data are presented in Chapter 7 examining the degree to which scores are corroborated by involved family members, and by an independent rater; the predictive validity of the PBI is assessed in Chapter 8.

7
Development of the Parental Bonding Instrument and the Parent Opinion Form

The development of the Parental Bonding Instrument (PBI) has been described in an earlier publication (Parker et al., 1979); it is summarized here before new data on its properties are presented.

DEVELOPMENT OF THE PBI

It can be argued (Parker et al., 1979), partly on the basis of studies reviewed in Chapter 6, that the parental contribution to bonding may be influenced to two principal source variables; an attempt was made to define and provide self-report scales for those two dimensions. An inventory of 114 items suggesting behaviors and attitudes of relevance was prepared; items were rejected if they did not produce well-distributed responses, if they correlated too highly with another item, or if they did not load clearly on the first few factors obtained in several screening principal components analyses.

In the final analysis of responses made by a heterogeneous nonclinical group, a limitation of two factors and a varimax rotation were imposed, and the factor loadings were examined. Items loading highest on the two factors were retained for the final scales, resulting in 12 care items and 13 overprotection items. The first factor, accounting for 28 percent of the total variance, was bipolar with factor loadings from +0.76 to −0.67. It clearly suggested a "care" construct, with items at one pole indicating affection, emotional warmth, empathy, and closeness, while items at the other pole suggested emotional coldness, indifference, and rejection. The second factor, accounting for 17 percent of the total variance, was bipolar with factor loadings from +0.71 to −0.58, and was termed an "overprotection" dimension, as items suggested several constructs relevant to overprotection. One pole of the second dimension was defined by items suggesting parental control, overprotection, intrusion, excessive contact, infantilization, and prevention of independent behavior, while the other was defined by items suggesting promotion of independence and autonomy (see Chapter 6). Close agreement between factor loadings for mothers and fathers on the comparable items suggested that the two dimensions reflect general parental characteristics, and that the items are of similar relevance to male and female parents. It is important to note that, for a number of reasons, the "overprotection" scale is now renamed the "protection" scale. The PBI and its scoring are presented in Appendix I.

At that time, the test–retest reliability of the inventory was assessed by having 17 subjects complete the PBI on two occasions 3 weeks apart. A Pearson correlation coefficient of 0.76 ($p<0.001$) was obtained for the care scale and 0.63 ($p<0.001$) for the protection scale. The split-half reliability of the PBI was assessed, and correlation coefficients of 0.88 and 0.67 (both $p<0.001$) were found for the care and protection scales, respectively.

Two attempts were made to assess the validity of the PBI as a measure of *perceived* parental characteristics. Three Thematic Apperception Test (TAT) cards were administered to a number of subjects and a content analysis of responses was made by Professor L. B. Brown. The three cards (7GF, GBM, and 2) suggested themes of separation and parental closeness. However, the responses consistently showed the expectation or stereotype that mothers are controlling, directly or indirectly, and suggested that TAT responses did not provide a useful basis for validation. Thus, 65 of the subjects in the nonclinical sample were interviewed jointly by a psychologist (Hilary Tupling) and by the present author, each subject being asked to discuss the emotional relationship they had with each parent, and the degree to which each parent had let them do "their own thing." The two raters independently assessed the content of those interviews and assigned a score from 5 to 1 for each parent's degree of "care" and "overprotection"; the interrater reliability coefficients on those two dimensions were 0.85 and 0.69 (both $p<0.001$), respectively. An estimate of the validity of the PBI as a measure of *perceived* parental characteristics was provided by correlating PBI scores with the raters' scores. The Pearson correlations for the two Care measures were 0.78 for rater 1 and 0.77 for rater 2, and for the two Protection measures they were 0.50 for rater 1 and 0.48 for rater 2 (all $p<0.001$).

In the original study normative data were obtained and the possible influences of several variables on PBI scores were studied. Patients and accompanying relatives attending several Sydney general practices were asked to complete a questionnaire comprising PBI forms and sociodemographic items. Responses made by 410 adults were analyzed and the mean scores are recorded (Appendix II). Scores on the Care and Protection scales correlated negatively for both mothers ($r = -0.47$) and fathers ($r = -0.36$). Respondents scored their mothers as more caring ($t = 8.3$, $p<0.001$) and as somewhat more protective ($t = 2.31$, $p<0.025$) than their fathers. Possible influences of the subjects' age, sex, and social class on PBI scores were examined separately. Only a weak positive association was found linking higher social class with higher maternal care scores. The possibility of an interaction between those predictor variables was examined subsequently by entering the three variables as independent ones in regression analyses, with PBI scale scores as dependent variables. Table 7-1 shows that the only significant effect is a link between higher social class and higher maternal care scores.

As several reports and commentators have suggested that the only child, in particular, may be at risk for maternal overprotection, any influences that family size might have on PBI scores was examined subsequently in a nonclinical group. Postgraduate students training at Sydney Teachers' College scored their parents on the PBI and provided details on family size and structure (the sample is described more fully in Chapter 16). The data returned by 252 students are shown in Table 7-2. There is a nonsignificant trend for only children to score their mothers as more protective than children with siblings. There is a nonsignificant curvilinear relation between paternal protection and family size, with only childen and children with many siblings scoring their fathers highest on protection. When a comparison is made of PBI scores for only children versus the remainder (i.e., those with one or more siblings), no differences are apparent on the care scale (maternal care = 26.8, paternal care = 22.7, for the remainder group), but only children scored both their mothers (17.9 vs. 15.0) and their fathers (15.4 vs. 13.6) as somewhat more protective than did the remainder.

FURTHER COLLECTIONS OF NORMATIVE DATA

Data Collection in Sydney, Australia

One of the aims in collecting PBI data was to provide control data for a number of case–control studies. Clearly, it would be ideal to collect control data from an appropriately selected sample of the general population, as general practice sampling runs the risk of having an excess of

Table 7-1
Influence of Age, Sex and Social Class on PBI Scores of General Practice Subjects, Sydney Sample

PBI Scale	Age		Sex		Social Class		All variables Entered into Equation	
	β Weight	Variance (%)	β Weight	Variance (%)	β Weight	Variance (%)	F Ratio	Variance (%)
Maternal care	−0.05	0.2	+0.02	0	−0.15	2.3	2.71*	2.6
Maternal protection	−0.7	0.5	−0.05	0.3	+0.05	0.2	1.00	1.0
Paternal care	0	0	+0.08	0.6	−0.09	0.7	1.40	1.4
Paternal protection	−0.04	0.2	+0.07	0.4	−0.03	0.1	0.71	0.7

*p < 0.05

Table 7-2
Influences of Family Size on PBI Scores (Sample of Postgraduate Teachers)

PBI Scale	Number of Siblings					F Ratio
	None ($n = 23$)	1 ($n = 71$)	2 ($n = 69$)	3–4 ($n = 71$)	More than 4 ($n = 18$)	
Maternal care	26.3	28.2	26.9	26.0	24.0	1.86
Maternal protection	17.9	14.1	15.2	15.5	15.3	1.19
Paternal care	23.5	25.2	22.8	20.5	21.3	3.01*
Paternal protection	15.4	13.9	12.5	13.7	16.0	0.98

*$p < 0.025$

those with psychological and psychiatric disorders compared to a community sample. For example, in samples of those aged 15–25 years in Western Australia, a case rate on the General Health Questionnaire (a measure of state psychological morbidity) of 18 percent was found in a community sample (Finlay-Jones & Burvill, 1977) and of 29 percent in a general practice sample (Finlay-Jones & Burvill, 1978). While the excess in the general practice sample is likely to reflect a large number of patients who score ephemerally as "neurotic" or as "psychiatric" cases as a consequence of stress associated with a physical disorder, it is also likely that there remains an excess of those with chronic neurotic disorders in general practice samples.

It is appropriate then to ask whether PBI data obtained by general practice sampling can be regarded as "good enough," or whether they are biased by an overrepresentation of psychologically disturbed patients. Thus it appeared useful to obtain and compare data from unscreened general practice patients and from patients screened for psychological morbidity. As the vast majority of psychiatric cases in community surveys appear to be depressed (Finlay-Jones, 1980), screening was designed principally to detect those who had had a significant depressive episode.

Method

Consecutive attenders of several Sydney general practitioners were to be asked to complete a PBI for each parent by a practice secretary, but practice demands prevented a consecutive collection. Subsequently, the general practitioner recorded their age, sex, and father's occupation, whether they had ever received psychiatric treatment or psychotropic medication, and whether they had had an episode of depression defined as follows:

> Have you ever had a period that lasted at least 1 week when you were bothered by feeling depressed, sad, blue, hopeless, down in the dumps, that you didn't care anymore, or didn't enjoy anything?

[This is the probe question from the Schedule for Affective Disorders and Schizophrenia (SADS) (Spitzer & Endicott, 1979) to detect the lifetime expression of a major depressive syndrome.]

Approximately 40 patients failed to return forms and another 11 forms were rejected as incomplete or clearly invalid. The responses of the remaining 212 patients who completed the forms were analyzed. Their mean age was 36.7 years (range 16–68 years), and there were 66 males and 146 females. The social class distribution, using the Congalton (1969) scale, was from highest to lowest: I = 7.4 percent, II = 25.5 per cent, III = 50.5 percent, and IV = 16.6 percent. PBI scores for the whole group corresponded closely with those obtained in the original Sydney general practice study (see Appendix II).

Results

Of the 212 respondents, 67 (32 percent) acknowledged an episode of depression as defined by the SADS probe; more females (36 percent) than males (20 percent) did so ($\chi^2 = 5.37$, df 1, $p<0.05$). Twenty-nine patients (14 percent) had had professional treatment for such an episode, again with a clear female preponderance (17 vs. 6 percent $\chi^2 = 4.67$, $p<0.05$); 27 (13 percent) had received psychotropic medication, and again there was a clear female preponderance (16 vs. 5 percent; $\chi^2 = 5.10$, $p<0.05$).

The 145 subjects who denied an episode of depression, treatment for depression, and psychotropic medication ("nondepressives") were compared with the remaining 67 "depressives" (Table 7-3). The two groups did not differ significantly in their scores on any PBI scale according to the nonparametric Z test. These findings suggest that there is no clear advantage in screening out "depressives" from routine general practice attenders in an attempt to reduce possible PBI biases accruing from an overrepresentation of psychologically disturbed patients.

Data Collection in Oxford, England

In order to examine the general applicability of the PBI, and to examine for demographic influences on PBI scores in another culture, normative PBI data were collected in Oxford, England.

Table 7-3
Comparison of PBI Scores of General Practice Subjects
Categorized as "Depressives" versus "Non Depressives"

PBI Scale	Depressives ($n = 67$)	Non-depressives ($n = 145$)	z test
Mean age (years)	37.6	36.3	0.83
Maternal care	26.8	27.0	0.52
Maternal protection	14.6	14.0	0.62
Paternal care	24.5	25.1	0.62
Paternal protection	13.7	11.8	1.80

Method

As in the Sydney study, data were sought from a series of consecutive attenders at several general practices in the Oxford region. The questionnaire included a PBI to be completed for each parent, along with questions to obtain the age and sex of each subject, and the occupation of the subject's father; the England and Wales Registrar General's classification was used to estimate social class. Secretarial staff were asked to present forms to consecutive adult attenders and to note the noncompliance rate, but forgetfulness, practice demands, and several other issues interfered. Some secretaries screened patients and excluded those who had minor language difficulties or those known to be "difficult."

The responses of 132 patients who completed forms anonymously were analyzed. Their mean age was 35 years (range 16–77 years), and there were 51 males and 81 females. The social class distribution, in descending social class order, of their fathers was class 1, 23 percent; class 2, 21 percent; class 3, 35 percent; classes 4 and 5, 21 percent.

Results

Mean scores on the Care and Protection scales correspond closely to Sydney data (see Appendix II). Mothers scored as more caring ($t = 4.46$, $p<0.001$) and somewhat more protective ($t = 2.56$, $p = 0.012$) than fathers. Care and protection scores were negatively correlated, with correlation coefficients of -0.44 ($p<0.001$) for mothers, and -0.20 ($p = 0.05$) for fathers. Regression analysis were performed to examine whether age, sex, and social class were associated with PBI scores. Table 7-4 shows that higher social class is associated with higher maternal care scores, and that fathers are more protective of daughters than of sons. The results are strikingly similar to those obtained in the Sydney study.

Table 7-4
Influence of Age, Sex, and Social Class on PBI Scores of General Practice Subjects, Oxford Sample

	Age		Sex		Social Class		All Variables Entered into the Equation	
PBI Scale	β Weight	Variance (%)	β Weight	Variance (%)	β Weight	Variance (%)	F Ratio	Variance (%)
Maternal care	+0.02	0.1	−0.04	0.2	−0.28	7.6*	3.2	7.9†
Maternal protection	+0.10	0.9	+0.03	0.1	+0.08	0.7	0.64	1.7
Paternal care	+0.02	0.1	−0.08	0.6	−0.01	0	0.25	0.7
Paternal protection	−0.03	0.2	+0.19	3.7†	+0.03	0.1	1.60	4.0

* $p < 0.01$; † $p < 0.05$

PBI VALIDITY STUDIES

While it can be argued that the perception and experience (i.e., the meaning) of parental characteristics are more important as possible causal influences on development than objective (i.e., actual) parental characteristics, it is nevertheless important to assess the degree to which the PBI assesses actual, and not merely perceived, parental characteristics.

Study 1

Method

Equal-sized subgroups of nonclinical and clinical subjects were selected to assess the degree to which PBI scores correspond with judgments made by another family member (Parker, 1981a). Diversity in data sources is recommended by Campbell and Fiske (1959) when analysis is to be made by the multitrait–multimethod matrix method and when the measuring methods are unlikely to be completely independent, as in the present study. The final sample comprised 15 university students, 7 members of a community service group, and 3 members of a mother's association in the nonclinical group, and 25 psychiatric outpatients in the clinical group. Those in the clinical group had the following clinical diagnoses: neurotic depression (12), anxiety state (5), personality disorder (5), manic-depressive psychosis (2), and schizophrenia (1). All patients were judged as being sufficiently well to understand the questionnaire and to distribute the forms to their siblings for completion. Forms were presented to a consecutive series of some 40 subjects in the nonclinical group and to 31 subjects in the clinical group before 25 completed forms were returned by siblings in each group in the stamped self-addressed envelopes.

Subjects and one of their nominated siblings were asked to complete PBI forms for each of their parents; then they were asked, based on their observations of their parents' behavior toward their sibling, to pretend to be that sibling and complete another set of PBI forms. Each was requested to ensure that he and his sibling completed the questionnaires independently and without discussion.

The mean age of the 50 subjects was 28 years (range 15–63 years), and of their siblings years 27 (range 15–68 years). Males and females were represented equally in both the subjects and siblings groups, although same-sex comparisons were made in only 58 percent of the comparisons.

Results

To assess validity by the multitrait–multimethod matrix several traits and several methods are required. In this study four different traits (maternal care, maternal protection, paternal care, paternal protection) were assessed by the following four different methods:

A). Subjects scoring their parents on the PBI as they remembered them
B). Subjects scoring their parents as they observed their attitudes and behaviors to the nominated sibling
C). Siblings scoring their parents on the PBI as they remembered them
D). Siblings scoring their parents as they observed their attitudes and behaviors to the subject.

The resulting multitrait–multimethod correlation matrix for the whole group of 50 subjects (as results were broadly comparable for the two subgroups) is shown in Figure 7-1. The relevant validity diagonals are diagonals III and IV (subjects' scores compared with scores for siblings pretending to be subjects; siblings' scores compared with scores for subjects pretending to be siblings). If the PBI is a valid measure of actual parental characteristics, then (assuming accurate reporting by the observers) there should be a high correlation between PBI scores by recipients and PBI scores returned by witnesses.

For validity to be demonstrated Campbell and Fiske (1959) suggest that several requirements need to be met. First, the entries in the validity diagonals should be significantly different from zero. Accepting a 5 percent level of significance, the critical value of r for the whole sample is 0.27. Examination of the relevant validity diagonals (III and IV) in Figure 7-1 reveals that this requirement is met in 7 of the 8 comparisons. Second, a validity diagonal value should be higher than the values lying in its column and row in the heterotrait–heteromethod triangles. This requirement is met by 7 of the 8 intercorrelations. Third, a validity diagonal value should correlate more highly with an independent effort to measure the same trait than with measures assessing different traits but employing the same method (i.e., values in the validity diagonal should exceed the values for that variable in the heterotrait–monomethod triangles). This requirement is met incompletely.

However, examination of the matrices for clinical, nonclinical, and combined groups suggested a contaminating influence of greater relevance. Intercorrelations in diagonals I and VI were generally higher than those in diagonals III and IV, suggesting that the subjects tended to score parents in a rather similar way *irrespective of whether they were asked to*

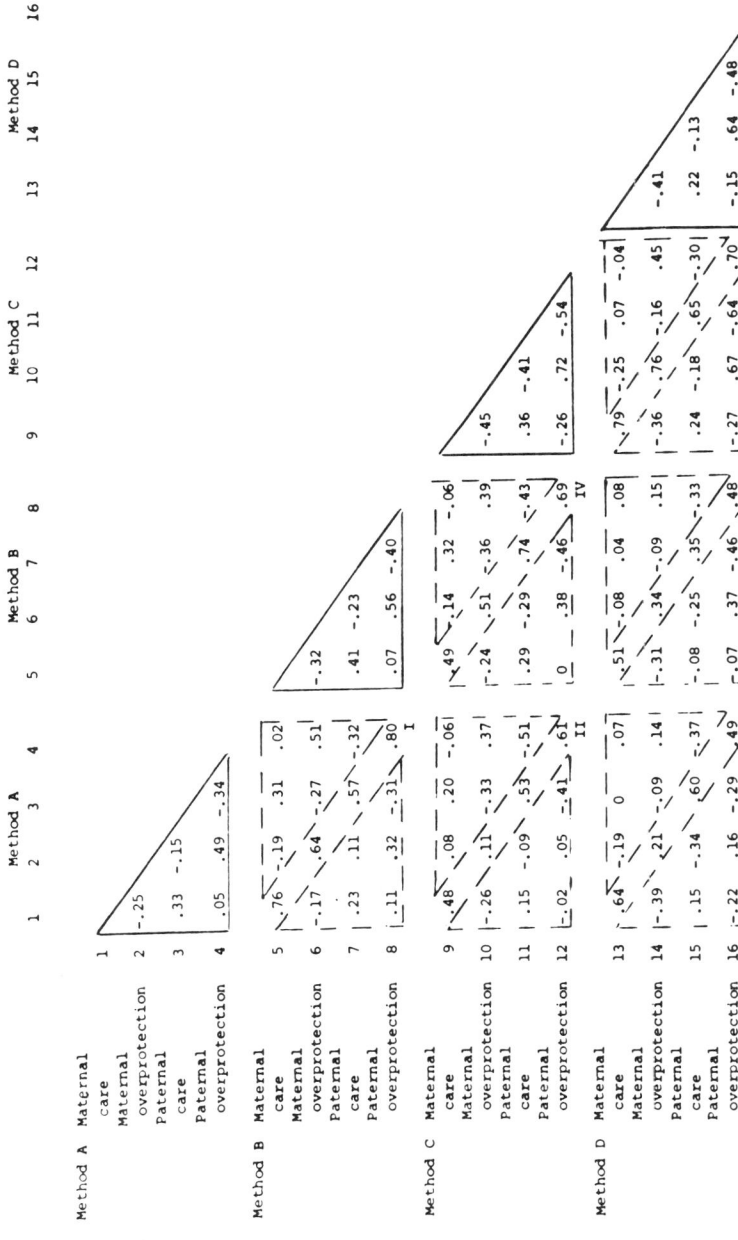

Figure 7-1. The multitrait–multimethod correlation matrix for all respondents. The validity diagonals are the six diagonals marked in Roman numerals, with diagonals III and IV being the principal diagonals under investigation. Each heterotrait–monomethod triangle is enclosed by a solid line, and each heterotrait–heteromethod triangle is enclosed by a broken line.

complete the test "for themselves" or "pretending to be a sibling." This explanation is preferred to one suggesting that results could be best accounted for by parents relating in a similar manner to all their children, as that possibility would require the highest correlations in diagonal II, a phenomenon not found in the present study.

Consideration of that issue raises another research issue—to what degree do subjects score parents on the PBI under the influence of some general perceptual set? If a general perceptual set influences reporting (whether it be a positive one such as "social desirability" or a negative one such as "plaintive set") it would act to bring out strong positive associations when parental care scores are intercorrelated, strong positive associations when parental protection scores are intercorrelated, and strong negative associations when care scores are intercorrelated with protection scores for the same parent. The mean coefficient strength (ignoring the direction of associations) is 0.31 in the clinical group and 0.43 in the nonclinical group. Such middle-order associations are not conclusive in resolving the issue, particularly when the coefficients would be boosted by other influences (e.g., a consensual parental style) apart from response biases. The difference between the mean coefficients for the clinical and nonclinical groups, if attributable to a difference in a response bias, might suggest that response biases are *less relevant* in groups of psychiatric patients. That issue is explored further in Chapters 9 and 17.

Finally, the crossover sibling design of the study allows some consideration of how closely sibings (reporting for themselves) approximate each other in their parental reports. For the combined group of clinical and nonclinical subjects, the intercorrelations are +0.48 (maternal care), +0.11 (maternal protection), +0.53 (parental care), and +0.61 (paternal protection). These associations possibly suggest some general consistency (apart from maternal protection) by parents in relating to their children. Clearly, many other factors (particularly child characteristics) would prevent absolute consistency, while still others (e.g., idealization of parents) would raise the intercorrelations. The lower figure on maternal protection was brought about solely by the clinical group; this raises the possibility that, if a response bias can be ignored, maternal protection may have been elicited by some characteristics of these children which may or may not have also contributed to their being in the clinical group.

While the present study finds some support for the view that PBI reports are reasonably consistent with witnesses' reports, the several contaminating influences that emerge suggest that a different approach to assessing the validity of the PBI as a measure of actual parental characteristics is required.

Study 2

Method

The present research issue is a component of a major study to be described later (Chapter 16); only a summary of the methodology is provided in this section. Students undertaking a postgraduate teacher training course were approached in class, and their participation in several studies, along with permission to interview their mothers, was sought (Parker, 1981a; Parker and Lipscombe, 1981). Provisional agreement was given by 199 of the 387 students, and these students completed several questionnaires, including the PBI, a trait depression measure (Costello & Comrey, 1967), and a state depression measure (Wilson & Lovibond, 1979). A random sample of 100 mothers was selected for interview: 75 of the mothers were subsequently interviewed at home, 21 interviews having been refused either by the mothers or students. The mothers were asked to complete a PBI as they believed they related toward their child in his or her first 16 years. At the completion of the interview the rater judged each mother on the basis of attitudes toward the index child expressed during the interview on the following possible components of maternal overprotection: excessive contact, infantilization, encouragement of dependency, control, and indulgence. In addition, the rater judged each mother on a general dimension of overprotection (scored on a 5-point scale), again on the basis of expressed attitudes during the interview.

Results

When students' PBI scores for their mothers are compared with the PBI scores of the mothers as they believed they had related to their child, significant correlations ($p<0.001$) are found on the Care and Protection scales, although the mothers scored themselves as significantly more caring ($p<0.001$) and as less protective ($p<0.01$) of their children than did the children themselves (Table 7-5).

The respective associations between PBI scores, assessed by the mothers and by their children, and depression levels were examined. Table 7-6 shows that higher depression scores in subjects, measured on both trait and state depression scales, are negatively associated with maternal care and positively associated with maternal protection, *whether judged by the subjects or by the subjects' mothers,* and that the respective correlations are strikingly similar in strength.

As the Protection scale of the PBI, and probably overprotection itself, encompasses several component characteristics, an attempt was made to see how well the total protection scores on the PBI discriminate

Table 7-5
Maternal PBI Scores Returned by Mothers (Scoring Themselves) and Students (Scoring Mothers)

PBI Scale	Mothers Scoring Themselves		Students Scoring Mothers		Intercorrelation of Scores by Mothers and Students
	Mean	SD	Mean	SD	
Maternal care	30.5	5.8	26.5	7.1	+0.44
Maternal protection	12.3	5.9	14.8	8.2	+0.55

From Parker, G. Parental reports of depressives: An investigation of several explanations. *Journal of Affective Disorders*, 1981, *3*, 131–140. Reprinted with permission of Elsevier Biomedical Press B.V.

subjects on those components of overprotection noted by Levy (1943). In order to perform these examinations two subgroups of mothers were formed:

1. "Overprotective mothers": those 15 mothers who scored 1 SD above the mean on the PBI protection scale completed by the index children
2. "Other mothers": the remaining 60 mothers whose children gave them a score of 22 or below on the PBI protection scale.

Table 7-7 shows the rater's mean scores (obtained at maternal interviews) for the mothers in the two groups on the suggested components of overprotection. Significance was tested for by the Mann-Whitney U test–Wilcoxon rank sum test. It can be seen that mothers in the two groups could be discriminated on three of the four behavioral dimensions regarded by Levy as indicating overprotection (infantilization, prevention of independent behavior, and excess of maternal control), while judge-

Table 7-6
Intercorrelation of Maternal PBI Scores Returned by Mothers (Scoring Themselves) and Students (Scoring Mothers) with Two Depression Measures

PBI Scale	Scorer	Intercorrelation	
		State Depression Scores	Trait Depression Scores
Maternal care	Students	−0.44*	−0.45*
	Mothers	−0.30‡	−0.35†
Maternal protection	Students	+0.30‡	+0.39*
	Mothers	+0.29‡	+0.33†

*$p < 0.001$; †$p < 0.01$; ‡$p < 0.05$

From Parker, G., Parental reports of depressives: An investigation of several explanations. *Journal of Affective Disorders*, 1981, *3*, 131–140. Reprinted with permission of Elsevier Biomedical Press B.V.

Table 7-7
Raters' Mean Scores for Mothers Assigned to Two Groups on the Basis of PBI Scores Returned by Index Children

Behavior Judged by Rater	Overprotective Mothers ($n = 15$)	Other Mothers ($n = 60$)	Z Test	Correlation of Rater's Scores and PBI Protection Scores (r)
Mother encouraged dependence	2.3	1.5	3.62*	+0.43*
Mother infantilized child	2.7	1.9	2.80†	+0.35*
Mother excessively indulged child	3.0	2.4	2.79†	+0.18
Mother excessively controlled child	3.3	2.7	2.52†	+0.30†
Mother sought excessive contact with child	2.3	2.2	0.52	+0.12
Mother overprotective (total impression)	3.5	2.3	3.59*	+0.44*

From Parker, G., & Lipscombe, P. Influences on maternal overprotection. *British Journal of Psychiatry*, 1981, *138*, 303–311. Reprinted with permission.
* $p < 0.001$; † $p < 0.01$

ment of excessive maternal contact by the rater did not discriminate the groups.

EXTRANEOUS INFLUENCES ON PBI SCORES

A number of irrelevant factors may influence self-report responses (see Wylie, 1961); social desirability and mood levels are common sources of bias.

Social Desirability Bias

The methodology is summarized here, as fuller details have been reported previously (Parker, 1977, 1979a). Sydney Teachers' College students ($n = 236$) scored their two most important parent-figures on the PBI and completed Form A of the Eysenck Personality Inventory (EPI) (Eysenck & Eysenck, 1964). The "lie" scale of that inventory is often regarded as a measure of the tendency to give socially desirable responses. On the "lie" scale of the EPI, 17 (7 percent) of the subjects scored 0; 140 (60 percent) scored 1–3; 35 (15 percent) scored 4; 27 (11 percent) scored 5; and 17 (7 percent) scored 6–9. A social desirability influence would be expected to be confirmed by high EPI lie scores being associated positively with parental care, and negatively with parental protection scores. Associations are in the expected direction ($+0.19$ and $+0.03$ with parental care, and -0.19 and -0.14 with parental protection scores) but are weak.

Liking of a Parent

The degree to which "liking" of a parent might be associated with scores was examined in a nonclinical group. In that study (reported more extensively in Chapter 16), 172 postgraduate students scored their parents on the PBI and were asked to score the degree to which they "liked" each parent on a 3-point scale ("a lot," "somewhat," "very little"). Greater liking of a mother was associated positively with maternal care scores ($r = +0.66$) and negatively with maternal protection scores ($r = -0.46$). Similar significant associations were found between greater liking of a father and paternal care ($r = +0.62$) and protection ($r = -0.42$) scores.

Level of Depression

The possibility that depression may influence the perception or recall of experiences has been mentioned frequently (e.g., Paykel et al., 1969) and requires consideration in relation to PBI scoring. The specific null hypothesis was as follows: level of depression does not influence scores on the PBI and, in such a study, a Type II error (accepting the hypothesis when it is false) might be committed by selecting too small a sample size. Applying the given standard error technique of Armitage (1971), which specifies a 95 percent confidence interval, it was estimated that a minimal sample size of 36 subjects would be required to avoid a Type II error.

Method

Patients consulting several psychiatrists and who had acknowledged depressive symptoms were asked to complete the PBI for each parent, and the Beck Depression Inventory (Beck et al., 1961), a self-report state depression measure. At a later time, when the psychiatrist judged each patient clinically to be either less or more depressed, the same forms were completed again. Only those subjects whose scores on the state depression scale differed by 5 or more points were included in the final sample.

Forty-six patients were screened before the final sample of 36 was obtained; 6 were excluded for returning similar scores on the depression scale at each assessment, and 4 for not completing the second set of forms. In the final sample there were 25 females and 11 males with a mean age of 36 years (range 18–63 years); 5 patients had been diagnosed clinically as having an endogenous depression, 5 a situational stress reaction, 7 an anxiety state, and 19 a neurotic or reactive depression. All but 1 scored highest on the depression scale at the first assessment. Scores obtained when subjects were most depressed ("high depression") were compared with scores returned by subjects when less depressed ("low depression"). The mean depression score during high depression was 24.4 (range 10–45) and was significantly higher ($t = 11.6$, $p<0.001$) than that returned (mean 6.9, range 0–34) at the low depression assessment. The mean interval between tests was 9 weeks.

Results

Table 7-8 shows that test–retest correlations of more than 0.87 were obtained for each PBI scale on the two test occasions. Since high test–retest correlations would be obtained if depression caused all the subjects to change their scores to a similar degree, correlated t tests were also performed, but no significant differences were found on any of the PBI scales. It can be concluded that level of depression does not influence PBI scores.

DISCUSSION OF THE PBI

The PBI was developed as a refined self-report scale measuring subjects' perceptions of the two dimensions identified as underlying parental attitudes and behaviors—care and protection. The care items define a

Table 7-8
Comparison of Subjects' PBI Scores on Two Occasions,
When Depressed and When Less Depressed

PBI Scale	Test–Retest Intercorrelation	High Depression		Low Depression	
		Mean	SD	Mean	SD
Maternal care	0.87*	19.5	11.6	20.8	10.1
Maternal protection	0.90*	19.8	10.3	18.5	11.3
Paternal care	0.92*	20.2	9.9	21.6	10.7
Paternal protection	0.87*	15.8	9.0	15.5	9.6

From Parker, G. Parental reports of depressives: An investigation of several explanations. *Journal of Affective Disorders*, 1981, *3*, 131–140. With permission of Elsevier Biomedical Press B.V.
*$p<0.001$

parental style that may range from one of affection, emotional warmth, empathy, and reciprocity to one of coldness, indifference, and neglect. The dimension is readily conceptualized (and supported by the split-half reliability and concurrent validity data) as a homogeneous one. The protection items suggest a dimension ranging from parental control, overprotection, intrusion, and infantilization to parental allowance of independence and the development of autonomy. In comparison to the care scale, it is less clear whether the protection scale reflects a homogeneous dimension, and it may be that "protection" is not the best label to apply to the dimension. Difficulty in defining that dimension is indicated in the initial study by lower interrater reliability and concurrent validity coefficients for that scale than for the care scale. It has been suggested that "control" may be a better label than "protection"; however, control would be a narrower construct, defining a parental style that is either authoritarian or authoritative (see Chapter 3), and which attempts to regulate and shape a child to a defined level of obedience or disciplined conformity. A controlling parent may or may not be intrusive or infantilize the child, but is rarely noted clinically to encourage dependency in a child. Thus, we see control as only a component of a wider dimension reflected in the scale, a scale that encompasses several related constructs and which historically (Levy, 1943) has been termed "overprotection."

Reliability

Several relevant properties of the PBI should be scrutinized. There are several components to reliability, but the most important is the extent to which the same results are obtained from one testing occasion to another. High reliability may not be demonstrated if a state disturbance is being measured. However, as the PBI is completed by subjects older than 16 years of age as they "remember" their parents in the first 16 years, consistency in reporting should be expected if the PBI is to be regarded as an acceptable measure.

The final scale was completed (Parker et al., 1979) by a small subgroup of the nonclinical sample on two occasions 3 weeks apart. The correlation coefficients of +0.76 for the care scale and 0.63 for the protection scale were acceptable. However, a later study (Parker, 1981a) of 36 depressed patients, tested when significantly depressed and when less depressed (on average 9 weeks apart), revealed much higher test–retest correlation coefficients—from 0.87 to 0.92. It is likely that the higher reliability coefficients in the clinical group, despite a longer test–retest interval, reflect the patients' greater motivation. The patients were quite likely to have completed PBI forms with the expectancy that the results would be important to their therapist and play some part in their assessment and therapy. The motivation of the volunteer nonclinical group might be expected to have been considerably lower. The patient study leads to two important conclusions: high reliability for the PBI has been demonstrated, and the PBI has been shown to be reliable in a clinical group. It should not be concluded, however, that it is necessarily reliable in all groups, whether psychiatric patients or others; in important studies its reliability should be assessed (as in the schizophrenia study reported in Chapter 8), as it seems clear that scoring is influenced by the motivation of the respondents.

While high reliability for the PBI has been demonstrated, observation over time has suggested that the wording of several items (i.e., items 2, 8, 14, 18, 24) may create confusion in some respondents because of the "double-negative" potential. The properties of an abbreviated PBI scale (with the five relevant items deleted) were therefore examined (see Appendix III).

Another issue is that the PBI appears to assume consistency of parental behavior over time. Clearly, parents may, in some instances, vary from one extreme of overprotection or care to the other during a child's lengthy period of development. There may be situations in which extreme variations occur (and several respondents have noted such details), but the author suspects that, despite appropriate shifts at developmental stages, parents have a tendency to relate to a child with some consistency over time. Thus it is assumed that the scales reflect a moment or product of innumerable specific experiences and some consistency over time. The truth of those propositions, however, can only be assessed by lengthy longitudinal studies.

Validity

Validity refers to the extent to which a test measures what it is supposed to measure. It is important to emphasize that the PBI was designed to be a phenomenological measure—to assess conscious perceptions, feelings, and cognitions of those two principal dimensions of parental characteristics (care and overprotection) that have been delineated in observational and factor analytic studies. The research emphasis is based on the premise that consequences of anomalous or optimal parenting are more likely to be related to the recipient's awareness or perceived reality of the parents rather than to actual parental characteristics. Thus PBI items emphasize assessment of attitudes more than behaviors, and are worded to invite subjective assessment by the recipient (e.g., "*Seemed* emotionally cold to me," "*Appeared* to understand my problems and worries").

A number of the problems involved in measuring phenomenological constructs have been considered by Wylie (1961). First, it may be useful to consider the construct validity of the PBI. What do the rating scales really measure? As suggested earlier, one scale appears to assess a dimension that can be clearly interpreted as one of parental care and embraces a number of closely interrelated attitudes and behaviors. The split-half reliability (really a measure of the coherence of the dimension) suggests that the scale encompasses a congruent dimension. The protection dimension, assessed similarly, appears to encompass a number of constructs that may not be homogeneous but that correspond clearly to the clinically defined portrait of the overprotective parent. In establishing construct validity it is important to examine whether other variables may be influencing scores. A number of factors may act as irrelevant response determiners. The possibility of a social desirability influence was therefore examined in a nonclinical group using the lie scale of the EPI, and only a weak influence was suggested.

It might be anticipated that the degree to which a child likes, cares for, or is hostile to a parent could influence PBI scoring in a negative or positive way, depending on the overall reaction to that parent. Moderate associations were observed in a nonclinical group linking "liking of" a parent with higher PBI care scores and lower PBI protection scores. The study design did not, however, allow any judgment as to the nature of those associations, and the degree to which any bias (e.g., "illusory glow," "plaintive set") may contribute to the associations cannot be assessed. The possible relevance of those two nominated biases in both clinical and nonclinical groups is explored further in Chapter 9.

The degree to which depression levels might influence PBI scores was examined for two reasons. As certain grades of depression appear to be strongly associated with PBI scores (see Chapter 9), it was important to ensure that the associations were not determined by *state* levels of depression (i.e., deviant PBI scores merely being a consequence of a depressed mood). The possibility that depression may influence the perception or recall of experiences is mentioned frequently. For instance, Paykel et al. (1969) suggest that "depressed patients' perceptions and reporting of events may be colored by the depressed mood." Blatt et al. (1979) report that clinical evidence suggests that changes in the parental representations of depressives are paralleled by changes in the clinical picture. Abrahams and Whitlock (1969), in a controlled study of the childlike experience of depressed patients, note that the depressed patients may have been in no fit state to give an unbiased account of their early lives. While the possibility of such an effect is acknowledged it is rarely studied. In the study carried out by Abrahams and Whitlock, an abbreviated version of the Bene-Anthony Family Relations Test was given to a subgroup 18 months or more later, and it was found that the patients' affective state did not influence scoring on that test. In a study by Schless et al. (1974), level of depression in a group of neurotic depressive inpatients was found to influence scoring on only 3 of 43 items in a life-event scale. The present study finds no support for the possibility that depression influences scoring on the PBI.

It is always difficult to establish the construct validity of a measure when many factors may have an influence on scores. However, the present studies are encouraging in suggesting that PBI scores are not significantly influenced by social desirability or a depressed mood.

While consensus of views does not necessarily establish or disprove validity (an issue that will be addressed shortly), the degree to which PBI scores correspond with semistructured interview questions assessing parental care and overprotection was considered. High correlations between interview ratings of parental care and PBI Care scale scores ($r = 0.77$ and 0.78) were encouraging. Lower intercorrelations were determined for the Protection scale ($r = 0.48$ and 0.50); while that difference could reflect a number of factors, it was the raters' impression that it reflected subjects having greater difficulty in understanding and responding to inquiries about parental overprotection.

It is concluded that the PBI is of acceptable reliability and validity as a measure of perceived parental characteristics. While designed as a measure of *perceived* and not necessarily of *actual* parental characteristics, assessment of its latter capacities is of considerable importance if it is to be used in studies assessing possible causal links between parental characteristics and developmental disorders. For instance, it could be that schizophrenics (as a consequence of a cognitive disturbance) perceive and hence report their parents as less caring and as more overprotective than they were in reality. In a case–control study, the PBI might be entirely accurate in measuring the perceptions of the schizophrenics and the controls, and differences between the two groups might be significant; but it could only be concluded that the schizophrenics *perceived* their parents in a distinctive way, not that the schizophrenics *actually* were recipients of distinctive parenting.

Thus there appeared to be a need to assess the degree to which PBI scores represent actual parental characteristics. Brown and Rutter (1966) note that it is doubtful practice to accept subjective reports blindly when, as a consequence of a variety of personality and attitudinal factors, they may be influenced by several response biases. They suggest that the accuracy of such reports can be assessed by comparing accounts of the same events by different participants. If the reports correspond it can be concluded that they accurately reflect actual happenings. Platt (1980) criticizes that view. He suggests, first, that high agreement between reports does not necessarily indicate the validity of the measure but represents a consensus in reports which might occur for reasons other than validity (e.g., respondents discussing their reporting with each other, or aspects of the subculture promoting sharing of perceptions giving spurious agreement in reports). Therefore, agreement between reports may tell us little or nothing about what actually happened. Second, Platt notes that low agreement between reports does not necessarily imply that the measure has poor validity. Subjective feelings of each observer may distort reports. On the other hand, each observer may attend to different issues that, although accurately reported, might result in low agreement between the reports.

Despite these reservations, accounts by different participants were compared. The first study required siblings to be the reporters; it was designed to assess the degree to which reported parental characteristics (specifically, scores on the PBI) correspond with observers' scores. In those comparisons that might be regarded as assessing validity (i.e., subjects' PBI scores correlated with siblings pretending to be those subjects), reasonable correlations were found: the mean correlation coefficient was +0.46 for the clinical group and +0.57 for the nonclinical group. These coefficients are higher than those generally found when validation of self-report measures is attempted using rating by others (Crandall, 1976). However, a strong contaminating influence was noted: subjects had difficulty in discriminating their own parental experiences from their siblings' when they were asked to score the PBI pretending to be that sibling. These findings are of relevance to other researchers attempting to measure aspects of the phenomenological world, as they suggest that observers cannot be regarded as objective reporters.

In a second study, respondents completed the PBI in the orthodox way and their mothers were asked to complete the PBI as they remembered their earlier attitudes and behaviors toward their child. Advantages accruing from having assessment made by someone intimately involved with the subjects over the lengthy period of childhood and adolescence are likely to be counteracted by subjective distortions, as the raters could hardly be regarded as "independent." The mothers scored themselves significantly higher on the Care scale, and significantly lower on the Protection scale than did their children. This may have emerged from the children scoring their mothers in a "negative" manner on the PBI and/or from the mothers' attempt to portray themselves in a favorable way. Nevertheless, the correlations between mothers' and childrens' scores were significant. These results, along with the results from the reciprocal comparison of siblings' scores, suggest some consensus in reports; it would be unwise, however, in view of Platt's (1980) comments, to claim that they demonstrate the validity of the PBI as a measure of actual parental characteristics.

Further assistance with this important issue comes from two further analyses. Mothers in a nonclinical group were divided, on the basis of PBI scores returned by their children, into "overprotective" and "other" mothers. Each was interviewed by a rater, blind to the PBI scores, who rated each mother on overprotection in general and on five possible components of overprotection. Mothers designated "overprotective" by receiving high PBI protection scores could be discriminated on all of the characteristics rated except "excessive contact." Furthermore, (as reported in Chapter 16), when the mothers scored themselves on the PBI protection scale the designated "overprotective" group returned a significantly higher mean score than the "other" mothers (16.5 vs. 10.8, $Z = 4.2$, $p<0.001$).

In a further analysis, PBI scores returned by the students, and then by the mothers rating themselves, were intercorrelated with the students' depression scores. Maternal care and protection scores correlated significantly with trait and state depression scores of the subjects, *whether the mothers scored themselves or were scored by their children,* and the correlations were strikingly similar. Thus, higher depression scores were returned by those who perceived their mothers as less caring and/or as overprotective, and by those whose mothers judged themselves as showing these parental characteristics.

There would appear to be two likely explanations of these findings. First, the PBI scale provides a reasonably accurate picture of *actual* parental characteristics, at least in a nonclinical group. Second, it is possible that in those families in which the students were most highly depressed, both the students and their mothers, in searching for an explanation, may have scored the PBI with a negative bias, bringing about the significant associations. The second possibility seems unlikely in a nonclinical group but must be conceded.

What can be concluded about the validity fo the PBI? First, it appears to be acceptable as a measure of *perceived* parental characteristics. Second, there is considerable support for the view that it is also an acceptable measure of *actual* parental characteristics, but closure on this issue will require further studies and will probably rely on establishing the predictive validity of the measure. Third, the properties have been examined more comprehensively (in terms of reliability and validity) than any other measure of parental characteristics. Fourth, findings from the several validity studies have relevance to other inquiries assessing the validity of aspects of the phenomenological world.

Additional Considerations

When the PBI data collected in Sydney and Oxford are compared, striking similarities are apparent: mean scores on the four scales are similar; mothers are reported as more caring, and as somewhat more protective than fathers; there is a significant association linking higher maternal care scores with higher social class; and neither the age nor the sex of the respondent has an influence on PBI scores.

How well do these findings agree with previous observations and reports? Maccoby and Jackin (1974), in a comprehensive literature review of sex differences, note that the most widely studied dimension of parent–child relationships is a warmth versus rejection dimension, and that girls are more likely than boys to report affection. Furthermore, they suggest that on a restrictiveness versus granting of autonomy dimension there is a trend for parents to be more restrictive of boys in preschool years. Becker (1964) reviews several studies suggesting that mothers use more psychological control than fathers (especially with girls), and that the opposite-sex parent is more likely than the same-sex parent to grant autonomy to the child.

The relationship between sex of recipient and scale scores of several parental characteristic measures is examined in a number of studies. Droppleman and Schaefer (1963) compared reports by young adolescents on the CRPBI (see Chapter 6) and found that both sexes scored their mothers as significantly more protective and intrusive than their fathers. Roe and Siegelman (1963) gave the PCR (see Chapter 6) to a nonclinical group of adults. No sex difference was found on scales suggesting overprotective characteristics. Raskin et al. (1971), using the abbreviated version of the CRPBI with normal adults, found higher scores for mothers on the "negative control" factor. Perris et a!. (1980) using the EMBU (see Chapter 6) with a nonclinical group, found mothers scored as significantly more "overprotective" and "overinvolved" than fathers.

If sex differences are found it is often difficult to assess whether they are an artifact of the scale or reflect real differences. For instance, it is possible to design a scale of items assessing overprotection which might only be relevant to mothers and/or daughters; such an artifact, if not corrected in the scoring, would result in females (mothers and/or daughters) scoring higher than males. Such an artifact is unlikely with the PBI, as the factor loadings, on both the care and protection scales, were similar for mothers and for fathers. It appears then that higher scores for mothers on both scales of the PBI reflect real differences between the sexes, and are consistent in general with the literature.

Several studies (e.g., Heckscher, 1967; Kardiner and Ovesey, 1951; McCord et al., 1962) have suggested that parental care is less, and maternal overprotection uncommon in lower class families. A number of reasons have been suggested: economic pressures, greater likelihood of the mothers being employed, and family size are all plausible explanations. The only social class effect noted in the PBI normative studies is a positive and weak association between social class and maternal care—which could reflect a real effect or a social desirability response in scoring by the recipients.

Ordinal position has often been considered in regard to overprotectiveness. Hagenauer and Tucker (1979) state that parents of first and only children "tend to be overprotective." Edington and Wilson (1979) have similar views about the parents of only children, and state that it may be especially true of the long-awaited child of older parents who is often subjected to "parental smothering and intrusiveness." Howe and Madgett (1975) report that only children were more likely than others referred to the London Psychiatric Hospital to have both their parents described as overprotective in the case notes. Weller et al. (1976) hypothesize that overprotection of the first-born results in greater anxiety and dependency. They tested (providing dilemmas to assess the degree to which subjects were likely to favor risk or cautious action) 177 Israeli kibbutz youths and 198 city youths. Results suggested that first-born and only child city youths were more cautious than later born city youths, while ordinal position did not influence scores in the kibbutz youths. They interpret the results as supporting their hypothesis arguing that child-rearing practices in the kibbutz acted against the common response by parents to first-born children.

When ordinal position was examined in a nonclinical group in the present study no differences were suggested on the PBI Care scales, whereas only children scored both their parents higher on the Protection scale than the remaining subjects. Thus, while PBI scores appear to be either unrelated or weakly linked to some demographic variables, the associations appear to be generally consistent with previous reports.

Several other findings in the normative groups should be noted. When scores on the Care and Protection scales (for both parents) were intercorrelated there was a consistent negative association linking higher protection scores with low, rather than with high, care scores. This is an important finding when overprotection is variably conceptualized (see Chapter 3) as reflecting an excess of care, an insufficiency of care, compensation for unconscious hostility, or denial of rejecting attitudes.

The crossover sibling study provides some data on the degree to which siblings (reporting for themselves) experienced similar parental characteristics. For the combined group of clinical and nonclinical subjects, the associations suggest a moderate degree of parental consistency, with the clear exception being in the degree of maternal protection offered to those in the clinical group. The exception may well reflect certain characteristics of those in the clinical group; perhaps their behavior in childhood elicited greater protection from their mothers.

The same study provides data allowing consideration of how closely subjects score each of their parents on the two scales. Maternal and paternal care scores correlated 0.15 in the patient group and 0.57 in the nonclinical group. Maternal and paternal protection scores correlated 0.30 in the patient group and 0.69 in the nonclinical group. The weaker correlations in the clinical group suggest less concordance in parental styles and/or a differential response bias between the two groups. It is suggested in Chapter 9 that social desirability biases may be weakened in clinical groups.

USES OF THE PBI

The PBI provides care and protection scores for parents or designated parent-figures. In most situations the raw scores are adequate for researchers interested in assessing these fundamental parental dimensions. However, as noted earlier, scores on the two scales are usually found to be negatively associated (i.e., a higher parental protection score is more usually associated with a lower parental care score). In some studies researchers may be more interested in examining parental care and protection as pure dimensions; it would then be appropriate to partial out any contributions made by one dimension to the other, thereby creating "uncontaminated" scores. Whereas, a researcher who wishes to study possible determinants of overprotective mothering, as clinically defined, would accept that overprotection involves some defi-

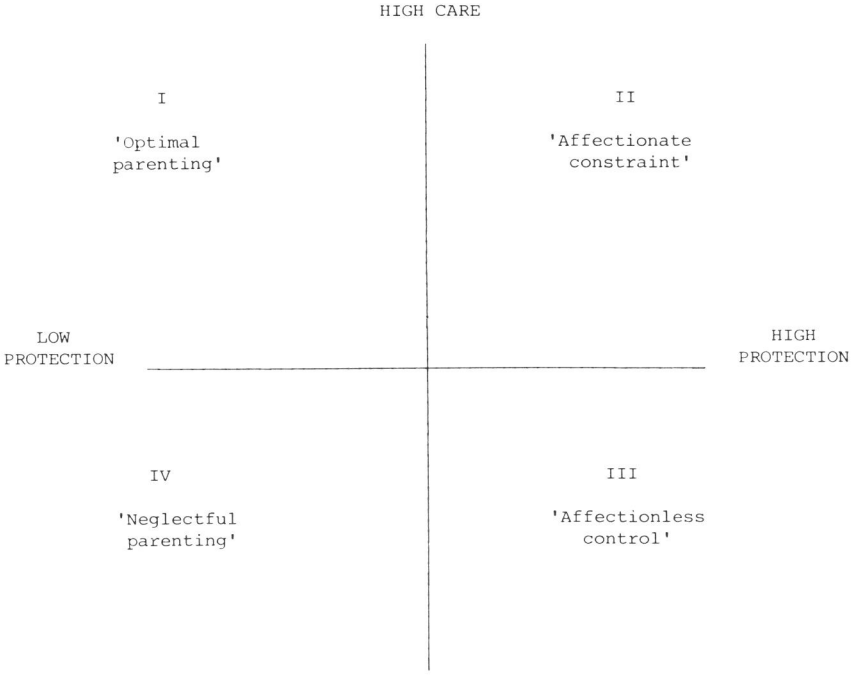

Figure 7.2. The four quadrants allowed by the PBI. From Parker, G., Fairley, M., Greenwood, J., Jurd, S., & Silove, D. Parental representations of schizophrenics and their association with onset and course of schizophrenia. *British Journal of Psychiatry*, 1982, *141*, 573–581. Reprinted with permission.

ciency of care as well as high protection (in PBI terms), and raw PBI scores would be appropriate.

The scales may be used together as a "bonding" instrument, allowing four broad styles of parenting to be examined (Figure 7-2). The first quadrant (high care–low protection) is conceptualized as reflecting "optimal parenting"; the second quadrant (high care–high protection) is conceptualized as "affectionate constraint"; and the third quadrant (low care–high protection) is conceptualized as "affectionless control." In developing the PBI it was suggested that the fourth quadrant (low care–low protection) might be conceptualized as reflecting "absent or weak bonding," but it is now suggested that the term "neglectful parenting" may be more useful. Normative data from the Sydney general practice studies can be used to create quadrants by intersecting the Care and Protection scales at their means. For mothers, the mean care score is 27.0

and the mean protection score is 13.5; for fathers the mean care score is 24.0 and the mean protection score is 12.5.

Theoretically, a parent–child bond will reflect contributions made by the child, the parent, and the resulting interaction. The title Parental Bonding Instrument reflects two relevant issues: it is designed to assess the parental contribution to a parent–child bond; and it attempts to clarify the structures of significance that appear central to "bonding," as bonding, in the absence of empirical data, remains essentially a concept.

PARENTAL OPINION FORM: A MATERNAL SELF-REPORT MEASURE OF OVERPROTECTION

Although a number of researchers have included an overprotection scale in maternal self-report inventories (e.g., Pitfield & Oppenheim, 1964; Zuckerman et al., 1958b); it cannot be said that the validity of any such measure has been established (see Chapter 6). In this section the development of such a scale and the assessment of its properties are reported.

Method

Thirty-five items suggesting maternal overprotection, intrusion, excessive contact, infantilization, prevention of independent behavior, excessive discipline, and overindulgence were collected from clinical notes and from appropriate inventories. The subjects were asked to complete a questionnaire by checking the rating for each item that best expressed their view. ("strongly agree," "agree," "disagree," or "strongly disagree").

Mothers attending five Sydney general practices were asked by the practice secretary if they would complete the questionnaire anonymously while waiting to see their doctor; 150 forms were distributed and 117 were returned and completed sufficiently for analysis. The mean age of the respondents was 35.5 years (range 20–68 years). They had a mean number of 2.1 (range 1–5) children. In 49 percent their youngest child was less than 5 years of age; in 24 percent it was 6–10 years old; in 13 percent it was 11–16 years old; and in 15 percent it was 16 years of age or older.

Results

Five items were deleted from further analysis as they elicited a poor response spread. Several principal component factor analyses of the 30-item data suggested that a 4-factor solution was the most coherent and that another 10 items could be deleted on the basis of weak factor loadings. In the final factor analysis, a 4-factor limitation and an oblique rotation were imposed (the 4 factors accounting for 47.5 percent of the variance) and the pattern matrix was examined.

Items loading on the factors were used to derive 4 scales. The first factor was bipolar, accounted for 16.7 percent of the variance, and appeared to reflect the relative right of the mother or the child to make decisions affecting the child. In effect, high scores on this "control" scale were returned by mothers who affirmed that they should choose the style of their children's clothes and that children should not talk back to, or set their will against, parents. They did not consider that children should be allowed to refuse to eat certain foods, select television programs, or disagree with parents, or that children need some babying (factor loadings for the items ranged from +0.57 to −0.63). The second factor was unipolar, accounted for 12.6 percent of the variance, and included those items in which the mother clearly sought to keep a close watch on the child; it was labeled "watchfulness." Those who scored high on this scale agreed, for instance, that children should not keep secrets from parents, that the doctor should always be called in for an unwell child, and that a mother should attend immediately to a crying child (factor loadings for the scale items ranged from +0.46 to +0.72). The third factor was bipolar with loadings from +0.82 to −0.44, accounted for 9.5 percent of the variance, and involved a discipline versus indulgence dimension; it was labeled "discipline." High scorers on this dimension agreed that a mother should be firm and strict (three items) and disagreed with sheltering a child or giving extra support to a clinging child. The final factor was unipolar, with a highest factor loading of +0.62, and accounted for 8.2 percent of the variance. High scorers on this scale indicated that they had difficulty in allowing a child's move to independent functioning and that they had a need for a mutually exclusive relationship with the child; it was labeled "dependency." Intercorrelations of the four factors revealed a weak correlation ($r = +0.23$) between the first and third factors, as might be expected from the labels, while weak correlation coefficients ranging from 0 to +0.06 for the remaining factors suggested their independence.

Several possible influences on the final questionnaire, termed the Parent Opinion Form (Appendix IV), were assessed within the general practice sample. A series of regression analyses established that scale scores were not significantly influenced by maternal age, by the number of children in a family, or by the age of the youngest child. Mean scores were as follows: control, 10.2 (SD 2.3); watchfulness, 5.9 (SD 1.9); discipline, 9.2 (SD 2.5), and dependency, 4.7 (SD 1.6).

Assessment of Reliability and Validity

The reliability of the measure was assessed in a separate study in which several groups of mothers, comprising both clinical and nonclinical subjects, were asked to complete the measure on two occasions; 32 subjects completed the forms, at a mean interval of 10 weeks. Consistency in scoring was examined by determining the percentage agreement in scoring within 1 point on both occasions (and by examining the strength of Pearson correlation coefficients). Results were as follows: control, 72 percent ($r = 0.35$, $p<0.025$); watchfulness; 78 percent ($r = +0.56$, $p<0.001$); discipline, 72 percent ($r = +0.80$, $p<0.001$); dependency, 78 percent ($r = +0.66$, $p<0.001$); and for the total scale (scores within 4 points of each other), 94 percent ($r = +0.67$). Mean total scale scores on the two occasions of testing were 27.1 (SD 2.7) and 26.7 (SD 3.1).

The concurrent validity of the questionnaire was assessed by comparing subjects' scores with scores returned on the protection scale of the PBI by their children. A nonclinical group of 75 mothers of students undertaking a postgraduate teacher training course was selected. The group and its representativeness on a number of sociodemographic and parental variables are described in Chapter 16.

Two types of comparisons were made to assess validity. First, total scores on the Parent Opinion Form returned by the mothers were correlated with PBI protection scores returned by their children; the correlation was low ($r = +0.27$, $p<0.01$). Second, a comparison was made of two subgroups of mothers. On the basis of PBI scores returned by their children, the mothers were designated as "overprotective" (15 mothers who received a score of at least 23 on the PBI Protection scale) or "other" (60 mothers who received a score of 22 or less on the PBI Protection scale). Scores on the Parent Opinion Form for those two groups were compared using a nonparametric test of significance. Although there was a consistent trend for the "overprotective" mothers to score higher on all scales of the Parent Opinion Form, significance was achieved only for the control scale ($Z = 2.6$, $p<0.01$) and for the total scale score ($Z = 3.59$, $p<0.001$). The mean total scores returned by those in the two groups differed by less than 5 points, suggesting that the Parent Opinion Form is unlikely to discriminate highly. In contrast, as shown earlier (see Table 7-7), when a rater assessed the mothers in the two groups on the basis of attitudes expressed toward the index child during the interview, the two groups were readily discriminated.

DISCUSSION OF PARENTAL OPINION FORM

As noted in Chapter 6, there have been several attempts to develop a self-report measure of maternal overprotection, and the relevance of the earlier research is suggested by the fact that a number of the items in the final questionnaire were derived from the other measures. The present measure comprises items that appear to be direct, but the more subtle ones failed to load clearly in the factor analyses. The present measure is more refined and its properties have been examined more extensively.

In the selection of items, the view that overprotection comprises a number of component attitudes and behaviors was accepted. The factor analyses support this approach and the final scales comprise relatively independent dimensions that reflect components of overprotection described by many clinicians and researchers. Subsequent testing with the scale produced some negative comments by respondents, with two principal objections: the forced-choice scale was too restrictive; and responses were dependent on the age of any relevant child. The first complaint is one common to similarly designed questionnaires, and is met almost as frequently as the opposite complaint that some scales offer far too many choices. The second objection was investigated in the development of the measure with scale scores not being influenced by the age of the child or by other variables of theoretical relevance, including maternal age or the number of children of the respondent.

The test–retest correlation coefficients suggest that mothers complete the questionnaire with acceptable consistency. However, when scores were compared against PBI scores the correlation coefficient ($r = +0.27$) demonstrated only a weak association and suggested that the mothers and/or the children were rather inaccurate raters of maternal overprotection. As discrimination on the relevant PBI scale has been shown (Table 7-7) to be confirmed by an independent rater, doubt must then be expressed about the capacity of the Parent Opinion Form to provide a valid representation of a mother's overprotectiveness.

There are two reasons these largely negative results are reported. First, there was a need to assess whether a maternal self-report measure might be superior to the PBI as a measure of maternal overprotection; this possibility can now be rejected. Second, study findings raise general questions about maternal attitude inventories and their likely susceptibility to response biases; there are many such inventories, but their validity is rarely assessed.

PART III

Research Studies

As reviewed in Part I, parental overprotection has been described in association with a wide variety of psychiatric, psychosomatic, and psychological disorders, and it is frequently implicated as a causal factor in the onset or course of such disorders. The principal aim of the research studies reported here is to evaluate (1) whether parental overprotection is overrepresented in several distinct disorders and (2) whether parental overprotection can be related to several dimensions of personality. The first inquiry necessitates a case–control approach. This can be a powerful research technique but interpretations may, at times, appear limited. Clearly, evidence of parental overprotection in those cases with the disorder does not allow any conclusion that overprotection is a necessary causal antecedent of the disorder. For instance, any demonstrated overprotection may merely be a parental reaction to the early expression of a disorder in a child. Such a mechanism has been proposed for a number of disorders and, as documented earlier (Chapter 4, Disorders in Childhood), has been clearly implicated as relevant to chronic childhood illness. A more complex methodology than the orthodox case–control comparison is required if the issue of antecedent and consequence is to be examined; one such research plan is adopted in a study of asthmatics (Chapter 12).

By conducting a series of studies (Chapters 8–11) of "neurotic" and "psychotic" disorders one can assess the relevance of parental overprotection as a risk factor to the broad types of psychiatric disorder. *Relative risk* and *attributable risk* are important epidemiological indices that are rarely used in psychiatric research. Paykel (1978) defined the concept of relative risk as a measure of the "association between exposure to a particular factor and risk of a certain outcome" and suggests that its application to psychiatric research may be productive. More specifically, it is the ratio of the incidence of disease in persons exposed to the risk factor to the incidence in those not so exposed. Relative risk can be estimated from case–control data; for the present inquiry, the formula is as follows:

$$\text{Relative risk} = \frac{a \times d}{c \times b}$$

where a is the number of cases describing an overprotective parent, b is the number of cases not describing an overprotective parent, c is the number of controls describing an overprotective parent, and d is the number of controls not describing an overprotective parent. Relative risk calculations of assignment to the quadrants allowed by the PBI permit assessment of the relevance of broad parental styles to several distinct disorders.

In other studies (Chapter 9, 10, 14) correlational analyses are employed, such as when the relevance of parental overprotection to personality variables (e.g., self-esteem, dependency) are under study. While such analyses may say something about the strength of an association, they say nothing about the nature of the association. Thus an association between dependency in a group of subjects and the reporting of parental overprotection could result from parental overprotection determining dependency, or it could be that those with dependent traits elicit higher levels of parental overprotection. Complex analyses are required to consider whether demonstrated associations reflect "real" or spurious relationships, and whether the associations might be brought about by one or more underlying variables; but the reported research analyses are restricted largely to determining whether or not associations exist.

In a number of studies (Chapters 9, 10, 14), multiple regression analyses are used to determine the degree to which PBI scale scores predict scores on outcome variables. Unless otherwise stated, the standard regression method is used. This method results in each variable being "treated as if it had been added to the regression equation in a separate step after all other variables had been included" (Nie et al., 1975). The incremental variance is examined to obtain an estimate of the variation attributable to each PBI variable.

While the PBI is used throughout as a measure of parental overprotection, scale scores are handled in several different ways and it is important to argue for that degree of flexibility at this stage. Raw scores on the Protection scale are used to provide some estimate of the degree to which a parent is overprotective or not. However, as noted earlier, scores on the Care and Protection scales are negatively associated, so that, in effect, high protection scores have a low care component. That care component may or may not be parceled out, depending on whether the research is endeavoring to assess overprotection *per se* or overprotection as operationally defined by a high score on the PBI Protection scale. The third option exercised in the research is to regard parental overprotection as a syndrome. As noted earlier, four quadrants are produced by intersecting the two PBI scales (Fig. 7-2), and two labeled "affectionless control" and "affectionate constraint," reflect differing types of overprotection; the former appears to correspond closely to many of the clinical descriptions of the overprotective parent. Thus the relevance of affectionless control is examined closely in all the case-control studies using relative risk estimates.

While maternal overprotection is far more commonly noted or implicated than paternal overprotection in clinical descriptions and research studies, the relevance of both is examined in the comparative studies.

As cultural variations in parental behaviors, and more specifically in overprotection, have been described, differences in PBI scores are examined in two sizable Australian subcultures of Jewish and Greek schoolchildren (Chapter 15). Finally, a key aim of the research is addressed in Chapter 16, in which possible determinants of maternal overprotection are examined in a nonclinical group.

8
Schizophrenia

As noted in the American Psychiatric Association (1980) *Diagnostic and Statistical Manual of Mental Disorders* (DSM-III), the limits of the concept of schizophrenia are unclear. Some definitions have included longitudinal features such as a deteriorating course or a poor prognosis. Cross-sectional features have, at times, been so vague and nonspecific as to result in falsely positive diagnoses of schizophrenia. Perhaps as a consequence, DSM-III provides a rather strict list of essential features for the diagnosis of schizophrenic disorders: the presence of certain psychotic features during the active phase of the illness; characteristic symptoms involving thought, affect, volition, and other psychological processes; deterioration from a previous level of functioning; onset before the age of 45 years; and a duration of at least 6 months.

Schizophrenic psychoses are somewhat more loosely defined in the World Health Organization (1978) *International Classification of Diseases* (ICD-9), where it is suggested that such a diagnosis should not be made unless there are characteristic disturbances in, preferably, two of the following areas: thought, perception, mood, conduct, and personality.

HISTORICAL OVERVIEW

While it is most commonly argued that the etiology of schizophrenia is multifactorial with a strong genetic basis, there has been increasing recognition of the relevance of social factors (Wing, 1978), with the early parental environment as a focus of clinical and research interest. Certainly, the concept of the schizophrenogenic mother has been evocative, persistent, and powerful in influencing views of both the etiology and treatment of schizophrenia. The concept has not died, despite many attempts to bury it, and has probably been given a new lease on life by British researchers such as Brown and Leff who have suggested the relevance of a related concept—high "expressed emotion" in key relatives—as a predictor of schizophrenic relapse.

The term "schizophrenogenic mother" was introduced "almost as an aside" (Hirsch & Leff, 1975) by Fromm-Reichmann (1948) when she wrote: "The schizophrenic is painfully distrustful and resentful of other people, due to the severe early warp and rejection he encountered in important people of his infancy and childhood, as a rule, mainly in a schizophrenic mother." In a later paragraph she suggests that the schizophrenic perceives such characteristics "actually, or by virtue of his interpretation," allowing the possibility that the schizophrenic may have merely judged, rather than have been exposed to, maternal rejection. The term "schizophrenogenic mother" has subsequently been used to describe a variety of maternal characteristics that are said to be associated—causally, in the view of many observers—with the development of schizophrenia. For instance, Lidz et al. (1964) incorporate overprotection within the definition when they describe mothers whom they held to be the schizophrenogenic mothers of the literature. They picture such women as seeking completion of their life (and compensation for attendant dissatisfactions) through their children. Such a mother "commonly projects her own insecurity onto the child and becomes overprotective of him" so that she hinders the child in "differentiating and from gradually achieving a sense of autonomy." Nevertheless, as McGhie (1961a) states, beyond a general agreement that the schizophrenogenic mothers tend to lack emotional warmth, and that they attempt to manipulate others, there is a "distinct lack of detail behind the clinical stereotype."

It would be inappropriate to review the family studies in great detail, as many reviews have been published (Frank, 1965; Hirsch & Leff, 1975: Jacob, 1975; Liem, 1980; Wynne, 1981; Parker, 1982b), but an attempt is made to chart the general direction of the clinical research explorations. It is important to emphasize that this review attends principally to those elements said to be central to the concept of the schizophrenogenic mother (e.g., overprotection and low care) rather than the family theories or the studies suggesting disordered marital relationships and disordered communication patterns in the parents of schizophrenics. The imputed parental variables are considered first in relation to the onset of schizophrenia and second in relation to the course of schizophrenic disorders.

Studies Relating Parental Characteristics to the Onset of Schizophrenia

The first clinical study of relevance was conducted by Kasanin et al. (1934), who studied the childhood history (noted in hospital case records) of 45 schizophrenic patients. They state that there was evidence of maternal rejection of 2 patients, and maternal overprotection of 33 patients, overprotection being defined by criteria developed by Levy (1931). The authors acknowledge that overprotective mothers might have been overrepresented in the sample as such mothers tend to be good historians, and a good history was required for the patients to be selected in the sample. They confirm associations between overprotection and variables described and held to be determinants by Levy, but emphasize that there appeared to be good evidence of interaction in the overprotective process. Thus they propose that the biological inferiority of the individual destined to develop schizophrenia results in the child having a number of physical defects and anomalies that might elicit overprotection; in addition, in feeling inferior and in looking and yearning for maternal overprotection, the child meets "the over-protective parent more than half way." Hirsch and Leff (1975) note that the authors' recognition of the circularity of cause and effect was lost sight of by subsequent workers for some time.

In 1938 Despert reported findings from a study of 29 children admitted to the New York Psychiatric Institute with a diagnosis of schizophrenia. He states that in 19 of the cases there was a consistent parental pattern: the mother is "aggressive, overanxious, oversolicitous, while the father plays a very subdued role." He speculates that such a matriarchal pattern might merely reflect a cultural influence, as 19 of the children had Jewish parents. A similar pattern is reported by Hadju-Gaines (1940), who describes an "identical environmental constellation" in 4 female schizophrenic patients, in that they had a "cold, rigorous, sadistically aggressive mother" and a "soft, indifferent, passive father." The author notes that such a parental pattern is not necessarily specific for schizophrenia, being relevant for neurotic patients as well.

Subsequent uncontrolled studies (Tietze, 1949; Reichard & Tillman, 1950; Clardy, 1951; Wahl, 1954 & 1956) appear to confirm the general tenor of those early reports. Tietze (1949), on the basis of a biased sample of 25 intelligent mothers of schizophrenic patients, provides a vignette of the schizophrenogenic mother: "All mothers were overanxious and obsessive, all are domineering. . . . It is the subtly dominating mother who appears to be particularly dangerous to the child." One of the uncontrolled studies conducted by clinicians at the Yale Psychiatric Institute and led by Lidz has been highly influential. Their observations are based on the intensive study of 17, largely middle-class, families.

They estimate that about one-half of the mothers of schizophrenic males "engulfed and intruded" and that such a mother was "unable to set boundaries between herself and her child, while treating her husband as a secondary figure." Female schizophrenic patients were most likely to have mothers who "were protective and frequently extremely intrusive." (Lidz et al., 1964). They suggest (Lidz et al., 1957) that schizophrenic patients have been exposed to either marital schism or skew. *Schism* refers to the failure on the part of the parents to achieve complementarity of purpose or role reciprocity, while *skew* describes serious psychopathology of one marital partner dominating the home. In their sample the dominant parent was usually the mother, who was distinguished by her intrusiveness, while the father could be distinguished by being ineffectual or disturbed.

Thus, as Frank (1965) notes, "an overwhelming number" of such studies "describe a familial pattern characterized by a dominant, overprotective but basically rejecting mother and a passive, ineffectual father." These studies have a large number of methodological weaknesses, including (variably) small sample sizes, the retrospective nature of the analyses, reliance on case notes, selective inclusion of subjects introducing sample biases, the possibility of observer or rater bias, and failure to define strict criteria for parental disturbance. No conclusions can be made about the frequency or the distinctiveness of a certain parental type or family style in the absence of an adequate control group.

One further caveat must be noted at this stage, although it is one that is not limited to the uncontrolled studies. As numerous studies (e.g., Kendell *et al.*, 1971) have shown, until recently, schizophrenia was diagnosed more widely in the United States than in the United Kingdom and, in the former nation, such a diagnosis encompassed neuroses and personality disorders. Many of those considered in the United States studies may have had psychiatric disorders other than schizophrenia. This important issue could be resolved by reinterviewing those in the original samples and evaluating the earlier diagnosis using the more rigorous diagnostic criteria that have been introduced in recent years. The Yale Psychiatric Institute sample would be suitable for such a reassessment, as results from those studies have been highly influential, no formal diagnostic reassessment of that sample has been conducted, and most of the patients are readily contactable (Lidz, personal communication, 1981).

Case–control and correlational studies have not clarified the research issue to any great degree; several representative studies are noted. Gerard and Siegel (1950), who conducted open-ended interviews with the close relatives of 71 hospitalized schizophrenic patients and with relatives of students who were completing high school, noted a "heightened relationship" between the schizophrenic patient and the mother (or mother substitute), evidenced by excessive contact, prolongation of maternal functions, and the relative precluding of other social contacts. This characteristic (which would seem to foreshadow the concept of "high expressed emotion", discussed shortly) was rated as marked for 91 percent of the schizophrenic patients and none of the controls. Prout and White (1950) Mark (1953) and Zuckerman et al. (1958a), found overprotection to be of varying relevance in their controlled studies. In the last study scores on an "authoritarian-control" scale were influenced by the level of education of the mother. Hirsch and Leff (1975) suggest that this finding, also reported in a number of other studies, demonstrates the importance of controlling for social class and education.

Kohn and Clausen (1956) interviewed 45 schizophrenic patients and their relatives. Only the higher class schizophrenic patients differed from matched controls in reporting their mothers as playing a strong, and their fathers a weak, authority role. Lane and Singer (1957) also found evidence of a clear social class effect in a controlled study. Differences were shown to be based largely on a tendency for the middle-class schizophrenic patients to verbalize negative judgments of maternal domination and rejection, while those in the lower class showed denial of hostility and overidealization of their mothers.

Garmezy et al. (1961) had 30 schizophrenic patients and 15 nonpsychiatric controls from general hospital wards score their parents on child-rearing attitudes and practices as they remembered them in early adolescence. The schizophrenic patients scored both their parents as dominating, more overprotective, and more ignoring of them than the parents of controls. Similar findings were reported by Lu (1961).

McGhie (1961a) notes both the methodological limitations of many of the studies and the consistency in findings: "Most investigations describe the mother's attitude to her schizophrenic offspring as over-protective although this term is seldom clearly defined." He suggests that in conducting such research much care needs to be directed toward allaying the anxiety of parents, who may feel responsible for their child's psychiatric problems, if a valid picture of the family situation is to be obtained. In his own study of the mothers of schizophrenic and neurotic patients, and of controls, he assessed the mothers over 6 sessions, and gave them considerable reassurance. He remains unimpressed that the mothers of the schizophrenic patients were distinctly "overprotective" and, in fact, argues that "overprotection is more typical of the early background of the neurotic than of the schizophrenic." However, on a modified version of the child-rearing attitude questionnaire used by Mark (1953), the mothers of the schizophrenic patients could be differentiated from the mothers of neurotic patients and controls in showing a tendency to endorse more strongly those items suggesting restrictive control of the child (McGhie, 1961b).

It is perhaps appropriate to consider a number of other methodological issues at this stage. In none of the studies considered were the raters unaware of the designation of the subjects (as patients of controls), so that the risk of unconscious observer bias was not circumvented. As noted for the uncontrolled studies, it remains to be established that all the patients had disorders that could be categorized confidently as schizophrenia by contemporary diagnostic criteria. Another concern relates to the PARI, the parent attitude scale used most commonly in the research. Heilbrun (1960) asked schizophrenic and normal women to score their mothers on that scale, and then had the mothers score for themselves. The patients scored their mothers in the direction of greater dominance than the controls, but no group differences were found for mothers scoring themselves. The nature of this discrepancy has not been examined with any rigor. Finally, differences between schizophrenic patients and nonpsychiatric controls could be determined by many factors (e.g., patient status) other than the categorical presence of absence of schizophrenia. The last issue can be investigated to some degree by comparing the family environment of schizophrenics and patients with other psychiatric disorders. Several studies (McKeown, 1950; Alanen, 1958 & 1960; Fisher et al., 1959; Costello et al., 1968) have employed such a strategy, producing varying results but generally finding anomalous parental characteristics as common, if not more common, in the families of neurotics when compared to schizophrenic patients.

If the parental characteristics of those with schizophrenia were established as distinctive and anomalous, it would then be necessary to establish whether they precede the development of schizophrenia in the child (and may therefore be a causal factor) and/or whether they are a reaction to schizophrenia or prodromal schizophrenic disturbance in a child. Several studies (O'Neal and Robins, 1958; Waring and Ricks, 1965; Gardner, 1967) have pursued the second issue by examining child guidance case records collected earlier in those who were later diagnosed as having a schizophrenic disorder, and found anomalous parenting variously overrepresented in the patient and control groups. While such studies are said to have the advantage of using data collected on patients (and their parents) before they developed schizophrenia (see Hirsch & Leff, 1975), none of those studies did, in fact, establish that the children did not have schizophrenia, or at least some prodromal disturbance, at the time they attended the child guidance clinic. If the children were already evidencing psychotic or prepsychotic symptoms, and such a possiblity would be highly likely, then the studies cannot be said to have resolved the research issue under examination (i.e., whether parental anomalies are primary or merely secondary to disorder in the child). At least one study Wender et al. (1971) suggests that both processes may operate.

Another research strategy has been to observe, record, and code the interactions of schizophrenic and control families as they engage in free interaction or as they carry out designated tasks. Jacob (1975) notes that 29 studies of this type were conducted during the years 1961–1973, but that the majority fail to satisfy five of the six criteria he argues are required. Summarizing studies of dominance (although the degree to which "dominance" may equate with "control" and "overprotection" cannot be stated), Jacob notes that of the 17 studies conducted, 7 reveal no reliable group comparisons, 5 suggest dominance to be distinguishable in a certain family member (variably the mother or the father, and variably in the patient and in the control group), and the remaining 5 produce inconclusive as well as inconsistent results. By comparison, studies of disturbed nonschizophrenic and control families show greater consistency in suggesting that fathers are more influential and less submissive in normal families, while a maternal hierarchical pattern is more distinctive in the disturbed families.

Studies Relating Parental Characteristics to Schizophrenic Relapse

Based on an earlier study (Brown et al., 1958), indicating that schizophrenic patients who return to parental or marital households have a higher relapse rate in the first year after discharge from hospital than those who go to another setting, Brown et al. (1962) commenced a longitudinal study of 128 male schizophrenic patients just prior to their discharge. The patients' relatives were interviewed to assess their expectations before discharge. The patient and a "key" relative (usually wife or mother) were interviewed 2 weeks after discharge, and the relationship between the patient and that key relative was assessed on "commonsense signs, such as content of speech, tone of voice, and gestures." Finally, relatives were interviewed after 1 year if the patient had not been readmitted, or at readmission if that had occurred. During the 1-year study, 41 percent of the patients were hospitalized and 52 percent were judged as having deteriorated in behavior. Deterioration was associated positively with the degree of emotion expressed by the key relative toward the patient at the earlier assessment, with the degree of hostility evidenced then, and nonsignificantly with the degree of dominance shown by the relative toward the patient.

A composite measure of family functioning was constructed by assigning key relatives to a "high emotional involvement" group (as judged by ratings of the relatives' behavior), while the remaining relatives were assigned to a "low emotional involvement" group. Of those exposed to the former type of relative, 76 percent deteriorated, while for those exposed to the latter the deterioration rate was 28 percent; the difference was reflected in the readmission rates (56 vs. 21 percent).

The authors had hypothesized that patients would deteriorate if discharged to a home where an involved family member evidenced high expressed emotion, hostility or dominating behavior. However, their assessment of the family milieu 2 weeks after, rather than before discharge allows another explanation (which also would account for the findings in the researchers' earlier study): that patients most likely to relapse were the most disturbed at discharge and so elicited more negative responses from relatives. The authors acknowledge that "some of the high emotion showed by relatives was elicited by the patient's disturbed behaviour at discharge," and that there are explanations other than a causal one linking deterioration with high emotional involvement in a relative.

In a later study Brown et al. (1972) pursued the important issue as to whether emotional arousal in a relative might actually cause schizophrenic relapse. Key relatives (usually spouses or parents) were interviewed while the patient was in the hospital to assess expressed emotion (EE). Interviewers judged the relatives on several parameters: the number of critical comments, hostility, dissatisfaction, warmth, and emotional overinvolvement. (On some parameters the relative's emotional response to *any* family member was assessed, on others only responses to the patient were rated; emotional overinvolvement was rated only in the case of parents). Assignment to a high EE group was made using only three of the ratings (in a *post hoc* way, by relating individual scale scores to relapse): seven or more critical comments, marked overinvolvement of parents, and hostility—although 35 of the 42 patients were assigned on the basis of the first parameter only. Of the 101 schizophrenic patients, 35 relapsed in the follow-up period, extending 9 months after discharge—58 percent of those having a high-EE relative, and 16 percent of those having a low-EE relative. On the separate measures of critical comments, hostility, and parental overinvolvement, a significant association was found with relapse.

As work impairment and behavioral disturbance during the 2 years before the relevant admission were both strongly associated with EE, the authors considered whether poor prehospital functioning was linked by an underlying process with relapse and also elicited high EE in relatives, but data analyses suggested that relatives' EE independently contributed to relapse.

The authors found that the patients living with the high-EE relatives at the time of the key admission appeared most susceptible to protective drug effects. A further finding was that among those who spent more than 35 hours per week in face-to-face contact with a relative, the relapse rate was 79 percent if the relative was high EE, compared to 12 percent if the relative was low EE. For those living with a low-EE relative, the duration of face-to-face contact made no difference.

In discussing the study the authors note that the most measurable component of EE is the number of critical comments made by the key relative about the patient, but that the other components of "emotional overinvolvement" and "hostility" are also important.

In considering the determinants of the relatives' degree of EE, the authors postulate a circular effect between EE and behavior in the patient, and speculate that a socially intrusive relative acts in such a way as to overstimulate the patient, so that residual or latent thought disorder becomes manifest in psychotic phenomena.

While the authors demonstrated that levels of EE in relatives were independently associated with relapse in schizophrenic patients, a process other than a causal one could explain the association. It could be that of those patients destined to relapse elicited, by the severity of their disorder or by other features, higher levels of EE in relatives at the time of admission and EE assessment. The more general issue, that EE may be reactive to characteristics in the patient, is considered by Brown et al. (1972). They note that the parents' degree of EE was minimally correlated with emotion expressed by those parents to their spouses, and that for those patients who improved most markedly over the 9 months, the greatest reduction in number of relatives' critical comments occurred.

Vaughn and Leff (1976), interested as to whether the results could be replicated with another sample of schizophrenic patients and whether the factors were specific for schizophrenia, studied 37 schizophrenic and 30 depressed neurotic patients on admission following a relapse. They made two basic assumptions: that EE as scored is a reasonable indicator of everyday family relations, and that the attitude shown by the relative toward the patient is representative of an enduring relationship over time. They state that findings by Brown et al. (1972) "appeared to justify those assumptions" but, as has been noted above, the latter study showed poor stability in EE over time. As noted later, Vaughn and Leff's first assumption—accepting the validity of the EE measure as an indicator of ongoing family relations—has not been established.

In their study the involved relative was interviewed shortly after the patient was admitted and after the mental state had been assessed by the Present State Examination (PSE); the PSE was repeated 9 months after discharge from hospital. Relapse of the schizophrenic patients was assessed by the same criteria as those in the previous study (a change in categorical assignment on the PSE measure, or judgment of a "marked exacerbation" in schizophrenic symptoms by a psychiatrist unaware of the earlier EE ratings). Relapse in the depressed patients consisted of significant symptoms of depression on the PSE or an episode of depression in the intervening period. In the schizophrenic group, those with a high-EE relative (involving in this study six or more critical comments and/or marked emotional overinvolvement) had a relapse rate of 48 percent, while those with a low-EE relative (one to five critical comments; emotional overinvolvement not marked) had a 6 percent relapse rate—a highly significant difference. The study confirmed the earlier finding that the relapse rate was lower in the high-EE group if there was low face-to-face contact between the patient and the relative, and if the patient took phenothiazine medication.

In the depressed group the number of critical comments made by relatives (but not scores on the other two indices of high EE—hostility and marked emotional overinvolvement) discriminated the group in terms of relapse: depressed patients whose relatives made two or more critical comments had a relapse rate of 67 percent, whereas those whose relatives made less than two critical comments had a 22 percent relapse rate.

The authors suggest that their study showed that psychiatric patients other than those with schizophrenia are also affected by qualitiative aspects of their emotional relationships with key relatives, but also point out the varying relevance of criticism, protective mechanisms, and coping devices in schizophrenic versus depressed patients. In regard to schizophrenic patients the study confirmed that a "high degree of emotion expressed by the relative at the time of key admission" is a strong predictor of symptomatic relapse.

In a 2-year follow-up report of that group (Leff & Vaughn, 1981), the relapse rate for the schizophrenic patients with high-EE relatives continued to be higher than for those with low-EE relatives, but the prophylactic effect of medication was no longer evident for those in the high-EE group. The authors state that this finding supports their earlier assumption that "the attitude shown by the relative toward the patient during the interview is representative of an enduring relationship over time."

Tarrier et al. (1979) sought to determine if the various findings could be linked to physiologic arousal. They obtained 21 schizophrenic patients in the community who had had their relatives rated on the EE measure in the Vaughn and Leff (1976) study 2 years earlier, and 21 matched controls, for testing on several measures of psychophysiological functioning with and without the appropriate relative present. The number of spontaneous fluctuations in skin conductance was found to be the most discriminating measure. On initial recording all groups (high-EE patients, low-EE patients, controls) showed high arousal levels when the subjects were alone. Over the next half hour the control subjects progressively reduced their arousal level, and it rose only briefly on entry of the relative. In contrast, the arousal level remained high in both schizophrenic groups until the relative entered, when the arousal level dropped in the low-EE group and remained high in the high-EE group. Differences between the various groups disappeared over subsequent testing. The importance of this study is that it demonstrated psychophysiological differences between the three groups in a normal situation, and suggested that patients categorized as having a low- or a high-EE relative differed 2 years later on an assessment of biological arousal.

While the authors do not speculate on possible factors determining that association there are two, not mutually exclusive, strong possibilities: first, that high EE in an involved relative results in greater psychophysiological arousal in a schizophrenic patient; and, second, that the link may be a hereditary one, with higher levels of arousal being reflected in the high EE scores of the relatives and in the failure of the patients to habituate to initial testing. If that explanation is correct, it would suggest that any link between high-EE relatives and schizophrenic relapse is not a causal one but an epiphenomenon due to high levels of arousal influencing high EE and relapse independently. Perhaps a more plausible model is a combination one which assumes both a hereditary link and an interactive environmental process. Thus, in high-EE families where relapse is frequent, the patient and the relative have high levels of arousal that dispose both involved members to stressful social interactions, producing higher levels of arousal in the patient and increasing vulnerability to florid schizophrenic symptoms.

In a similar study (Sturgeon et al., 1981), patients with an acute episode of schizophrenia were tested in a videotape studio (the relatives' EE was assessed 1 week beforehand). The patients from low-EE homes habituated to the experimental situation in the presence of their key relative, while those from high-EE homes did not.

Thus a series of studies has established that high EE (as measured) in an involved family member is a predictor of schizophrenic relapse, but, as noted in this review and as stated by Leff and Vaughn (1981), "it does not resolve the problem of the direction of cause and effect." High EE is then best regarded as a risk factor (i.e., a measurable characteristic predictive of future illness, but not necessarily a causal influence).

Kuipers (1979) notes that over 20 years of research the concept of EE has evolved and changed: "It is now a measure of the number of critical remarks and the level of overinvolvement, spontaneously expressed by the relative in the course of a factual interview." EE is rated not only by what is said but also by the way things are said—raters are required to note differences in the speed, pitch, and intensity of speech, and to a lesser degree, facial expression and gestures. A critical comment is one that expresses dislike, resentment, or disapproval of the patient or his behavior and must have a vocal component "more intense than mere *dissatisfac-*

tion." Kuipers defines emotional overinvolvement as "a tendency to overprotect, to overdramatize incidents, go into excessive and inordinate detail, and show emotional distress in the interview." In recent work (Vaughn & Leff, 1976) high-EE families have been defined as those with a rating of marked emotional involvement or six or more critical comments.

Kuipers notes that while the original researchers obtained high interrater reliability data, their validity data are, in fact, reliability data. She suggests that validity could be tested against an external criterion, as done by Tarrier et al. (1979) and Sturgeon et al. (1981). She suggests that while adequate evidence for the validity of EE ratings has not yet been demonstrated, the predictiveness does make it likely that the ratings do reflect important and subtle aspects of the home atmosphere. She reviews some of the characteristics of high-EE families revealed in content analyses, and concludes that ratings of EE appear to be a way of assessing different attitudes and coping responses in relatives who are faced with disturbed behavior in a schizophrenic family member.

Even with the new shortened version, an average of 4 hours per individual is required to rate EE. As Kuipers notes, "EE remains an esoteric measure," but it has an immediate practical use as a clinical screening device to determine those families most likely to benefit from intervention to reduce relapse rates in their schizophrenic family members.

PBI STUDY

Thus, while observers on both sides of the Atlantic have frequently imputed characteristics of overprotection and rejection as signal features of the mothers of schizophrenic patients, critical reviews and psychological test evaluations in case–control studies have generally been more guarded in suggesting acceptance of such a view. For instance, Hirsch and Leff (1975) conclude in their review that "the characteristics of overprotection and hostile rejection cannot be sustained." The present review has served to evaluate the caliber of previous research and to suggest methodological weaknesses that require consideration in conducting such research.

The present study was conducted with a number of considerations in mind. First, the PBI may, as a measure with acceptable properties, bring greater rigor to the inquiry. Second, by using a case–control approach the relevance of a particular parental style may be assessed both within the cases and the controls, to determine if it is overrepresented in the parents of schizophrenic patients. Third, as the PBI quadrant low care–high protection appears to describe a parental style resembling the expression of high EE, an attempt should be made to determine whether PBI scores predict the longitudinal course of schizophrenia (at least in regard to hospital readmission). Fourth, as a corollary, it appeared useful to assess whether PBI scores might predict the age of onset of schizophrenia (or at least the age of initial hospitalization), an issue that had not been addressed previously. Finally, the relevance of paternal, as well as maternal, characteristics were assessed.

Method

An attempt was made to include all schizophrenic patients admitted consecutively to two psychiatric units in general hospitals and to two state psychiatric institutions, until an adequate sample size had been obtained (Parker et al., 1982). Inclusion required a clinical diagnosis of schizophrenia sustained over the admission. In addition, all patients had to satisfy diagnostic criteria for schizophrenia, delineated by Spitzer et al. (1975), which have been demonstrated (Kendell et al., 1979) as successful in discriminating schizophrenic disorders from other disabling psychotic illnesses.

The patients were requested to complete a PBI for each parent on two occasions: shortly after admission ("test"), and when judged clinically as having improved to a significant degree ("retest"). On both occasions the rater assessed the severity of their clinical disturbance using both a 3-point scale ("extremely disturbed," "moderately disturbed," or "minimally disturbed") and the Brief Psychiatric Rating Scale (BPRS) (Overall & Gorham, 1962). All but a few patients were able to complete the PBI forms at the more disturbed phase of assessment. The raters, all psychiatric registrars, also collected the following data: sex of patient, age at present admission, age at first hospitalization, father's occupation (to determine social class), and the likelihood of schizophrenia in a parent. The accuracy of the last piece of information was not established. A history (obtained from the patients) of an admission to a psychiatric hospital and probable delusional beliefs were the principal features resulting in a parent being categorized as possibly having had a schizophrenic illness.

All but 3 of the patients were discharged within the first phase of the study, and 9 months after discharge the raters determined whether the patients had been readmitted to any psychiatric hospital during the interim period. In addition, an attempt was made to establish whether patients had been discharged to their parents or not, whether there had been contact between the patient and parents since discharge, and whether the patients had been discharged on, or continued on neuroleptic medication. The raters were blind to the PBI scores for the duration of the study.

Seventy-eight subjects completed both sets of forms (12–15 were unwilling or unable to complete the forms); of those 78 sets, 6 were rejected as showing clear scoring anomalies or as being incomplete. The final sample comprised 40 male and 32 female schizophrenics with a mean age of 31.8 years (range 17–68 years); 24 percent were first admissions. Paternal social class distribution, according to the Congalton (1969) scale, was as follows: I, 12.7 percent; II, 29.6 percent; III, 43.7 percent; and IV, 14.1 percent. The mean age at first admission was 25.7 years (range 15–52 years). A history of "possible schizophrenia" was obtained for 12 (17 percent) of the patients' mothers and 10 (14 percent) of the patients' fathers; 1 patient had both parents so assigned. Thus, the morbidity risk of possible schizophrenia in the parents was 29 percent in the sample.

Patients were matched exactly for sex and social class, and similarly for age (31.8 versus 31.5 years), with controls attending several general practices in Sydney (their selection is described in Chapter 7).

Readmission or not in the 9 month period following discharge was established by the raters with some confidence for 69 of the 72 subjects in the sample: 24 (35 percent) were readmitted, with a mean duration after discharge of 14.1 weeks (SD 10.0 weeks). Whereas 97 percent had been discharged on neuroleptic medication, the raters assessed that only 65 percent were likely to have received it continuously, that 26 percent had definitely ceased that medication, and that the remainder had probably ceased their medication over the follow-up period. Although 25 patients (35 percent) had been discharged to live with their parents, many of those did not remain with their parents during the follow-up period; 41 (60 percent) had had some degree of contact with their parents during that period. Those having contact with their parents did not differ from the remainder by sex ($\chi^2 = 0$), but were clearly younger (26.1 versus 40.5 years) and were far more likely to be readmitted (49.0 versus 13.4 percent; $\chi^2 = 10.78$, df 1, $p<0.01$). In addition to common tests, the nonparametric Z test is used where appropriate, Z being a normally distributed statistic transformed from the Mann-Whitney statistic U.

Results

Reliability of the PBI

The test–retest reliability of the PBI was assessed within the patient sample to determine whether schizophrenia or fluctuations in its severity might significantly impair the measure's reliability. At initial testing 97 percent of the patients were judged as extremely or moderately disturbed; the mean BPRS score was 52.0 (range 30–77), and the mean score on one BPRS item which appeared relevant for the present inquiry—the degree of conceptual disorganization—was 4.5. At retesting (the mean test–retest duration was 3.4 weeks), only 41 percent were judged as extremely or moderately disturbed; the mean BPRS score was

Table 8-1
Mean PBI Scores of Schizophrenic Patients and Matched Controls

PBI Scale	Patients ($n = 72$)		Controls ($n = 72$)
	Test	Retest	
Maternal care	23.6*	24.2†	27.2
Maternal protection	14.7	14.4	13.2
Paternal care	20.5†	20.7†	23.9
Paternal protection	14.7†	14.9†	11.9

Adapted from Parker, G., Fairley, M., Greenwood, J., Jurd, S., & Silove, D. Parental representations of schizophrenics and their association with onset and course of schizophrenia. *British Journal of Psychiatry*, 1982, *141*, 573–581.
*$p<0.01$; †$p<0.05$

34.0 (range 18–53) and the mean BPRS score for conceptual disorganization was 2.5. Comparison of the mean PBI scores at test and retest showed significant (all $p<0.001$) correlation coefficients: maternal care, $r = 0.77$; maternal protection, $r = 0.73$; paternal care, $r = 0.58$; paternal protection, $r = 0.69$). The data in Table 8-1 show that the mean scale scores are strikingly similar for the two assessment periods.

In order to compare broad types of parental bonding, the mothers and the fathers of both the patients and the controls were assigned to quadrants allowed by the PBI (Fig. 7-2). The stability of assignment of parents to the quadrants was then examined. Consistent assignment was noted for 68 percent of the mothers and 70 percent of the fathers. As the risk posed by having one or more parent allocated to the low care–high protection quadrant is of interest, the consistency of that assignment was assessed and calculated to be 86 percent, with 62 of the 72 patients completing all forms being assigned either to the "at risk" or to the "not at risk" group on both occasions. While these results suggest satisfactory stability, it is shown later that the incomplete consistency has an influence on the readmission analyses.

Case–Control Comparisons

The data in Table 8-1 show that the patients scored both parents as less caring than did the controls, and on both occasions of testing. While the patients scored both parents as more protective, this was significant only for the fathers (on both occasions).

The assignment of parents to PBI quadrants is shown in Table 8-2. The patients tend to differ from the controls on both occasions of

Table 8-2
Assignment of Parents to PBI Quadrants by Schizophrenic Patients and Controls

Assessment and Group Parent	High Care–Low Protection	High Care–High Protection	Low Care–Low Protection	Low Care–High Protection	χ^2
Test					
Patient Mother	21 (0.6)	13 (0.8)	9 (1.0)	28 (1.8)*	3.03
Control Mother	29	15	9	19	
Patient Father	16 (0.5)	10 (0.8)	17 (1.1)	26 (2.0)	4.40
Control Father	26	12	17	7	
Retest					
Patient Mother	19 (0.5)	16 (1.1)	11 (1.3)	26 (1.6)	3.41
Control Mother	29	15	9	19	
Patient Father	11 (0.3)	18 (1.8)	13 (0.7)	27 (2.1)	10.03†
Control Father	26	12	17	17	

Modified from Parker, G., Fairley, M., Greenwood, J., Jurd, S., & Silove, D. Parental representation of schizophrenics and their association with onset and course of schizophrenia. *British Journal of Psychiatry*, 1982, *141*, 573–581.
*Relative risk estimates are shown in parentheses.
†$p<0.02$

testing in paternal assignment; the consistent difference is that the fathers of the patients are most likely to be assigned to the low care–high protection quadrant, and least likely to be assigned to the high care–low protection quadrant. A similar trend exists in the assignment of mothers by the patients.

The relative risk estimates quantify the relevance of those broad parental styles to the patients; when test and retest calculations are compared, they are consistent except for paternal assignment to the high care–high protection quadrant. They reveal that the patients were less likely to experience high care–low protection (with the estimate being less than unity), that a high care–high protection parental style is not consistently overrepresented, and that the patients were more likely to experience low care–high protection. Male and female patients were equally likely to assign parents of the same and opposite sex to that quadrant. The relative risk for the patients assigning either one or both parents to the low care–high protection quadrant is 2.1.

PBI Scores for the "Schizophrenic" Parents

As a consequence of genetic factors, anomalies in parental characteristics might be a reflection of schizophrenia in a parent. Scores returned by the 12 patients whose mothers were judged as possibly having had

Table 8-3
Mean Age at First Hospitalization for Schizophrenic Patients Assigning Parents to Each PBI Quadrant

Assessment and Parent	High Care–Low Protection	High Care–High Protection	Low Care–Low Protection	Low Care–High Protection	F Ratio
Test					
Mother	25.7	26.3	34.0	22.8	4.88*
Father	26.1	28.0	27.4	22.7	1.66
Retest					
Mother	25.0	27.3	30.9	23.0	2.99*
Father	24.1	28.5	26.4	22.8	1.98

Adapted from Parker, G., Fairley, M., Greenwood, J., Jurd, S., & Silvoe, D. Parental representations of schizophrenics and their association with onset and course of schizophrenia. *British Journal of Psychiatry,* 1982, *141,* 573–581.
*$p < 0.05$

schizophrenia were compared with scores returned by the remainder. Similar comparisons were made between 10 patients whose fathers had possibly had a schizophrenic illness and the remainder of the sample. Significant differences were not noted (Z values ranged from 0.01 to 0.84) and no clear trend was suggested in an examination of both test and retest data for the patients.

PBI Scores and Age at Initial Hospitalization

The next series of analyses assessed whether PBI quadrant scores were associated with the age of the patients at initial psychiatric hospitalization. In Table 8-3 the mean age at first admission is shown for those assigning their parents to the different quadrants allowed by the PBI. When the mean ages are subjected to analyses of variance, the distribution of admission ages against different maternal styles is significant on both occasions of testing. Table 8-3 shows clearly that scoring a parent to the low care–high protection quadrant is associated with the lowest mean age at admission.

While these differences are of interest, clear interpretation is difficult when PBI analysis does not concede interactional effects in regard to the contributions made by both parents. Thus, a very simple approach is adopted of comparing those who assigned one or more parent to the low care–high protection quadrant against the remainder. The mean age at first admission for those in the former group (22.6 years) is 6.1 years lower than that of the latter group (28.7 years) for test data ($Z = 2.72$,

$p<0.001$). For the retest data, the age difference is reduced to 4.6 years but remains significant ($Z = 2.26$, $p<0.025$).

Capacity of PBI Scores to Predict Readmission

As noted above, 24 (35 percent) of the patients were readmitted during the follow-up period of 9 months. The sex of the patient did not influence readmission ($\chi^2 = 0.1$), nor did age (25.8 vs. 25.9 years). Several analyses were conducted to assess whether or not PBI scale scores collected before discharge might predict subsequent readmission. First, raw PBI scores for the readmitted group were compared with the scores for the remainder of the sample: there was a trend for readmitted patients to score their parents low on care and high on protection. These trends were more pronounced in two subgroups: significance was achieved for low maternal care at retest in the subgroup of those having parental contact ($Z = 2.01$, $p<0.05$) and the subgroup of those discharged to live with their parents ($Z = 1.97$, $p<0.05$).

Second, readmission rates for those who assigned one or more parent to the low care–high protection quadrant were compared with readmission rates of those who did not assign either parent to that quadrant. The rate of readmission is considerably higher in the former group (Table 8-4); discrimination is more marked when retest, rather than test PBI scores are used, and discrimination is most marked in that subgroup of patients having parental contact after discharge. Whether or not readmission relates to PBI scores in those having no contact with parents during the follow-up period is clearly of interest, but as only 3 of the 26 patients having no parental contact were readmitted, such an analysis is inappropriate. It should be emphasized that for those in contact with their parents after discharge, the readmission rate was 75 percent for those assigning one or more parent to the low care–high protection quadrant on retest and 25 percent for those who did not so assign a parent.

Discussion

Several methodological issues are considered first. As noted earlier (Chapter 7), a minimum sample of 36 subjects is required to avoid a Type II error in using the PBI measure. Thus the total sample was of a sufficient size to demonstrate significant differences if they did, in fact, exist. Although the properties of the PBI have been assessed in nonclinical and neurotic patient groups, reexamination appeared important in this study when the conceptual disorganization of schizophrenic patients might be expected to influence self-reporting. Certainly, a number of patients were unable and/or unwilling to complete the forms. Furthermore, 6 of the 78 patients who filled out the forms did so incompletely or made obvious

Table 8-4.
Readmission Rates for Schizophrenic Patients With Versus Without Parents in the Low Care–High Protection Quadrant

Group	Assessment	One or Both Parents in Quadrant		Neither Parent in Quadrant		χ^2
		No. Readmitted	No. Not Readmitted	No. Readmitted	No. Not Readmitted	
Whole sample ($n = 65$)	Test	16 (70*)	19	7 (30*)	23	3.54
	Retest	16 (70*)	18	7 (30*)	24	4.25†
Patients discharged to live with parents ($n = 24$)	Test	7 (64)	7	4 (36)	6	0‡
	Retest	8 (73)	5	3 (27)	8	1.61‡
Patients having contact with parents after discharge ($n = 39$)	Test	15 (75)	11	5 (25)	8	1.29
	Retest	15 (75)	8	5 (25)	11	4.36†

Adapted from Parker, G., Fairley, M., Greenwood, J., Jurd, S., & Silove, D. Parental representations of schizophrenics and their association with onset and course of schizophrenia. *British Journal of Psychiatry*, 1982, *141*, 573–581.
*Percentage of all readmissions.
†$p<0.05$
‡After applying Yates' correction.

scoring anomalies. The percentage unable to complete the form is possibly higher among acutely disturbed schizophrenics than in nonclinical groups, but it must be remembered that the study was designed also to determine whether the severity of schizophrenic disturbance influenced PBI scores. Despite considerable reduction in disturbance, the test–retest reliability coefficients for the PBI scales ranged from 0.58 to 0.77; these are middle-order correlations not much lower than those calculated in a nonclinical group, but considerably lower than those calculated (0.87–0.92) in a clinical group of depressives (see Chapter 7). Test–retest consistency of assigned parental style quadrants allowed by the PBI was 68 percent for mothers and 70 percent for fathers. For the most important assessment—the allocation by a schizophrenic of one or more parent (versus neither parent) to the low care–high protection quadrant—consistent assignment occurred in 86 percent of the cases. While the reliability of the PBI in a group of schizophrenics is acceptable, readmission was differentially predicted by test and retest data (the latter discriminating more highly). It can be concluded that acute schizophrenic disturbance does influence completion of the PBI, and that greater disturbance lowers the predictive validity of the PBI measure.

Thus it would be more appropriate to consider findings in relation to PBI scores completed when the patients were less disturbed. In the case–control comparisons the schizophrenic patients were likely to score their parents, and particularly their fathers, as less caring and as more protective. Assignment of parents to the quadrants permitted by the PBI allowed the relevance of the concept of the schizophrenogenic mother, as one deficient in care and as overprotective, to be assessed. When relative risk was used as an estimate of the magnitude of the effects, the risk of a schizophrenic assigning a mother to the quadrant was 1.6, and for fathers it was 2.1, while the risk of those assigning at least one parent to that quadrant was 2.1. While these levels of risk are worthy of note (in exceeding unity), they are less striking than for several other disorders, principally neurotic ones, as is shown in Chapter 17. Further analysis of the data from the present study reveals that 33 percent of the controls and 53 percent of the schizophrenic patients assigned at least one of their parents to the low care–high protection PBI quadrant. Thus the perception of a parental style of "affectionless control" which corresponds closely to the vignette of the schizophrenogenic mother (hostility, rejection, control, and intrusion), appears to be neither specific to nor markedly overrepresented in the schizophrenic sample. This finding appears to explain the frequent clinical observation of such a parental style, and yet its inconsistent relevance in case–control studies of schizophrenic patients.

It is appropriate to speculate on the nature of the slightly increased risk of this parental style in the present study; three possible explanations are noteworthy. First, such a parental style may be a consequence of schizophrenia or preschizophrenic disturbance in the child, or of treatment; that is, parents may respond to such an illness or to the treatment of their child by being more protective yet less caring. Second, it is possible that such a parental style may be a characteristic of those parents who have schizophrenic disorders themselves and carry the schizophrenic gene less manifestly. However, no support for a link between that parental style and schizophrenia in the parent was found in the present study—although the assessment of schizophrenia in a parent (being based on historical information) may not have been accurate. Third, such a parental style may be a causal influence increasing any diathesis (genetically or otherwise determined) to schizophrenia.

The possibility that such a parental style of "affectionless control" might influence the onset and the course of schizophrenia should be examined at this stage. One of the key findings in the present study—which seems not to have been examined or demonstrated previously—is that schizophrenic patients who assigned at least one parent to the relevant PBI quadrant had their initial psychiatric admission 4–6 years earlier than the remainder of the sample. While age at initial hospitalization cannot be regarded as synonymous with age of onset of schizophrenia, a reasonable correlation must be conceded. Furthermore, PBI data collected during hospital admission were highly discriminating in predicting subsequent relapse (or, at least, rehospitalization) for those who had some contact with their parents after discharge. Both findings, but more importantly the prospective data, support a causal process, but other noncausal explanations must be conceded. For instance, the link may reflect a hereditary factor with two independent consequences—a certain parental style in the parents and a relapsing type of schizophrenia in the child—creating a spurious association between parental style and schizophrenic relapse. Moreover, there may be certain personality characteristics in schizophrenic patients destined to relapse that result in their effectively assigning parents to the relevant PBI quadrant. A causal process is suggested, however, by 2 recent studies (Fallon et al., 1982; Leff et al., 1982), where intervention directed at high-EE families both lowered the EE of the involved family members and the relapse rate of the schizophrenic patients.

Two important conclusions are worthy of emphasis. First, the PBI appears to be a highly efficient predictor of schizophrenic relapse, and is certainly simpler to administer than the EE measure; second, and as a corollary, the prospective study demonstrates the predictive validity of the PBI.

9
Depression

The term "depression" may be used to describe a mood, a symptom, a syndrome, or a disease entity. A depressed mood is probably a universal experience (Kiloh, 1968); community research reveals a high prevalence (Parker, 1977). In the latter review it was suggested that the central feature of depression is a lowering of mood, while its quality suggests sadness, loneliness, despair, self-criticism, pessimism, hopelessness, and helplessness along with a lowering of self-esteem. When a depressed mood is distinctive, in terms of its severity, duration, or phenomenology (e.g., morbid guilt), then a depressive syndrome, reaction, or specific disease entity may exist, but it must be conceded immediately that the boundary between nonclinical and clinical disorder has resisted clear definition (Roth & Kerr, 1970).

Although there is still "no consensus of opinion" (Kendell, 1976) about how depressive disorders should be classified, the evidence from a number of published studies suggests that the debate "has been conclusively decided in favour of the binarian school" (Eysenck, 1970). That view, that there are two principal types of depression, has been supported by principal components analyses (e.g., Kiloh et at., 1972) and cluster analyses (e.g., Paykel, 1971). A psychotic (endogenous) type appears to be distinguished by a "restricted range of clinical manifestations" (Kiloh et al., 1972) and by "severity of illness" (Paykel, 1971). Several conceptual divisions of this type of depression have been proposed, but in recent years Leonhard's (1959) proposal (modified somewhat by North American researchers) of the polarity concept has achieved wide acceptance. *Bipolar illness* is now said to occur in a patient who has had a manic episode, with or without depression, while *unipolar illness* refers to the occurrence of at least one depressive illness (James, 1981). This type of depression is classified in the ICD-9 (WHO, 1978) as *manic-depressive psychosis* (with manic, depressed, and circular expressions). The binary view of depression is rejected in DSM-III (APA, 1980), which does not include a "manic disorder" category. Instead, the category *Bipolar disorder* is used if there is an episode of mania. The endogenous type of depression is likely to be diagnosed as a *major depression;* it is distinguished by, in part, a dysphoric mood and by the existence of a number of symptoms present for at least 2 weeks. Furthermore, this type of depression has an additional subclassification as *melancholia* (indicating a "typically severe form of depression and features of endogenous depression as defined by other diagnostic systems").

While there is considerable evidence to suggest that psychotic depression (synonyms are: endogenous depression, manic-depressive psychosis, melancholia, etc.) is a categorical biological illness with a restricted range of clinical manifestations consistent with an imputed genetic or biochemical basis (Kiloh et al., 1972), the "other type" of depression is more difficult to assign as an illness or to consider as a homogeneous disorder. Termed *neurotic depression* in ICD-9, *dysthymic disorder* in DSM-III (but also capable of being classified as a *major depressive episode, cyclothymic disorder, atypical depression*), and *reactive depression* by many clinicians, it may be distinguishable from "normal depression" only by variably defined determinations of severity and duration. It would appear to be a dimensional entity depicting ways patients use their defence mechanisms to cope with concurrent environmental stress (Kiloh et al., 1972).

Many claims have been made that the two principal types of depression may be differentiated by several psychological, biochemical, and genetic variables, their response to several treatment modalities, and a number of clinical features. Despite increasing awareness of the relevance of such considerations and increasing sophistication in attempts to make such a distinction (e.g., the dexamethasone suppression test), it still cannot be asserted that the two principal types can be readily distinguished.

In any assessment of the relevance of parental characteristics to later depression there appear to be three important issues. First, the common practice of sampling possibly heterogeneous types of depression may introduce a methodological error and also obscure important associations. Furthermore, in assessing the relevance of an early environmental variable (e.g., parental characteristics) it would be useful to examine its comparable relevance to depressive disorders in which biological vulnerability differs widely. Thus separate groups of "psychotic" and "neurotic" depressives might best be studied, with bipolar depressives (i.e., those having had a manic episode) being selected for the "psychotic" group, as they may be distinguished more confidently than unipolar depressives from the neurotic depressives. Finally, as the distinction between "normal" depression and clinical depression remains unclear, it would be useful to study nonclinical as well as clinical groups.

The proposition that variables in the parent–child relationship predispose a child to later depression has been maintained for a long time by a number of theorists; this literature is reviewed by Becker (1974). More specifically, and of relevance to this inquiry, a large number of clinical reports and investigations indicate that depressed patients report their parents as providing an insufficiency of care or as being overprotective (Blatt et al., 1979). Some of the literature is described briefly below.

According to Mendelson (1974), analysts, "from the days of Abraham through Klein to Jacobson," express a recurring theme that "adult depressive illnesses recapitulate early infantile parathymias or disappointments." Bibring (1953) suggests that an insufficiency of parental love and approval in infancy fixates the infant to feelings of helplessness and predisposes to depression. Jacobson (1964) holds that excessive parental frustration of needs for care and affection result in feelings of inferiority and self-disparagement. The neoanalyst Adler (1924) suggests that depressives perceive their parents as depriving them of spontaneous and genuine regard, sometimes beneath a veneer of oversolicitude. The cognitive theorist Beck (1967) holds that depressives had parent-figures who disparaged their worth and so came to value themselves similarly. Sandler and Joffe (1965) argue that the child who fails to "individuate" and obtain independence from parental figures is "prone to react to later disappointments with depression."

A few representative studies should be noted. Wilson (1951) studied a dozen families with a manic-depressive member using a modified Fels Questionnaire (and general population data from the Fels Institute). The diagnosis was made on loose clinical criteria and some patients with "superimposed schizophrenic features" were included. He concludes that the patients had faced more restrictive parental attitudes and had had less freedom than children in families without the disease. Cohen et al. (1954) conducted an uncontrolled study of 12 manic-depressive patients; they suggest that the mothers had indulged their infants' dependency needs and punished their moves to autonomy. Gibson (1958) was unable to replicate those findings in a study of 27 manic-depressive patients; data were collected from a questionnaire completed by the therapist, and a control group of 17 schizophrenics (not matched for sex, age, or race) was used. Munro (1966) compared 153 depressed inpatients (comprising "endogenous" and "neurotic" types) with 163 general hospital outpatients (having excluded those with an affective disorder) and reported an incidence of a "disturbed relationship" with a parent in 32 percent of the depressives and 18 percent of the controls.

Abraham and Whitlock (1969) interviewed and gave a modified Bene-Anthony Family Relations Test to a heterogeneous group of depressives and to controls (after excluding mental disorder in the latter). The entire depressive group was more likely to report unsatisfactory family relationships than the control group, and there was a steady increase in such reporting as "one progresses through the group of patients from manic-depressive psychoses to neurotic depression." Examination of their data suggests that the manic-depressive group cannot be distinguished from the controls by the quality of the family relationships, but the authors fail to make such an unequivocal statement.

Raskin et al. (1971) studied a mixed group of 548 hospitalized depressives and 254 "normal" adults chosen from various hospitals (including psychiatric ones). The subjects were asked to describe their parents as remembered in adolescence and complete an abbreviated version of Schaefer's (1965) CRPBI. The depressed patients rated both parents as having been less positively involved in their activities and having used more negative control. Jacobson et al. (1975) assessed similar numbers of "neurotic" and "psychotic" inpatient depressives and compared their interview and questionnaire (unvalidated) data with similar data from groups of outpatient depressives and nonclinical controls. The "normals" were the least likely to have experienced parental abuse, shaming, rejection, and overprotection. The authors conclude that their results offer empirical evidence to support an association of depriving child rearing practices with adult depression. Blatt et al. (1979) assessed levels of depression and parental representations in a nonclinical adult group. Intensity of depression was related to qualities attributed to the parents and, in particular, to a lack in parental nurturance, support, and affection.

On the basis of these studies it would be fair to agree with Becker (1974) that "variabilities in subject sampling, the scarcity of replications, and dearth of logically interrelated studies do not yet provide a firm base for empirical generalizations or theoretical clarification." Diagnostic criteria are often unclear or unstated, it is possible that heterogeneous types of depression have often been sampled, sample sizes have frequently been inadequate, control groups have often been absent or inappropriate, and the assessments of parental characteristics have often relied on measures with unevaluated properties.

The research studies to be reported here were designed to attend to such methodological issues.

Table 9-1
Study 1: Mean PBI Scores of Depressive Patients and Matched Controls

PBI Scale	Neurotic Depression ($n = 50$)		Manic-Depression ($n = 50$)	
	Patients	Controls	Patients	Controls
Maternal care	19.9	28.3*	25.9	25.6
Maternal protection	19.1	14.3†	14.0	13.2
Paternal care	14.7	25.2*	21.8	23.5
Paternal protection	16.4	13.9	12.7	11.5

From Parker, G. Parental characteristics in relation to depressive disorders. *British Journal of Psychiatry*, 1979, *134*, 138–147. Reprinted with permission.
*$p<0.001$; †$p<0.01$

Study 1: Patients with Clinical Depressive Disorders

The aim of this study was to test the proposition that depressives perceive their parents as being deficient in care and/or as being overprotective and to examine its relevance for distinct types of depression, variably with imputed biological and environmental origins.

The methodology and results of this study are summarized, as they have been considered more extensively elsewhere (Parker, 1977, 1979a). In this study 50 neurotic depressive outpatients (15 males, 35 females; mean age 31 years) and 50 bipolar manic-depressive patients (25 of each sex; mean age 44 years, selected principally from a lithium clinic at the University of Sydney), comprised the two samples. Subjects were requested to complete PBI forms about their natural parents and the scores were compared with PBI scores for matched (age, sex, and paternal social class) controls from the first Sydney general practice study (Parker et al., 1979).

The data in Table 9-1 show that the neurotic depressive patients perceived both parents as less caring and, in addition, perceived a slight excess (significant only in relation to mothers) of parental protection. In contrast, the manic-depressive patients did not score their parents in a distinctive way.

Parental assignment by the patients and controls to the quadrants allowed by the PBI is shown in Table 9-2. The manic-depressive patients assigned their parents in a similar manner to the controls; the relative risk calculations, in approximating unity, suggest that they were no more and no less likely to report high care–low protection or low care–high protec-

Table 9-2
Study 1: Assignment of parents to PBI Quadrants by Depressive Patients and Controls

Group	Parent	High Care–Low Protection	High Care–High Protection	Low Care–Low Protection	Low Care–High Protection	χ^2
Neurotic depressive patients						
Patient	Mother	8 (0.4)	6 (0.2)	6 (1.6)	30 (4.7)*	16.78†
Control	Mother	16	18	4	12	
Patient	Father	4 (0.1)	5 (0.6)	15 (3.1)	26 (2.8)	20.61†
Control	Father	22	8	6	14	
Manic-depressive patients						
Patient	Mother	18 (1.2)	5 (0.6)	7 (0.6)	20 (1.4)	1.78
Control	Mother	16	8	10	16	
Patient	Father	17 (1.2)	10 (1.3)	13 (1.1)	10 (0.6)	1.39
Control	Father	15	8	12	15	

From Parker, G. Parental characteristics in relation to depressive disorders. *British Journal of Psychiatry*, 1979, *134*, 138–147. Reprinted with permission.
*Relative risk estimates are shown in parentheses; †$p<0.001$

tion. In contrast, the neurotic depressive patients were unlikely to assign their parents to the high care–low protection quadrant: they were more likely to assign them to the low care–low protection, but most likely to assign them to the low care–high protection quadrant. The relative risk of a neurotic depressive patient assigning one or more parents to the high care–low protection quadrant was 0.2; for the low care–high protection quadrant it was 6.7 (76 percent of the patients and 32 percent of the controls assigned at least one parent to this quadrant).

Study 2: A Replication Study with Neurotic Depressive Patients

Since the results for the neurotic depressive patients are so striking a replication study was undertaken involving 125 neurotic depressive patients and 125 matched general practice controls together with 125 matched general practice controls screened to ensure that they had not had an episode of depression.

Results were broadly consistent with those from the first study with the relative risk of neurotic depressive patients assigning one or both parents to the low-care–high-protection quadrant being 3.2 and 3.4 (in comparison to the two respective control groups). Clear sex differences were apparent, however, with patients scoring the same-sexed parent more deviantly (i.e., less care and greater protection) than the parent of the opposite sex (Parker, 1983, in press).

The capacity of a low PBI care scale score (i.e. a score of less than 10) was shown in several analyses, with 31 percent of the patients and 2 percent of the "nondepressive" controls scoring one or both parents in such a way.

The study design did allow for examination of a possibly relevant response bias. Henderson et al. (1981) suggest the importance of "plaintive set" in creating spurious associations between predictor variables and neurotic symptoms as outcome variables. Thus, it could be that the deviant scores for the depressed patients reflect their greater propensity for complaining, resulting in their scoring parents as both less caring and as more protective on the PBI. Such a possibility would be supported by the finding of strong negative associations between care and protection scores for the same parent, strong positive associations between care scores for both parents, and strong positive associations between protection scores for both parents. However, for those relevant intercorrelations (Table 9-3), associations are weakest, rather than strongest, in the patient group. This finding suggests that any general bias is acting more strongly in the control group than in the patient group — whether it be a positive (e.g., social

Table 9-3
Study 2: Intercorrelation of PBI Scale Scores in Patient and Control Groups

PBI Scales Compared	Neurotic Depressive Patients	General Practice Controls	Non-depressive Controls
Maternal care with maternal protection	−0.28	−0.42	−0.43
Maternal care with parental care	+0.16	+0.57	+0.58
Maternal protection with paternal protection	+0.41	+0.61	+0.65
Paternal care with paternal protection	−0.24	−0.41	−0.32

desirability) or a negative (e.g., plaintive set) bias. It is worth drawing attention to a study by Lewinsohn et al. (1980), who interpreted their results as suggesting that depressives lose the "illusory warm glow" of normals and tend to perceive the world more, rather than less, realistically. Thus the stronger associations in the control groups are more likely to reflect a stronger "social desirability" or "illusory glow" bias in those groups, or a stronger "plaintive set" bias in the patients which counteracts the opposing positive bias.

Study 3: Nonclinical Group

In order to examine the degree to which PBI scores are associated with depression levels in a nonclinical group, a study of students at Sydney Teachers' College, was conducted.

Method

The subjects were trainee teachers who had previously obtained a bachelor's degree and the methodology has been described elsewhere (Parker, 1979a–d). A high level of cooperation with the anonymous questionnaire was obtained; 236 (124 female, 112 male) of the 242 students approached returned completed questionnaires; the mean age was 24 years. Over 90 percent had been raised principally in Australia.

Depression was defined as "a significant lowering of mood, with or without feelings of guilt, hopelessness and helplessness, or a drop in one's self-esteem or self-regard"; 223 students (95 percent) acknowledged having had such an episode, with a mean of 6.3 episodes reported over the preceding 12 months. The most usual duration of such episodes was minutes in 8 percent, hours in 39 percent, days in 39 percent, weeks in 6 percent, and months in 8 percent. The relevance of a number of commonly suggested precipitants (see Becker, 1974) was assessed in regard to such episodes. Precipitants (and the relevant theory) were life events (life events theory); disparity between realization and idealization of goals and standards (cognitive theory), disruption and distancing in interpersonal relationships (object loss theory), and an overall decrement in positive reinforcers (behavioral theory). The linking of any one precipitant to any theoretical school does not deny that there are clear overlaps. The Costello and Comrey (1967) trait depression scale, measuring "a person's tendency to experience a depressive mood," was given. Self-esteem was assessed by the Rosenberg (1965) scale, alienation by the Middleton (1963) scale, and neuroticism and extraversion by the EPI (Eysenck and Eysenck, 1964). Permanent separation from parents in the first 16 years was assessed, and a 9-item version of Rotter's locus of control measure derived at the School of Psychology, University of New South Wales, was administered for a subsidiary study, which is described later.

Respondents were asked to nominate their two most important parent-figures in childhood and complete a PBI for each. Mothers were nominated by 75 percent as the more, and by 24 percent as the less important parent-figure, while fathers were nominated by 23 percent as the more, and 67 percent as the less important parent-figure. Grandmothers were the next most frequent relative to be nominated by the respondents. The biological mother was not nominated by 4, and the biological father was not nominated by 23 of the respondents. Twenty-seven subjects had been permanently separated from a biological parent before the age of 16 years; the mean age at separation was 8 years.

Results

PBI care and protection scores for the nominated parent-figures were separately intercorrelated with other variables (Table 9-4). Lower parental care scores for either parent are associated with higher trait depression, lower self-esteem, and higher alienation scores. Higher parental protection scores for either parent are associated weakly with higher trait depression scores. Higher scores on several expressions of depression and anxiety are associated with higher parental protection scores for the more important parent only.

Mean scores of the variables under examination were compared for those assigning their parents to the different PBI quadrants and to a

Table 9-4
Study 3: Product Moment Correlation Coefficients of PBI Care and Protection Scores for Each Parent Versus Main Variables

Variable	More Important Parent		Less Important Parent	
	Care	Protection	Care	Protection
Trait depression	−0.28*	+0.22*	−0.33*	+0.21†
Number of depressive episodes in preceding 12 months	−0.15‡	+0.18†	−0.13	+0.13
Self-esteem	+0.22*	−0.23*	+0.24*	−0.07
Alienation	−0.20†	+0.16‡	−0.28*	+0.13
Trait anxiety	−0.10	+0.25*	−0.22*	+0.04
Neuroticism	−0.09	+0.25*	−0.24*	+0.11
Extraversion	+0.12	−0.04	+0.08	−0.04

*$p<0.001$
‡$p<0.05$
†$p<0.01$

"middle" position containing approximately one-fifth of the total sample (Tables 9-5 and 9-6). Differences were examined using analyses of variance. Inspection of the tables suggests two positions to be clearly associated with the highest morbidity (low care–high protection) and with the lowest morbidity (high care–low protection) on the several continuous variables, the results were more striking in relation to the more important parent.

These findings suggest, but in no way prove, that low parental care and, to a lesser degree, parental overprotection may predispose nonclinical subjects to greater depressive experience in adult life. If they do so, this may occur in a direct fashion, or they may require interaction with a precipitating stress, as Brown and Harris (1978) have suggested in regard to a number of other psychological vulnerability factors. The present study allows some examination of that proposition, both in regard to PBI variables and to a number of other suggested variables. Data, necessarily based on subjects' memories and perceptions, were collected on the relevance of several key precipitants to episodes of depression. The data in Table 9-7 show that situations suggesting disruption of, or distancing in, an interpersonal relationship were acknowledged as being most likely to precipitate depression.

The reasons for studying several variables other than the PBI variables should be briefly stated. Self-esteem is a hypothetical construct referring to an individual's assessment of the degree to which he is capable, significant, successful, and worthy (Coopersmith, 1967). A fall in

Table 9-5
Study 3: Mean Scores on Main Variables for Respondents Assigning the More Important Parent to Five PBI Positions

Variable	Middle	High Care–Low Protection	High Care–High Protection	Low Care–Low Protection	Low Care–High Protection	F Ratio
n	40	40	47	66	43	
Trait depression	30.7	28.8	32.9	36.5	37.9	4.00†
Number of depressive episodes in preceding 12 months	6.0	4.5	6.0	5.8	10.2	1.96
Self-esteem	1.2	1.2	1.6	1.5	2.1	3.47†
Alienation	2.1	1.9	2.1	2.3	2.7	2.16
Neuroticism	10.9	10.0	11.8	9.7	12.3	2.57‡
Extraversion	11.3	12.4	12.7	11.8	11.7	9.86

Adapted from Parker, G. Parental characteristics in relation to depressive disorders. *British Journal of Psychiatry*, 1979, *134*, 138–147.
†$p<0.01$; ‡$p<0.05$

Table 9-6
Study 3: Mean Scores on Main Variables for Respondents Assigning the Less Important Parent to Five PBI Positions

Variable	Middle	High Care–Low Protection	High Care–High Protection	Low Care–Low Protection	Low Care–High Protection	F Ratio
n	42	39	52	62	41	
Trait depression	30.4	28.0	32.6	37.4	39.2	5.93‡
Number of depressive episodes in preceding 12 months	4.4	6.7	3.8	5.1	11.8	4.07*
Self-esteem	1.4	1.2	1.3	1.9	1.9	2.57§
Alienation	1.9	1.9	1.9	2.5	3.0	6.13‡
Neuroticism	10.7	9.7	10.4	11.9	12.8	3.04†
Exraversion	12.4	12.8	11.7	10.7	11.8	1.67

Adapted from Parker, G. Parental characteristics in relation to depressive disorders. *British Journal of Psychiatry*, 1979, *134*, 138–147.
*$p<0.01$; †$p<0.02$; §$p<0.05$; ‡$p<0.001$

Table 9-7
Study 3: Likelihood of Several Situations Precipitating Depressive Episodes

Precipitant (actual wording)	Principal Theoretical Dimension Tapped	Likelihood of Association with Depression			
		"Frequently"	"May sometimes"	"Might rarely"	"Not known to depress me"
The break-up of an important relationship	Object loss	84	76	30	25
Being rejected or distanced in a relationship	Object loss	63	72	44	32
A fall-off in support to my self-esteem	Behaviorist	48	71	57	42
Failure to obtain an important goal	Cognitive	38	95	48	32
Failure to live up to my own standards	Cognitive	49	73	42	51

From Parker, G. Vulnerability factors to normal depression. *Journal of Psychosomatic Research*, 1980, *24*, 67–74. Reprinted with permission.

self-esteem is perhaps the key characteristic of the depressive experience (Bibring, 1953), and it is likely that those with a low inherent self-esteem are more susceptible to potential precipitants of depression, and especially to those that reflect directly on self-esteem.

Eysenck (1967) claims that the Eysenck Personality Inventory measures relatively stable personality dimensions of Neuroticism and Extraversion, with Neuroticism scores reflecting lability of the autonomic nervous system and Extraversion scores reflecting cortical arousal. While Paykel et al. (1976) state that the content of the Neuroticism personality scale "mainly reflects lifelong habitual mood lability," any relationship between Neuroticism and sensitivity to potential precipitants of depression remains to be demonstrated.

Parental loss has been incriminated variably as predisposing to depression. The published studies and reviews (numbering more than 40) are notable for their inconsistent conclusions (Parker, 1979b).

The present study also considers whether an external locus of control increases vulnerability to depression following life events. Lefcourt (1976) suggests that there is an importance in the ability to exercise control and the ability to predict the occurence of aversive stimuli. Those with a more "internal" locus of control are said to be more resistant to influence and less likely to yield to external pressure.

Finally, as many studies (see Weissman & Klerman, 1977) suggest that the prevalence of depression is higher in women, any sex difference in susceptibility to life events is assessed.

A stepwise multiple regression analysis was performed to determine the degree to which the several variables predicted the likelihood of respondents to report depression following the several listed precipitants. The incremental contribution of each variable can be seen in Table 9-8 in which F values are reported. It can be seen that for each precipitant, neuroticism levels were the clearest (and for four of the five precipitants significant) predictors of acknowledged depression. Self-esteem and sex appeared the next most important predicators. Parental protection scores were of relevance to only one precipitant, while low parental care scores were irrelevant to all precipitants. (Only PBI scores for the more important parent were entered as the clearer relevance of that figure has been suggested earlier in the study). Findings with the PBI variables suggest that if low parental care and high parental protection scores predispose the recipient to later depression, then any induced vulnerability does not require interaction with a precipitant.

Study 4: Another non-clinical Group

This study was designed to reassess the relationship between PBI scores and trait depression scores but differed in two clear ways. First while the preceding study had assessed the relevance of nominated parent-figures, the hardy tradition of only considering natural parents was preserved in this study. Second, sex of parent–sex of recipient associations were assessed.

Method

The methodology, described more fully elsewhere (Parker, 1977, 1979c), is summarized. All first-year psychology students at the University of New South Wales who were attending seminars during 1 week in early 1977 were asked to complete PBI measures for both parents and the Costello-Comrey mood measures. Hypotheses were not disclosed. While the response rate was not determined formally, it was informally reported that very few of the students declined to complete the forms. Eight forms were subsequently rejected as incomplete or possibly invalid, and an

Table 9-8

Study 3: Degree to Which the Variables Predicted the Likelihood of Respondents to Report Depression in Response to Several Precipitants (F ratio values tabulated)

Precipitant (actual wording)	Sex of Respondent	Permanent Separation from Biological Parent	PBI Scores Low Care	PBI Scores High Protection	Neuroticism	Extraversion	Respondent's Self-Esteem	External Locus of Control	Overall F
The break-up of an important relationship	2.2	0.3	0.8	1.0	10.6*	0.7	1.1	0	2.5‡
Being rejected or distanced in a relationship	6.1‡	0.8	0	1.7	17.9*	1.9	1.5	0.2	6.0†
A fall-off in support to my self-esteem	8.0*	0.7	2.5	0.9	18.2*	0	6.4‡	0	7.2‡
Failure to obtain an important goal	0.6	0.6	0.1	0.8	3.4	0	1.4	0	1.6
Failure to live up to my own standards	3.0	1.1	3.8	4.0‡	13.9*	0	9.3†	0	6.6†

From Parker, G. Vulnerability factors to normal depression. *Journal of Psychosomatic Research*, 1980, 24, 67–74. With permission.
*$p<0.001$; †$p<0.01$; ‡$p<0.05$

Table 9-9
Study 4: Mean Scores on Trait Depression Measure for Subjects who Assigned Parents to Five PBI Positions

Parent	Middle	High Care–Low Protection	High Care–High Protection	Low Care–Low Protection	Low Care–High Protection	F Ratio
Mother	36.5	27.6	32.0	35.0	43.7	10.85†
n	50	95	44	62	35	
Father	37.5	29.7	28.3	34.4	35.4	4.45‡
n	56	78	39	61	43	

From Parker, G. Reported parental characteristics in relation to trait depression and anxiety levels in a non-clinical group. *Australian and New Zealand Journal of Psychiatry*, 1979, *13*, 260–265. Reprinted with permission.
†$p<0.001$; ‡$p<0.005$

analysis was made of the remaining 289 questionnaires completed by 191 female and 98 male students having a mean age of 22 years.

Results

On the basis of PBI scores, parents were assigned, in effect, to four broad PBI positions or to a "middle" group (determined statistically to receive one-fifth of the sample). The data in Table 9-9 show that in respect to mothers the quadrant high care–low protection was associated with the lowest mean levels of depression, while the quadrant low care–high protection was associated with the highest. A similar trend was noted in association with paternal scores.

These analyses are somewhat limited by ignoring parental interactional effects. Therefore, multiple regression analyses were undertaken to examine the contribution made by each independent variable in predicting depression scores. In Table 9-10 separate multiple regression analyses are summarized for male and female respondents (and for the combined group). A low maternal care score is the only significant predictor of higher depression scores, for both males and females, and the variance it accounted for is in the order of 10 percent for each sex.

Study 5: Adopted Group

The possibility that a link between PBI and depression scores might merely reflect a hereditary influence is an issue worthy of investigation—associations might reflect a more central genetic influence causing independent outcomes (e.g., anomalous PBI scores and higher depression in recipients), with any associations between the two outcomes being spurious.

Table 9-10
Study 4: Multiple Regression Analyses Assessing Degree to Which PBI Scores Predicted Trait Depression Scores, by Sex of Parent and Sex of Respondent

PBI Scale	Female Respondent			Male Respondent			Both Sexes		
	r	F Ratio	Variance (%)	r	F Ratio	Variance (%)	r	F Ratio	Variance (%)
Maternal care	−0.31	10.9*	9.7	−0.33	2.6	10.6	−0.30	15.5*	9.3
Maternal protection	+0.21	2.4	1.2	+0.25	0.9	0.9	+0.15	0.2	0.1
Paternal care	−0.15	0.04	0.1	−0.30	2.6	2.7	−0.20	1.7	0.6
Paternal protection	+0.03	1.1	0.1	+0.19	0.09	0.4	+0.09	0	0
Multiple R	+0.33	5.56*	11.2	+0.38	3.59†	14.6	+0.32	7.6*	10.0

*$p<0.001$; †$p<0.01$

Method

In order to investigate such a possibility an appeal was made through a women's magazine for adoptees (Parker, 1982a). Any bias accruing from a possibly greater likelihood of dissatisfied adoptees responding would not affect the results as the principal examinations were to be within-group associations. Over 3000 adoptees responded to the appeal. A questionnaire was sent to 200 of those seeking to participate. The selection was not a random one. As few males made contact, all males making contact were included, as were those who responded earlier to the appeal. At no time, whether in the initial appeal or in the questionnaire sent to the target group, were the hypotheses under examination stated. Of the 162 questionnaires returned, 34 of those returned were rejected on one of several grounds (e.g., questionnaire incomplete, subject fostered rather than adopted), and 19 were returned after the cut-off time for analysis. Information returned by the remaining 109 subjects was coded for analysis.

The adoptees were asked to complete a questionnaire and to note their age, sex, and occupation, the occupation of their adopting father, their age at the time of adoption, and whether they had had any contact with their biological parents in childhood and adolescence. They were requested to complete a PBI for each adopting parent, and the Costello-Comrey (1967) trait depression questionaire.

The mean age of the 109 respondents was 33.0 years (range 18–60 years), and there was a marked female preponderance (88.1 percent) of respondents; 63 (58 percent) had been adopted within the first month after birth. Only 9 (8 percent) had had any contact with a natural parent in the first 16 years.

Results

Mean scores on the several scales of the PBI were as follows: paternal care, 25.2 (SD 9.7); paternal protection, 14.5 (SD 8.8); maternal care, 24.9 (SD 10.0); and maternal protection, 16.8 (SD 9.2).

PBI scores for the adopting parents were correlated against the depression scale scores for the respondents (Table 9-11). Higher depression scores are associated negatively with parental care and positively with parental protection scores, although, in a simple multiple regression analysis, only a low maternal care score is a significant predictor of higher levels of depression.

Correlations between PBI and depression scores for a subgroup of those adopted within the first month were also examined to exclude the possibility of an artifact being introduced by the biological parent having

Table 9-11
Study 5: Multiple Regression Analysis Assessing Degree to
Which PBI Scores Predicted Trait Depression Scores

PBI Scale	r	β Weight	F Ratio	Variance (%)
Maternal care	−0.47*	−0.37	9.3†	22.0
Maternal protection	+0.37*	+0.15	1.4	1.1
Paternal care	−0.25†	−0.03	0.1	0
Paternal protection	+0.11	−0.06	0.3	0
Multiple R	+0.48		7.5*	23.1

Adapted from Parker, G. Parental representations and affective disorders: Examination for an hereditary link. *British Journal of Medical Psychology*, 1982, 55, 57–61.
*$p<0.001$; †$p<0.01$

had some contact with the child. Associations within the subgroup were at least as strong as those within the whole sample (for maternal care, −0.50; maternal protection, +0.37; paternal care, −0.25; and paternal protection, +0.21).

DISCUSSION

Five studies have been conducted examining the relevance of parental variables to several types and grades of depression. The overall results support the strategy of attempting to preserve boundaries between several expressions of depression. Neurotic depressives and those in nonclinical groups with greater depressive experience reported less parental care and greater parental protection. In contrast, patients with bipolar manic-depressive disorder could not be distinguished from matched controls. Those differential results offer further support for the binary view of depression. As distinct PBI scores were not recorded by the manic-depressive patients, there is no support for the view that manic-depressives experience parental overprotection and/or decrements in parental care either before the onset of, or as a response to, the disorder.

The results in the nonclinical and neurotic depressive groups may reasonably be considered together. In two studies, neurotic depressive patients, as a group, reported considerably less parental care and somewhat more protection than did the matched controls, and the relative risk estimates of exposure to the parental style of affectionless control suggested its clear overrepresentation. The replication study found also that neurotic depressives were more likely to score the same-sex parent as less caring and as more protective. These findings were supported further in one of the nonclinical studies (Study 4) when the simple correlations were examined, although in the regression equations low maternal care remained the best PBI predictor of high depression scores in both sexes. Findings support Becker's (1964) review suggesting that the same-sex parent is less likely than the opposite-sex parent to grant autonomy to the child.

The clear relevance of the parental style affectionless control to greater depressive experience was evident in both the neurotic depressive and in the nonclinical studies assessing depression as a continuous variable. In both the clinical studies more than two-thirds of the patients, compared to one-third of the controls, reported exposure to one or more parents effecting that parental style. In the Teachers' College study (Study 3), those assigning nominated parent-figures to that quadrant scored highly on trait depression, incidence of depression, alienation, and neuroticism measures, and low on a self-esteem measure. A replication study of psychology students (Study 4) confirmed the principal findings. Several analyses suggest that low parental care is more strongly associated with depression than is higher parental protection, and in the replication study of neurotic depressive patients (Parker, 1983) a low PBI care score (i.e., 10 or less for either parent) was shown to be highly sensitive (in that there were few false positives) in distinguishing patients from controls.

Several explanations of these findings can be considered. First, it is possible that the results from the initial clinical neurotic depressive group could be biased. As most of the patients were treated by the author, it is possible that they gave back the author's interpretation rather than their own account of their parents. That possibility appears unlikely because replication was achieved in a second study with the sample chosen from patients attending 14 psychiatrists.

Second, bias could be introduced by matching against inappropriate controls. If depressives are overrepresented in general practice control groups it is likely that differences in case–control studies of depressives will be minimized. The possible relevance of such a bias was examined in the second clinical study by comparing the neurotic depressive patients with a group of unscreened general practice controls and with controls selected in a separate study after those with a history suggesting a depressive disorder were screened out. The findings (Parker, 1983) suggest that any such biases were trivial or nonexistent, and that the unscreened general practice controls were appropriate to use as a criterion group in the case–control comparisons.

Third, the results could be brought about by the dependent variables, depression, influencing the independent PBI variables. Causality is only supported if an association is undirectional (Susser, 1973). However, as described in Chapter 7, the possibility that depression levels influence PBI reporting was tested in a separate study and not supported.

Finally, it is possible that another variable influences both greater depressive experience and PBI scoring. Henderson et al. (1981) suggest three personality attributes of relevance: anxious attachment or dependency, neuroticism, and plaintive set. Some comments may be made about the possible relevance of each to the present findings.

It is often suggested (e.g., Chodoff, 1972) that depressives have unduly dependent premorbid characteristics, although the relative contributions made by constitutional and environmental factors to any greater dependency are less clear. It is possible that the future depressive, as a consequence of premorbid dependency traits, may elicit affectionless control from a parent. Such a possibility was investigated in a study reported elsewhere (Parker, 1981a). In that study a nonclinical group of subjects scored their mothers on the PBI, and themselves on trait and state measures of depression and on 12 items of the dependency scale of the Depressive Experience Questionnaire (Blatt et al., 1975). Their mothers were interviewed and asked to rate those children in early childhood on parameters of "shyness and timidity" and "independence." The associations linking higher depression scores with low maternal care (-0.44 and -0.45) and with greater maternal protection ($+0.30$ and $+0.39$) were not influenced when the several ratings of childhood and adult dependency were partialed out. Thus, the possibility that greater dependency, whether as a childhood and presumably constitutional characteristic, or as an adult characteristic (constitutionally or environmentally based), influences associations between PBI scores and depression scores is unlikely.

Henderson et al. (1981) state that neuroticism, as measured by the Eysenck Personality Inventory, is widely accepted as an index of vulnerability to neurotic disorder. Indirect support for that proposition is given in Study 3, in which regression analyses established that the EPI neuroticism score was the best of eight suggested vulnerability factors. Thus, it could be that the relevant associations between PBI scores and depression are determined by neuroticism levels. That possibility can be examined by analyzing appropriate data from Study 3. Trait depression scores correlated -0.28 ($p < 0.001$) with PBI care scores and $+0.22$ ($p < 0.001$) with PBI protection scores for the more important parent. After the effect of neuroticism scores was partialed out, trait depression scores correlated -0.27 ($p<0.001$) with care scores and $+0.14$ ($p<0.02$) with protection scores. For the less important parent, controlling for neuroticism reduced the correlation between trait depression scores and raw care scores from -0.33 to -0.27 and reduced the correlation between trait depression scores and protection scores from $+0.21$ to $+0.11$. These findings suggest that neuroticism levels are not creating any spurious association between PBI care scores and depression. As their partialing out does weaken associations between PBI protection scales and depression, this could suggest their partial relevance to that dimension, but it does not establish the nature of that association. For instance, it is just as possible that parental overprotection *causes* higher neuroticism levels as it is that higher neuroticism levels may *cause* parents to be scored as more protective on that PBI scale.

The relevance of plaintive set, or a propensity to complain, in the depressed patients could not be so readily assessed as a determinant of the associations, as there is no measure of this personality characteristic. The logic suggested in the present inquiry is that if neurotic depressive patients have a greater tendency to complain than controls, then intercorrelations of appropriate PBI scale scores should reflect that phenomenon by showing stronger associations between scores returned by the patients than by the controls. In fact, the opposite phenomenon was observed, the mean coefficient being 0.27 in the neurotic depressives compared to 0.50 in both the control groups. It would seem unwise to interpret those results as evidence of a more marked plaintive set in the controls than in the patients. It is suggested that if plaintive set is more relevant to the depressives, then it acts to counteract any social desirability or illusory glow tendency engaged in by nondepressives.

Finally, the possibility that associations between PBI scores and depression might reflect a hereditary factor was assessed in a study of adoptees and no support was found. The possibility that low parental care and parental overprotection act as causal influences on the development of the nonbiological forms of depression would appear worthy of close assessment when appropriate noncausal explanations have been assessed and found wanting. It is likely that a causal process would be best assessed by a prospective study. The importance of assessing the relevance of causality is emphasized by the fact that the relative risk estimates and variance accounted for in regression analyses indicate that the parental variables are not trivial ones.

If parental overprotection and low parental care are causal influences on later depressive experience, then subsidiary results from one study (Study 3) allow some comments on the nature of that process. In that study, analyses were made to assess whether certain risk factors to depression were likely to act independently of precipitating factors or whether they were vulnerability factors in the sense suggested by Brown and Harris (1978)—that is, while they may predispose to depression, they require the presence of a precipitant or provoking agent to produce depression. The important negative finding was that PBI care and protection scores (in comparison to neuroticism and self-esteem scores, and to female sex) were not suggested as vulnerability factors. This is perhaps surprising since it is often suggested that an individual's capacity to overreact to particular stimuli may follow past losses and exposure to negative attitudes (Brown & Harris, 1978). If that view is valid, it might have been expected that those subjects who had experienced less parental care would have reported greater sensitivity to the precipitants or provoking agents involving rejection and distance within, or ending of, an interpersonal relationship. That expectation was not supported by the analyses. Thus, if parental overprotection and low parental care increase vulnerability to depression, it would appear that they do so directly and that they do not make the recipient any more sensitive to precipitating or provoking life stresses.

Any further contemplation of possible causal mechanisms is left until Chapter 17.

10
Anxiety

Pathological or morbid anxiety is commonly diagnosed as *anxiety neurosis* although that term is not included in the more recent classificatory systems. In ICD-9 (WHO, 1978) such disorders are classified as *anxiety states* and defined as conditions reflecting "Various combinations of physical and mental manifestations of anxiety, not attributable to real danger and occurring either in the attacks or as a persisting state." In DSM-III (APA, 1980) *anxiety disorders* is one of the diagnostic classes of neurotic disorders and comprises three subgroups: *phobic disorders, anxiety states* (or *anxiety neuroses*), and *obsessive-compulsive disorders.* The essential features of the second subgroup (300.01) are said to be recurrent panic or anxiety attacks with associated features of varying degrees of nervousness and apprehension between attacks. It is stated in DSM-III that *separation anxiety disorder* in childhood and sudden object loss apparently predispose to the development of an anxiety state. The essential feature of separation anxiety disorder in childhood, according to DSM-III, is excessive anxiety on separation from major attachment figures or from home and other familiar surroundings. It is suggested that children with this disorder "tend to come from families that are close-knit and caring" and that neglected children are underrepresented.

While constitutional factors are held to play the major role in determining any vulnerability to anxiety neurosis, the proposition that psychosocial factors may predispose a child to greater anxiety in later life has been considered by a number of theorists and clinicians. It is noted in a major British textbook of psychiatry (Slater & Roth, 1969) that: "If the growing child is subjected to feelings of fear . . . as for instance when he

Anxiety   175

is brought up by a stern and rigid parent, he may come to have a very generalised susceptibility to anxiety" (p. 89). In Chapter 4 there are a number of references to the view that overprotective parenting is linked with higher levels of anxiety in children, but there has been little empirical assessment of that proposition.

In this chapter several studies of patients with a clinical diagnosis of anxiety neurosis and of nonclinical groups are reported. These studies were designed to examine the proposition that adults with significant anxiety have been exposed to pathogenic parental experiences.

STUDY 1: PATIENTS WITH AN ANXIETY NEUROSIS

Method

The sample comprised 50 consecutive outpatients diagnosed clinically as having an anxiety neurosis (Parker, 1981b). Those patients with marked phobic symptoms, those with a first episode, and those with a history that could be interpreted as reflecting merely a situational stress reaction were not included in the sample. The majority of patients described recurrent episodes going back to early adolescence or early adulthood, with symptoms such as fear, poor concentration, faintness, tremor, fears of going mad, and irritability. The following data were extracted from each patient's file: age, sex, father's occupation (to determine social class), and whether the patient acknowledged a history of school refusal in childhood or adolescence. Patients were matched for age, sex, and paternal social class with controls selected from the Sydney general practice study (Parker et al., 1979) to allow comparison of PBI scores.

Results

There were 34 females and 16 males, and the mean age was 30 years (range 16–56 years); 20 (40 percent) had a positive history of school refusal.

The PBI scores (Table 10-1) show that the anxiety neurotic patients perceived both parents as less caring and as more protective than did the controls. Parental assignment to the PBI quadrants by the patients and controls is compared in Table 10-2. It can be seen that the patients were least likely to assign their parents to the high care–low protection quadrant, and were most likely to assign their parents to the low care–high protection quadrant. The relative risk of a patient assigning one or more parent to the low care–high protection quadrant was 3.9.

Table 10-1
Study 1: Mean PBI Scores for Anxiety Neurosis Patients and Matched Controls

PBI Scale	Patients	Controls	t-test
Maternal care	21.2	27.2	3.31*
Maternal protection	19.6	13.3	4.42†
Paternal care	18.0	25.0	4.09†
Paternal protection	17.4	12.0	3.07*
Parental care	39.9	52.1	4.11†
Parental protection	37.2	25.7	4.67†

From Parker, G. Parental representation of patients with anxiety neurosis. *Acta Psychiatrica Scandinavica*, 1981, *63*, 33–36. Reprinted with permission.
*$p < 0.01$; †$p < 0.001$

Table 10-2
Study 1: Assignment of Parents to PBI Quadrants by Anxiety Neurotic Patients and Controls

Group	Parent	High Care– Low Protection	High Care– High Protection	Low Care– Low Protection	Low Care– High Protection	X^2
Patient	Mother	6 (0.2)*	9 (0.7)	7 (1.5)	27 (3.1)	10.9‡
Control	Mother	18	12	5	14	
Patient	Father	4 (0.1)	10 (2.3)	10 (1.8)	23 (2.3)	17.3†
Control	Father	22	5	6	14	

*Relative risk estimates are shown in parentheses.
†$p < 0.001$; ‡$p < 0.02$

Table 10-3
Study 1: Mean PBI Scores for Patients with a School Refusal History and Remaining Patients

PBI Scale	School Refusal Patients	Remaining Patients	t test*
Maternal care	23.4	19.7	1.25
Maternal protection	20.9	18.6	0.81
Paternal care	20.1	16.6	1.27
Paternal protection	16.8	17.7	0.32
Parental care	43.6	37.3	1.56
Parental protection	37.9	36.7	0.29

From Parker, G. Parental representations of patients with anxiety neurosis. *Acta Psychiatrica Scandinavica*, 1981, *63*, 33–36. Reprinted with permission.
*All comparisons nonsignificant

PBI scores for patients with a history of school refusal were compared with those for the remaining patients (Table 10-3). There was an insignificant trend for those with a history of school refusal to report more parental care and more parental protection.

STUDY 2: NONCLINICAL GROUP

Method

In order to examine the degree to which PBI scores were associated with levels of anxiety in a nonclinical group, a study of 236 Teachers' College students (described in Study 3 Chapter 9) was conducted. The subjects were asked to nominate their two most important parent-figures during childhood and adolescence and complete PBI questionnaires for each. Two measures of anxiety were completed by the respondents: the Costello-Comrey (1967) trait anxiety scale, which is claimed by the authors to "measure a predisposition to develop anxious-affective states," and the neuroticism scale of Form A of the EPI (Eysenck & Eysenck, 1964).

Results

When PBI scores were correlated with the anxiety measure scores (Table 10-4), higher protection scores for the more important parent-figure, and lower care scores for the less important parent-figure, were linked weakly with higher scores on the anxiety measures.

A further analysis compared the mean anxiety scores for those who assigned parents to broadly distinctive parental styles. In this study a "middle" group was created in addition to the four quadrants and, by using a partialing out procedure, the axes for the two PBI scales were

Table 10-4
Study 2: Intercorrelation of PBI Scores and Measures of Anxiety for a Nonclinical Group

Parent-Figure	PBI Scale	Neuroticism r	Trait Anxiety r
More important	Care	−0.09	−0.10
More important	Protection	+0.25*	+0.25*
Less important	Care	−0.24*	−0.22*
Less important	Protection	+0.11	+0.04

*$p < 0.001$

Table 10-5
Study 2: Mean Anxiety and Neuroticism Scores for Subjects Assigning Parents to Each PBI Position

Parent-figure	Scale	Middle	High Care–Low Protection	High Care–High Protection	Low Care–Low Protection	Low Care–High Protection	F Ratio
More important	Anxiety	26.5	25.3	29.5	26.4	30.6	2.28
More important	Neuroticism	10.9	10.0	11.8	9.7	12.3	2.57†
n		40	66	47	43	40	
Less important	Anxiety	27.8	24.9	26.0	31.3	30.0	3.13*
Less important	Neuroticism	10.7	9.7	10.4	11.9	12.8	3.04*
n		42	62	52	41	39	

*$p < 0.025$; †$p < 0.05$

made orthogonal. The data in Table 10-5 show that, for three of the four analyses, those who assigned a parent-figure to the low care–high protection position scored highest on the continuous measures of anxiety. By comparison, but again for three of the four analyses, the lowest mean scores on the measures of anxiety were most likely to be returned by those who rated a parent-figure as belonging to the high care—low protection position.

STUDY 3: ANOTHER NONCLINICAL GROUP

Method

This study was essentially a replication of the former study, although rating was restricted to natural parents. The study involved 289 psychology students, who completed PBI scores for each parent and the Costello-Comrey trait anxiety scale, and has been described more fully in Study 4, Chapter 9.

Results

A comparison of PBI positions and trait anxiety scores (Table 10-6) shows that the position low care–high protection was associated with the highest levels of anxiety when examined in relation to mothers and intermediate levels when examined in relation to fathers.

Multiple regression analyses were then conducted to determine whether higher levels of anxiety might relate more to the PBI scores for mothers or for fathers. Separate simple multiple regression analyses were

Table 10-6
Study 3: Mean Trait Anxiety Scores for Subjects Assigning Parents to Each PBI Position

Parent	Middle	High Care–Low Protection	High Care–High Protection	Low Care–Low Protection	Low Care–High Protection	F Ratio
Mother	28.2	24.5	29.2	26.3	32.7	5.13*
n	50	95	44	62	35	
Father	29.7	29.7	26.6	28.3	28.9	4.12†
n	56	78	39	61	56	

From Parker, G. Reported parental characteristics in relation to trait depression and anxiety levels in a non-clinical group. *Australian and New Zealand Journal of Psychiatry*, 1979, *13*, 260–265. Reprinted with permission.
*$p < 0.001$; †$p < 0.01$

Table 10-7
Study 3: Multiple Regression Analyses Considering Degree to which PBI Scores Predict Trait Anxiety Scores, by Sex of Parent and Sex of Respondents

PBI Scale	Female Respondents			Male Respondents			Both Sexes		
	r	β Weight	Variance (%)	r	β Weight	Variance (%)	r	β Weight	Variance (%)
Maternal care	−0.06	−0.05	0.4	−0.34	−0.23	11.8	−0.25	−0.17*	6.1
Maternal protection	+0.20	+0.31†	3.1	+0.28	+0.15	1.0	+0.23	+0.16*	2.6
Paternal care	−0.09	−0.05	0.5	−0.43	−0.43*	8.7	−0.14	−0.05	0.2
Paternal protection	+0.06	−0.05	0.3	+0.23	−0.07	1.0	0	−0.10	0.3
All (multiple R)	+0.21		4.3	+0.47		22.5	+0.30		9.2

*$p < 0.01$, †$p < 0.025$

Anxiety 181

conducted for male and female respondents (and the combined group) to examine whether there is any relevant interaction between sex of child and sex of parent. PBI scores are clearly stronger predictors of anxiety levels in males (accounting for 22.5 percent of the variance) than in females (4.3 percent of the variance). While the only significant predictor of higher anxiety levels in females was higher maternal protection scores, higher anxiety scores in males were predicted both by lower maternal and by lower paternal care scores.

STUDY 4: ADOPTED GROUP

The possibility that the link between PBI scores and anxiety might reflect a hereditary influence is an important one. For instance, higher neuroticism as a hereditary factor might cause a parent to adopt an uncaring and overprotective parental style, and it might cause higher levels of anxiety in a child, thereby producing a spurious associations between the two sequelae. As discussed in Chapter 9, such a possibility can be assessed by studying adoptees (who score their adopting parents on the PBI), in whom such a hereditary influence cannot operate. If, in this study, PBI scores for the adoptive parents are not associated with trait anxiety levels in the adoptees, than it is possible that the associations described in the earlier studies were spurious ones, reflecting a hereditary influence.

Method

The methodology is described in Chapter 9. Data completed by 109 subjects were examined; 63 (58 percent) of the respondents had been adopted in the first month after birth. As in the previous studies the Costello-Comrey trait anxiety scale was used to assess the dependent variable, anxiety.

Results

Higher anxiety scores are associated negatively with parental care scores and positively with parental protection scores, although they are significant only in relation to the mothers (Table 10-8). Correlations were reexamined for those in the subgroup of the first-month adoptees to exclude any possibility of contact with, and influence by, biological parents: they were at least as strong as for the whole group (maternal care, $r = -0.39$; paternal care, $r = -0.12$; maternal protection, $r = +0.30$; paternal protection, $r = +0.10$). In the whole sample the regression

Table 10-8
Study 4: Multiple Regression Analysis
Assessing Degree to Which PBI Scores
Predicted Trait Anxiety Scores

PBI Scale	r	F Ratio	Variance (%)
Maternal care	−0.36*	7.5†	12.7
Maternal protection	+0.26†	0.3	0.2
Paternal care	−0.12	0.5	0.5
Paternal protection	+0.07	0	0
All (multiple R)	+0.36	3.9	13.5

From Parker, G. Parental representations and affective disorders: Examination for an hereditary link. *British Journal of Medical Psychology*, 1982, 55, 57–61. Reprinted with permission.
*$p < 0.001$; †$p < 0.01$

equation established that low maternal care was the only significant predictor of higher anxiety scores, accounting for approximately 13 percent of the variance.

DISCUSSION

The four studies described in this chapter assess the relationship between parental representations, as reflected by the PBI, and the expression of several grades and/or types of anxiety. The first study, an orthodox case–control comparison, established that anxiety neurosis patients are distinguished from controls by reporting less parental care and greater parental protection. As with neurotic depressives, the anxiety neurotics were highly unlikely to assign their parents to the high care–low protection PBI quadrant and were most likely to assign parents to the low care–high protection quadrant. Specifically, 74 percent of the patients and 42 percent of the controls scored one or more parent to the latter quadrant.

In three studies correlational analyses were performed to examine associations between PBI scores and scores on the same continuous measures of trait anxiety, the Costello–Comrey scale. In the two studies in which the sex of the parent was assessed in the analyses—psychology students scoring their natural parents (Study 3) and adoptees scoring their adopting parents (Study 4)—the several correlations were similar across the two groups, respectively: maternal care, $r = -0.25$ and -0.36; maternal protection, $r = +0.23$ and $+0.26$; paternal care, $r = -0.14$ and -0.12; paternal protection, $r = 0$ and $+0.07$. Thus higher levels of anxiety were associated with maternal, but not clearly with paternal, PBI scores. Multiple regression analyses suggested that low maternal care was the PBI variable of greatest relevance to higher levels of anxiety. In the psychology students (Study 3), low maternal care (when examined for the whole group) predicted 6.1 percent of the variance in anxiety levels, while in the adoptees (Study 4), it predicted 12.7 percent of the variance—and was the only significant predictor in both cases. However, the large number of subjects in Study 3 allowed analyses for male and female respondents and a striking difference was suggested: for female respondents only higher maternal protection scores significantly predicted higher levels of anxiety, while for male respondents only low paternal care scores were significant predictors. Furthermore, the amount of variance accounted for by PBI variables was very different for female (4.3 percent) and male (22.5 percent) respondents. Until these findings are replicated any attempt at interpreting the different associations between PBI scores and anxiety for males and females would be unwise.

Assignment by respondents of parents and parent-figures to PBI quadrants was assessed in two of the nonclinical studies (2 and 3). Findings were broadly consistent with those from the clinical study in that the highest levels of anxiety were reported by those assigning a parent to the low care–high protection quadrant.

Several explanations of the findings are noteworthy. First, children with an anxious temperament might elicit less parental care and greater parental protection. Results from the clinical study (Study 1) are then of interest: 40 percent of that sample acknowledged significant episodes of school refusal, behavior that is often the early expression of anxiety in a child or adolescent. Those acknowledging school refusal showed a nonsignificant trend to score both parents as *more* caring and their mothers as more protective than did the nonphobic patients. This finding would suggest that the early expression of anxiety in a child (at least when inferred from a history of school refusal) may elicit a differential parental response, but not the one reported for the whole patient sample. Nevertheless, childhood anxiety may be manifested in many ways apart from school refusal, so that this explanation cannot be confidently rejected by the school refusal data.

Second, it may be that those with an anxious or neurotic temperament score their parents with a negative bias on the PBI. Henderson et al. (1981) have considered the relevance of Gruenberg's notion of plaintive set (whereby certain individuals will seize any opportunity to complain) as an explanation of negative judgments of social relationships by neurotic patients. Such a possibility should be assessed in longitudinal studies, and must be conceded at this time.

Third, associations could be spurious ones reflecting a hereditary factor. For instance, higher neuroticism as a hereditary factor might cause a parent to be deficient in care and to be overprotective, and it might cause higher levels of anxiety in a child, thereby producing spurious associations between two independent outcomes. The fourth study was designed to assess that possibility. The confounding effect of a hereditary influence would be suggested if the adoptees' levels of anxiety were not correlated with PBI scores for the adopting parents. However, as comparison across the several studies shows, the correlations were generally stronger than those found in studies involving subjects scoring natural parents. While it is not entirely appropriate to compare associations across different study groups, the comparative strengths of the correlations in the study of adoptees suggest strongly that a hereditary influence does not bring about the associations.

Finally, it may be that low parental care and high parental protection (affectionless control) may be antecedent causes of anxiety in adult life. There are many ways by which those parental characteristics might aid such a process, although the author favors a process suggested by Ainsworth et al. (1971) and by Bowlby (1973), whereby deficient parenting interferes with the dynamic balance between attachment and exploratory behaviors, promoting what Bowlby terms "anxious attachment." However, considerations of a causal process are left to the final discussion in Chapter 17.

11
Phobic States

Phobic states are defined in ICD-9 (WHO, 1978) as "neurotic states with abnormally intense dread of certain objects or specific situations which would not normally have that effect." In DSM-III (APA, 1980), *phobic disorders* comprise one of the three subgroups of anxiety disorders and are subdivided into *agoraphobia, social phobia,* and *simple phobia.* Marks (1969) considers that phobic states can conveniently be divided into phobias of stimuli external to the patient (agoraphobia, social phobias, animal phobias, miscellaneous specific phobias) and phobias of stimuli internal to the patient (illness phobias and obsessive phobias). Agoraphobia and social phobias are probably the two most common phobic disorders seen by psychiatrists, and comprised 68 percent of all phobias in a Maudsley Hospital, London, series (Marks, 1969). Only these two phobias are considered further in this chapter, in view of their preponderance and because atypical parental characteristics (considered shortly) have been held to be of relevance to these disorders.

The agoraphobic syndrome mainly affects women and has many synonyms (Marks, 1969), including *phobic anxiety state* and *phobic-anxiety-depersonalization syndrome.* Fears center around going out but may generalize to many other situations. Items tapping the agoraphobic dimension in a fear survey schedule include "traveling alone by bus or coach," "walking alone in busy streets," "going into crowded shops," "going alone far from home," and "large open spaces" (Marks and Mathews, 1979).

Social phobias have a similar incidence in men and women (Marks, 1969) and the phobic situation is restricted to social activities. Items tapping the social phobia dimension in the Fear Survey Schedule of Marks and Mathews (1979) comprise "eating or drinking with other people," "being watched or stared at," "talking to people in authority," "being criticized," and "speaking or acting to an audience."

The etiology of phobic disorders remains unclear, although there is much to recommend a multifactorial view. Marks (1969) considers that phylogenetic influences, age, sex, personality, cultural influences inside and outside the family, physiological variables, trauma and stress, modeling experience, and learning theory may all be of varying relevance to individual cases.

A number of reports have suggested that those with phobic disorders have been recipients of parental overprotection. Terhune (1949) considered 86 (2.5 percent) of his psychoneurotic patients to have a "severe phobic syndrome." He observes that "the phobic person is one who has been overprotected, brought up 'soft,' usually by neurotic parents, on one of whom they are still emotionally dependent." He holds that as a consequence of such rearing they lack adequate psychological preparation for living, and, faced with the more stressful exigencies of living, they "regress to a childish level of adjustment." He suggests that neurotic parents should realize that they are psychologically infectious insofar as their apprehensive children are concerned, and that they should seek treatment to learn not to overprotect their children.

Tucker (1956) considered the features of 100 patients seen over the course of 1 year presenting with "varying degrees of anxiety, somatic symptoms, and hysterical and obsessive-compulsive tendencies"; he judged a dependent relationship to the parents, and usually to the mother, to be present in 77 of the 100 patients, and notes "The background is that of insecurity in childhood as a result of parental strife, lack of parental affection, overprotection and overcriticism by parents."

Bowlby (1973) suggests that there are probably four patterns of interaction in the families of agoraphobics, on the basis of studies of school refusing children. In Pattern A there is clear evidence of a dominant and controlling parent, usually the mother, and Bowlby cites studies by Roth (1959), Snaith (1968), Terhune (1949), and Webster (1953) in support. While noting such a clear pattern, Bowlby is unable to suggest its origins.

Reports and views such as those described above have stimulated a number of controlled studies. Snaith (1968) compared 27 phobic patients who had a primary fear of going away from home or other shelter (agoraphobics) with 21 phobic patients whose primary fear focused on another situation or object and found a similar incidence of overprotection. Solyom et al. (1974) studied 47 phobic outpatients at a Montreal hospital; 92 percent had been diagnosed clinically as having agoraphobia and the remainder a specific phobia. On the basis of interview information, 44 percent of the phobic patients and 28 percent of selected controls were judged to have had overprotective mothers, a nonsignificant trend.

In a later study, Solyom et al. (1976) hypothesize that agoraphobia is a reactivation of early attachment behavior, "made more than usually tenuous by the presence of an overprotective mother." In order to investigate the relevance of maternal overprotection, they first developed a 50-item Maternal Overprotection Questionnaire (MOQ) whose validity was supported when 10 mothers rated as overprotective by a treating psychiatrist scored significantly higher on completing the scale than 10 mothers judged not to be overprotective. The researchers compared the total MOQ scores of the 21 mothers of agoraphobics (mean 25.5) with those returned by the 10 mothers judged to be overprotective (mean 15.9) and the 10 mothers judged not to be overprotective (mean 10.9). In a second analysis they compared scores of 18 agoraphobic mothers with normative data obtained from 222 women in five subscales of the PARI questionnaire. The differences in the means suggested agoraphobic mothers to be more overprotective but were not significant. In a third analysis they found that MOQ scores correlated positively with scores on an anxiety measure (the IPAT), although the level of the association was not described. The authors conclude that overprotection may be a manifestation of the mother's general anxiety. "As a consequence of her anxiety, she strives to keep her offspring away from all (in her view) potentially dangerous situations and/or to keep him constantly within her purview".

Buglass et al. (1977) compared the early childhood experiences of 30 agoraphobic housewives with matched general practice controls screened for absence of psychiatric symptoms. While the relevance of parental overprotection was not directly assessed, the authors found evidence of a dependency conflict (defined as a conscious awareness by the individual of being dependent on her mother but resenting the state of dependency) in eight of the patients and in none of the controls.

A review of the literature considered in this chapter and in Chapter 4 suggests a possible relevance of parental overprotection to certain phobic disorders. Interpretation of the findings is clouded by the researchers' failure to concede the view suggested by Marks (1969) that separate phobic conditions can be differentiated. If parental overprotection is of differing relevance to several phobic disorders, then the aggregation of possibly heterogeneous subgroups of phobic disorders may have prevented clarification. Parental overprotection has been assessed loosely in most studies, and adequate control or comparison groups have been lacking in a numer of the studies.

In the present study an attempt is made to improve on some of those methodological weaknesses by extending work commenced by Shaw at the Oxford Psychological Treatment Research Unit, Oxford, England. Shaw (1976) studied subjects who had been referred to the unit by general practitioners and psychiatrists in response to a letter describing and offering treatment for agoraphobia and social phobia. Subjects were accepted for study if they had either of those phobias as a main complaint, had had their phobia for at least 1 year, and scored 5 or more on a 9-point modified Fear Survey Schedule (Marks and Mathews, 1979). The 144 subjects satisfying these criteria were assigned as agoraphobics or social phobics according to their clinical features and scores on the phobia rating scale. Assessment of earlier parental attitudes and behaviors was made with a structured interview and by the use of self-rating scales, although the reliability and validity of those assessment techniques were not determined.

The phobic group described greater parental deprivataion and poorer relationships with parents than did a control group of orthopedic patients matched by age, sex, and social class. The relevance of parental overprotection was not assessed. In addition to delineating differences in the parental attitude of phobic patients, Shaw's controlled study found that parents of agoraphobic patients differed from parents of social phobic patients on a number of parental attitude scales. Shaw felt that these different parental attitudes might account in part for the different expression of the phobias. It appeared to be worthwhile to extend Shaw's work using the PBI in order to assess more precisely the relevance of parental overprotection and insufficiency of parental care.

METHOD

The study was conducted while the author was on study leave at the Department of Psychiatry, Oxford University, and has been described in greater detail (Parker, 1979d). Questionnaires were sent to 123 of the 144 patients assessed by Shaw 5–7 years previously; 50 had been assigned as agoraphobics and 73 as social phobics. Questionnaires were not sent to those 21 subjects who had either requested no further contact or whose addresses were no longer known. Data on social class, agoraphobic and social phobic scores, and item scores on self-reports (measuring perceived maternal affection, paternal affection, dependency on others, and approval by others) were collected from Shaw's notes for each patient.

Eighty-one patients (40 agoraphobics, 41 social phobics) replied to the questionnaire, giving a reponse rate of 66 percent (80 percent of the agoraphobics and 56 percent of the social phobics). There were 52 females and 29 males with a mean age of 39 years (range 20–71 years). Their social class (using the England and Wales Registrar General's classification) was as follows: class 1, 11 percent; class 2, 25 percent; class 3, 47 percent; class 4 and 5, 17 percent.

Respondents were compared with nonrespondents on several relevant variables. The two groups could not be distinguished by age ($t = 1.46$), self-report of maternal affection (median test = 0.37), self-report of paternal affection (median test = 0.63), or sex ($\chi^2 = 0$). The respondents had a lower social class (median test = 6.37, $p<0.05$), scored higher on the agoraphobic rating scale (median test = 11.01, $p<0.001$), and lower on the social phobic rating scale (median test = 6.36, $p<0.05$) than nonrespondents at the initial assessment 5–7 years earlier.

Controls for the present study were selected from two general practices in the Oxford Region as described in Chapter 7. Patients and controls were matched exactly for sex and approximately for age and social class. There were no significant differences between the age of the patients (mean 39.1) and that of the controls (mean 37.8 years) and their social class was similar (median test = 0.73, NS). On the basis of the descriptive studies referred to earlier, it was hypothesized that phobic patients would score their parents as less caring and as more protective than controls, and that they would be more likely to assign their parents (in particular, their mothers) to the quadrant of low care–high protection.

Several analyses were performed. A comparison was made between the whole phobic group and the controls. However, as Marks (1969) notes, separate phobic conditions can be differentiated on the basis of clinical, questionnaire, and psychophysiological variables. It thus appeared appropriate to consider the influence of parental antecedents on separate subgroups of social phobics and agoraphobics if the two groups could be differentiated with some confidence.

RESULTS

A comparison of the whole phobic group with the controls was made first (Table 11-1). The phobics scored both parents as significantly less caring and as significantly more protective than did the controls.

However, a pooled comparison of phobics appeared inappropriate when a comparison was made of those designated by Shaw as agoraphobics and those designated as social phobics (Table 11-2). Designated agoraphobics scored near zero for social phobic symptoms, while designated social phobics had low agoraphobic scores. The product moment correlation coefficient for scores on those two scales was -0.63, further suggesting differentiation of the two phobic disorders. Furthermore, the designated agoraphobics, compared to social phobics, were older, developed their phobia at an older age, were more likely to be female, judged

Table 11-1
PBI Scores of Whole Phobic Group and and Matched Controls

PBI Scale	Phobics		Controls		
	Mean	SD	Mean	SD	t test
Maternal care	21.0	8.0	26.7	7.8	4.39†
Maternal protection	15.9	8.5	13.0	7.8	2.06*
Paternal care	18.9	9.8	23.8	8.8	3.38†
Paternal protection	13.5	8.8	11.1	5.8	1.98*

*$p < 0.05$; †$p < 0.001$

themselves as more "dependent on others," and judged themselves as "more approved of by others." These findings suggested that separate analyses should be performed for those categorized clinically as agoraphobics or as social phobics by Shaw.

The case–control comparisons (Table 11-3) show that while the agoraphobics scored their parents as less caring, this was significant only in relation to the mothers. By comparison, social phobics scored both their parents as less caring and as more protective than controls; therefore, it appeared worthwhile to determine those components of overprotection most clearly associated with social phobic symptoms. This was

Table 11-2
Comparison of Respondents Categorized as Having Agoraphobia or Social Phobia

Variable	Agoraphobia ($n = 41$)	Social Phobia ($n = 40$)	Test
Mean age (years)	42.5	35.7	$t = 3.25$**
Mean age of onset of phobia (years)	26.5	17.3	$t = 4.65$†
Median social class	3.0	2.6	Median test = 2.94
Sex			
Females	36	26	
Males	5	24	$\chi^2 = 20.22$†
Median agoraphobic rating score	3.5	0.1	Median test = 60.62†
Median social phobic rating score	0.9	2.8	Median test = 24.61†
Self-rating of "approved of by others"	2.5	3.0	$t = 2.24$*
Self-rating of "dependent on others"	2.0	2.8	$t = 2.45$*

From Parker, G. Reported parental characteristics of agoraphobics and social phobics. *British Journal of Psychiatry,* 1979, *135,* 555–560. Reprinted with permission.
*$p < 0.05$; **$p < 0.01$; †$p < 0.001$

Table 11-3
Mean PBI scores of Phobic Patients and Matched Controls

Phobic Group and PBI Scale	n	Patients	Controls	t Test
Agoraphobics				
Maternal care	41	19.9	27.2	4.14†
Maternal protection	41	14.0	13.6	0.23
Paternal care	39	21.0	24.5	1.65
Paternal protection	39	13.0	11.9	0.61
Social phobics				
Maternal care	40	22.1	26.2	2.16*
Maternal protection	40	17.7	12.4	2.54*
Paternal care	36	16.7	23.0	3.30**
Paternal protection	36	14.1	10.1	2.48*

From Parker, G. Reported parental characteristics of agoraphobics and social phobics. *British Journal of Psychiatry*, 1979, *135*, 555–560. With permission.
*$p < 0.05$; **$p < 0.01$; †$p < 0.001$

attempted by correlating the social phobic score of each social phobic subject against his score on each high protection item of the PBI for each parent. Higher social phobic scores were most strongly associated with the infantilization items ("Did not want me to grow up"; "Tended to baby me") for each parent, but significance was achieved only in relation to the mothers (Table 11-4).

In order to compare broad types of parenting, the assignment of parents by the patients and controls to the PBI quadrants was examined. The results of separate analyses for the agoraphobics and social phobics are shown in Table 11-5. The agoraphobics differ from controls in paren-

Table 11-4
Intercorrelations Between Total Social Phobic Scores and Individual PBI Protection Items for Social Phobic Patients

PBI Protection Scale Item	Mothers	Fathers
8. Did not want me to grow up	+0.33*	+0.20
9. Tried to control everything I did	+0.10	+0.04
10. Invaded my privacy	+0.12	0
13. Tended to baby me	+0.38†	+0.20
19. Tried to make me dependent on her/him	+0.20	−0.04
20. Felt I could not look after myself unless she/he was around	+0.22	−0.14
23. Was overprotective of me	+0.21	+0.13

*$p < 0.025$; †$p < 0.01$

Table 11-5
Assignment of Parents to PBI Quadrants by Agoraphobic Patients, Social Phobic Patients, and Matched Controls

Group	Parent	High Care–Low Protection		High Care–High Protection		Low Care–Low Protection		Low Care–High Protection		χ^2
Agoraphobics										
Patient	Mother	9	(0.3)§	2	(0.2)	11	(7.1)	19	(3.6)	20.86*
Control	Mother	21		10		2		8		
Patient	Father	14	(0.9)	4	(0.5)	7	(0.8)	14	(1.9)	2.00
Control	Father	15		7		8		9		
Social phobics										
Patient	Mother	9	(0.4)	6	(0.5)	5	(0.7)	20	(4.7)	9.56‡
Control	Mother	16		10		7		7		
Patient	Father	5	(0.2)	2	(0.5)	11	(0.8)	18	(4.0)	12.43†
Control	Father	14		4		13		5		

*$p < 0.001$; †$p < 0.01$; ‡$p < 0.05$
§Relative risk calculations are shown in parenthesis.

tal assignment of their mothers, who are overrepresented in the two low care quadrants, but do not differ in assignment of their fathers. The relative risk of agoraphobics assigning a parent to the quadrant of low care–high protection (i.e., the relevant quadrant suggested by the literature review) was 3.6 for mothers, 1.9 for fathers, and 3.3 for assigning either one or both. The social phobics differed significantly from controls in the assignment of both their mothers and their fathers. They were most likely to assign parents to the quadrant low care–high protection, the relative risk for the latter assignment being 4.7 for mothers, 4.0 for fathers, and 9.0 for assigning either one or both.

DISCUSSION

A response rate of 66 percent is acceptable for a group of patients initially seen 5–7 years previously.

Information recorded at that time was used to established that respondents did not differ from nonrespondents in judging the degree of maternal or paternal affection, which were important variables for the present study. Very few of the agoraphobics had changed their address in the preceding 7 years, and 80 percent replied to the questionnaire. By comparison, only 56 percent of the social phobics responded, and of the nonrespondents most had moved from their last address and not left a forwarding address. This finding of a differential mobility between the agoraphobic and social phobic subjects suggests another difference between the two groups.

While the whole phobic group scored their parents on the PBI scales as less caring and as more protective than controls, comparisons of the social phobics and agoraphobics on several measures suggested some independence of the disorders. Separate analyses showed a differential relevance of PBI scale scores. Social phobics scored both parents as low on care and high on protection, while agoraphobics differed from controls only in scoring lower maternal care.

PBI quadrant assignment of the agoraphobics' parents produced some interesting and potentially misleading findings. The relative risk of their assigning a mother to the quadrant suggested by the literature (i.e., low care–high protection) was 3.6, which would appear, in part, to support the views of Bowlby (1973) and other commentators that agoraphobics are frequently under the domination of an overprotective mother. However, it was established that the mothers of agoraphobics were also overrepresented in the quadrant of low care–low protection, the relative risk of their assignment being 7.1. This seeming paradox in the agoraphobics' assignment of mothers to PBI quadrants reflecting marked differences in protection is accounted for to some degree by the very low care scores they returned against their mothers. PBI quadrant assignment of fathers by the agoraphobics was not distinctive.

Quadrant assignment by the social phobics contrasted with that of the agoraphobics in that it more closely corresponded with the distribution found in anxiety neurotics and neurotic depressive groups. Specifically, the social phobics were highly unlikely to assign either of their parents to the quadrant high care–low protection and most likely to assign parents to the quadrant low care–high protection: 75 percent of the social phobics (versus 25 percent of the matched controls) assigned one or both parents to the quadrant, giving an extremely high relative risk of 9.0. The distinctive results for the two phobic disorders clearly support the approach of examining social phobic and agoraphobic subgroups as separate entities, and raise doubts about earlier studies that made no attempt to ensure that only agoraphobic patients comprised particular samples.

The case–control findings could reflect a number of influences, and several important ones are considered briefly. First it may be that phobics (before or after the development of their phobia) elicit differential parental responses. It is unlikely that the low maternal care reflects a response to the development of agoraphobia, as 85 percent of the agoraphobics developed their phobias after the age of 16 years. As 53 percent of the social phobics dated the onset of their phobia before the age of 16 years, it is possible that PBI scores could reflect a parental response to social phobia in a child. To investigate that possibility, PBI scores for those who developed the phobia before 16 years were compared with the scores of the remainder. Parental assignment to PBI quadrants did not differ for the two groups, in regard to either mothers ($\chi^2 = 3.58$, df 3) or fathers ($\chi^2 = 4.82$, df 3).

If we can assume that the phobics adhered to the PBI instructions (to score a parent as remembered in the first 16 years), then it is more likely that any anomalous parental style is an antecedent to, rather than a consequence of, phobic symptoms in childhood; that is, if social phobics elicit differential parental responses, then the parents are responding to prephobic characteristics of the children rather than childhood phobias.

Second, if a plaintive set or a mood disturbance influenced reports, then it is likely to be of greater relevance to the social phobics (who, in effect, scored both parents negatively) than to the agoraphobics (who were distinguished from the controls on only one of the four PBI scales). It would appear reasonable to propose that social phobics might have a tendency to judge relationships in a negative way, either as a constitutional characteristic or as a consequence of personality features associated with a being a social phobic.

Third, it is possible that the phobics' view of the parents could be determined by a phobic disorder in the parent influencing their caring and protectiveness. Based on discussions with the patients, Shaw had judged 16 of their mothers and 16 of their fathers to have a phobic disorder. However, no significant differences were found when PBI scores for "phobic parents" were compared with those for "nonphobic parents." The only trend suggested (by the maternal care scores for the phobic parents being 24.5 versus 20.1 for the nonphobic parents) would indicate that if a phobia influences parental characteristics it does so in quite the opposite way to that anticipated—increasing rather than decreasing maternal care.

Finally, a causal process may underlie the associations. In Chapter 5 it was noted that an indifferent or rejecting parent may increase a child's attachment behavior. Thus the finding of a marked decrement in maternal care for the agoraphobics is of considerable relevance. However, further explorations of causality are left to Chapter 17.

12
Asthma

Asthma is defined by McFadden and Austin (1977) as "a disease of airways that is characterized by increased responsiveness of the tracheobronchial tree to a multiplicity of stimuli." Those authors point out that about one-half of the cases develop before 10 years of age and, from an etiological standpoint, it is a heterogeneous disease. There are *allergic* and *idiosyncratic* subgroups; the idiosyncratic asthmatics have no personal or family history of allergy, negative skin reactions to intradermal injection of appropriate antigens, and normal serum levels of immunoglobulin E. McFadden and Austin state that emotional stress may "cause reflex bronchoconstriction by activation of vagal efferent pathways and appears to be a factor in initiating some asthmatic episodes."

A psychosomatic basis to childhood asthma has often been presumed from clinical observations and studies of parents, and the vignette of the asthmatogenic mother as an overprotective and controlling figure is not an uncommon one. Block et al. (1966) comment that many clinicians have described such a mother as "a decisive, traumatic, pathological agent in the child's environment, contributing to the development of (and) exacerbation of the child's allergic symptoms" and "many clinicians agree that the asthmatogenic mother is rejecting, dominating, overprotective, insecure and suffering from feelings of inadequacy." Such a view is broad (in implicating that parental style as a factor in both the *onset* and to the *course* of asthma), and nonspecific (in generalizing such an etiological factor to such a heterogeneous disorder).

There are two principal reasons it appears to be important to assess the relevance of parental overprotection to asthma: the validity of the vignette of the asthmatogenic mother requires close examination, and childhood asthma is a good example of the group of disorders most associated with maternal overprotection in the literature–chronic childhood illness (see Chapter 4). In addition, it would be important to assess whether overprotection, if demonstrated, tends to be associated with increased or decreased parental care.

The relevance of parental overprotection to asthma has been assessed in a number of studies, which are briefly reviewed.

Fitzelle (1959) compared the parents of 100 asthmatic children with the parents of 100 nonallergic children brought to a medical center with "diverse problems." No differences were found on parents' attitudes toward child-rearing, but the research design did not allow (by comparing parents of asthmatics with parents of children with other problems) for any statement to be made as to whether parents of asthmatics are any more dominant or possessive of their children. Purcell and Metz (1962) used the PARI (Schaefer & Bell, 1958) to measure parent attitudes and found that a group of rapidly remitting asthmatics had more punitive and authoritarian parents than a group of steroid-dependent asthmatics, who, in turn, did not differ from a nonclinical control group. Block et al. (1964), arguing against any presumption of homogeneity within psychosomatic samples, compared 35 asthmatic children scoring below the mean on a composite measure of allergic predisposition with the 27 scoring above the mean. Children who scored as having a low allergic predisposition were rated by their parents as significantly more rebellious, clinging, intelligent, jealous, nervy, and whiny, whereas their mothers were judged (on the basis of interviews, observation, and projective tests) as being overly dependent on their asthmatic child for satisfaction of their own needs, and showed a trend to be more intrusive and to allow the child less autonomy than those in the other group. The authors conclude that such mothers lacked "maternal behaviors" and that they fitted the concept of the asthmatogenic mother described in the literature and impute a relevance for these parental characteristics to the illness.

In a subsequent paper, Block et al. (1966) asked 14 psychiatrists, psychologists and pediatricians who had a special interest in asthma to rate their conceptions of a hypothetical mother of an asthmatic child, using an 100-item Q-sort technique (the clinical Q-set). Intercorrelations of the descriptions suggested poor agreement in views. A factor analysis was interpreted as suggesting that the 14 clinicians saw "three distinct personality syndromes which separately, or in conjunction, characterize the asthmatogenic mother." After further analysis, the authors conclude that clinicians generally tend to agree that the asthmatogenic mother is concerned with her own adequacy, is self-defensive and is protective of others. The possibility that the study design might have elicited a description of a stereotype rather than a valid description of mothers of asthmatic children is rejected by the authors.

Byrne and Murrell (1977) sought to determine if the mothers of asthmatics were highly anxious and overprotective of their children. A questionnaire of 50 items, assessing the ways in which people may respond to stressors and 20 items assessing maternal qualities, was generated. Mothers of asthmatic children and control mothers of children without asthma or any other chronic illness were requested to choose the degree to which the items referred to them. Separate principal component analyses of item scores were conducted for the two groups. Factor 1 for both groups suggested an anxiety dimension. Factor 2 for both groups described maternal qualities. The authors note that the factor for the mothers of asthmatics indicated "an obsessional quality not unlike the notion of over-protective maternal behaviour," while the factor for the control mothers suggested little obsessional over-concern. The authors interpret those findings as supporting the view of Purcell et al. (1969) that the obsessional and overprotective quality of the mothers' behavior acts to reinforce and thus prolong the occurrence of asthmatic symptoms in the child.

Several studies (reviewed by Purcell et al., 1969) have shown that substantial percentages of children lose their asthmatic symptoms rapidly when removed from the family home but relief from an overprotective parental system has not been proposed as a direct cause.

In a general review, Purcell and Weiss (1971) note that parents frequently report a deep sense of guilt for having produced or fostered the development of asthma in a child, and propose that guilt may be one of the antecedents of the commonly observed overprotective maternal attitudes toward the asthmatic child.

A review of the literature suggests that parents (and particularly mothers) of asthmatic children are often described as overprotective, and some writers have incriminated parental overprotection as a causal influence on the frequency and severity of asthmatic attacks—a view glorified by the concept of asthmatogenic mothers. While there is some evidence suggesting that the mothers of child asthmatics are overprotective, and are seen by clinicians as overprotective—despite varying interpretations of what might constitute overprotection and sometimes imprecise measures of that dimension (Werry, 1979)—evidence of a causal process is lacking. The present study was designed to determine if asthmatics have experienced parental overprotection (using a more rigorous measure of overprotection than those used in previous studies), and, if so, whether overprotection can be more readily viewed as an antecedent to, and thus a possible cause of asthma, or whether overprotection is more likely to be a consequence of asthma. As the relevance of parental overprotection to

Table 12-1
Comparison of Patients, Their Siblings, and the Controls on Several Variables

Group	Sex		Age (years)		Ordinal Position		
	M	F	Mean	Range	Eldest	Middle	Youngest
Patients	20	30	33.7	14–62	18	20	12
Siblings	22	28	34.0	13–65	13	25	12
Controls	20	30	33.9	16–61	—	—	—

From Parker, G., & Lipscombe, P. Parental overprotection and asthma. *Journal of Psychosomatic Research*, 1979, *23*, 295–300. Reprinted with permission.

asthma in general was to be studied, there was no attempt to select only those subjects reputed to have psychological asthma as opposed to allergic asthma.

METHOD

It was decided to study a sample of 50 asthmatics and their nonasthmatic siblings (Parker & Lipscombe, 1979b). To obtain that sample, 214 asthmatics were screened at the asthma clinic at Royal Prince Alfred Hospital, Sydney, to see if they satisfied the following criteria: development of asthma in childhood, age 14 years or over, and one or more nonasthmatic siblings living in Australia. In addition, 2 patients with language difficulties and 2 patients with no memory of their mother were excluded during the study. Each of the remaining 67 patients were asked to complete a PBI form for each parent, and their age, sex, ordinal position, and father's occupation (to determine social class) were noted. Their permission to contact a nonasthmatic sibling was obtained, and that sibling's consent was sought by telephone or by letter. Patients and siblings were told that the study sought to assess the parental experiences of asthmatics and their siblings. Screening ceased when forms had been returned by 50 siblings, giving a 75 percent response rate.

The sample comprised 30 females and 20 males with a mean age of 33.7 years. Controls were selected from the Sydney general practice group (Parker et al., 1979). They were matched exactly with the patients and their siblings on the Congalton (1969) scale of paternal social class, the distribution being as follows: I, 6 percent II, 12 percent; III, 60 percent; IV, 22 percent. There was a similar ordinal pattern for the patients and their siblings (Table 12-1). No significant differences were found between the three groups on age or sex distribution.

The principal analyses were made by means of planned contrast repeated measures of analysis of variance using the PSY program (Hewson

Table 12-2
Mean PBI Scores of Patients, Siblings, and Controls

PBI Scale	n	Patients	Siblings	Controls
Maternal care	50	26.0	26.6	27.3
Maternal protection	50	15.4	13.5	12.1
Paternal care	44	22.4	21.7	24.2
Paternal protection	44	14.4	10.5	11.5

& Bird, 1977). The first analysis sought to determine if the asthmatics scored distinctly on the PBI scales, and the subsequent analyses sought to consider the nature of any differences.

RESULTS

Mean scores for the three groups on the PBI scales are shown in Table 12-2. Six patients and their siblings were unable to complete PBI forms for their fathers due to his early death or separation. Maternal protection scores for those 6 patients (19.2) were higher than those for the remaining 44 patients (14.9). Maternal protection scores for their 6 siblings (12.7) were similar to those for the remaining siblings (13.6). These results suggested that maternal protection scores of the patients, but not of their siblings, might be influenced by early paternal loss. It appeared to be important to consider that possible confounding influence in the subsequent analyses.

The first planned contrast analysis (Contrast A) examined if asthmatics reported different parental characteristics when compared with controls. The asthmatics scored their mothers ($F = 6.02$, $p < 0.05$) and their fathers ($F = 5.32$, $p < 0.05$) higher on the PBI protection scale, but maternal care ($F = 0.88$, not significant) and paternal care ($F = 1.33$, not significant) scores did not differ. The analysis was repeated after the 6 patients who had been permanently separated from their fathers at an early age were removed. The remaining 44 patients scored their mothers as more protective than the control ($F = 3.39$), but this fell just short of the 5 percent significance level.

The nature of the greater parental protection reported by the asthmatic patients was considered by two further contrasts. First, protection scores reported by patients were compared with those of their siblings. If parental overprotection is a consequence of a child developing asthma, it would be anticipated that patients would score significantly higher than their siblings on the PBI protection scale. Contrast B in Table 12-3 pro-

Table 12-3
Planned Contrasts Examining Nature of
Greater Parental Protection

PBI Scale	n	F Ratio for Contrast B*	F Ratio for Contrast C†
Maternal protection	50	1.80	0.82
	44	0.71	0.53
Paternal protection	44	6.20‡	0.35

From Parker, G. & Lipscombe, P. Parental overprotection and asthma. *Journal of Psychosomatic Research,* 1979, *23,* 295–300. Reprinted with permission.
*Patients contrasted with their siblings; †Siblings contrasted with the controls; ‡$p < 0.05$. All others were not significant.

vides statistical support for that proposition for the fathers and a nonsignificant trend for the mothers. That trend was less apparent when those 6 patients who had faced early permanent separation from their fathers were excluded, leaving 44 cases for analysis (Table 12-3). If parental overprotection is an antecedent parental style, it would be anticipated that parents of asthmatics would be overprotective of all their children, so that the nonasthmatic siblings would report greater overprotection than controls. Contrast C in Table 12-3 provides no support for that possibility.

The assignment of parents to PBI quadrants is summarized in Table 12-4. The only significant difference in the distributions exists between maternal assignment of the asthmatics and their siblings, with the asth-

Table 12-4
Assignment of Parents to PBI Quadrants by Patients, Siblings, and Controls

Parent	Group*	High Care–Low Protection	High Care–High Protection	Low Care–Low Protection	Low Care–High Protection
Mother	Asthmatics	14	9	8	19
	Siblings	27	4	3	16
	Controls	20	12	6	12
Father	Asthmatics	12	11	8	13
	Siblings	19	4	10	11
	Controls	18	12	10	9

*Asthmatics compared to siblings: $\chi^2 = 8.58$, mothers; 5.23, fathers.
 Asthmatics compared to controls: $\chi^2 = 3.34$, mothers; 1.94, fathers.
 Siblings compared to controls: $\chi^2 = 6.61$, mothers; 4.00, fathers.
($\chi^2 = 7.82$ is required for significance at the 5 percent level).

matics being far less likely to assign their mothers to the quadrant of high care–low protection, and somewhat more likely to assign mothers to the other three quadrants. The data also suggest that asthmatics were more likely than controls to report low care–high protection, with relative risks of 1.9 for both parents, but no more likely to report high care–high protection, with relative risks of 0.7 for mothers and 1.0 for fathers.

DISCUSSION

The study was developed to take in all asthmatics attending a large asthma clinic who developed their illness in childhood. While it is clear that asthma may be induced by a large number of disparate factors, the study was not designed to favor or exclude those subjects in whom psychosocial factors may have played a part in increasing any vulnerability to asthma. Such an approach minimizes the chance of detecting disturbances in family interactions, but it does provide an overall estimate of their relevance to asthma. It is likely that the subjects included in the present study are representative of asthmatics in general in regard to etiological factors, but they may differ in having a more persistent and more severe expression of the condition.

Minuchin et al. (1975) propose a model of childhood psychosomatic illness which postulates that "certain types of family organization are closely related to the development and maintenance of psychosomatic symptoms in children." They delineate four transactional characteristics in families with asthmatic children: enmeshment, overprotectiveness, rigidity, and lack of conflict resolution. Block et al. (1966), on the basis of their review, argue for the concept of the asthmatogenic mother (as rejecting, overprotective, etc.) and hold that such a parental style contributes both to the onset and the maintenance of asthmatic symptoms.

The present study sought first to determine whether asthmatics would score their parents on the PBI as suggested by the vignette and, if so, whether such a parental style was more likely to be an antecedent to, or consequence of, asthma in the child. The case–control comparisons showed no support for the view that parents are clearly rejecting of their children, whether they are asthmatics or not. They did suggest, however, that the asthmatics had been recipients of greater parental protection than those in the control group. The finding that the fathers of the asthmatics were perceived as significantly more protective than control fathers is an interesting one, as most commentators have drawn attention to maternal overprotection only. As mothers, rather than fathers, are more likely to accompany their child for medical consultations it is hardly surprising that clinical observers have selectively attended to maternal overprotection.

The relative risk estimates of assigning a parent to the quadrant that might best approximate the description of the asthmatogenic parent (i.e., low care–high protection) were 1.9 for mothers, 1.9 for fathers, and 2.1 for assigning one or more parent. By exceeding unity they provide some support for the clinical description. However, the study sought to be more amibitious than merely quantifying that risk, by seeking to assess whether such a parental style preceded or followed the development of asthma.

While it must be conceded that there can be selective overprotection of certain children as a consequence of child, parent, or interactional factors, it might be anticipated as a general process that, if overprotection precedes the development of asthma, overprotection would be effected toward nonasthmatic as well as the future asthmatic child. More specifically, we would expect, in the present study, both the asthmatic and the nonasthmatic sibling groups to have scored parents significantly higher on the PBI protection scale than the control group. As the nonasthmatic siblings did not so differ from the controls, there is little to support the view that parental overprotection is an antecedent cause of the disease. By contrast, if parental overprotection is elicited by asthma in a child, then PBI protection scores for asthmatics should be significantly higher than scores for controls, while scores for the nonasthmatic siblings should approximate to those of the controls; these findings were demonstrated in the present study. Thus the "consequence" hypothesis in regard to parental overprotection is supported. It is suggested that overprotection is an adaptational response to a child with a chronic, unpredictable illness arousing high levels of anxiety in parents. These findings have important implications, both in consideration of the etiology of asthma and in regard to assessing the frequently described association between parental overprotection and chronic childhood illness. It is of interest to note further that the overprotection is unlikely to be caring in type, with the PBI parental style of affectionless control being the only overprotective quadrant overrepresented.

The issue of whether parental overprotection is related to the maintenance of asthma in childhood, as suggested by Minuchin et al. (1975), was not considered in the present study but is one that is worthy of close research. Clinicians often suggest that enforced periods of separation of the asthmatic child from its overprotective parent (rejoicing in the name of 'parentectomy') are beneficial. One research approach might be to study the longitudinal course of two groups of asthmatic children, matched in regard to asthma, but differing in judged extremes of parental overprotection.

13
Transsexualism

Benjamin (1966) notes that the phenomenon "of anatomic males feeling themselves to be women and anatomic females feeling themselves to be men and wanting to 'change sex' has existed in rare individuals since time immemorial." Green (1974) reviews historical evidence (reported by Hippocrates, Philo, and Juvenal) and cross-cultural studies (in Western and Eastern cultures) to conclude that the desire to adopt the opposite sex-role has been noted in numerous cultures, has an early age of onset and an apparent lifelong endurance.

The term transsexualism was used first in 1953 by Benjamin in a lecture describing the disorder (Benjamin, 1966). Although not defined in ICD-9 (WHO, 1978), *transsexualism* is defined in DSM-III (APA, 1980): "The essential features of this heterogeneous disorder are persistent sense of discomfort and inappropriateness about one's anatomic sex and a persistent wish to be rid of one's gentials and to live as a member of the other sex." It is stated that transsexualism should not be diagnosed if there is an intersex or genetic abnormality, and if the disturbance is symptomatic of another mental disorder such as schizophrenia.

Wålinder (1968) also suggests a definition with a number of criteria: (1) a sense of belonging to the opposite sex, of having been born into the wrong sex, of being one of nature's extant errors; (2) a sense of estrangement from one's own body, with all indications of sex differentiation being considered as afflictions and as repugnant; (3) a strong desire to resemble the opposite sex physically via therapy, including surgery; and (4) a desire to be accepted by the community as belonging to the opposite sex.

In considering predisposing factors the DSM-III manual suggests that extreme, excessive and prolonged physical and emotional closeness between an infant and mother, and a relative absence of the father during the earliest years, may contribute to the development of this disorder in the male. Several reports and studies, considering whether transsexuals have been exposed to parental overprotection and to deficiencies in parental care, are reviewed briefly below.

Ball (1967) compared 30 transsexuals with 30 homosexuals, 30 exhibitionists, and 94 neurotic patients, all subjects being male. Parental deprivation (undefined by the author) in the first 5 years was reported more often by transsexuals than those in the other groups. The transsexuals were more likely than the exhibitionists and the neurotics to report their mothers as dominating. Ball describes the typical father of the transsexual as either inadequate, incompetent, seriously preoccupied, withdrawn from contact with his children, or driven into a subservient role by a wife who had usurped his position and taken a controlling role. Ball suggests that the mother's role remained something of an enigma.

In an uncontrolled study, Stoller (1969) reports data from evaluative interviews with male transsexuals (5 were 6 years of age or younger). He suggests that male transsexuals were exposed to a particular type of "domineering, overprotective mother" who gave their sons a blissful closeness, and that they had a psychologically absent father. The essential pattern was too much mother, too little father. Hoenig et al. (1970) studied 50 transsexual subjects attending the Department of Psychiatry at Manchester. In 70 percent of cases the patients came from "stable families with close family ties."

Prince and Bentler (1972) obtained data from 502 readers of a transvestite journal and attempted to differentiate a group of transsexuals within the whole sample. They suggest that the possible transsexuals were very much like the majority of "true transvestites" in regard to family factors. They note that although broken homes, poor father image, and dominant mothers are generally listed as etiological factors, they found no evidence to support their relevance to members in the sample.

Pauly (1974) reviews much of the relevant literature incriminating an unhealthy parental relationship in the family dynamics of transsexuals, but points out the lack of any systematic or confirmatory study. Green (1974) obtained a sample of 38 boys aged 3–10 years who showed an "unusual degree of feminine behavior," and who were thus regarded as being at high risk for later atypical sex-role development. He determined 10 parental factors as of possible relevance to transsexualism, including materal overprotection, inhibition of boyish rough-and-tumble play in early years, excessive maternal attention and contact leading to lack of separation and individuation of a boy from his mother, maternal dominance in a family with a powerless father, and the father being physically or psychologically absent.

In a more recent report Uddenberg et al. (1979) compared the parental experiences of 12 male transsexuals seeking sex reassignment with a sample of male military conscripts. Data from interviews, although the latter were not standardized for the two groups, suggested that the transsexuals were more likely to report "unsatisfactory contact" (undefined) with parents in childhood, adolescence, and adulthood.

While there is some consistency in these reports suggesting, at least in regard to males, that the fathers of transsexuals are rejecting and emotionally uncaring, and that the mothers are unduly caring, overinvolved, and overprotective, these conclusions must be treated with some reservation; the study designs reveal various weaknesses, with the definition of a transsexual being particularly debatable in several studies. The present study was designed to clarify these issues by examining a large number of male transsexuals, and by comparing the male transsexuals with both male and female control subjects on the PBI.

METHOD

Thirty male transsexual subjects who presented as outpatients to Prince Henry Hospital, Sydney, comprised the sample (Parker & Barr, 1982). All subjects were applicants for, but not had received, sex reassignment surgery. All had been judged as potential candidates for such surgery, none had received a significant psychiatric diagnosis such as schizophrenia or intellectual retardation, and all had been diagnosed as transsexuals by the psychiatrist involved in the surgical reassignment program. Nearly all had taken estrogen medication. The majority had had homosexual, while a small number had had heterosexual, experiences.

All subjects completed the PBI for each parent and their scores were compared with those returned by the general practice controls (Parker et al., 1979). Members of the two groups were matched exactly for age and paternal social class. In view of the unique characteristics of transsexuals, the subjects were compared both with male controls and with female controls. The mean age of the subjects was 30.9 years (range 17–55 years) and their social class grouping according to the Congalton scale (1969) was as follows: I, 6.7 percent; II, 23.3 percent; III, 60.0 percent; IV, 10 percent.

RESULTS

Comparison of the transsexuals with male controls on PBI scores showed that transsexuals scored their fathers as significantly less caring and as more protective (Table 13-1). A trend to score their mothers

Table 13-1
Mean PBI Scores of Transsexuals, Male Controls, and Female Controls

PBI Scale	Transsexuals	Male Controls Means	t test	Female Controls Mean	t test
Maternal care	23.9	25.2	0.6	26.4	1.3
Maternal protection	16.8	14.8	1.0	14.8	0.9
Paternal care	16.5	23.0	2.9*	23.0	3.0*
Paternal protection	16.5	12.1	2.3†	13.5	1.6

From Parker, G., & Barr, R. Parental representations of transsexuals. *Archives of Sexual Behavior*, 1982. *11*, 221–230. With permission of Plenum Publishing Corp.
* $p<0.01$; † $p<0.05$

similarly was not significant. Comparison of the subjects with the female controls revealed similar findings apart from paternal protection scores no longer being significant.

In order to compare broad parental styles, assignment of parents to PBI quadrants was compared for the patients and the controls (Table 13-2). There was no significant difference between the subjects and the controls in assigning mothers, but a significant difference in assigning fathers. Fathers were clearly, and mothers somewhat, more likely to be assigned to the low care–high protection quadrant, and the risk of the transsexuals assigning one or more parent to that PBI quadrant was 3.3.

Contrary to expectations, fathers but not mothers had been scored highly on the protection scale; it thus seemed important to perform an item analysis to determine the most relevant components of the overprotection. The mean scores returned by transsexuals and controls for each item of the PBI scale are shown in Table 13-3. Median test analyses

Table 13-2
Assignment of Parents to PBI Quadrants by Transsexuals and Male Controls

Group	Parent	High Care–Low Protection	High care–High Protection	Low care–Low Protection	Low care–High Protection	X^2
Patient	Mother	7 (0.8)	4 (0.6)	3 (0.7)	16 (1.7)*	1.18
Control	Mother	8	6	4	12	
Patient	Father	1 (0.1)	2 (0.3)	8 (0.8)	19 (4.7)	11.04†
Control	Father	7	6	9	8	

Adapted from Parker, G., & Barr, R. Parental representations of transsexuals. *Archives of Sexual Behavior*, 1982, *11*, 221–230.
*Relative risk estimates are shown in parentheses; † $p<0.02$

Table 13-3
Comparison of Scores Returned by Transsexuals and Controls on Each Item of the PBI Protection Scale

PBI Protection Scale Items	Scores for Mothers			Scores for Fathers		
	Patients	Male controls	Female controls	Patients	Male controls	Female controls
3. Let me do those things I liked doing	1.3	0.8	1.1	1.6	0.9*	0.9*
7. Liked me to make my own decisions	1.1	0.9	1.2	1.4	0.9†	1.0
8. Did not want me to grow up	1.1	1.1	0.9	0.6	0.5	0.9
9. Tried to control everything I did	1.2	1.4	1.2	1.4	1.0	1.1
10. Invaded my privacy	1.2	1.0	1.0	1.2	0.5*	0.7
13. Tended to baby me	1.1	1.3	0.9	0.6	0.3	1.1
15. Let me decide things for myself	1.3	1.2	1.1	1.4	1.0	1.1
19. Tried to make me dependent on her/him	1.2	0.9	1.1	0.9	0.6	0.7
20. Felt I could not look after myself unless she/he was around	1.2	1.0	1.0	1.0	0.6	0.5
21. Gave me as much freedom as I wanted	1.7	1.5	1.6	2.1	1.3‡	1.1‡
22. Let me go out as often as I wanted	1.8	1.4	1.4	2.1	1.2*	1.4
23. Was overprotective of me	1.2	1.4	1.2	0.7	0.8	1.1
25. Let me dress in any way I pleased	1.9	1.8	1.4	2.1	1.6	1.4

From Parker, G., and Barr, R. Parental representation of transsexuals. *Archives of Sexual Behavior*, 1982, *11*, 221–230. With permission of Plenum Publishing Corp.
*$p<0.05$, median test; †$p<0.02$, median test; ‡$p<0.01$, median test.

revealed no differences between the two groups in the rating of mothers. It is interesting that no difference in scores is evident for the item referring directly to maternal overprotection, or the item "let me dress in any way I pleased." Several significant differences were found between the groups in the rating of fathers. Compared to male controls, the transsexuals rated their fathers as less likely to let them do those things they liked doing, as less likely to allow them to make their own decisions, as unlikely to give them as much freedom as they wanted, as more likely to invade their privacy, and as less likely to let them go out as often as they wanted. Those differences were maintained or weakened only minimally when comparison was made against the female controls. Clearly, the fathers of the transsexuals differed from the controls in being perceived as offering less freedom and less encouragement to independence and autonomy, and it was these items of the PBI scale that resulted in the transsexuals scoring their fathers significantly higher on the total protection scale. On the specific item referring to paternal overprotection no differences between transsexuals and controls were found.

DISCUSSION

This study assessed the parental representations of transsexuals and found that male transsexuals, when compared with matched controls, remembered their fathers in earlier years as deficient in care and as somewhat overprotective. A weak trend to score their mothers similarly was not significant. Both parents, but particularly fathers, were more likely to be assigned to the affectionless control PBI quadrant.

These findings could be accounted for in a number of ways. First, such a response could reflect a specific negative response set against parents, most marked against their fathers, or reflect a more general response set to judge all relationships in a critical or negative way.

Second, the transsexuals may have scored their mothers with a social desirability set so as to prevent true differences on maternal care and protection from emerging; such a possibility seems unlikely but must be conceded.

Third, the PBI could be an accurate portrayal of transsexuals' parents on those dimensions. While mothers of transsexuals are said to be especially caring and overprotective of their child, as noted earlier, such observations have been based in the main on clinical reports, usually uncontrolled and often concerning young, effeminate boys rather than definitive transsexuals. It is likely that maternal overprotection and excessive or unusual maternal care may be common in those who reach clinical attention as children; but it may be somewhat risky to impute such features as then relevant to transsexualism.

Green (1974) makes a point that is of relevance to any consideration of the present lack of differences between the transsexuals and the controls in the scoring of mothers—that the mothers would have to be perceived as caring and as expressing desirable goals if they were to provide a role model for their transsexual sons. Thus, if a mother were to be too deviant (at least in fundamental parental characteristics) the child might be disinclined to identify too closely. If findings from this study are replicated, then it would appear unlikely that maternal overprotection is a deleterious influence on the development of core gender identity. It is far more likely, and supported by studies of intersexed children (Green, 1969), that gender identity is established principally by clear and unambiguous raising of a child as belonging to one or the other sex. Thus one would expect specific parental maneuvers, such as encouraging feminine behavior in the early years and interaction with the child as if he were a girl, to be more influential than the more general parental dimensions of care and protection in any causal process linking parental characteristics with transsexualism in a boy.

This study does confirm the common observation that fathers of transsexuals provide an insufficiency of care. Reasons for low parental care were not explored in the present study. They might include a primary deficiency in the fathers, a response to early effeminacy in their sons, or a secondary consequence of factors in the marital interaction. However, rather than the fathers being psychologically "absent," as suggested in the literature, they scored higher than control fathers on the protection scale and were overrepresented in the affectionless control quadrant of the PBI. Item analysis showed that the fathers in the two groups differed on several items reflecting a rather homogeneous dimension. In essence, it appeared that the fathers of transsexuals were perceived as being less able to allow the development of independence and autonomy in their sons. The finding that paternal protection scores for the subjects approximated those for female controls more closely than those for male controls could suggest the fathers had acted toward their sons as if they were daughters in terms of overprotectiveness, or that the subjects acted toward their fathers as if they were girls, thereby eliciting that degree of protection appropriate in such circumstances. Either way, the results clearly suggest the relevance of further close study of the fathers of transsexuals.

14
Dependency, Hypochondriasis, and Utilization of Primary Physicians

Care-eliciting behavior is defined by Henderson (1974) as "a pattern of activity on the part of one individual which invokes from another responses which give comfort." Henderson distinguishes normal and pathological care-eliciting behaviors, principally on the basis that the latter are disruptive for the individual and/or those around him, but notes that both have a common aim of bringing important others closer. He suggests that care-eliciting behaviors have their origin in the attachment behaviors of infancy, with the repertoire of behaviors enlarging during childhood and adolescence, and that such behaviors have evolutionary importance. As noted in Chapter 5, Bowlby (1977) argues that, in normal development, exploratory behavior is antithetical to attachment behavior in a child. On theoretical grounds it might then be supposed that parental overprotection would act to reduce exploratory behavior in a child (with resulting effects on its competence, autonomy, and capacity to develop relationships of mutuality) as well as increase any diathesis to pathological care-eliciting behaviors.

In adults, dependency, hypochondriasis, and excessive utilization of primary physicians may well reflect pathological care-eliciting expressions, and parental overprotection is often implicated as a determinant of each. In Chapter 3 and 4 a number of references are given for the proposition that parental overprotection renders a child dependent and hypochondriacal. Freedman et al. (1975) state that recipients of overprotection are conditioned not to want to leave a protected environment so that they "crave dependency and develop an overly dependent relationship with helping professionals" (Martin, p. 1737). Thus dependency, hypochon-

Dependency, Hypochondriasis, and Utilization of Primary Physicians

driasis, and general practitioner utilization form the focus of research attention in this chapter.

As well as assessing parents in terms of their PBI scores, it appeared important to make some attempt to assess parental responses to illness in the subjects when children. Such a methodology allows assessment to be made of any broad links between fundamental parental dimensions (as assessed by the PBI) and responses made to an ill child and, in addition, allows consideration of whether scores on the outcome variables might relate more to PBI scores or to "illness response" scores.

METHOD

Instruments

As noted above, parental care and protection scores were assessed with the PBI. To assess parental response to illness in childhood, subjects were provided with a (written) vignette of an illness that might have physical and/or psychological origins and might have resisted clear interpretation by parents. The instruction was as follows:

> Children often have mild headaches, abdominal pains and other discomforts. Looking back on your childhood, when you had pains or discomforts of that type, how would your mother/father have reacted? Put a mark somewhere along the line that best describes her/his usual reaction.

Visual analogue scales were used to measure four perceived parental attitudes (sympathy, concern, anger, and likelihood that the child had a real rather than an imaginary illness) and two perceived behavioral responses (likelihood to call the doctor, and likelihood to keep the child home from school). Respondents could score a parent between the following anchor points:

He/she was:	As sympathetic as anyone could be	Totally unsympathetic
	Totally unconcerned	As concerned as anyone could be
	As angry as anyone could be	Not at all angry
He/she would:	Always call the doctor	Never call the doctor
	Always keep me home from school	Always make me go to school
	Always act as if I had a worrying physical illness	Always act as if I had an imaginary illness

To assess dependency in the adult subjects 12 items from the dependency scale of the Depressive Experiences Questionnaire (Blatt et al.,

1975) were selected that appeared least likely to imply disapproval or disparagement, and most likely to reflect need for care, personal closeness and security in affectional bonds. All items are scored on a 7-point scale ranging from "strongly agree" to "strongly disagree".

Hypochondriasis was measured by the 9-item "general hypochondriasis" subscale of the Illness Behavior Questionnaire developed by Pilowsky and Spence (1976).

Procedure

Patients attending three Sydney general practices were asked to complete the series of self-report questionnaires (Parker & Lipscombe, 1980). Fifty-five patients were excluded as they were outside the age range of 21–65 years, and a further 17 refused to take part. The lower age limit had been imposed in an attempt to obtain patients with developed patterns of attenders. The final sample comprised 64 female and 36 male subjects with a mean age of 36.4 years (SD 13.0 years); 35 subjects were from one practice and 32 from each of the other two practices. The social class of the study group was slightly higher than that of the Sydney general population. The estimates of a subsample ($n = 36$) of their general practice visits over the preceding 12 months were compared against the number of visits recorded in practice files and were found to correlate ($r = 0.88$, $p < 0.001$). The mean number of visits estimated by patients in the preceding 5 years was 23.2, and the number of the visits in those two periods correlated moderately ($r = 0.66$, $p < 0.001$), suggesting some consistency in patterns of attendance.

RESULTS

Mean scores on the PBI were similar to normative data obtained in its development (see Appendix II): paternal care, 24.6 (SD 8.2); paternal protection, 12.8 (SD 7.6); maternal care, 27.5 (SD 6.8) and maternal protection, 14.5 (SD 8.2). On the visual analogue scales only one significant sex difference was noted: male subjects were more likely than female subjects to report their fathers as responding to their illnesses as if they were imaginary. Present age of subjects had an influence on only one dimension, with older patients reporting their mothers ($F = 4.05$; df 2, 92; $p = 0.02$) as more likely to keep them home from school. The mean score on the dependency measure was 54.0 (SD 8.8), the mean on the hypochondriasis measure was 2.1 (SD 2.1), and the mean number of visits to the general practitioner in the preceding year was 6.2 (SD 8.1).

Assessment of the degree to which the three dependent measures

Dependency, Hypochondriasis, and Utilization of Primary Physicians 213

might be related to each other was made first. Hypochondriasis scores correlated +0.13 with the number of general practice visits and +0.18 with dependency scores, while the number of general practice visits correlated +0.04 with dependency scores. The possibility that these low correlations could have emerged from skewed distributions in scores was investigated but not confirmed. In summary, results from the several analyses suggested a trend for hypochondriasis scores and number of general practice visits to be weakly and positively associated, a weak positive association between hypochondriasis and dependency scores, but no association at all between the number of practice visits and dependency scores.

As in previous studies using the PBI the care and the protection scales were negatively associted ($r = -0.50$ for mothers and -0.31 for fathers). To assess any relationship between parental illness responses and more general characteristics of care and overprotection, any protection component to the PBI Care scale scores and any lack of care component to the Protection scale scores were partialed out. Associations between care and protection (as independent parental dimensions) and visual analogue scores reflecting parental response to illness in a child are presented in Table 14-1. Results suggest that parents who were perceived as caring (in that they received a high score on the derived PBI Care scale) were perceived as having been highly caring of their child during illness, as unlikely to regard the child's illness as imaginary, as likely to call the doctor, and as less likely (particularly in the case of fathers) to respond with anger. Mothers perceived as protective (i.e., high scorers on the derived PBI Protection scale) were remembered as responding with anger to childhood illness, while protective fathers were remembered as likely to send the child to school.

Single-order correlations (r) between parental variables and subjects' scores on the three dependent measures (dependency, hypochondriasis, and utilization of general practitioner) are given in Table 14-2. In addition, the degree to which parental variables predict scores on each dependent variable was assessed by performing separate stepwise multiple regression analyses, and examining the variance explained. The more important trends and significant findings are summarized in Table 14-3.

The possibility that higher scores on any of the three dimensions might represent a categorical subgroup and be distinguished from the others in terms of parental characteristics was assessed. Thus subjects scoring higher than 1 SD on each scale were compared with the remaining subjects on the parental measures. The significant differences found on the visual analogue scales are listed in Table 14-4; none were found on the PBI scales.

Finally, PBI quadrant assignments of parents were examined for those scoring highest and those scoring lowest (dichotomized around the

Table 14-1
Relationship Between PBI Scores, Indicating Independent Parental Characteristics, and Visual Analogue Scores, Indicating Parental Responses to Illness

PBI Scale	Sympathy	Concern	Anger	Suggest Illness Imaginary	Call Doctor	Keep Child Home from School
Maternal care	+0.21*	+0.27†	−0.13	−0.06	+0.12	+0.03
Maternal protection	−0.03	+0.08	+0.18*	+0.06	−0.06	−0.15
Paternal care	+0.48**	+0.45**	−0.34**	−0.19*	+0.33**	+0.08
Paternal protection	−0.06	−0.04	+0.09	+0.03	−0.11	−0.28†

From Parker, G., & Lipscombe, P. Early parental characteristics as influences on adult dependency, hypochondriasis and utilization of primary physicians. *British Journal of Medical Psychology*, 1980, 53, 355–363. With permission.
*$p<0.05$; †$p<0.01$; **$p<0.001$

Table 14-2
Three Multiple Regression Analyses Assessing Influence of Parental Variables on Dependency Scores, Hypochondriasis Scores, and Number of General Practice Visits in Preceding Year

Parental Variable	Dependency		Hypochondriasis		General Practice Visits	
	r	Variance (%)	r	Variance (%)	r	Variance (%)
PBI scale: ongoing parental characteristics						
Maternal care	+0.03	0.6	+0.09	4.2*	−0.02	0.1
Maternal protection	+0.13	0	0	0	+0.07	0
Paternal care	+0.18	3.5	−0.14	3.0	−0.06	0
Paternal protection	+0.28	7.9†	+0.26	9.7†	+0.15	0.8
Visual analogue: mother's response to illness						
Sympathy	−0.04	1.2	+0.01	1.8	−0.08	2.1
Concern	0	0.3	+0.14	1.2	+0.01	0.4
Anger	+0.07	0.2	+0.01	0.5	−0.04	0.5
Suggest illness imaginary	−0.05	2.2	−0.24	1.0	−0.15	2.7
Call doctor	+0.14	2.8	+0.30	8.8†	+0.22	4.7*
Keep home from school	−0.08	1.1	+0.15	0	−0.16	7.1*
Visual analogue: father's response to illness						
Sympathy	+0.27	0	+0.13	2.8	−0.11	0.1
Concern	+0.17	0.6	+0.12	0.9	+0.09	2.4
Anger	−0.14	0.5	−0.13	0.9	+0.12	0.5
Suggest illness imaginary	−0.26	1.8	−0.05	0.5	+0.12	0
Call doctor	+0.27	11.2**	+0.09	0	−0.05	2.6
Keep home from school	+0.07	0.6	+0.15	0.2	−0.10	0.4
Total		34.5		35.5		24.4

From Parker, G., & Lipscombe, P. Early parental characteristics as influences on adult dependency, hypochondriasis, and utilization of primary physicians. *British Journal of Medical Psychology*, 1980, 53, 355–363. With permission.
*$p<0.05$; †$p<0.01$; **$p<0.001$

Table 14-3
Summary of Regression Analyses Reported in Table 14-2

High-Scoring Outcome Variable	Predictors	
	PBI Results	Visual Analogue Results
Dependency	Father caring and protective	Parents call doctor, and treat illness as real
Hypochondriasis	Father protective but low on care	Father shows sympathy
	Mother caring	Mother calls doctor, and shows sympathy
General practice utilization	—	Mother less likely to allow child to stay home from school, but more likely to call the doctor and treat the illness as real

From Parker, G., & Lipscombe, P. Early parental characteristics as influences on adult dependency, hypochondriasis, and utilization of primary physicians. *British Journal of Medical Psychology,* 1980, 53, 355–363. With permission.

mean) on each of the three independent variables (Table 14-5). Relative risk estimates were not calculated for the low care–low protection quadrant as the low cell numbers could create quite spurious estimates. The only significant difference in PBI quadrant distribution occurs for the dependency variable in the assignment of mothers. The relative risk calculations suggest the clearest difference to be an overrepresentation of the mothers of the highly dependent subjects within the low care–high protection quadrant. For the remaining comparisons assignment of parents by high scores is not clearly overrepresented in that quadrant. Instead, the quadrant most likely to have parents of high scorers overrepresented is the high care–high protection one.

DISCUSSION

Before considering the relationships between parental ratings and the dependent variables, several important reservations must be expressed. The usual and important limitations of accepting retrospective judgments of parental attitudes and behaviors is of key relevance. Moreover, a large number of analyses were performed—a procedure that runs the risk of achieving significance by chance. In addition, as routine general practice patients were assessed it is unlikely that many "deviant" patients (in terms of the dependent variables) were included, reducing the likelihood of demonstrating strong associations. Finally, there are likely to be many

Table 14-4
Comparison of High Scorers (>1 SD) on
Care-Eliciting Dimensions with the Remainder:
Significant Differences in Visual Analogue Scores

Outcome Measure	Visual Analogue Results** for High Scorers	z test
General practice utilization	Mother more likely to call the doctor	2.6*
Hypochondriasis	Mother more likely to treat illness as real	3.2*
	Mother more likely to call the doctor	2.5†
	Mother more likely to keep the child home from school	2.0‡
	Father more likely to keep the child home from school	2.0‡
Dependency	Mother more likely to keep the child home from school	2.0‡
	Father more likely to call the doctor	2.2‡

From Parker, G., & Lipscombe, P. Early parental characteristics as influences on adult dependency, hypochondriasis, and utilization of primary physicians. *British Journal of Medical Psychology,* 1980, 53, 355–363. With permission.
‡$p<0.05$; †$p<0.025$; *$p<0.01$
**High scorers on the outcome measures distinguished themselves by these perceptions of their parents' responses to their illness as reflected in visual analogue scale results.

factors of greater relevance to the outcome variables (and especially to general practice utilization rates) than parental variables. Clearly, the present study is no more than an exploratory one, suggesting areas possibly worthy of more rigorous attention. For that reason a large number of analyses were performed and reported to suggest potential directions for future research. Nevertheless, it would be unwise, in the absence of replication, to consider any other than the broad findings.

Two such findings are worth emphasizing. First the study suggests that parental responses to childhood illness are associated with the broader dimensions of care and protection that have been the major interest in the research studies. Parents who were perceived as caring on the PBI were remembered as responding to illness in their children with care and concern, and as likely to seek medical attention for them. By contrast, parents who were rated as overprotective on the PBI were re-

Table 14-5
Assignment of Parents to PBI Quadrants by High and Low Scorers on the Three Outcome Variables*

Variable and Group	Parent	High Care–Low Protection	High Care–High Protection	Low Care–Low Protection	Low Care–High Protection	χ^2
Dependency						
High scorers	Mother	15 (0.6)†	6 (0.5)	1	21 (3.8)	8.86**
Low scorers	Mother	21	11	4	9	
High scorers	Father	13 (0.5)	16 (2.7)	5	9 (0.9)	4.54
Low scorers	Father	20	8	7	10	
Hypochondriasis						
High scorers	Mother	14 (1.0)	10 (2.8)	1	9 (0.6)	4.50
Low scorers	Mother	22	7	4	21	
High scorers	Father	8 (0.4)	10 (1.2)	8	8 (1.2)	7.14
Low scorers	Father	25	14	4	11	
General practice utilization						
High scorers	Mother	14 (0.7)	7 (0.8)	4	14 (1.2)	3.17
Low scorers	Mother	22	10	1	16	
High scorers	Father	12 (0.6)	13 (1.7)	6	8 (0.9)	1.99
Low scorers	Father	21	11	6	11	

*Sample reduced after deleting those who only scored one parent. †Relative risk estimates are shown in parentheses. **$p<0.05$

membered as responding with anger and as likely to send their children to school rather than allowing them to stay home. The latter results may seem somewhat surprising, for it might be imagined that overprotective parents would be more likely to keep a possibly sick child home from school. Perhaps this response reflects the "control" construct of the protection PBI scale. However, the associations could merely reflect an overall perception of the parent influencing ratings on the scales.

The second general finding was that scores on the three outcome measures were associated more strongly with parental responses to illness than with PBI scores when the variance estimates were examined. This finding is speculated on shortly.

Findings in regard to the three outcome variables are of interest. The suggestion that overprotected children develop an overly dependent relationship with helping professionals was noted earlier; it has also been suggested that those exposed to deficiencies in parental caregiving may subsequently seek surrogate care from a health care provider, their general practitioner. The present study examined whether subjects who considered they had experienced anomalous parental care and/or parental protection visited their general practice more frequently than those exposed to more optimal parenting: no support for either proposition was found. The finding that those subjects with high general practice utilization rates remembered their mothers as responding to their childhood illnesses by being likely to call the doctor might suggest a modeling response.

While the study did not confirm the view that deficiencies in parental characteristics promote dependency on helping professionals, it must be acknowledged that only one aspect of dependency on a general practitioner (i.e., utilization rate) was examined. It may be that those exposed to parental anomalies depend on health professionals in ways other than by excessive attendance, perhaps in their perception of, and psychological reliance on primary care physicians. Unfortunately, the study did not assess evaluative aspects of patient–physician interactions.

By comparison, two PBI variables (high parental protection and high maternal care) predicted higher hypochondriasis scores, as did one visual analogue score (mother being highly likely to call a doctor when the child was ill). In addition, high scores on the hypochondriasis measure were most likely to assign their mothers to the high care–high protection quadrant, suggesting that they were likely to be recipients of a caring form of overprotection. The visual analogue scores of those who scored highest on the hypochondriasis measure suggest that there was a highly vigilant response by the mothers and that they were more likely to accept somatic complaints as "real" (directly and in their greater likelihood to keep the child home and to call a doctor). Baker and Merskey (1982) compared

PBI scores of hypochondriacal patients and matched controls. While the two groups did not differ on parental care scores, the hypochondriacal patients scored their mothers 75 percent higher and their fathers 35 percent higher on the protection scale. That result and the present study therefore suggest that parental overprotection is relevant to hypochondriasis but that the overprotection is not associated with an insufficiency of parental care, as found for the neurotic disorders considered in Chapters 9, 10, and 11.

Variable associations between PBI scores and dependency were found. In the regression analysis higher paternal protection and higher paternal care scores were predictors of higher dependency scores (and explained 11.4 percent of the variance). PBI quadrant assignment (when subjects were dichotomized on the basis of dependency scores) confirmed that highly dependent subjects were most likely to allocate their fathers to the high care–high protection quadrant (the relative risk was estimated at 2.7). Visual analogue scores suggested that in response to somatic symptoms in childhood the fathers of the more highly dependent subjects showed a highly sympathetic response and were likely to respond to the illness, directly and indirectly, as if it were "real." While a maternal relevance was not suggested by the regression analysis, PBI quadrant assignment showed that highly dependent subjects were most likely to assign their mothers to the quadrant low care–high protection (relative risk was 3.8).

Until the results are replicated and clarified it would be unwise to draw other than tentative conclusions regarding the findings linking dependency and hypochondriasis levels with parental reports. First, it could be that the more dependent and hypochondriacal subjects showed such traits in childhood and elicited such differential parental characteristics. Such an explanation would support Henderson's (1974) view that dependency and hypochondriasis have a care-eliciting component.

Second, associations could be determined by a more general genetic factor such as anxiety. Higher levels of anxiety in a family could both influence parental characteristics and promote higher levels of hypochondriasis and dependency in children. Such a possibility of a shared familial variable rejects any causal process.

The third explanation presupposes a causal process linking certain parental characteristics with higher level of hypochondriasis and dependency. Bianchi (1971), in a study of patients with a disease phobia, found evidence of parental oversolicitude, overprotection, and excessive babying. He suggests that phobic disorder is more likely in those programmed to regard disease as an imminent risk and that parental overprotection promotes a sense of personal vulnerability. The vignette of childhood illness given to subjects in the present study was purposely vague, but was one that a pediatrician would regard as reflecting emotional stress in most instances (Apley et al., 1978). Accepting that most children will experience such symptoms in childhood, it is likely that their interpretation of those symptoms will be influenced by parents' responses. It is known that cultural factors produce wide variations in illness behavior (Zborowski, 1952), and families are, in effect, minicultures capable of influencing a child's interpretations of the salience and severity of ths symptoms. It is conceivable that parents who overprotect a child and/or respond selectively with greater solicitude to its illness promote a sense of vulnerability and insecurity in their child, thus promoting dependency. By responding to the illness as if it were a "real" physical illness of some severity and requiring external medical help, they encourage a somatic interpretation of stress symptoms and so promote any hypochondriacal tendency.

A feature distinguishing high scorers on all outcome variables from remaining subjects in the present study was that high scorers remembered one or more of their parents as more likely to call the doctor in response to childhood illness. The origins and impact of that parental response would appear worthy of greater consideration.

The present study suggests a relevance for early parental experiences in the expression of dependency, hypochondriasis, and recourse to medical treatment. If Henderson's suggestion that such expressions have a care-eliciting component can be accepted, then the study suggests several ways in which that component may be related to child-rearing practices.

15

Cross-Cultural Studies of Parental Overprotection: Jewish and Greek Families in Australia

Although cultural variations in parental behaviors have long been noted (Erikson, 1965; Mead, 1955), most reports have been descriptive. Anecdotal reports of parental overprotection within certain cultural or racial groups are common, yet remain unverified by objective studies.

The present studies were designed to determine if the degree of parental overprotection varied within separate Australian subcultures and, if so, the origins and implications of any differences. It is generally agreed that methodological difficulties in cross-cultural research are reduced by selecting groups within the same national framework, and by selecting subcultures that are sizable and identifiable within the wider culture. Jewish and Greek families resident in Sydney were therefore selected for study. The vignette of the Jewish mother as overprotective, intrusive, and controlling is a commonly drawn one, although there would appear to be only one research attempt at quantification. In that study (Fernando, 1975), maternal overprotection was equally common among Jews and Protestants in both depressed and normal groups, although the reliability and the validity of the overprotection measure were not established. In support of the decision to study Greek subjects was a finding from a separate study (Chapter 16), that subjects judged as overprotective were more likely to be born in Greece or Italy.

Before the particular studies are described, some general comments should be made about the circumstances of Greek and Jewish families in Australia. The Australian population was relatively culturally homogeneous prior to the World War II. In the late 1940s, as the population declined in number, the Australian Government initiated an intensive immigration program, seeking migrants from Greece and a number of other countries. Whereas only 0.5 percent of the New South Wales population was Greek-born in 1940, extensive immigration increased the proportion of Greek-born to 1.8 percent in 1954 and to 8.7 percent in 1977 (Bottomley, 1979). From 1945 to 1968 nearly 200,000 Greeks migrated, so that at present they form the second largest ethnic group in Australia.

As Bottomley notes, emigration has a long history in Greece, the majority of Greeks having lived away from Greece since the third century B.C. By having a concept of a "community of Hellenism" not restricted by geographical boundaries (termed *ethnos*), overseas Greeks have successfully established communities and developed institutions that preserve traditions. By maintaining ties with their homeland, by having a distinctive and comprehensive culture, and by having a number of ethnically defined institutions (e.g., the Greek Orthodox Church), the Greek popoulation forms a large, highly organized minority in Australia. By maintaining their cultural patterns in Australia, the Greek population maintains what Bottomley (1979) termed a partial universe within Australian society.

The family is a basic element in the Greek cultural framework. Central values are an honorable family reputation and respect for the parents. Men are expected to be manly, assertive, and courageous, while women are required to be chaste and restrained. Bottomley (1979) notes that relationships within the family are authoritarian.

Bottomley states that Greek attitudes to children had been poorly studied and that only scrappy comparative evidence is available. She draws attention to the relative informality of Australian families when contrasted with the authoritarianism of Greek families. Greek girls are closely restricted, and the sexes segregated. Marriage is by arrangement and there is no dating in the traditional sense. By comparison, Australian adolescents are comparatively unrestricted—they are allowed to date and choose their spouses freely.

Bottomley (1979) studied 23 second-generation Greeks, ranging in age from 21 to 40 years. The majority volunteered that "Greek-style" kinship traditions were valuable enough to be worth preserving in Australia. There were few exceptions to this view, although one woman described the close-knit family as a "strait-jacket."

Thus it would appear that there is a continuity of Greek traditions in Australia, that those traditions are maintained for positive reasons, and that they provide meaning, communication, and social networks. If Greek parents are more overprotective of their children, evidence might be anticipated within second-generation Greek children matched against an appropriate Australian group.

According to Bergman (1978), there were at least seven Jewish convicts, if not more, in the First Fleet, and by 1840 more than 800 Jewish convicts had been transported to New South Wales and at least 200 to Van Dieman's Land. Most were descendants of poor Europeans who had migrated to England in the 18th century to escape persecution, and some 98 percent of the convicts were of Ashkenazi (Western Jewish) stock. While the first Jewish organization (a burial society) in Australia was formed in 1817, and Jewish worship established by 1820, the establishment of a "proper and officially recognised Jewish congregation" (Bergman, 1978) had to wait the arrival of the free settlers in 1828, and the first rabbi in 1831. The first synagogue was established in Sydney in 1832, and a more permanent one opened in 1844.

Bergman points out that Australian Jews never had to face the challenges of emancipation faced by their brethren in Europe as Australian Jewry needed no emancipation. Immigration prior to 1850 was slow, but the first immigration wave occurred in the following decade as a consequence of gold discoveries. A second wave occurred in the last years of the 19th century following persecution of Jewish people in Eastern Europe. Another wave occurred after World War I, and a further one between 1933 and 1947 (when approximately 9,000 came to Australia) following Nazi persecution in Europe.

Data from the 1971 Australian Census suggest that there are about 70,000 Jewish people in Australia, with Sephardic Jews representing a clear minority.

Bergman describes the current Jewish community as largely a middle-class one; members neither drink nor gamble much, have a comparatively high living standard, support the arts, welfare organizations, and the State of Israel, and have a minimal crime rate. Encel and Buckley (1972), as well as Medding (1968) have commented on the marked ethnic commitment by the Australian Jewish community.

The present study considers whether Jewish children in Australia experience an overprotective parental network. There are several reasons Jewish parents might be seen by their children as overprotective. As suggested at the beginning of this chapter, Jewish parents (and mothers in particular) are often described as overprotective. In addition, it might be imagined that any ethnic group subject to persecution and decimation might invest in and protect their youth as a consequence. Certainly, there is some anecdotal support for the view that Jewish parents in Australia are seen as overprotective, with Medding (1968) noting overindulgence as well as attempts to smother the younger generation. Finally, and nonspecific to Jewish groups, it may be that immigrants, as a consequence of migration, are more likely to overprotect their children.

METHOD

Study 1: Greek Families

Permission to study all school students in years 11 and 12 was obtained from the principals of two high schools in Sydney regions reputed to have a high proportion of Greek residents (Parker & Lipscombe, 1979a). The principals of a boys' school (Enmore) and of a girls' school (Marrickville) gave permission for data to be collected anonymously during designated class time. All students in those classes, apart from those with poor English, were asked to complete a PBI form for each parent and note their own age, ordinal position, family composition, and years in Australia, the mother's country of birth, and the father's occupation (to determine social class).

Data were collected from 120 boys at Enmore Boys High School. Analysis was restricted to 104 as 16 forms were incomplete or incorrectly filled in. When classified according to their mother's country of birth, there were 47 Greek, 19 Australian, and 17 Yugoslav students; 13 other countries were listed as the place of birth for the mothers of the remaining 21 boys. Data were collected from 179 girls at Marrickville Girls High School, and 2 incomplete forms were deleted. Classified by their mother's country of birth, there were 78 Greek, 27 Australian, 18 Portugese, 16 Yugoslav, 8 Lebanese, and 7 British students. The mothers of the remaining 23 girls had been born in another 13 countries.

Study 2: Jewish Families

The principal of a Jewish private school in Sydney was contacted to obtain a group of Jewish adolescents (Parker & Lipscombe, 1979a). He gave permission for data to be collected anonymously from students in years 11 and 12 at that school; all were Jewish and day pupils. Students were requested to note their age, sex, ordinal position, years in Australia, parents' ages, and father's occupation (to determine social class), and to complete a PBI for each parent. The principals of two private schools in the same region allowed contact with students in the same years to provide anonymous control data. In addition to providing similar data, those in the control group were requested to note their religion and if they were boarders. Forms completed by Jewish students and by boarders in the control group were excluded from analysis.

Data from 81 Jewish students and from 74 non-Jewish controls were compared. Sixty-four percent of the Jewish students had been born in Australia and only 11 (14 percent) had migrated to Australia in the preceding five years. By comparison, 78 percent of the controls had been

Table 15-1
Comparison of Groups on Sociodemographic Variables

Variable	Study 1		Study 2	
	Greek Students	Australian Controls	Jewish Students	Non-Jewish Controls
Number	125	46	81	74
Mean age (years)	16.3	16.1	16.6	16.3
Sex (M:F)	47:78	19:27	37:41	37:37
Mean social class	3.5	3.2	1.8	1.9
Mean number of siblings	2.0	2.8	1.7	1.8
Ordinal position				
Only	8	3	7	11
Eldest	51	11	26	12
Middle	26	11	23	22
Youngest	33	18	24	29

born in Australia and only 2 (3 percent) had migrated to Australia in the preceding five years.

RESULTS

The data in Table 15-1 show that the control groups were adequate in each study in terms of age, social class (Congalton scale), and sex ratio. The Jewish students could not be distinguished in ordinal position from their controls ($\chi^2 = 6.3$, df 3, NS), nor the Greek students from their controls ($\chi^2 = 4.7$, df 3, NS).

Study 1

PBI scores revealed no differences on parental care scales; on the parental protection scales, the Greek girls scored both their mothers and their fathers approximately 70 percent higher than the Australian controls (Table 15-2). These findings suggested that it might be useful to compare the scores returned by the Greek and Australian girls on each protection item of the PBI scale to determine whether Greek parents are overprotective in distinctive ways. As shown in Table 15-3, on all 6 items suggesting the encouragement of independence and autonomy (items 3, 7, 15, 21, 22, and 25), the Greek girls scored both their parents lower than did the Australian girls, with the differences being significant for 8 of the 12 comparisons. On the 7 items assessing components of protection (items 8, 9, 10, 13, 19, 20, and 23), the Greek girls scored their parents higher than did the Australian girls on all but one comparison; significant differences

Table 15-2
Study 1: Mean PBI Scores of Greek Students and Australian Controls

	Males			Females		
PBI Scale	Greek Students	Australian Controls	t test	Greek Students	Australian Controls	t test
Maternal care	26.7	27.5	0.42	28.0	28.8	0.44
Maternal protection	14.7	13.7	0.55	16.6	9.9	4.07*
Paternal care	22.6	21.8	0.38	24.0	26.6	1.56
Paternal protection	14.7	12.2	1.15	17.4	10.4	4.25*

*$p < 0.001$

were found for 9 of the 14 comparisons. Significant differences on the item analyses were found for both parents on 3 items, suggesting that the Greek girls clearly saw both parents as generally overprotective (item 23), as encouraging dependency (item 19), and as tending to baby them (item 13, an infantilization item). Significant differences were found on the control item (item 9) for fathers only, and on intrusion (item 10) and infantilization (item 20) items for mothers only. Only 1 of the 13 items did not appear to differentiate the Greek and Australian girls; this was an infantilization item (item 8) assessing whether parents did not want their child to grow up.

After differences had been demonstrated between the Greeks and Australians, further analyses were performed to determine if there was any evidence of an acculturation effect, as 59 percent of the Greek children had been born in Australia. Scores on the parental protection measures for the Australian-born and the remaining Greek students were compared (Table 15-4): results showed that the Greek students born in Australia did not score their parents differently than those born outside Australia on the protection scales.

Parental protection scores of Greek students who were born in Australia, Greek students who came to Australia in early childhood (up to 6 years of age), and Greek students who came to Australia in late childhood (after the age of 6 years) were then compared. The results (Table 15-5) suggest a curvilinear relationship linking protection scores with length of stay. Those Greeks who migrated in early childhood tended to score both parents higher on protection than those who were born in Australia, who in turn scored their parents as more protective than those who migrated to Australia in later childhood.

Finally, PBI quadrant assignment of parents of the Greek and of the control students was examined (Table 15-6). As the numbers in many of the cells are small, the statistical analyses should be considered with some

Table 15-3
Study 1: Comparison of Scores Returned by Greek and Australian Girls on Each Item of the PBI Protection Scale

PBI Protection Scale Item	Mothers			Fathers		
	Greek	Australian	χ^2	Greek	Australian	χ^2
3. Let met do those things I liked doing	1.9	2.3	2.04	1.4	2.3	12.6†
7. Liked me to make my own decisions	1.7	2.3	6.01*	1.4	2.3	8.08**
8. Did not want me to grow up	0.8	0.6	0.30	0.9	1.0	0.03
9. Tried to control everything I did	1.2	0.7	1.46	1.2	0.6	7.28**
10. Invaded my privacy	1.1	0.5	8.77**	0.8	0.4	3.32
13. Tended to baby me	1.4	0.6	9.06**	1.2	0.8	4.25*
15. Let me decide things for myself	1.7	2.3	7.40**	1.4	2.1	10.58**
19. Tried to make me dependent on her/him	1.4	0.6	6.15*	1.1	0.5	8.96**
20. Felt I could not look after myself unless she/he was around	1.1	0.6	5.04*	0.8	0.7	0.56
21. Gave me as much freedom as I wanted	1.3	1.7	4.97*	1.0	1.6	3.27
22. Let me go out as often as I wanted	1.3	1.9	10.40**	0.7	1.8	17.63†
23. Was overprotective of me	1.6	0.8	6.78**	1.6	0.9	6.25*
25. Let me dress in any way I pleased	2.2	2.3	0.73	2.1	2.7	1.82

From Parker, G., & Lipscombe, P. Parental characteristics of Jews and Greeks in Australia. *Australian and New Zealand Journal of Psychiatry*, 1979, *13*, 225–230. With permission.
*$p < 0.05$; **$p < 0.01$; †$p < 0.001$

Table 15-4
Study 1: Mean PBI Scores of Australian-Born Greeks and Greeks Born Outside Australia

Group	PBI Scale	Australian-born Greeks	Greek Students Born Outside Australia	t test*
Total	Maternal protection	16.2	15.4	0.59
	Paternal protection	16.3	16.5	0.18
Boys	Maternal protection	13.9	16.4	1.85
	Paternal protection	14.1	15.3	0.79
Girls	Maternal protection	17.3	15.6	0.97
	Paternal protection	17.0	18.0	0.53

From Parker, G., & Lipscombe, P. Parental characteristics of Jews and Greeks in Australia. *Australian and New Zealand Journal of Psychiatry*, 1979, *13*, 225–230. With permission.
*All differences were not significant.

caution. Significant differences in PBI quadrant assignment were found for all analyses except for the male students scoring their fathers. Relative risk analyses produced interesting findings. Both the male and female Greek students were less likely to assign their parents to the high care–low protection quadrant. They were somewhat more likely (and especially for the Greek girls scoring their mothers) to assign parents to the low care–high protection quadrant. They were most likely to assign their parents to the high care–high protection quadrant.

Table 15-5
Study 1: Influence of Varying Length of Residence in Australia on Parental Protection Scores of the Greek Students

PBI Scale	Born in Australia ($n = 61$)	Migrated at Age 0–6 years ($n = 26$)	Migrated After Age 6 years ($n = 26$)	F Ratio
Maternal protection	16.0	17.5	13.3	2.45
Paternal protection	16.4	18.9	12.9	5.06*

From Parker, G., & Lipscombe, P. Parental characteristics of Jews and Greeks in Australia. *Australian and New Zealand Journal of Psychiatry*, 1979, *13*, 225–230. With permission.
*$p < 0.01$

Table 15-6
Study 1: Assignment of Parents to PBI Quadrants by Greek Students and Australian Controls

Parent	Sex of Child	Group	High Care– Low Protection	High Care– High Protection	Low Care– Low Protection	Low Care– High Protection	χ^2
Mother	Female	Greek	25 (0.3)*	24 (5.9)	2	24 (2.5)	14.8**
		Control	15	2	4	4	
	Male	Greek	11 (0.2)	12 (1.8)	11	13 (1.1)	8.0†
		Control	9	3	0	4	
Father	Female	Greek	20 (0.3)	24 (5.4)	4	27 (1.4)	9.3†
		Control	13	2	3	7	
	Male	Greek	11 (0.7)	12 (5.5)	10	14 (1.3)	3.7
		Control	5	1	6	4	

*Relative risk estimates are shown in parentheses. They were not calculated for the third quadrant due to small cell numbers.
**$p < 0.01$; †$p < 0.05$

Study 2

Both the Jewish boys and the Jewish girls scored their mothers as less caring than did the controls (Table 15-7). On the protection scales the only difference was that the Jewish girls rated their fathers as less protective than fathers of the controls

PBI quadrant assignment of parents (Table 15-8) showed no significant differences in the distribution of the two groups. However, relative risk calculations showed that the female Jewish students were somewhat more likely to assign their mothers to low care–high protection quadrant. There is no clear suggestion of any greater risk of assigning a parent to the high care–high protection quadrant—the expression of a caring form of overprotection.

Table 15-7
Study 2: Mean PBI Scores of Jewish Students and Non-Jewish Controls

	Boys			Girls		
PBI Scale	Jewish Students	Non-Jewish Students	t test	Jewish Students	Non-Jewish Students	t test
Maternal care	27.9	30.7	2.41*	27.8	32.0	2.37*
Maternal protection	13.2	10.8	1.37	11.5	10.9	0.40
Paternal care	26.2	25.8	0.31	28.3	26.0	1.34
Paternal protection	10.8	9.3	1.08	9.1	12.7	2.59*

*$p < 0.025$

Table 15-8
Study 2: Assignment of Parents to PBI Quadrants by Jewish Students and Non-Jewish Controls

Parent	Sex of Child	Group*	High Care–Low Protection	High Care–High Protection	Low Care–Low Protection	Low Care–High Protection	χ^{2**}
Mother	Female	Jewish	18 (0.9)†	6 (0.4)	6	7 (1.9)	7.00
		Control	19	13	1	4	
	Male	Jewish	17 (0.8)	5 (1.0)	3	7 (1.2)	0.40
		Control	19	5	2	6	
Father	Female	Jewish	23 (1.2)	5 (0.8)	5	4 (0.6)	1.34
		Control	21	7	3	6	
	Male	Jewish	21 (1.4)	4 (1.4)	3	4 (0.8)	1.49
		Control	19	3	6	5	

*Sample reduced after deleting those who only scored one parent; **All differences were not significant
†Relative risk estimates are shown in parentheses. They were not calculated for the third quadrant due to small cell numbers.

DISCUSSION

It is generally agreed that methodological difficulties in cross-cultural research are reduced by selecting groups within the same national framework. That approach was adopted in the two studies and considerable care was taken to select suitable controls in terms of age, sex, social class, and Sydney residence.

Contrary to expectation, there was no support for the anecdotal view that Jewish parents are distinctly overprotective. The only significant difference was that the Jewish girls scored their fathers lower than control fathers on the PBI protection scale. It would be unwise to suggest that this study disproves the myth when there are marked regional differences in Jewish customs and cultures. Two explanations of the generally negative findings can be offered. First, it may be that acculturation has occurred, a phenomenon whereby extensive borrowing of cultural elements takes place in the context of superordinate–subordinate relations between societies. Thus, any cultural tradition of parental overprotection may have been weakened by time and/or acculturation and is not relevant in this Australian group.

Second, it may be that the control students were selected to match the Jewish students *too* well, in parents being equally ambitious for, and overinvolved with, the children. In this sense, it has been said that Jewish people are "like everyone else . . . but only more so" (Encel, personal communication). Thus, when a control group is selected that matches the Jewish students in belonging to a high social class, in attending an expensive private school, and in perhaps having parents who were highly ambitious for their children, differences between the groups in reporting overprotection should perhaps not be expected. That explanation is not supported when the mean protection scores for the Jewish students is compared with our *general* control PBI data, (Parker et al., 1979), but could be supported by the care scale results; that is, while Jewish students scored their mothers as less caring than mothers of the matched controls, their maternal care scores were not distinctive compared to those of the Sydney general practice controls.

In the Greek family study high PBI protection scores were confined to the Greek girls. Quadrant assignment, however, showed that both the Greek boys and the Greek girls were more likely to assign their parents to the affectionate constraint quadrant, indicating a caring form of overprotection. The uncaring variant of overprotection, affectionless control, was slightly more likely for Greek girls scoring their mothers, but for no other comparison.

The failure to demonstrate significant differences on parental protection scores between those Greek students born in and those born out of Australia might suggest that overprotection is not a sequela of migration. However, there was a trend for those Greek students who came to Australia as babies or young children to score higher on the protection scale than Greek students who came at a later age and Greek students born in Australia. The possibility that overprotection is enhanced by migration with young children is worthy of closer study.

Results suggest clearly that Greek mothers and fathers are perceived by their daughters as overprotective and that this parental characteristic is not weakened by the broader Australian culture, at least for the first generation. In comparison with the study of Jewish students, this finding argues against acculturation in the Greeks and for the power of cultural mores to resist change despite exposure to a foreign culture. It is important to emphasize that the "overprotection" that is overrepresented in the Greek study is distinguishable from that documented in chapters 9–11, which consider neurotic disorders, in that it is associated with a sufficiency, rather than a decrement in parental care.

Finally, the study demonstrates that the PBI is sufficiently sensitive to discriminate cultural differences in parental overprotection.

16

Influences on Maternal Overprotection

In this chapter an attempt is made to consider a key issue: what factors in a mother, in her child, or in the mother–child interaction serve to promote maternal overprotection? Such a question might best be addressed by undertaking a longitudinal study, ideally commencing at least some years before the subjects had had their first child, and involving a large sample of clinical and nonclinical subjects. A number of constraints prevented this approach and resulted in a more limited one. A nonclinical group of middle-aged women was studied, each woman's degree of overprotectiveness being assessed by her child on the PBI.

Several expressions of overprotection were considered. First, overprotection was assessed using the Protection scale of the PBI as a continuous variable. Raw scores on that scale indicate lesser or greater degrees of protection, and overprotection was defined as a Protection scale score at or above a level determined on statistical grounds. As noted in Chapter 7, Protection scale scores are not independent of Care scale scores on the PBI. As high protection scores reflect low care, in part, there is a need to ensure against predictors of low care being isolated. Thus, some analyses were repeated with any care component effectively partialed out of the PBI protection score. Finally, a need was perceived to study influences on the development of the two overprotective syndromes delineated by the relevant quadrants, particularly the affectionless control one, which appears to delineate a risk factor most particularly to the neurotic disorders studied in chapters 9–11.

Among the possible research approaches, the option of studying mothers actively engaged in the care of young children was rejected as levels of overprotection might be influenced by ephemeral situational factors or reflect age-specific factors. As it seemed more useful to assess factors influencing overprotection as an enduring parental style, mothers were selected whose children had progressed beyond childhood and adolescence. PBI scores returned by a young adult group might be less likely to reflect acute situational factors and be more likely to provide an overall picture of the mother during the formative years of mother–child interaction.

As a group of postgraduate teacher trainees had been studied in another, and quite different, research program, it was expedient to select a group of mothers for study from members of that sample. Although not an ideal group, it was a statistically adequate sample of representative general population mothers; therefore, the possibility appeared remote that the composition of the group was so distinct as not to reflect factors influencing maternal overprotection, especially when within-group comparisons were made. Furthermore, the final sample was selected from available subjects on a random basis, with only one exclusion criterion (mother living outside the Sydney metropolitan area) being specified; this limited the possibility of sampling a unique group.

A nonclinical group was studied quite deliberately so that refined hypotheses might be tested subsequently in clinical groups. A lengthy, semistructured interview assessing retrospective information was developed. The validity of this procedure might be criticized as it has been shown on numerous occasions (Cox & Rutter, 1976) that reports about the past are subject to inaccuracy and distortion. Furthermore, it is also likely that mothers, when questioned about their maternal role, would tend to report in a favorable way. Such reservations should be noted now, although they will be addressed and answered to some extent in the discussion.

Perhaps a final reservation that should be noted at this stage is that a large number of variables are assessed; this procedure allows chance to bring about significant results. However, as Levy (1943) suggested a large number of variables to be relevant in his classic study of a clinical group, it appeared important that those and related issues be assessed in the study. From a statistical point of view, when the number of variables exceeds the number of subjects, extreme caution in interpretation is necessary. In defense of this practice, it should be stated that the aim of the study was to define a number of relevant factors (from a wider list of postulated and hypothesized ones) that might then be assessed and further refined by replication studies in clinical and nonclincal groups.

As noted above, in designing the semistructured interview an attempt was made to assess the relevance of variables suggested by Levy and other commentators, which are considered extensively in Chapter 3.

METHOD

Subjects

The Principal of Sydney Teachers' College was approached, and he offered access to those students who had previously obtained a Bachelor degree in Arts or Science, and who were undertaking a 1-year training course for primary or secondary school teaching (Parker & Lipscombe, 1981). Two lecturers from the College were asked by the Principal to prepare a list of lectures to be attended by all those students. It was agreed that the author would attend those scheduled lectures and that the students would not receive prior information of the study or of changes in their scheduled program.

In April–May 1978 the author attended 24 classes with a total of 396 students present and explained to each group that he wished to perform a 5-year longitudinal study with the principal aim of investigating the influence of social factors on their adaptation and on their depressive experience. A further aim was to obtain some information on their memories of their parents' early attitudes and behaviors. It was explained that interviews of some of their mothers would be sought to obtain historical information, particularly details of the trainees' early childhood development. The students were requested to complete a 3-page questionnnaire. This comprised separate PBI scales for each parent and a self-esteem scale (Rosenberg, 1965). Respondents were asked to provide their name, address, address of their mother, age, sex, age of each parent, occupation of their father (to assess social class), and the age and sex of all siblings. They were to state if they had "any objections if we contact you at a later stage to take part in the projected study."

Eleven of the trainee teachers did not return the questionnaires. Of the remainder, 102 declined to take part in the studies, 66 had mothers who were resident outside the Sydney metropolitan area, and 18 noted that their mothers had died. The remaining 199 consented (33 expressing reservations) to take part in the studies. Of those 199 volunteers, 100 were selected randomly using a table of random numbers. Each selected trainee was contacted by telephone and permission was sought for his or her mother to be contacted about arranging an interview. At that time, 12 students refused permission for their mothers to be contacted, 2 mothers were rejected as they lived outside the metropolitan area, and 2 mothers were rejected as language difficulties appeared insurmountable. Subsequently, the mothers were contacted to arrange an interview, being told that the researchers wished to study the family background of those trainees taking part in the longitudinal study: 75 agreed and 9 declined to be interviewed.

Scores returned by the 75 index students whose mothers were inter-

Table 16-1
Mean Scores of Students Whose Mothers Were Interviewed Compared with Mean Scores of Remaining Students on Initial Questionnaires

Variable	Mothers Interviewed ($n = 75$)	Remainder ($n = 310$)
Age of student (years)	22.5	23.6
Sex of student (male:female)	1:2.2	1:2.0
Ordinal position of student	1.8	1.4
Number of siblings	2.4	2.2
Self-esteem score	1.7	1.4
PBI scale		
Maternal care	26.5	26.7
Maternal protection	14.8	15.2
Paternal care	21.2	23.0
Paternal protection	12.6	12.9
Mother's age (years)	50.8	52.3
Father's age (years)	53.2	55.3
Mean social class of father (Congalton 4-point scale)	2.5	2.5

viewed were compared with those returned by the remaining 310 students on the initial questionnaire. Similar scores were found on all variables (Table 16-1), and it was concluded that the final sample was representative of the wider group initially screened.

Sociodemographic details of the mothers in the final sample are shown in Table 16-2. The mean age was 51 years (SD 5.6, range 42–65 years); 25 percent were born overseas, compared to 27 percent of the adult Australian population. The social class of the sample, whether assessed from their husbands' or their fathers' occupation, was slightly higher than that of the Sydney general population.

Recording of Data

An interview schedule, consisting of open-ended and precoded questions and a number of self-report instruments, was designed and pilot interviews were conducted. All interviews were conducted in the homes of the mothers by a psychologist, Penny Lipscombe, over a 7-week period commencing in July 1978. A translator was required to interview one Italian and four Greek mothers; for these women the self-report instruments were translated (and checked against back-translation by an additional translator) and presented in the same sequence used for the other mothers.

Table 16-2
Sociodemographic Details of Mothers Interviewed

Characteristic	No.	Percentage		
Nationality at birth				
Australian	56	75		
British	5	7		
Greek	4	5		
Italian	2	3		
Other	8	10		
Religion				
Protestant	45	60		
Roman Catholic	21	28		
Jewish	1	1		
Other	6	8		
Agnostic/Atheist	2	3		
Level of education completed				
Primary	10	13		
Intermediate	38	51		
Secondary	23	31		
Tertiary	4	5		
Marital status				
Currently married	67	89		
Currently widowed/divorced	8	11		

	Socioeconomic Class*			
Relation	I	II	III	IV
Husband	12	35	45	8
Father	5	35	49	9
(Sydney general population norms)	4	17	61	20

*Data from Congalton, A. *Status ranking list of occupation in Australia.* Melbourne: Cheshire, 1969.

After obtaining sociodemographic details, the interviewer assessed the family background, education, socialization, work, marital, obstetric, and sexual histories of the mothers. Information on the early development of the index child and the mothers' response to and involvement with the child was obtained.

At the completion of the general interview the rater judged each mother (on the basis of attitudes expressed during the interview) on the following possible components of maternal overprotection: excessive contact, infantilization, encouragement of dependency, control, and indulgence (each scored on a 5-point scale). On a similar basis, overprotection was assessed as a general dimension on a 5-point scale.

Self-report instruments were used for the following:

1. Assessment was made of each mother's judgment of normal milestones in childhood. The items being listed in the Results section.

2. Assessment was made of each mother's judgment as to when a child should be *allowed* to perform each of several independent behaviors and tasks (e.g., using matches, crossing a road alone). The full list of items is given in the Results section.

3. An attempt was made to assess each subject's inherent maternal responses. Subjects were asked to view a color plate of a radiant mother with a young and healthy looking baby, and imagine that they were the mother. Each subject then scored the degree ("definitely," "probably," "to some degree," "possibly," "definitely not") to which she agreed with 11 different statements assessing the intensity of several maternal responses such as concern, responsibility, wish to protect, etc. The full list of items is given in the Results section.

4. An attempt was made to assess each subject's inherent response to illness in a child. As it has been suggested that certain characteristics in a child (such as deformities, ugliness, unusual beauty) may elicit overprotection from some mothers, a projective device was used. Subjects were shown a picture of a baby with its head shaved, and surrounded by a worried and concerned mother, doctor, and nursing sister. Subjects were asked to imagine themselves as the mother in the photograph and reflect the intensity of several responses by scoring several items on a 5-point scale coded as for the previous test. The degree of certainty of serious illness, the warmth felt toward the child, and other responses were assessed. The full list is given in the Results section.

5. The mothers were asked to complete a PBI about themselves as they remembered their behaviors and attitudes to the index child in his or her first 16 years, in an attempt to assess the validity of the PBI. (Results from those analyses are given in Chapter 7). Subjects were asked to complete a PBI for both of their natural parents to assess the degree to which their own parents were seen as caring and overprotective.

6. Assessment of several personality characteristics was made. The Costello-Comrey (1967) trait anxiety scale, designed to measure any predisposition to anxious-affective states, was used. A Fear Survey Schedule, designed by Marks and Mathews (1979), was completed; it provides separate scores for agoraphobic, social phobic, and blood and injury phobias, as well as a composite score. A dependency measure was given, derived from those 12 items that had the highest factor loadings on the dependency scale of the Depressive Experience Questionnaire (Blatt et al.,

1975) and had face validity as a measure of intensity of needs for care, personal closeness, and security in affectional bonds. A self-report measure designed by Levine and Scotch (1978) allocating people along a Type A/Type B behavioral dimension was included. Friedman and Rosenman (1960) describe the Type A behavioral pattern as being marked by time urgency and competitiveness, and there is some evidence to suggest that Type A characteristics reflect an expression of anxiety. These several measures were included to test the author's hypothesis that overprotective maternal characteristics reflect an expression of high maternal anxiety. Another hypothesis, that overprotective maternal characteristics reflect obsessional personality traits (often defined as traits of orderliness, control, and inflexibility) was tested by two measures. Rotter (1966) designed a Locus of Control measure which he held determines the degree to which a subject judges that he controls the environment (internal locus) or perceives himself as sensitive to external pressures (external locus). Those with a more internal locus of control are said to be more resistant to influence and less likely to yield to pressure (Lefcourt, 1976). An abbreviated 9-item version of Rotter's scale, developed at the School of Psychology at the University of New South Wales was given to the subjects. In addition, the 14-item Lynfield Obsessional/Compulsive Questionnaire (Allen & Tune, 1975), assessing the degree to which subjects rate obsessions and compulsions as interfering in their daily life, was given.

Almost without exception the 75 mothers were cooperative at the interview. Few sought any further details about the research or asked to be informed about results. Some months after the interview the mothers were sent another questionnaire for completion and return. All responded to this request, which can be interpreted as confirming that the earlier interview had been neither alienating nor excessively intrusive, and that the goodwill of the sample had not been lost.

RESULTS

Interview Data

Interview data are summarized to provide a description of the sample.

Family Background

The mothers had a mean number of 2.9 (range 0–10) siblings. For the greater part of their first 16 years, 7 had an absent father and 2 an absent mother. Twenty-nine (39 percent) acknowledged that they had taken up a surrogate maternal role as a child in helping with household chores and the care of young children. This was done voluntarily by 11; the others did it because a parent was ineffective (9), because of pressure of a large family (8), or because a parent was absent (1); 15 stated that they enjoyed such role, 12 appeared neutral, and 2 acknowledged some resentment.

Education

The majority (64 percent) had completed their intermediate year of secondary school. Only 9 percent acknowledged an active dislike of school. Approximately 47 percent had their wish to continue their education frustrated: 12 had that wish frustrated by a parent's decision, 12 by economic circumstances, and 3 by marriage.

Employment

Only 29 percent were able to get the employment or educational choice they had sought at the time of leaving school. Once employed, the subjects had very stable work histories, 62 percent remaining in one job until marriage and only 1 spending less than 1 year in each position. Despite the initial frustrations faced by the majority, 68 percent rated their work as pleasurable and only 8 percent were dissatisfied. Almost equal numbers regarded their work as a career or as a means of filling in time until marriage; 59 percent worked after marriage, and only 16 percent of the sample expressed any dissatisfaction with their work status after marriage.

Socialization

A majority (88 percent) stated that they had made friends with ease at school, and 41 percent still kept in contact with such friends. Before marriage, 20 percent regarded themselves as loners and had no boyfriends, while 25 percent had had more than 4 boyfriends.

Marriage

The sample married at a mean age of 23.4 years (range 17–35 years). Subjects were asked to assess the relevance of a number of possible factors that attracted them to their future husbands. In rank order, with the most relevant reasons listed first, they noted the following qualities: dependable, intelligent, physically appealing, supportive, generous, capable of providing financial support, friendly and outgoing, ambitious, and dependent on subject. While most subjects married for reasons positive toward their husbands, 7 married to get away from home and 8 primarily in order to have a family; 2 Greek women had arranged marriages.

Children

At the time of marriage, 40 percent remembered a strong desire to have children and 7 percent a wish not to have children; the remainder considered their desire for children to be unremarkable. The sample nominated a mean of 3.3 (range 0–8) children as their ideal at marriage. While 23 percent felt their first child was born too soon, and 15 percent later than intended in the marriage, only 7 subjects considered that alteration to be of any importance. The index child was an only child in 20 percent, the eldest child in 45 percent, and the youngest in 17 percent of cases.

Obstetric History

Prior to the birth of the index child, 20 had problems in conceiving, 31 had one or more miscarriages, 1 had a stillbirth, and 1 had an abortion. The pregnancy of the index child was planned by 63. While 12 subjects remembered being distressed at being pregnant, this feeling abated for all but 1 mother. A complication of that pregnancy occurred in 27, and 8 had been unworried and only 5 worried by that event.

At the birth of the index child the mothers had been married a mean of 4.4 years (range 0–18 years); 15 mothers and 15 children had a perinatal complication of some sort, with 9 of the mothers being worried to at least some degree by either event. On first seeing their child, 11 percent felt at least some doubts about coping, 72 percent a significant sense of responsibility, and 9 percent little or no pleasure. In the postpartum period 1 remembered a severe, and 5 a mild depression. After the birth of the index child, 8 percent had problems in conceiving, 17 percent had miscarriages, 5 percent had abortions, and 1 percent had a stillbirth.

Developmental History of Index Child

In the first year, 13 percent of the children had a serious illness, 3 percent a serious accident, and 4 percent an operation. In their subsequent childhood years, 19 percent had a serious illness, 20 percent a serious accident, and 40 percent an operation. These events caused considerable concern to 30 mothers, moderate concern to 9 mothers, and were of little or no concern to 10 of the relevant mothers.

To assess the possibility that maternal overprotection might be elicited by early personality characteristics in the child, the interviewer asked each mother to rate her child during his or her early years on several characteristics. The frequency distribution of the mothers' responses to the several traits or dimensions assessed is shown in Table 16-3.

Eighty-four percent of the children were breast-fed. Data shown in Table 16-4 suggest that most of the index children began walking and

Table 16-3
Early Childhood Characteristics as Rated by Mothers

Description of Child	Mother's Assessment		
	"Markedly like my child" (%)	"Moderately like my child" (%)	"Not like my child" (%)
Clumsy	1	9	89
Shy/timid	20	25	55
Hesitant about going to school	8	7	85
Preferred playing by himself/herself	8	8	84
Independent	46	32	22
Physically frail	3	4	93
Sickly	0	1	99
Assertive	36	22	42

washing themselves at the expected time, but that they were more likely to be rated as advanced, rather than slow, in mastering several other developmental stages.

Marital and Social Relationships

Nineteen women acknowledged significant marital problems at one time or another; in order of frequency they were adultery on the part of the husband, extensive absence from the home by the husband, the husband preventing his wife pursuing her career, and excessive drinking by the husband. Only 1 woman reported any responsibility for a marital problem, stating she had placed her children before her husband. Overall, 83 percent stated that currently they were satisfied, and 7 percent unsatisfied with their marriage; the remainder were widowed or divorced. The majority had either a quiet social life with a few friends (47 percent)

Table 16-4
Development of Children as Rated by Mothers

Developmental Task	Usual Age of Mastery (Years)	Mothers Rating of Child Compared to Norm		
		Slow (%)	Normal (%)	Advanced (%)
Toilet trained	2–3	1	40	59
Feeding himself/herself	2	8	36	56
Washing himself/herself	3–4	16	47	37
Dressing himself/herself	4	11	42	47
Talking	2	4	47	49
Walking	1	31	53	16

or a minimal social life (33 percent); 9 women felt that the index child had reduced their social life. Fifteen percent reported the sexual relationship with their husband as unsatisfactory.

Assessment of the PBI as an Appropriate Measure of Maternal Overprotection

The validity of the PBI Protection scale as a measure of overprotection was assessed specifically within the sample. As the assessments are reported in Chapter 7 (see validity study 2), they are only summarized here. First, when subjects' PBI scores (i.e., mother's scores for themselves on the PBI) were correlated with the children's PBI scores, significant coefficients were returned, although the mothers scored themselves generally as less protective than did the children themselves (Table 7-5). Second, PBI protection scores, whether returned by the mothers or by the children, correlated significantly (and the levels of the associations were strikingly similar) with two dependent measures assessing state and trait depression in the children (Table 7-6). Finally, mothers distinguished as "overprotective" (described shortly) on the PBI were distinguished (at interview and with the rater being blind to PBI scores) as overprotective in general, and as evidencing most of the components of overprotection (Table 7-7) (dependency, infantilization, indulgence, and control) suggested by Levy (1943). These results suggested that the PBI could be accepted as an appropriate measure of maternal overprotection.

Distinctions Between Overprotective and Other Mothers

As the first step in considering possible influences determining maternal overprotection, two subgroups of mothers were formed:

- *Overprotective mothers:* those 15 mothers who were scored 1 SD above the mean on the PBI protection scale by their index child.
- *Other mothers:* the remaining 60 mothers whose children gave them a score of 22 or below on the protection scale.

The two groups were compared and contrasted on all study variables. The distributions of responses to all variables were examined first and decisions were made to retain scale scores, collapse scales to create more equally distributed responses, or delete variables, depending on the likely adequacy and usefulness of the data. Comparisons were made by chi square tests (using Yates' correction where appropriate) or by the nonparametric Z test, Z being a normally distributed statistic transformed from the Mann-Whitney statistic U. The latter test is appropriate for ordinal data and when there are two independent samples (one variable, two groups). It tests the difference in central tendency and is more powerful than the median test since it uses the rank value of each case, not just its location relative to the median.

Sociodemographic Details and Family Background

Several possibly relevant variables in the index child and in the mother are compared in Table 16-5. Sex of the child did not emerge as a significant variable. The possibility that only children might be overprotected was unlikely to emerge in the present study as only 2 of the index children were only children. There was a nonsignificant trend for the only/eldest children to have a mother in the overprotective mother group, but the ordinal position of the mothers themselves in the two groups was unremarkable. Mothers in the two groups differed in country of birth and religious upbringing, with the latter differences reflecting a preponderance of Greek Orthodox subjects in the overprotective group. When subjects born in Mediterranean countries (4 Greeks and 2 Italians) were excluded from the analysis, the significant differences on the nationality and religion variables no longer existed.

Mothers in the overprotective group were no more likely than the other mothers ($\chi^2 = 0.03$, df 1) to acknowledge having taken up a surrogate maternal role in their own childhood. However, there was a trend ($\chi^2 = 4.27$, df 2) for overprotective mothers who did take up such a role to report enjoyment, rather than to resent or be neutral about such a role.

Education

The overprotective mothers had a lower level of education than the other mothers ($\chi^2 = 6.50$, df 2, $p<0.05$), and this difference appeared to be accounted for completely by the lower education of the mothers of Mediterranean birth. No other differences were found or suggested on other education variables.

Employment

The overprotective mothers showed a nonsignificant trend ($\chi^2 = 4.80$, df 2) to report not reaching the work ambitions they had entertained at school. No other differences were found or suggested on variables assessing work stability, satisfaction, seeking a career before marriage, or employment after marriage.

Socialization

No differences were suggested on variables assessing degree of sociability, and number and enjoyment of close interpersonal relationships.

Table 16-5
Comparison of Overprotective and Other Mothers on Sociodemographic Variables

Variable	Overprotective Mothers	Other Mothers	Test
Children			
Age	21.6	22.8	$Z = 1.35$
Sex			
Male	3	20	$\chi^2 = 0.47$
Female	12	40	
Ordinal position			
Only/eldest	11	29	$\chi^2 = 3.07$
Second child	2	18	
Remainder	2	13	
Social class (from father's occupation)	2.3	2.6	$Z = 0.89$
Mothers			
Age at interview	49.5	51.2	$Z = 0.95$
Nationality			
Australian	8	48	$\chi^2 = 18.6^*$
Greek	4	0	
Italian	1	1	
English	1	4	
Other	1	7	
Religion			
Protestant	7	38	$\chi^2 = 21.5^*$
Catholic	2	19	
Jewish	1	0	
Other	5	1	
None	0	2	
Ordinal position			
Only child	2	7	$\chi^2 = 2.53$
Only daughter	2	18	
Eldest	4	12	
Middle	4	9	
Youngest	3	14	
Number of siblings	3.1	2.9	$Z = 1.06$
Father's social class	2.5	2.6	$Z = 0.24$
Age when married	23.6	23.3	$Z = 0.35$
Age at having index child	27.9	28.4	$Z = 0.63$
Age of husband at birth of index child	30.4	30.8	$Z = 1.04$
Years married when index child born	3.5	4.6	$Z = 0.91$

*$p < 0.001$

Marriage

Age at marriage did not distinguish the two groups. There was a trend for the overprotective mothers to acknowledge that they had been initially attracted to their future husband by his being "supportive" ($Z = 1.73$, $p = 0.08$), but none of the other descriptions of husbands discriminated the two groups of mothers. However, the overprotective mothers were much more likely to suggest that desire to be a mother was their main reason for marriage ($\chi^2 = 13.07$, df 2, $p<0.01$).

Children

There was a nonsignificant trend for the overprotective mothers to judge their desire for children at the time of marriage as being very strong ($\chi^2 = 3.6$, df 2). They also intended at that time to have more children than the other mothers ($Z = 1.99$, $p<0.05$). In spite of their intention, they had less children (mean 2.9) than the other mothers (mean 3.5), and there was a trend for them to report having less children than they had hoped for ($\chi^2 = 3.85$, df 2). Their index child was born an average of 13 months earlier after marriage than those of the other mothers, and even then the overprotective mothers were more likely to report that child as being born later than intended ($\chi^2 = 5.91$, df 2, $p = 0.05$).

Obstetric History

No differences were found for obstetric difficulties prior to the birth of the first child, although this could reflect the rarity of such problems for the whole sample. Overprotective mothers were no more likely than the others to report problems in conceiving ($\chi^2 = 0.09$, df 1), miscarriages ($\chi^2 = 0.47$, $df\ 1$), stillbirths ($\chi^2 = 0.57$, df 1), abortions ($\chi^2 = 0.80$, $df\ 1$), or an adoption ($\chi^2 = 0.02$, df 1).

In relation to the pregnancy involving the index child, there was a trend for the overprotective mothers to be more likely to report great pleasure ($\chi^2 = 2.60$, df 2), but there was no difference in remembered complications during pregnancy ($\chi^2 = 0.15$, df 1), at the perinatal period for the mother ($\chi^2 = 0.01$, df 1) or for the child ($\chi^2 = 0.01$, df 1), or in reporting a congenital abnormality in the child ($\chi^2 = 0.33$, df 1). In assessing their reaction to seeing the index child for the first time, overprotective mothers were more likely to report a great sense of responsibility ($\chi^2 = 8.03$, df 2, $p< 0.025$) but did not differ in their doubts about coping or remembered feelings of protection.

Developmental History of Index Child

Children of the overprotective mothers were no more likely to have serious illnesses, operations, or accidents in the first year, or in subsequent childhood years than children of the remainder.

There was a trend for the overprotective mothers to report the index child as shy and timid ($Z = 1.9$, $p = 0.06$), but the groups could not be distinguished on scores for clumsiness ($Z = 0.35$), hesitancy about going to school ($Z = 1.55$), assertiveness ($Z = 0.40$), independence ($Z = 0.91$), physical frailty ($Z = 1.15$), or other personality variables.

No differences were found in the initiation and duration of breast-feeding between groups. There was a trend for overprotective mothers to report their index child as slow in learning to feed ($\chi^2 = 4.76$, df 2) and to dress ($\chi^2 = 4.92$, df 2), but no differences were suggested in time required for toilet training, washing oneself, talking, or walking. Overprotective mothers were more likely to report their child as having problems in response to an item assessing general mastery of developmental tasks ($\chi^2 = 4.50$, df 1, $p < 0.05$).

Marital and Social Relationships

There was a trend for the overprotective mothers to report their marriage as unsatisfactory ($\chi^2 = 5.71$, df 2, $p = 0.06$), and a weak trend for that group ($\chi^2 = 1.12$, df 1) to score the sexual relationship with their husbands as unsatisfactory (approximately 27 percent of the overprotective mothers and 12 percent of the other mothers making that judgment). There was a nonsignificant trend for overprotective women to report that the index child had brought about a decrease in their social life ($\chi^2 = 2.28$, df 1).

Scores on the Self-Report Instruments

In Table 16-6 the scores on the self-report measures for the categorized subgroups overprotective and other mothers are compared; in addition, any associations in the whole sample between raw PBI protection scores assigned by the children and mothers' self-report scores are indicated by correlation coefficients.

With the most overprotective mothers categorized into one group, it is hardly surprising that they were scored significantly higher on the Protection scale; item analysis showed they could be most clearly distinguished by the following items: "Invaded my privacy" ($Z = 3.3$, $p<0.001$), "Tried to make me dependent on her" ($Z = 2.9$, $p<0.05$), "Was overprotective of me" ($Z = 2.6$, $p<0.01$), and "Tried to control everything I did" ($Z = 2.0$, $p<0.05$). It is interesting that their index children scored their mothers as significantly lower on care as well.

When asked to score themselves as they believed they had related to the index child, the overprotective mothers also scored themselves as significantly higher on the Protection scale but did not distinguish themselves on the Care scale. On the several self-report questionnaires completed by the mothers, the overprotective group could be distinguished from the other mothers by scoring significantly higher on the trait anxiety

Table 16-6
Mean Scores of Overprotective Mothers and Other Mothers, and Correlational Analyses for Whole Sample with PBI Protection Scores Intercorrelated with Maternal Self-report Scores

Self-Report Scale	Overprotective Mothers	Other Mothers	Comparison of Groups Z Test	Correlational Analyses* r
PBI scores for mothers' own parents				
Maternal care	24.4	26.8	1.47	$-0.20^{\dagger}$
Maternal protection	15.6	11.3	1.87	$+0.32^{\ddagger}$
Paternal care	24.5	24.2	0.25	-0.07
Paternal protection	15.1	12.2	0.88	$+0.18$
Trait anxiety scale	42.9	33.0	$2.76^{\ddagger}$	$+0.46**$
Fear Survey Schedule				
Agoraphobic subscale	3.5	3.1	0.41	$+0.04$
Social phobic subscale	8.9	7.6	0.71	$+0.19^{\dagger}$
Blood and injury subscale	8.7	5.2	$2.14^{\dagger}$	$+0.21^{\dagger}$
Total score	21.1	16.0	1.54	$+0.20^{\dagger}$
Dependency scale	53.5	52.2	0.60	$+0.14$
Type A/B scale				
Type A score	15.7	13.5	1.47	$+0.26^{\dagger}$
Anger out score	3.7	3.3	1.17	$+0.25^{\dagger}$
Total score	19.5	16.8	1.63	$+0.27^{\ddagger}$
Abbreviated Rotter scale	4.1	3.5	1.16	$+0.21^{\dagger}$
Obsessive-compulsive scale	18.1	13.3	1.42	$+0.31^{\dagger}$
Subjects' scoring of themselves on PBI for				
Protection	16.5	10.8	$3.48**$	$+0.55**$
Care	30.1	31.3	1.58	
PBI scores by index child				
Maternal care	30.1	31.4	0.8	
Maternal protection	16.5	10.8	$4.2**$	

Adapted from Parker, G., & Lipscombe, P. Influences on maternal overprotection. *British Journal of Psychiatry*, 1981, *138*, 303–311.
*Examining for associations between PBI protection scores assigned by the children and mothers' self-report scores.
$^{\dagger}p < 0.05$; $^{\ddagger}p < 0.01$; $**p < 0.001$

Influences on Maternal Overprotection

Table 16-7
Mean responses of Overprotective and Other Mothers to Questions Assessing Normal Milestones

Question: At what age, in months, can the average child	Overprotective Mothers	Other Mothers	Z Test*
Roll over	4.3	4.4	0.5
Crawl	7.5	7.7	0.4
Walk	12.4	12.3	0.1
Talk	19.5	19.6	0.2
Catch a ball	28.1	32.8	0.6
Pick up objects with fingers	6.9	6.7	1.0
Unwrap paper from a sweet	16.5	19.0	1.4
Use a knife and fork	42.9	38.7	0.6
Be dry during the day	19.3	22.7	1.5
Be dry during the night	24.8	29.3	1.7

*All differences were not significant.

scale, and on the blood and injury subscales of the Fear Survey Schedule; several nonsignificant trends may be noted in Table 16-6.

A correlational analysis (where, for the whole sample, maternal protection scores assigned by the children were correlated with the mothers' self-report scores) showed that the overprotective mothers scored their own mothers as more protective and lower in care, scored higher on anxiety, higher on several subscales of the Fear Survey Schedule, higher on Type A characteristics, higher on obsessionality, and as having a more external locus of control. The responses the two groups made to questions assessing mothers' judgments of the ages at which children might be expected to achieve various milestones are compared in Table 16-7. No significant differences were found, although mean scores suggest that the overprotective mothers expect children to master certain milestones (dexterity skills such as catching a ball and unwrapping a candy, and urinary continence) at a slightly earlier age than the other mothers.

In Table 16-8, however, there are clear differences between the groups in assessing ages when children should be "allowed to" engage in several independent behaviors with some risk to the child. There is a clear trend (with only the item about owning a bicycle providing an exception) for the overprotective mothers to nominate older ages for children; three of those differences are significant (Table 16-8).

In Tables 16-9 and 16-10 the results of the projective tests designed for this study are shown. In the first test (Table 16-9) the mothers were asked to imagine themselves as the mother in the picture depicting a happy and healthy mother and baby. The overprotective mothers were significantly more likely to express concern about their maternal capacity,

Table 16-8
Mean Responses of Overprotective and Other Mothers to Questions Assessing Allowance of Independent Behaviors

Question: At what age, in years, should the average child be allowed to	Overprotective Mothers	Other Mothers	Z Test
Use matches	8.9	8.1	0.8
Use a penknife	12.5	10.1	1.9*
Bathe alone without supervision	7.1	5.7	2.6*
Travel alone on buses	9.5	9.1	0.6
Own a bicycle	10.0	11.4	1.2
Go to a swimming pool alone	12.2	10.8	1.7
Cross a road alone	7.7	6.9	0.8
Go to school without a parent	7.5	6.4	2.2*

*$p < 0.05$

Table 16-9
Comparison of Responses by Overprotective Mothers and Other Mothers to Photograph of the Healthy Baby and Mother

Responses*	Overprotective Mothers	Other Mothers	Z Test
1. She feels completeness as a woman	4.6	4.4	0.3
2. She feels responsibility for the child	4.8	4.7	0.4
3. She feels concern about her capacity as a mother	3.7	2.7	2.2†
4. She feels sad that babies grow up so quickly	2.2	2.6	1.2
5. She feels concern that the child might become ill	3.3	2.6	1.5
6. She feels that there is now someone to share her world	4.7	3.8	2.9**
7. She feels warmth toward the child	5.0	4.9	1.0
8. She wishes to protect the child from harm in a in a difficult world	4.9	4.1	2.6**
9. She wishes to be physically close to the child	4.6	4.4	0.2
10. She wishes to keep the child as clean and neat as it is now	4.6	4.1	1.1
11. She wishes to know where the child is at all times	4.4	4.3	0.7

*Higher scores indicate respondents were more likely to agree with statement; †$p < 0.025$; **$p < 0.01$

Table 16-10
Comparison of Responses by Overprotective Mothers and Other Mothers to Photograph of a Mother and Her Bald Child in a Hospital Setting

Responses*	Overprotective Mothers	Other Mothers	Z Test[†]
1. She thinks that there is something seriously wrong with the child	3.7	3.9	0.8
2. She feels that the doctor and nurse know there is something seriously wrong with the child	3.7	3.8	0.2
3. She feels that the child is going to need extra care from her	4.4	4.2	0.1
4. She feels that the child is going to need extra protection from her	3.8	4.0	0.2
5. She believes that the child is going to need much more of her time	4.3	4.2	0
6. She feels a sense of warmth towards the child	4.6	4.7	0.4
7. She feels that the child might die	2.4	2.3	0.1
8. She feels a bit put off by the child's appearance	2.3	2.5	0.4

*Higher scores indicate respondents were more likely to agree with statement.
[†]All differences were not significant.

to feel they had someone with whom to share their world, and to wish to protect the child from harm. There is also a trend for them to express concern that the child might become ill (Table 16-9).

The responses of mothers in the two groups to the photograph of the ill-looking baby are compared in Table 16-10. No differences were found or suggested on items seeking to determine if overprotective mothers would be more likely to react to the threat of serious illness, or to be more overprotective, feel more warmth, or feel greater aversion than nonoverprotective mothers to an ill child.

The reported analyses, along with several others performed, suggested that numerous variables were associated with PBI Protection scale scores. Subsequent analyses sought to determine the relevance of those variables as possible determinants or correlates of maternal overprotection.

Possible Determinants or Correlates of Maternal Overprotection

Factor Analyses

As a first step a factor analysis was performed; variables were included if earlier analyses had shown them to be associated (or tending to be associated) with defined overprotection. The aim of these analyses was to examine the pattern of variables contributing to any maternal overprotection factor. The initial factor analysis included 49 variables, and the loadings on the first factor were examined to aid data reduction; 16 variables loaded clearly with the maternal protection score, so the factor analysis was repeated with only those variables being included. The first factor accounted for 25.4 percent of the variance and had an eigenvalue of 4.3. Loadings on this first unrotated factor (which conceptually appeared more coherent than the first factor obtained after varimax rotation) are shown in Table 16-11. Maternal protection scores did not load clearly on the four other factors with an eigenvalue in excess of 1.0.

The loadings would suggest that mothers rated as overprotective were likely to score their own parents as excessively protective and deficient in care on the PBI, to score highly on measures of anxiety (and to be anxious about their maternal capacities), to score highly on obsessionality and dependency (and to show projective evidence of wanting to share their world with a child), and to score highly on Type A characteristics. In addition, such mothers reported a strong desire to have their first baby, and gave evidence of overprotective capacities in response to the projective tests. They rated their child as slow in mastering a developmental skill (washing) and as low in independence.

This factor analysis, while providing a vignette of the overprotective mother, is limited in two ways: It is possible that there may be some redundancy if two or more of the variables are very highly intercorrelated. In addition, it remains unclear whether variables associated with maternal overprotection are possible "determinants" of overprotection or noncausal correlates or expressions of maternal overprotection. Subsequent statistical procedures, involving regression analyses, addressed the first issue only.

Regression Analyses

Several stepwise multiple regression analyses were conducted to assess relationships between the dependent variables, PBI protection scores, and the numerous independent or predictor variables. In a regression analysis employing the stepwise method one variable is chosen from the available independent variables at each step, the variable selected

Table 16-11
Factor Loadings on the Maternal Overprotection Factor in the Second Factor Analysis

Variable	Factor Loading
Mother's scoring of her own mother on PBI protection scale	+0.69
Trait anxiety score	+0.69
Obsessionality score	+0.59
PBI protection scores for mother (scored by child)	+0.58
Mother's scoring of her father on PBI Protection scale	+0.55
Total Fear Survey Schedule score	+0.50
Dependency score	+0.47
Total Type A score	+0.44
Mother responds to photo of a normal baby by reporting a wish to "protect the child from harm in a difficult world"	+0.38
Mother married principally to have a baby	+0.37
Mother responds to photo of a normal baby by feeling that there "is now someone to share her world"	+0.33
Mother remembering a strong desire for children at marriage	+0.26
Mother responds to photo of a normal baby by affirming "concern about her capacity as a mother"	+0.25
Mother rates index child as "independent" in early years	−0.35
Mother's scoring of her father on PBI Care scale	−0.41
Mother rates index child as quick in learning to wash	−0.42
Mother's scoring of her own mother on PBI Care scale	−0.48

being that one explaining the greatest amount of variance unexplained by those variables already in the equation. The process is repeated until all variables that meet designated statistical criteria have been considered. Inclusion levels defining minimal statistical criteria (i.e., minimum F ratios and tolerance values) may be specified, but this was not done in these analyses.

Three other issues relevant to regression analysis need to be considered. First, independent variables may correlate minimally with the dependent variable when a simple correlation is performed, but may receive a sizable weight in the regression equation. Independent variables were included in the analysis if they were associated, or even if they tended to be associated, with protection scores in the earlier analyses. Second, independent variables that had been scored on nominal scales were entered as "dummy" variables, as described by Nie et al. (1975). Third, an examination for multicollinearity (a situation whereby some or all of the independent variables are very highly correlated, thereby creating problems in regression analysis) was made.

Consideration was first given to possible determinants of maternal overprotection, although it is important to note that labeling of a variable as a possible "determinant" was made only on an intuitive basis. Thirty variables were investigated and the resulting correlation matrix was examined for instances of multicollinearity; several were found. Blood and injury subscale scores correlated $+0.81$, and social phobia scores correlated $+0.84$, with the total scores on the Fear Survey Schedule. Type A subscale scores correlated $+0.99$, and anger subscale scores correlated $+0.71$, with total scores on the Type A scale. Summed maternal and paternal PBI care scores correlated $+0.72$ with PBI care scores for mothers alone, while summed maternal and paternal protection scores correlated $+0.82$ with maternal, and 0.78 with paternal protection scores. Thus only the total scale scores of the Fear Survey Schedule and the Type A scale were entered, while PBI scores for each parent were entered separately.

The first five variables in the regression analysis (high trait anxiety, reporting a child as slow in learning to wash, reporting a child as having a problem with developmental milestones, being less likely to report a complication during pregnancy, and being born in Greece or Italy) accounted for 41 percent of the total variance in protection scores. As the fourth variable was paradoxical, in that overprotective mothers were less likely to report complications during pregnancy, rather than more likely, as suggested by Levy (1943), and as a nonevent is unlikely to be a determinant, that variable was not considered in the next analysis.

In that analysis the remaining four variables were examined in a further stepwise regression analysis. As shown in Table 16-12, these four variables were all highly significant individual predictors and remained significant when all had been entered into the equation, accounting for 36.6 percent of the variance in overprotection scores (multiple $R = +0.60$, overall F ratio $= 10.1$, $p<0.001$). Residuals in that equation were examined to ensure that underlying statistical assumptions had not been violated. The scatterplot showed a straight band pattern, suggesting relative freedom from abnormalities and only three cases (4 percent) lay outside 2 SD. Trait anxiety scores were clearly the best predictor, and the scattergram suggested a linear relationship with protection scores rather than any other pattern.

As in previous studies, maternal protection and care scores were negatively associated ($r = -0.58$, $p<0.001$). Such an association raised the possibility that the four predictor variables might be predictors of low maternal care rather than predictors of maternal protection. To examine this possibility, maternal care scores were added as a further independent variable, before the other predictors. This had the effect of partialing out any influence of low care on Protection scale scores, allowing predictors of overprotection as a "pure" dimension to be assessed. The effect of

Table 16-12
Final Regression Equations Assessing Best Predictors (Possible Determinants) of High PBI Protection Scores

Independent Variable	Simple Correlation r	Variables Entered Separately F Ratio	All Variables Entered Together			
			Before Entering Maternal Care Scores		After Entering Maternal Care Scores	
			F Ratio	Variance (%)	F Ratio	Variance (%)
Maternal care	−0.58				37.3*	33.8
Trait anxiety score for mother	+0.46	20.0*	20.0*	21.5	14.0*	10.8
Mother reported child as slow in learning to wash	+0.39	14.4*	7.1†	7.0	2.9	1.9
Mother reported child as having a problem with developmental milestones	+0.31	10.1*	4.6**	4.2	6.8†	4.9
Mother born in Greece or Italy	+0.36	11.4*	4.1**	3.9	5.3**	3.6

Adapted from Parker, G., Lipscombe, P. Influences on maternal overprotection. *British Journal of Psychiatry*, 1981, *138*, 303–311.
* $p < 0.001$; † $p < 0.01$; ** $p < 0.05$

adding maternal care scores is shown in Table 16-12. Trait anxiety, mother reporting child as having a problem with developmental milestones, and mother born in Greece or Italy remain as significant predictors, while mother reporting the child as being slow in learning to wash has been weakened. These four predictors, then, were not merely predicting low maternal care.

Consideration was next given to regression analyses that considered variables that might be regarded more as correlates, rather than as determinants, of maternal overprotection. Twenty-six independent variables were selected for the initial investigation, and again the stepwise method of regression was used, with dummy variables being created for data scored on nominal scales. Several variables that had been considered in the previous analyses of possible determinants were included in the present analyses as their relevance as possible determinants or correlates could be suggested only on an intuitive basis and remained unclear. Care scores for the mothers were not included in the initial regression analysis as it was felt more useful to examine the relevance of other possible correlates before adding maternal care. The correlation matrix of independent variables was examined and no instances of multicollinearity were found.

The first seven variables each contributed at least 2 percent to the variance in PBI protection scores and together accounted for 42.1 percent of the variance (Table 16-13). The second highest predictor, the mother reporting the child as having problems with developmental milestones, is one that had been considered in the list of possible determinants and found to be a significant predictor in that analysis.

In the earlier regression analyses trait anxiety had been shown to be a highly significant predictor of protection scores. It appeared useful to examine the possibility that some of the predictors might achieve significance as a consequence of their being expressions of anxiety; that is, it could be that anxious women, as a consequence of their anxiety, seek supportive husbands, marry principally to have a baby, report their child as having difficulty with developmental milestones, and project their need for support in concerns about being a mother in certain situations. This would result in such variables being associated spuriously with PBI protection scores as a consequence of their being expressions of an anxious personality.

To determine whether the seven predictors were merely expressions of anxiety, two analyses were performed. First, predictors were correlated against anxiety. Second, anxiety scores were added to the list of independent variables in a further regression analysis, thereby partialing out any influence that anxiety might exert on the predictor variables to bring about an association with PBI protection scores. When trait anxiety

Table 16-13
Multiple Regression Analyses Assessing the Effect of Introducing Trait Anxiety Scores to the Seven Best Predictors (Possible Correlates) of Maternal Protection Scores

Independent Variable	Before Entering Trait Anxiety Scores		After Entering Trait Anxiety Scores	
	F Ratio	Variance (%)	F Ratio	Variance (%)
Trait anxiety			19.8**	21.5
Mother married principally to have a baby	10.2*	12.4	1.0	0.7
Mother reported child as having problems with developmental milestones	8.7*	9.6	8.0†	6.4
Mother responded to photo of happy child by affirming a feeling that there "is now someone to share her world"	7.3*	7.3	7.1†	6.3
Mother attracted initially to husband as he was "supportive"	5.6†	5.3	10.5†	10.1
Mother responded to photo of happy child by affirming "concern about her capacity as a mother"	4.7**	4.3	4.1**	3.0
Mother reported having less children than desired initially	3.1	2.6	3.6	2.6
At marriage mother had a very strong desire for children	2.5	2.2	5.1**	3.9

*$p < 0.001$; †$p < 0.01$; **$p < 0.05$

scores for the mothers were correlated separately against each of the five predictors, no significant associations were found, with the strength of the associations ranging from 0.11 to 0.20. The effect of adding anxiety to the regression analysis is shown in Table 16-13. The predictor, marrying principally to have a baby, is clearly influenced by trait anxiety as it drops from being markedly significant to a nonsignificant predictor when anxiety is partialed out. The other variables do not seem to be influenced by anxiety levels.

As noted earlier, maternal PBI protection and care scores were strongly and negatively associated. Overprotective mothers are clearly seen as low in care, and the relationship is a striking one. In assessing possible determinants, assessment should be made of the possibility that the suggested correlates of maternal overprotection are not instead correlates of low maternal care. Assessment was made by adding PBI maternal care scores to the list of predictors and repeating the regression analysis. Only reporting the child as "having problems with milestones" and responding to the projective test by agreeing that there was "someone to share her world" remained significant predictors.

The several analyses reported allow some closure on the first two issues addressed by the research, i.e., what variables are the best predictors of high PBI protection scores, both in their raw form and after partialing out any contribution made by low care. There is a third issue that is important to consider. Studies reported in earlier chapters have suggested that the PBI defines two quadrants (high care–high protection and low care–high protection) that reflect rather contrasting types of parental overprotection. Thus the final inquiry in this study was to determine what variables are associated with those parental styles, and especially low care–high protection, the high-risk quadrant.

On the basis of PBI scores returned by the index children, the mothers were assigned (using the same allocation scores as used in the earlier studies) to the four PBI quadrants. For variables of possible relevance, scores of those assigned to the quadrants were compared using one-way analyses of variance. The more important findings, several of which should be highlighted, are presented in Table 16-14. The blind ratings for several components, and for a general assessment of maternal overprotection made by the interviewer support and extend the earlier comments on the validity of the PBI. As suggested in Chapter 7, excessive maternal contact does not appear to be a component of either overprotective style. Second, the somewhat paradoxical earlier finding that overprotective mothers may be both more controlling and more indulging is clarified. Excessive control is associated most clearly with low care–high protection, while excessive indulgence is associated most clearly with high care–high protection. Third, the two quadrants that define overprotection contrast most strikingly with the remaining two quadrants compared to any other combination, suggesting that the variables rated by the interviewer (apart from excessive contact) are important component constructs of maternal overprotection, irrespective of the degree of maternal care.

Those assigned to the low care–high protection quadrant were more likely than high care–high protection (and other) quadrant mothers to show evidence of high "maternal drive," although variable distributions were not significantly different. Child variables (e.g., being shy, timid, dependent, or slow in mastering milestones) did not show a clear association with any maternal style. Responses to the projective test of the happy mother and baby were significant for three variables, and mean scores suggest that they relate most to protection and that care, whether high or low, does not contribute to the difference. Mothers in the two overprotective quadrants were similarly anxious, likely to report their child as slow with milestones, and likely to respond to the projective test by reporting a strong wish to protect the child in a difficult world. However, these overprotective groups differed from each other in several interesting ways. Those assigned to the high care–high protection quadrant were more indulgent in their parenting, had higher dependency scores on the personality measure, were more likely to score on the projective test as regarding the baby as someone to share their world, and scored as having a more external locus of control. Those assigned to the high care–low protection quadrant were more controlling in their parenting, reported a stronger desire for children as well as a wish for more children at marriage, and reported a higher degree of responsibility toward the baby on the projective test.

DISCUSSION

Several of the methodological reservations expressed in the introductory portion of this chapter should be noted briefly again. The study was cross-sectional rather than longitudinal, limiting considerations of causality. Moreover, there was considerable reliance on anamnestic and self-report data, a procedure risking distortion and inaccuracy, particularly when the mothers were studied many years after their involvement with young children. Finally, a large number of variables was studied, a procedure allowing chance to bring about significant results. However, the aim of the study was to assess the relevance of a wide variety of postulated and possible variables, so that a refined list might be examined subsequently. A prospective study will allow firmer conclusions about a causal link to be made. Replication of key aspects of the present study is

Table 16-14
Mean Scores on Possible Relevant Study Variables for Mothers Assigned to the Different PBI Quadrants

Variable	High Care–Low Protection ($n = 30$)	High Care–High Protection ($n = 11$)	Low Care–Low Protection ($n = 8$)	Low Care–High Protection ($n = 26$)	F Ratio
Age at marriage	23.6	23.5	23.0	23.1	0.13
Desire for children at marriage	2.2	2.1	2.2	2.6	2.73**
Estimated ideal number of children when married	3.4	2.5	2.9	3.6	1.15
Actual number of children	2.0	2.2	2.4	2.0	0.56
Years married when first child born	4.4	5.5	4.6	3.8	0.49
Remembered index child as					
Shy and timid	1.5	1.4	2.1	1.8	2.22
Independent	2.5	1.6	2.4	2.1	4.30†
Frail	1.1	1.2	1.4	1.0	2.44
Index child's milestones‡					
Feeding	2.6	2.2	3.0	2.3	3.37**
Washing	2.4	1.9	2.5	2.0	3.69**
General problems	1.2	1.4	1.0	1.4	2.47
Rater's judgment of mother at interview					
Sought excessive contact with child	2.0	2.5	2.1	2.3	1.37
Infantilized child	1.7	2.2	1.9	2.5	3.29**
Encouraged dependency	1.2	1.8	1.7	2.0	6.63*
Excessively controlled	2.5	2.6	2.6	3.1	2.61**
Excessively indulged	2.4	3.0	2.2	2.5	2.21

Overprotective (general impression)	2.0	2.7	2.4	3.2	6.51*
Mother's response to projective test of happy mother and baby					
Feels responsible for the child	4.8	4.5	4.2	4.9	3.59**
Feels there is now someone to share her world	3.7	4.6	3.4	4.2	3.00**
Wishes to protect the child from harm in a difficult world	4.2	4.5	3.4	4.5	2.70**
Personality measures					
Trait anxiety	30.6	39.2	30.2	40.0	4.17†
Fear Survey Schedule					
Agoraphobia subscale	3.2	4.1	1.6	3.2	0.57
Social phobia subscale	6.2	10.1	6.7	9.2	1.98
Blood and injury subscale	5.0	6.5	4.4	7.3	1.23
Total score	14.4	20.7	12.7	19.7	1.64
Dependency	51.6	58.4	49.0	52.2	1.46
Type A total score	16.3	20.0	14.0	18.9	3.66**
Locus of control	3.2	4.8	3.9	3.6	2.47

‡Lower scores indicate child slower in mastering milestones.
*$p < 0.001$; †$p < 0.01$; **$p < 0.05$

also required in clinical groups as it is by no means certain that overprotection in such groups can be equated with overprotection in the present nonclinical group.

The validity of the PBI as a measure of actual, and not merely, perceived overprotective parenting was assessed within the sample. Comparison of those mothers who received high protection scores on the PBI with remaining mothers (as described in Chapter 7) showed that members of the two groups could be discriminated on three of the four characteristics suggested by Levy (1943) as indicating overprotection: infantilization, encouragement of dependency, and "lack or excess of maternal control."

The last finding, whereby the overprotective group of mothers received both higher indulgence and higher control scores from the rater appeared paradoxical, but was clarified by examining interviewer ratings of mothers assigned to different PBI quadrants. The highest control scores were returned by mothers assigned to the low care–high protection quadrant, while the highest indulgence scores were returned by those assigned to the high care–high protection quadrant. Contrary to Levy's suggestion, excessive maternal contact did not appear to be a component of maternal overprotection. Further support for the validity of the PBI Protection scale, and for the ongoing propensity of overprotective mothers to be overprotective, was shown by responses to the projective test of the healthy mother and baby and to a question assessing when a mother should allow independent behaviors in her child. It is worth noting here that the developmental constraints exerted by overprotective mothers do not emerge from any incorrect knowledge of child development.

Thus, despite differing approaches, there appeared to be broad agreement between Levy and the present inquiry in defining maternal overprotection. To date, Levy's study has provided the only comprehensive theory of maternal overprotection. Findings from the present study support aspects of his theory but differ perhaps in allocating the relative contribution by the child and the mother, and in indicating the key relevance of maternal anxiety.

After the appropriateness of dividing the sample into overprotective and other mothers was demonstrated, the relevance of a number of factors suggested by Levy was assessed. Levy suggests that overprotective mothers were likely to have taken up a surrogate maternal role in early childhood by attending to housework and the care of siblings. Describing this characteristic as "responsible," Levy concluded that it was evidence of strong maternal behavior from an early age. The present study did not demonstrate an early surrogate role in the overprotective mothers, but there was a trend for overprotective mothers who had been required to take such a role to report enjoying it.

In Levy's clinical study there were 19 boys and 1 girl, a difference he accounted for, in part, by suggesting that a male child enhances a strong maternal drive. However, almost all psychiatric disorders in childhood are commoner in boys (Rutter et al., 1970), and it could be that the sex difference in Levy's study reflected the pattern of referrals to the child guidance clinic. Again, as boys are more likely than girls to reflect disturbance behaviorally, and as Levy's subjects were brought to the clinic principally for behavioral problems, it may be incorrect to assume that maternal overprotection is necessarily of greater relevance to sons than to daughters. As noted in Chapter 3, Sebald (1976) concedes that the suggested preponderance of sons may be an artifact reflecting saliency, so that while both sons and daughters may be equally affected by overprotection the consequences in daughters may not be interpreted as distinctive or noteworthy.

Levy reported that overprotective mothers had experienced a prolonged period of anticipation before having their first child, as a consequence of experiences (e.g. sterility, miscarriages) thwarting or threatening the possibility of pregnancy. The present study found no support for that view when obstetric and conception difficulties, miscarriages, and stillbirths were examined. It is true that the overprotective mothers were more likely to report that the index child had been born later than intended, but this finding does not establish that the child *was* delayed, in comparative terms. The fact that the children were born earlier in the marriage (when compared with children of the other mothers) suggests that if the period of anticipation is unusual, then it is in terms of the intensity of the desire for children rather than in duration, as advanced by Levy.

Levy also argued that the experience of life-threatening illness in the child aided the development of maternal overprotection. In this study serious illnesses, operations, and accidents in the first and in subsequent years did not differentiate the two groups. Unfortunately, assessment was not made of *chronic* childhood illness, which, if the asthma findings (see Chapter 12) are valid, may be the more important characteristic or promoting factor.

Levy noted that most of his overprotective mothers had experienced a lack of maternal love. He suggested that such an "affect hunger" acted to promote an overprotective relationship, with the mother expressing her exaggerated need for love in the relationship with her child. If that were so it might be expected that such mothers would also show an insatiable need for love in their marital relationship, but Levy reported that the mothers, in monopolizing their child, tended to exclude their husbands, who were, in general, submissive and stable. Levy's proposition of affect hunger in the mothers might appear to be supported by findings in the present study (group comparison, correlational, and factor analytic) showing that the more overprotective subjects reported less parental care and greater parental protection in their own development. However, as these variables were not significant predictors in the final regression equations (perhaps because a higher order predictor determined the associations), this study does not support the view that affect hunger is likely to be a primary causal factor. Although there was a trend for the overprotective mothers to rate their marriage and their sexual relationships with their husbands as unsatisfactory, no clear picture of the husbands' personality was obtained in the present study. This is a clear limitation when the husbands of overprotective mothers are generally (see Chapters 2 and 3) described as at least submissive and compliant, if not effectively absent fathers.

Theoretically, maternal overprotection might be promoted or elicited by the child, by mother, by mother–child interactional, or by extraneous factors. Culture is an example of the last and appeared relevant in the present inquiry. Mothers who were born in Mediterranean countries received a mean protection score of 27.3 (range 20–33), and all but 1 were allocated to the overprotective group. The possibility that this is an artifact of their small number (i.e., 5) or of most having required translated questionnaires is unlikely, for the study reported in Chapter 15 has suggested the relevance of parental overprotection in the Greek culture.

The possibility that factors in the child may have elicited overprotection was assessed in a number of ways. In the semistructured interview the mothers were asked about their child's clumsiness, shyness and timidity, dependency, physical frailty, and degree of sickliness in early childhood. Furthermore, milestones of walking, talking, toilet training, feeding, washing, and dressing were assessed. The incidence of serious illnesses, operations, and accidents in the early years was assessed. Finally, the mothers were asked to respond to a photograph of a bald child surrounded by medical attendants. Findings suggesting a contribution by the child were few. There was a trend for the overprotective mothers to report their child as shy and timid, and, in the final regression equations, the more protective mothers were likely to report their child as slow in learning to wash and having problems with developmental milestones. These findings could be interpreted as suggesting that certain childhood characteristics elicit overprotection, but could be equally well explained by overprotective mothers being more inclined to conceive of difficulties in their child.

Levy's theory of maternal overprotection presupposes a "constitutionally maternal personality" exposed to certain psychological forces. Results from the present study support his view that overprotective mothers have a strong "maternal drive" and perhaps clarify its characteristics somewhat. The results also suggest strongly that personality characteristics in the mother are linked with overprotection. These two points should be examined more closely.

Levy argued, almost entirely on the basis of animal experiments, that aggressive behaviors are integral components of maternal behavior and that a high maternal drive develops at the expense of femininity. He argued that because the overprotective mothers in his study demonstrated aggressive and helping tendencies from chiidhood that these were the features of a strong endogenous maternal drive.

Evidence of a strong maternal drive in the overprotected group in the present study was suggested by a number of factors: compared to the other group they sought marriage principally to have children, they tended to judge their desire for children to be higher at the time of marriage, they desired a larger family size at that time, their first child was born earlier, and even then, they were more likely to report the child as being born later than intended. Despite all this they appeared to experience greater doubts about their maternal capacities, whether in relation to their own child or to a neutral stimulus, as shown by their responses to the photograph of a healthy child. They remembered a greater sense of responsibility on first seeing the index child and in the end they had fewer children. Such findings might suggest that the realities of mothering result in overprotective mothers limiting the size of the family. However, they could be interpreted as supporting Levy's comment that the arrival of a child may, in some overprotective women "represent a complete fulfilment . . . (and) . . . preclude further pregnancies" (p. 119). That interpretation, along with the finding that overprotective mothers in this study were highly likely to respond to the photograph of the healthy baby by affirming "that there is now someone to share her world," raises the question as to whether the strong desire to have a child is best regarded as a strong maternal drive or as a reflection of some other need, for instance, to have a special type of companion. While the nuances of the greater maternal drive in overprotective mothers were not studied in the present inquiry, further explanations are clearly suggested.

Scores for the mothers on several measures suggested that overprotection is related most closely to personality characteristics of the mother. Correlational analyses associated higher protection scores most clearly with high scores on the trait anxiety measure but also with higher scores on the obsessionality, Type A, social phobia, blood and injury phobia, and locus of control scales. It is likely that these measures reflect a number of interrelated constructs including anxiety, neuroticism, fearfulness, time urgency, control, rigidity, and sensitivity to external pressure, but that the central construct is anxiety or neuroticism. The central role of anxiety is suggested both by the strength of its association with overprotection scores and by the finding that the other personality measures that loaded high on the maternal overprotection factor no longer remained significant predictors of protection scores in the several regression equations after anxiety scores had been entered.

Before considering the relevance of anxiety further, it is perhaps worth drawing attention to several other variables that loaded highly on the maternal overprotection factor and were nonsignificant predictors in the regression equation. Overprotective mothers were highly likely to report their own parents as overprotective and deficient in care, and scores for their mothers on the PBI Protection scale had, in fact, the highest factor loading of any variable. Such a finding linking overprotective parenting over two generations is an important one. It would be easy to suggest that the experience of overprotection is a modeling influence on the recipient's own relationship with her child; but as noted earlier, those variables were not significant in the regression analyses, suggesting that parental overprotection in two or more generations may be independent consequences of a more important variable.

Although, as noted on several occasions, the cross-sectional study design disallows examination of causal processes, there appeared to be some merit in attempting to assemble significant predictors of maternal overprotection, in terms of their likelihood (on an intuitive basis) to be determinants or merely correlates. In the regression analyses examining possible determinants the final predictors were few in number. Trait anxiety was clearly the best predictor and, in fact, accounted for 21.5 percent of the variance. Of considerable importance, since it is established that Protection scale scores on the PBI reflect a low care component, was the subsidiary analysis showing that anxiety levels remained a powerful predictor of overprotection when any low care component was, in effect, partialed out. The greater relevance of anxiety levels to overprotection than to low care was revealed in the examination of mean anxiety scores for mothers assigned to PBI quadrants. The two high protection quadrants were associated with distinctly higher scores on the trait anxiety measure than the two remaining quadrants, with the low care–high protection quadrant having a mean anxiety score only approximately 2 percent higher than the high care–high protection quadrant.

Clearly, the association between anxiety and protection scores could be interpreted in several ways:

1. The nature and the consequences of an overprotective mother–child relationship could lead to higher levels of anxiety. This seems unlikely because one analysis showed that one characteristic distinguishing the overprotective mothers (marrying principally to have a baby) was clearly influenced by trait anxiety levels, suggesting that higher levels of anxiety were evident before they had a child.
2. Maternal overprotection may be a consequence of, or an expression of, anxiety in a mother.
3. Both maternal overprotection and higher levels of anxiety may be secondary to some other determinant (e.g., life trauma), with each being either (a) independent or (b) associated consequences.

Explanations 2 and 3b are favored by the author. The following process might then be proposed: certain women are disposed to overprotective mothering as a consequence of high levels of anxiety and associated personality characteristics. Largely as a consequence of their anxiety (whether constitutionally based or acquired), they seek to protect and control their child as they protect and control themselves. Such an explanation could be tested by conducting a longitudinal study of primiparous women, assessed for anxiety, with serial assessment of the mother–child relationship. Furthermore, support for the hypothesis might be obtained by lowering anxiety in mothers who were highly anxious and overprotective, and assessing whether overprotective characteristics were weakened. Although Levy made a passing observation that maternal anxiety was manifested in some of the components of overprotection, he did not argue for any key role of anxiety in cases of maternal overprotection, which he thought resembled in part an "obsessional neurosis." If the hypothesis is correct that anxiety in a mother is a key determinant of her capacity to be overprotective, then there would be clear implications for preventive and clinical interventions.

Finally, PBI quadrant assignment suggested differences between the two styles of overprotection. Those mothers assigned to the low care-high protection quadrant differed from those assigned to the high care-high protection quadrant in showing evidence of a stronger maternal drive at marriage, in scoring higher on feelings of responsibility to the baby in the projective tests, and were perceived as very controlling in their parenting. Mothers in this quadrant are thus distinctive in being controlling and responsible, in addition to providing an insufficiency of care. Those in the other overprotective quadrant were perceived as indulging, were dependent (as determined by a personality measure and by the projective test) and scored as having a more external locus of control, the last characteristic suggesting a greater sensitivity to influence as capacity to yield to external pressure (Lefcourt, 1976).

In summary, the study implicates a maternal contribution (effected principally through levels of maternal anxiety) as the major influence on an overprotective mother-child relationship, but also suggests that child variables (e.g., slowness or difficulties with developmental milestones) and cultural influences may make a contribution.

17
Conclusion

A number of issues considered earlier are brought together in this chapter with an attempt at synthesis.

COMPONENTS OF PARENTAL OVERPROTECTION

First, it would seem reasonable to conclude that there is quite a high censensus in defining parental overprotection when clinical observations, literary descriptions, and factor-analytic studies are considered. "Protective," "vigilant," and "restrictive" parental attitudes and behaviors are clearly prominent. Most often the parent appears to be protecting the child excessively against real or imagined danger, but the restrictions on the child's graduated progress to independence may reflect other influences. For instance, some overprotective parents seem to wish for an exclusive dyad with their child, and restriction of the child is perhaps a consequence of the resulting symbiotic bond. "Overpossessiveness," i.e., with the parents being unwilling to relinquish their grasp on their child, is a clear feature and is probably related to the constructs already mentioned.

A "control" dimension appears to be highly relevant. An excess of control is evident in the more malignant and uncaring style of overprotective parenting, and delineated by the "affectionless control" PBI quadrant. Such a high degree of control may be related to the protective and restrictive components, or it may reflect an authoritarian parental personality with an emphasis on conformity and discipline. Such high levels of control are likely to be manifested overtly. In a minority of overprotective mothers there may be a lack of control, according to Levy (1943). The present research delineated such an overprotective style within the "affectionate constraint" PBI quadrant and demonstrated that it is a style marked by caring indulgence of the child and associated with personality characteristics in the mother of dependency and an external locus of control. Because of these several differences and because the two overprotective parental styles seem differentially associated as risk factors to adult disorders it would appear important to distinguish these two subtypes theoretically and in research inquiries. The present inquiry has assessed the relevance of both in quantifiable terms by using relative risk estimates.

"Prevention of independent behavior" and "infantilization" of the child appear to be key constructs. Such parental characteristics are manifested in obvious attempts to cushion a child against adversity and stress, in babying the child, and in restricting all components of the child's socialization. An important component, often ignored by commentators, is the parental tendency to "isolate the child" from the influence of others. The child's father is commonly excluded or negated, as are peers, teachers, and other important socialization figures. An overprotective mother often invokes connotations of "dominance" and "power." Such mothers are often described as dominant in the marital relationship, are seen by their children as the parent "who gets things done" and are larger than life in the imagery of their child. Although some commentators, such as Levy, regard maternal overprotection as synonymous with "excessive maternal care," most emphasize an insufficiency of care, love, and warmth as allied with parental overprotection. Love, if present, is commonly interpreted as being compensation for guilt over an earlier desire to reject the child. Expressions of care are often described as mechanical and manipulative, and love is often conditional on the child doing "the right thing."

The present research suggests strongly that there is both a highly caring overprotective style and an overprotective style distinguished by an insufficiency of care. Other constructs appear less relevant or are less obvious. They include "vicarious gratification," with the parent seeking to obtain an identity, or to live, through the child. There is a suggestion in the literature that some overprotective parents relate to their child in such a way as to "mystify the child" about its needs, feelings, and wants. Finally, there is a suggestion by Levy that "excessive contact" with the child is a characteristic, but such a possible component has not been stressed by other commentators and was not supported in the present inquiry.

MEASUREMENT OF PARENTAL OVERPROTECTION

The second issue to be considered is whether parental overprotection can be measured. In Chapter 6 various measures that have been used to rate parental overprotection were reviewed. Almost all have been pencil-and-paper tests, and most "overprotection" scales have been a component of much broader parental attitude/behavior inventories. Some measures require a child to score the parent (for current or remote characteristics), some require the parent to complete self-ratings, and a few allow ratings to be made by trained observers. It was noted in Chapter 6 that only rarely had the properties of such measures been subject to any critical assessment.

As a consequence, one of the key aims of the present research was to develop a satisfactory measure of parental overprotection. A self-rating questionnaire, the Parent Opinion Form, was designed as a measure to be completed by mothers (Chapter 7). Despite the face validity of the items and of the subscales (control, watchfulness, discipline, and dependency) the measure appeared less than satisfactory. Test–retest consistency, while reasonable for total scale scores, was not satisfactory for the subscale scores, perhaps because each scale had only a few items. The validity of the measure was assessed by comparison with scores returned on the PBI protection scale by children of the subjects, and agreement, examined in several ways, was low. While low agreement could reflect a weakness in one or both measures, comparisons suggested that the Parent Opinion Form was the measure more subject to a response bias, presumably social desirability. These findings are consistent with previous attempts to validate self-report measures of maternal overprotection that are completed by mothers.

The second measure, the Parental Bonding Instrument (Chapter 7) clearly generates more confidence. The decision to develop a subjective measure was made on the basis that, if parental characteristics have an influence on a child's development, it is probable that it is the child's perception and interpretation of those characteristics that is more influential, rather than "actual" characteristics divorced of context and meaning to the recipient. In adopting such an approach it must be conceded immediately that any potential for response bias will be increased by a self-report measure. It is then important to assess to what degree such scores relate to actual parental characteristics (making the rather large assumption that the latter can be measured). The reason this is so important was briefly illustrated in Chapters 6 and Chapter 7. Links between a valid measure of actual parental characteristics and an outcome variable support the possibility of a causal process, while links between scored perceptions of parents and an outcome variable may reflect nothing more than a certain personality style influencing both the parental reports and scores on the outcome variable. The issue is examined more closely after a few general comments about the PBI.

As in most previous factor analytic studies of parental attitudes and behaviors, care and protection dimensions were the two principal source variables in the developmental studies. The final 13 items contributing to the Protection scale of the PBI have face validity in that they assess the following constructs: control, overprotection, intrusion, infantilization, and prevention of independent behavior at one pole, and, at the other pole, the promotion of independence and autonomy. The split-half reliability figures suggest that the Care scale is more congruent than the Protection scale—the latter presumably embracing several constructs—but that both have a high degree of internal consistency. Several test–retest reliability studies have been conducted to assess the consistency of PBI scoring over brief intervals, and 5-year reliability data will emerge shortly. Very high reliability coefficients in a sample of clinically depressed patients (Chapter 9) were interpreted as supporting the reliability of the PBI in clinical groups, and (when compared with findings in a nonclinical group) as indicating that motivation exerts an influence on consistency in scoring. While an acceptable reliability was demonstrated in a group of schizophrenic patients (Chapter 8), it was also demonstrated that the level of clinical disturbance had a slight influence on scoring.

The reliability data and comparison of PBI scores against parental ratings made by independent interviewers, suggest that the validity of the PBI is acceptable when considered as a measure of *reported* parental characteristics. However, as noted above, it is highly important to determine the degree to which PBI scores reflect *actual* parental characteristics. As described in Chapter 7 two studies were undertaken to assess the degree to which PBI scores correspond with scores returned by family observers. In a sibling cross-over study, middle-order associations were generally obtained, with higher correlations than those usually reported when raters have been used to validate self-report measures. However, the study also demonstrated that subjects have difficulty in discriminating their own parental experiences from those of their siblings.

In a second study, with PBI scores being completed by subjects in a nonclinical group and by their mothers (as they believed they had related to their child), middle-order correlations were again determined, but mean scores suggested a response bias, with either the mothers portraying themselves in a favorable way and/or the children scoring their mothers with a negative bias. The possibility that any link between PBI scores and depression levels might merely reflect a response bias in the respondents was effectively rejected in the second study. Associations between low maternal care and depression, and between maternal protection and depression, were significant whether maternal characteristics were judged by the subjects or by the mothers themselves, and the relevant correlations were strikingly similar, indirectly supporting the validity of the PBI as a measure of actual parental characteristics. The predictive validity of the PBI was demonstrated in a longitudinal study of schizophrenic patients: scores for those subsequently having contact with parents after hospital discharge predicted readmission to hospital (Chapter 8).

The validity of the PBI Protection scale as a measure of "actual" characteristics was further supported by reports from an external rater in a nonclinical group (Chapter 7). Mothers assigned to an overprotective group on the basis of PBI scores given by their children scored themselves distinctly higher on a modified PBI form than the remaining mothers and were discriminated by the rater (blind to PBI scorings) on six of seven constructs assessing overprotection. While there is evidence to suggest that the PBI is of acceptable validity, as a measure of both actual and perceived parental characteristics, it would be unwise to conclude that such a finding might apply across all clinical and nonclinical groups when the relevance of extraneous factors may vary considerably.

The degree to which several extraneous factors might infuence the construct validity of the PBI was considered in several studies. While mean PBI scores in a group of depressed (Chapter 7) and in a group of schizophrenic patients (Chapter 8) did not differ significantly with improvement in clinical state, PBI scores collected when the patients had improved were shown to be the better predictor of readmission in the second study. "Liking" of a parent appeared to be strongly associated with PBI scores (Chapter 7). However, the degree to which "disliking" a parent *causes* a negative bias in scoring, and the degree to which the experience of an insufficiency of parental care and/or parental overprotection *causes* the parent to be disliked remain to be established.

The relevance of social desirability was considered in several studies in Chapter 7 and 9. The possibility of an opposing response bias (plaintive set) was also considered. Examination of correlation matrices of PBI scores showed higher correlation coefficients in a control than in a patient group. If this general difference reflects a response bias rather than more discordant parenting in the latter group, two explanations are most likely: first, that nonclinical subjects show, in responding to the PBI, a more marked social desirability set than those with clinical disorders; and, second, that clinical subjects have a more marked plaintive set, which, in effect, counteracts any social desirability bias. Both expla-

Conclusion

nations may be supported by the suggestion (Lewinsohn *et al.*, 1980) that depressives' reports may be the more realistic as they have lost the illusory warm glow enjoyed by normals. As the relevance of several possible response biases to PBI scoring cannot be specified, potential biases should be controlled by design or analysis in research studies where appropriate.

Parental overprotection may be defined and measured in several ways using the PBI. One may regard the Protection scale as a continuous variable with high *raw* scores (defined arbitrarily or statistically) indicating the experience of parental overprotection. However, raw PBI protection and care scores are negatively correlated (as found by Jillings et al., 1976, in a rather similar inquiry), suggesting that an insufficiency of care may be a component of overprotective parenting so defined. Such an association has implications for the design of research studies. If the researcher is interested in overprotection *per se*, divorced of its lack of care component, then partialing out procedures may be required.

A third option is to examine assignment of parents to the quadrants allowed by the PBI. Such an approach defines an "optimal parenting" quadrant of high care and low protection, a "neglectful parenting" quadrant, and two overprotective quadrants. The "affectionless control" quadrant reflects a parental style of overprotection and low care, corresponds with the malignant overprotective (e.g., schizophrenogenic, asthmatogenic) parent of the literature, and has been demonstrated as a risk factor in a number of the current research studies. The "affectionate constraint" quadrant reflects a parental style of caring and indulgent overprotection and has been shown, in the current research, to be of some relevance in the study of Greek children, and of possible relevance both to hypochondriacal and dependent adults.

It is unlikely that the PBI comes to terms with interaction between parents and it was not designed to do so. Summing raw scores for mothers and fathers can, at best, be regarded as an approximation of parental care or protection and is probably only efficient in those subjects who return extreme scores. Consequently, an epidemiological approach to this issue has been adopted in the research reported here. Assuming that assignment to the low care–high protection quadrant represents a positive risk factor to certain developmental disturbances, and assignment to the high care–low protection quadrant represents a negative risk factor, various permutations and combinations allow a number of risk estimates. While many might be examined, the research suggests that it may be most useful to estimate the risk of the disorder or the outcome if the child is exposed to a mother, a father, or one or more parent meeting the criteria for a positive or negative risk factor.

ASSOCIATION OF PARENTAL OVERPROTECTION WITH SPECIFIC DISORDERS AND PERSONALITY CHARACTERISTICS

Based on the conclusion that the PBI delineates two distinct types of parental overprotection, the research assessed their relevance to a number of disorders and personality characteristics. Such a wide approach appeared to be relevant because, despite various definitions, parental overprotection has been incriminated as a causal influence on most psychiatric disorders, and as producing a wide range of other untoward sequelae. In a general review (Chapter 4) and in separate research chapters, the claims that overprotection may lead to schizophrenia, manic-depressive psychosis, anxiety, depression, phobic disorders, hypochondriasis, borderline personality, anorexia nervosa, drug and alcohol dependence, homosexuality, transsexualism, and even psychiatric referral itself, were noted. Implicated links with so-called psychosomatic disorders (e.g., peptic ulcer, rheumatoid arthritis, asthma, diabetes), with certain personality traits (e.g., dependency, insecurity, shyness, narcissism, inhibition), and with illness behavior e.g., overutilization of medical services) were documented.

As Susser (1981) notes, the detection of harmful environments is a classic public health strategy that can be applied to the social as well as to the physical or biological environment. In an attempt to assess whether parental overprotection, and not merely maternal overprotection, provides a harmful environment, those disorders most incriminated as sequelae of parental overprotection were examined. The proposition, that parental overprotection is pathogenic, would be supported, but not proved, if case–control comparisons provided evidence of parental overprotection being overrepresented in subjects with such disorders. Susser (1981) states that the "case–control design is efficient and parsimonious." In this general overview the clearest information is likely to be provided by examining the relative risk of "cases" assigning parents to the PBI quadrants delineating the two broad types of parental overprotection. As noted in the Introduction to Part III, relative risk is the ratio of the incidence of cases among those exposed to the risk factor, to the incidence among those not exposed. The ratio, more exactly defined as the relative odds or cross-products ratio, is a measure of association; as it is independent of the sample size, it allows ready comparison of the various study groups. The relative risk for subjects with designated psychiatric disorders assigning each of their parents to the overprotective quadrants is shown in Table 17-1. It is clear that the high care–high protection (affectionate constraint) quadrant is irrelevant to all the psychiatric disorders. However, such a parental style was clearly overrepresented in the study of Greek children and was suggested as of possible relevance to the more hypochondriacal and dependent subjects studied in Chapter 14. Fur-

Conclusion

Table 17-1
Summary of the Incidence of Parental Overprotection* in Case–Control Studies of Designated Psychiatric Disorders

	Low Care–High Protection			High Care–High Protection		
Disorder	Mother Only	Father Only	One or More Parent	Mother Only	Father Only	One or More Parent
Social phobia	4.7	4.0	9.0	0.5	0.5	0.5
Depressive neurosis						
Study 1	4.7	2.8	6.7	0.2	0.6	0.3
Study 2	2.2	2.1	3.3	0.7	0.9	1.0
Anxiety neurosis	3.1	2.3	4.3	0.7	2.3	0.9
Agoraphobia	3.6	1.9	3.3	0.2	0.5	0.3
Transsexualism	1.7	4.7	3.3	0.6	0.3	0.8
Schizophrenia	1.6	2.1	2.1	1.1	1.8	1.0
Manic-depressive psychosis	1.4	0.6	1.2	0.6	1.3	1.5

*Reflected in the relative risk of patients assigning parents to the two relevant PBI quadrants.

thermore, anxiety neurosis patients with a history of school refusal, and therefore likely to have shown "dependency," were shown to be more likely to report both more parental care and protection (Chapter 10). In the past, such a parental style has been described as "indulging," as opposed to "controlling" overprotection. However, as the present studies provide no clear evidence to suggest that those with psychiatric disorders are more likely to assign parents to that quadrant, such a parental style is unlikely to be distinctly pathogenic. By contrast, the low care–high protection (affectionless control) quadrant shows elevated relative risks for a number of the disorders, and the risks for assigning parents to that quadrant for those with "neurotic" disorders, such as social phobia, depressive neurosis, anxiety neurosis, and agoraphobia, are clearly higher than the risks for those with "psychotic" disorders, such as schizophrenia and manic-depressive psychosis). In fact, it can be argued that the risks for the two latter disorders are slight, trivial, or nonexistent. This general finding is clearly of interest in view of the fact that genetic and biochemical influences are usually implicated as of most relevance to the latter disorders, while psychosocial influences are more likely to be incriminated in the etiology of neuroses.

When comparison is made with the magnitude of effects found generally in psychiatry, some of the relative risk estimates for the affectionless control quadrant are quite high. For instance, Paykel (1978) examined several studies and calculated the relative risk for depressives to report life events (generally conceded as highly relevant to depression to range from 4.0 to 6.5. Thus affectionless control, with a relative risk ranging as high as 9.0, is not a trivial risk factor to neurosis.

Another finding worth drawing attention to is that any overrepresentation of affectionless control is not the prerogative of mothers. In fact, for transsexualism the risk of the disorder is increased by a factor of 5 if the patient is exposed to that paternal style, while exposure to that maternal style increases the risk of the disorder by less than 2. However, some caution is appropriate in suggesting any greater relevance of maternal or paternal affectionless control to any one disorder; when Study 2, Chapter 9 (of neurotic depressive patients) showed that patients were most likely to report anomalous parenting from same-sexed parent, suggesting that the relative proportion of the sexes in any sample may contribute to the relative importance of anomalous maternal or paternal characteristics.

The research has established that PBI scores define a parental experience of affectionless control that is a risk factor to certain psychiatric disorders, but individual studies were not designed to establish the nature of that risk. Rather than reiterate possible explanations considered in the individual research studies, broad explanations are considered here. First, it is possible that the PBI is not a valid measure of actual parental characteristics and that a personality characteristic in subjects might cause them both to assign a parent to the affectionless control quadrant and to score high on measures of neurotic or other disturbance. The PBI validity studies (especially the study showing that higher trait depression scores for subjects were associated with mothers' judgment of themselves on the Care and Protection scales, Chapter 7) suggest that that explanation is unlikely. Nevertheless, it must be remembered that such studies were conducted principally in nonclinical groups and the relevance of extraneous biases may vary across clinical and nonclinical groups. Second, it is possible that extraneous variables may have intruded, confounding associations or creating spurious associations. In various studies (especially the depression studies, Chapter 9), several possible influences (e.g., social desirability, neuroticism, genetic factors) were examined and excluded, but clearly it is never possible to test or control for all the possible variables that might explain the observed associations.

Finally, it is possible that the risk ratios have accurately quantified the incidence of affectionless control to several important psychiatric disorders. If the last possibility is correct, then there may be many determinants of any increased incidence. For instance, it is possible that children destined to develop neurotic or other disorders may elicit such a parental style. While that possibility was examined and not supported in the anxiety and depression studies (Chapters 9 and 10) it must be conceded. Although the research has concentrated on examining one participant only in the parent–child dyad, future research should clearly recognize and investigate the transactional issues involved. It is necessary to establish whether affectionless control is merely a consequence of, rather than an antecedent to, several disorders. Such a mechanism is clearly suggested in the literature examining chronic childhood illness. As childhood asthma appears to represent an appropriate paradigm for chronic childhood illness, the relevance of such a mechanism was assessed (and supported) in the present inquiry by using a rather more elegant study design than that adopted for the other studies (Chapter 12). Alternatively, parental overprotection may be a cause of the disorder influencing its onset and/or its course, and numerous mechanisms could be implicated. Clearly, longitudinal studies are required to elaborate the nature of the varying associations and to establish causal mechanisms.

POSSIBLE EFFECTS OF AFFECTIONLESS CONTROL

Assuming for the moment that a parental style of affectionless control *is* a causal influence on the later development of neurosis, some speculation on intervening processes would appear to be in order. It is argued first that such a proposal is highly consistent with, but adds to, contemporary analyses of the sequelae associated with bonding anomalies.

In Chapter 5 there was an extensive consideration of the mother–child tie and the ontogeny of social relationships. While an ethological, evolutionary view—as argued by Ainsworth, Bowlby, and others—was emphasized, it was demonstrated that such a view is not incompatible with the reports of others (e.g., Mahler) who emphasize intrapsychic, as opposed to behavioral, aspects of separation and individuation.

There are a number of parallels between the current research and the views of one seminal thinker, John Bowlby. Bowlby (1977) states that the key point of his thesis is that there is a strong causal relationship between an individual's experiences with his parents and his later capacity to make affectional bonds. According to Bowlby, the main variables are the extent to which a child's parents (a) provide him with a secure base, and (b) encourage him to explore that base. Bowlby defines those parental characteristics in greater depth. Parents require an intuitive and sympathetic understanding of a child's attachment behaviors, should respond to the child's wishes for love and care, but also should respect the child's desire to explore and extend his relationships with peers and other adults. Bowlby suggests that many children grow up with parents who do not provide these conditions, and he lists several patterns of pathogenic parenting. They include parental unresponsiveness to a child's care-eliciting behavior, parental disparagement and rejection, parental threats not to love or to abandon a child as a way of controlling a child, and induction of guilt in a child. He notes, in addition, that some individuals may be exposed to a parent, and usually the mother, who exists pressure on the child to act as an attachment figure for her, thus inverting the normal relationship."

The most important consequence of such pathogenic parenting is said by Bowlby to be "anxious attachment," with the child being anxious, insecure, overdependent, or immature and, under stress, disposed to develop neurotic symptoms, particularly depression or a phobia. Those who, in addition, have a parent who inverts the parent–child relationship by seeking the child as an attachment figure are said to be likely to become overconscientious and guilt ridden, as well as anxiously attached, and Bowlby (1977) suggests that the majority of cases of school phobia and agoraphobia probaby arise as a consequence of such interactions. While he suggests that some recipients may show an opposing pattern of "compulsive self-reliance," such recipients are also apt to decompensate under stress and present with psychosomatic symptoms or depression.

It is readily apparent that the PBI measures those parental parameters described by Bowlby as key variables. Bowlby's emphases on decrements in parental care and on parental failure to allow a child to explore progressively away from a secure parental base clearly suggest a pathogenic parental style resembling that demarcated by the PBI affectionless control quadrant, which has been shown in these studies to be strongly associated with neurotic disorders. Patients with anxiety neurosis, depressive neurosis, social phobia, or agoraphobia were highly likely to assign one or more parent to the affectionless control quadrant, the relative risks ranging from 3.3 to 9.0. Furthermore, highly dependent subjects were much more likely to assign their mothers to this quadrant. It is important to emphasize that the present research findings are consistent in general terms with Bowlby's notation, and amplify it by defining a pathogenic parental style and by quantifying associations with appropriate disorders; but they should not be regarded as demonstrating "attachment theory." This issue is addressed again shortly. It is concluded that (1) the present research findings offer empirical support for Bowlby's observational data linking pathogenic parenting with neurotic sequelae in the recipient, (2) the research has defined and offers a simple method for quantifying the parental environment that increases the risk for future neurosis in a child or adult, and (3) the link between the parental style of affectionless control and maladaptive, neurotic development is not a trivial one.

Some of the less striking and negative findings are now considered. The suggestion that parental overprotection is irrelevant to manic-depressive psychosis is an important negative finding. It raises doubts about previous studies that have implicated such a parental style as an etiological factor to that mental disorder. Furthermore, it supports the binary view of depression because the results contrast strikingly with those found in the neurotic depressive groups and in the nonclinical studies of depression. While the schizophrenic patients were somewhat more likely to assign their parents to the affectionless control quadrant, the relative risk of that assignment was not much above unity and certainly far less than the risks calculated in the neurotic disorder groups. Unfortunately, the study design disallows any conclusions as to whether that parental style is weakly overrepresented as an antecedent to, and/or as a consequence of, schizophrenia or preschizophrenic disturbance in a child. Historical and longitudinal data suggested, however, that such a parental style may be of some relevance to the actual onset and to the course of schizophrenia; if so, this does not negate the clear genetic influence that is implicated in schizophrenia. Instead it is suggested that, in those who are vulnerable genetically to schizophrenia a certain parental environment may promote precipitation of a schizophrenic episode. It is unfortunate that a similar longitudinal study was not undertaken with the manic-depressive group of patients. It would seem important to assess whether parental affectionless control has any similar relevance to the onset or course of the biological subtypes of depressive disorders, whether they are bipolar or unipolar in expression.

Thus the present research findings may be speculatively interpreted as suggesting that a parental style of affectionless control may be irrelevant to certain psychiatric disorders (e.g., manic-depressive psychosis), be an antecedent to and a possible causal influence on other psychiatric disorders (e.g., neuroses), be a consequence of chronic disorder in a child (e.g. asthma), and be a possible stressor to those vulnerable to certain psychiatric disorders as a consequence of genetic influence (e.g., schizophrenia).

The studies assessed the proposition that the Jewish and the Greek parental style is a distinctly overprotective one. In the study of Jewish school children, the only evidence of overprotection was that the daughters were more likely to assign their mothers to the affectionless control quadrant. The relative risk of that assignment was only slightly increased (1.9), and the numbers in the quadrant were so few that this result should be treated with some reservation. In the study of Greek schoolchildren there was again a slightly increased likelihood of the daughters assigning their mothers to that quadrant, the relative risk being 2.5. However, the Greek girls and boys were far more likely than controls to assign their mothers and their fathers to the affectionate constraint quadrant. Thus, while the study provided evidence of an overprotective parental style in the Greek sample, it is important to note that the nature of the overprotection was qualitatively different than the more pathogenic overprotective style discussed previously.

SOURCES AND MECHANISMS OF MATERNAL OVERPROTECTION

A separate inquiry, into perhaps one of the most important issues of the current research, concerned possible origins of overprotective maternal characteristics. A comprehensive study of a nonclinical group of mothers assessed (Chapter 17) the relevance of those factors suggested by Levy (1943) and a number of other possible influences. There was strong evidence that protective characteristics related most clearly to factors in the mother, although child characteristics and cultural influences were not entirely without relevance. Trait anxiety appeared to be the key maternal factor, with a strong linear association between maternal protection and anxiety scores ($r = +0.46$); in the final regression analysis examining possible determinants, anxiety scores accounted for 20 percent of the variance in maternal protection scores. Furthermore, similar high levels of anxiety were found for mothers assigned to the affectionless control and the affectionate constraint quadrants.

Until now the possible relevance of anxiety has not been developed. While Levy (1943) suggests, almost in parenthesis, that maternal anxiety is manifested in three of the components of overprotection (excessive contact, infantilization, and prevention of independent behavior) he does not implicate anxiety in his speculation on the possible origins of overprotection. Several clinical reports, however, have alluded to the possible relevance of anxiety. Mahler et al. (1975) note that during the rapprochement subphase (see Chapter 5) some mothers "shadow" their children as a consequence of "their protracted doting and intrusiveness rooted in their own anxiety." Barker (1976) comments on "excessive parental anxiety" associated with maternal overprotection, while Rutter (1977), suggests that overprotection may arise from some "forms of emotional disturbance" in parents. In a research study Solyom et al. (1976) suggest that overprotection may be a manifestation of the mother's general anxiety. In Chapter 3 Bowen's (1976b) views on the central role of maternal anxiety in creating a dysfunctional family system were discussed. In particular, Bowen describes the development of a triangle in which the mother (anxious, dependent, and inadequate but perceived as dominating and aggressive) seeks to fuse with the child, to leave the father an outsider.

While there is a need to replicate the research findings, particularly in clinical groups, the possible central role of anxiety should be considered further at this time. If a general relationship exists linking higher levels of anxiety or arousal with such a stereotyped social behavior as parental overprotection, it might be expected to be demonstrated in subhuman primates. Supportive evidence can be martialed. In Chapter 5 attention was drawn to the comment by Rosenblum (1971) that, in macaque monkeys, maternal protection is increased when the mother becomes agitated, both in the presence of a social threat or danger and even when no apparent external provocation exists. Observations by van Lawick-Goodall (1971) of free-ranging chimpanzees provide further anecdotal support for the proposed link. She describes one chimpanzee mother, Flo, as being "relaxed in her relations" while another mother, Olly, was "tense and nervous in her relationships with others of her kind." Generally, "Flo was a far more easy-going and tolerant mother than Olly." The author describes several episodes in which Olly rushed up to take her daughter, Gilka, away from the males in the group when there was no risk of aggression. She comments; "Some mothers appear to be overcautious, and repeatedly 'rescue' their infants from situations which do not seem to be dangerous at all."

Two findings—that overprotective mothers tend to be anxious, and that there is an association between maternal overprotection and anxiety in the recipient—could suggest a simple noncausal explanation: anxiety in the mother (inducing her overprotectiveness) and anxiety in the recipient are merely independent consequences of a genetic influence. A separate study (Chapter 10) provided data rejecting the view that the link is always determined by a hereditary influence. In a nonclinical group of adoptees, anxiety in the children and PBI scores for the adopting parents were associated at least as strongly as in the studies in which subjects rated natural parents on the PBI.

If the central importance of anxiety is conceded, then other findings in Chapter 16 become somewhat easier to explain. The strong maternal drive (evidence by marrying principally to have a baby, etc.) in overprotective mothers is likely (and was confirmed in a regression analysis) to be influenced by higher levels of anxiety. Clinical experience would support the view that anxiety encourages a mother to seek comfort in a relationship with a "safe, helpless" companion, when other relationships (parents and husband, according to that study) are perceived as unsatisfactory. Moreover, higher levels of anxiety may explain the tendency of the overprotective mothers to have fewer children than originally anticipated and their tendency to express doubts about their maternal capacities on projective tests. Finally, it may explain (by causing the overprotective mother to have a low threshold for concern about her child) the finding that overprotective mothers tended to judge their children as being slow or having difficulties with developmental milestones in early years.

Results from the study of asthmatic children (Chapter 14) are also relevant. While the asthmatics scored their parents higher on the protection scale, the analyses suggested strongly that the parents were not primarily overprotective, and that overprotection was more likely to be a consequence of the child developing asthma. It appears reasonable to assume then, particularly when the studies on chronic childhood illnesses are reviewed (Chapter 4), that parental overprotection may be elicited by the arousal of anxiety in the parent in such circumstances.

The studies were designed to consider whether, rather than how, maternal overprotection might be associated with certain sequelae in children, but some speculation on the second issue may be appropriate. It is likely that the high protection and the low care components of the more malignant overprotective parental syndrome exert their influence in different ways. Parental care appears to influence a child's intrinsic level of self-esteem and self-worth (Coopersmith, 1967; Parker, 1978). A child exposed to indifferent or rejecting parents is liable to introject their assessment of its worth, and the resulting low self-evaluation and insecurity is said to make the child vulnerable to later episodes of anxiety and depression. By contrast, the protective element is likely (see Chapters 3 and 5) to delay the usual socialization process by restricting graduated tasks that promote competence and autonomy.

In Chapter 5 the various important influences on socialization—parents, siblings, other family members, peer group, schools—were considered in some depth. Considerable data were referenced or reviewed to suggest that an overprotective parent tends to encourage an exclusive relationship with the child and acts so as to preclude all other socializing influences. Such mothers tend to have few children, their husbands are said to be ineffective or are negated, they discourage the influence of peers (for example, in the child's early years, by placing restrictions on playing with, visiting, or entertaining other children), and they are jealous, dismissive, or otherwise negating of schoolteachers. Insufficiently or inappropriately socialized, the recipient is thus liable to decompensate when faced later with adult responsibilities or stresses.

Seligman (1975) draws attention to similarities between learned helplessness in animals and depression in humans; his concept, rather than the model, is worth noting briefly. Seligman reports data suggesting that it is not trauma *per se,* but the inability to control the trauma that increases any diathesis to learned helplessness. Perhaps in a similar way, the recipient of parental protection is less likely to believe that he or she can act or have a significant influence on the environment, having in their earlier years been prevented from exerting control over the environment. Abramson et al. (1978) suggest that learning that outcomes are uncontrollable results in motivational, cognitive and emotional deficits. The motivational deficit consists of retarded initiation of voluntary responses, and a depressed affect is a consequence of learning that outcomes are uncontrollable.

The view that parental overprotection exerts a strong pathogenic influence by restricting or slowing socialization is supported by Levy's data on the effectiveness of treatment methods used with his overprotected subjects. There were three broad treatments: (1) psychotherapy, for the mother, to assess dynamics and give insight into her overprotective attitude and effects on the child; for the father, to show him the importance of taking a more active family role; and for the child, to discourage maladaptive responses and encourage him or her to be more responsible; (2) educational therapy, which consisted essentially of suggestions and demonstrations as to how to handle the child; and (3) environmental or manipulative therapy, which sought to make the mother and child more independent of each other. In the last treatment model the independent socialization of each member of the triad was encouraged or organized. Levy (1943) comments that the last intervention had "a telling effect in a number of cases," that educational therapy was next in importance, and psychotherapy was least valuable.

A research interest of high priority would be to determine if parental overprotection has any primary influence on basic attachment processes as they were defined in Chapter 5. Sufficient evidence was reviewed to suggest that an infant is equipped with a number of evolving repertoires which are increasingly interactive with environmental stimuli, and which serve to promote attachment to a caregiver. In that chapter a number of views were presented to suggest that, if optimal attachment occurs, there develops between the two parties what has been variously termed "synchrony," "reciprocal interaction," "mutual modification of behavior," and "mother–infant equilibrium" (Osofsky & Connors, 1979). It was noted that, as early as 10 days of life, the infant seeks to regulate the interaction and the synchrony. A maternal contribution to synchrony is reflected optimally by sensitivity, acceptance, cooperation, and accessibility (Ainsworth et al., 1971). "Insensitive" mothers tend to impose their own needs, may ignore rather than be accessible, and interfere rather than cooperate.

Some evidence was given that is thought provoking when considered with the present research results. Osofsky and Connors (1979) report that high maternal anxiety interferes with the development of synchrony. Second, observational data suggest that a young infant employs primitive defense mechanisms when overstimulated. It might be imagined that anxious mothers would have greater difficulty in establishing synchrony (due to difficulties in relaxing with the baby and perhaps by overstimulating the baby and being more intrusive). Thus anxious, overprotective mothers may be less able or likely to allow optimal attachment to develop. Bowlby (1969) argues that the psychological importance of attachment is that it leads to the sensory experience of warmth, food, and protection, to a decrease in arousal level, and, as a consequence, it *promotes* detachment, socialization, and exploratory play. As noted earlier in this chapter, pathogenic parenting is associated with anxious attachment by the child, who is seemingly more vulnerable to neurotic disorders.

The views in the present research that anxiety is of key relevance to overprotective parenting and that parental anxiety may influence the development of attachment at a very early age, have a number of important implications. First, the findings suggest that it might be possible to predict overprotective parenting even before the individual takes up an active parenting role. Second, if maternal anxiety has a deleterious influence on the development of attachment, then corrective intervention may have a primary preventive role. A prospective study, led by Dr. Bryanne Barnett, is addressing the latter issue: Sydney women are being screened on a trait anxiety measure shortly after having their first child. Follow-up data will determine whether high maternal anxiety predicts overprotectiveness, and a comparison of appropriate target groups who have received treatment or nonintervention should establish whether, and what, interventions are associated with more optimal mother–child relationships.

Illness, frailty, deformity, and a special beauty in the child have all been suggested as child factors that may elicit overprotection in a mother. The present research sought to determine to some degree whether child factors might be of relevance to maternal overprotection. In the nonclinical group the overprotective mothers did not show distinctive responses to a projective test involving a photograph of an ill child, and their children could not be distinguished by the incidence of serious illnesses, operations, and accidents in earlier years. Nevertheless, two variables were significant in the final regression analysis examining predictors of high protection scores—reporting the child as being slow in learning to wash, and reporting the child as having problems with developmental milestones. As noted in Chapter 17, this could support the view that certain childhood characteristics elicit overprotection, but could also be accounted for by the overprotective mothers being more observant, and even more critical, of their children. The study by van Lawick-Goodall of free-ranging chimpanzees noted earlier can be used to illustrate the possibility that certain infant characteristics may elicit overprotection. Flo, the chimpanzee who was described as a relaxed mother, changed her maternal style when she had another infant later in life (van Lawick-Goodall, 1967). That baby, Flint, was unable to cling properly due to a deformity of his right foot, and was slower in adopting the dorsal position for riding on his mother. For longer than usual periods, Flo supported Flint while carrying him and resisted his attempts to crawl away from her. Rather than reach out and touch him at such times she was far more likely to gather him in. Her holding back of Flint could be distinguished readily from the behaviors of other mothers, and Flint's initial separation from his mother was unusual in that he was pulled away by his sister Fifi.

Although some child characteristics may have a potential to elicit overprotection, it remains to be established whether they do so by increasing anxiety in the mother or whether they act by an independent mechanism.

FINAL CONSIDERATIONS

Although close consideration of treatment issues was not the intent of the present research, one issue is worth addressing on theoretical grounds. It appears that attempts to correct or to ameliorate overprotective parenting have tended to concentrate on the protective aspects of the parental style (e.g., Levy, 1943). However, as the more malignant style of overprotection involves an insufficiency of care, it may be important for therapists to direct their attention toward that component as well.

Finally, adopting a wider perspective, it would appear to be reasonable to ask whether parental overprotection is advantageous. Having marshaled an impressive array of disorders postulated as sequelae of overprotection, such a question may appear paradoxical; yet, parental overprotection would be advantageous on evolutionary grounds if it aided survival. Dimond (1980) argues that it would be advantageous to have some members of a group programed to be "anxious types" or to have an anxious personality, as this would promote the survival of the group. Thus an anxious personality may be a severe disadvantage to the relevant individual but the intense watchfulness that goes with it has probably been of great benefit in the past to the social group. By virtue of the watch-keeping behaviour of some "the rest of the society had the burden of continual vigilance lifted . . . When the individual is on the look out for a predator in its natural environment, it has to remain vigilant, but in groups some animals can be vigilant while others carry out other life-maintaining activities" (Dimond, 1980).

The proposal that an anxious, overprotective parental style may be of immense advantage to the social group, particularly in a hostile environment when demands on vigilance might be expected, thus makes common sense in terms of evolutionary theory. However, the advantages of an anxious, overprotective parental style are no longer clear when, as a consequence of the nuclear family and other social strictures, the "group" is no longer an extant unit. Parental overprotection has probably always acted to the disadvantage of the individual, but in contemporary society, where malignant parental influences may not be diffused or counteracted by an effective, immediate, and supportive social group, overprotection may operate more readily as a risk factor to neurotic dysfunction.

Appendices

Appendix I

The Parental Bonding Instrument and Its Scoring (Scores for the Care scale are shown in Arabic numerals; scores for the Protection scale are shown in Roman numerals)

Female/Male Parent Form: This questionnaire lists various attitudes and behaviors of parents. As you remember your MOTHER/FATHER in your first 16 years would you place a check in the most appropriate brackets next to each question.

	Very like	Moderately like	Moderately unlike	Very unlike
1. Spoke to me with a warm and friendly voice	(3)	(2)	(1)	( )
2. Did not help me as much as I needed	( )	(1)	(2)	(3)
3. Let me do those things I liked doing	( )	(I)	(II)	(III)
4. Seemed emotionally cold to me	( )	(1)	(2)	(3)
5. Appeared to understand my problems and worries	(3)	(2)	(1)	( )
6. Was affectionate to me	(3)	(2)	(1)	( )
7. Liked me to make my own decisions	( )	(I)	(II)	(III)
8. Did not want me to grow up	(III)	(II)	(I)	( )
9. Tried to control everything I did	(III)	(II)	(I)	( )
10. Invaded my privacy	(III)	(II)	(I)	( )
11. Enjoyed talking things over with me	(3)	(2)	(1)	( )

12.	Frequently smiled at me	(3)	(2)	(1)
13.	Tended to baby me	(III)	(II)	(I)
14.	Did not seem to understand what I needed or wanted	( )	(1)	(2)
15.	Let me decide things for myself	( )	(I)	(II)
16.	Made me feel I wasn't wanted	( )	(1)	(2)
17.	Could make me feel better when I was upset	(3)	(2)	(1)
18.	Did not talk with me very much	( )	(1)	(2)
19.	Tried to make me dependent on her/him	(III)	(II)	(I)
20.	Felt I could not look after myself unless she/he was around	(III)	(II)	(I)
21.	Gave me as much freedom as I wanted	( )	(I)	(II)
22.	Let me go out as often as I wanted	(III)	(I)	(II)
23.	Was overprotective of me	( )	(II)	(I)
24.	Did not praise me	( )	(1)	(2)
25.	Let me dress in any way I pleased	( )	(I)	(II)

*From Parker, G. Parental characteristics in relation to depressive disorders. *British Journal of Psychiatry*, 1979a, *134*, 138–147, and from Parker, G., Tupling, H., & Brown, L.B. A parental bonding instrument. *British Journal of Medical Psychology*, 1979, *52*, 1–10.

Appendix II
Normative PBI Data Obtained in Several Nonclinical Studies

Study	n	Maternal PBI						Paternal PBI					
		Care			Protection			Care			Protection		
		Mean	Median	SD	Mean	Median	SD	Mean	Median	SD	Mean	Median	SD
Sydney general practice (Chapter 7)	410	26.9	28.6	7.3	13.3	13.2	7.4	23.8	24.1	7.6	12.4	11.3	7.4
Sydney general practice (Chapter 9)	210	27.0	28.0	6.4	14.2	12.7	7.9	24.9	25.1	6.9	12.5	11.7	6.8
Sydney general practice (Chapter 14)	100	27.5	28.3	6.8	14.5	13.9	8.2	24.6	26.6	8.2	12.8	11.7	7.6
Oxford (U.K.) general practice (Chapter 7)	132	27.1	28.5	7.3	12.5	11.8	7.3	23.7	24.4	8.8	11.0	10.5	6.4
Vermont (U.S.A.) general practice data*	463	25.2	26.9	8.3	13.3	12.6	7.1	22.5	23.1	8.9	12.7	11.7	7.6
Teachers' College students (Chapter 7)	387	26.7	27.4	6.7	15.1	14.3	7.7	22.6	23.3	8.1	13.3	12.5	7.7
Psychology students (Chapter 9)	286	27.1	28.3	7.3	14.3	13.1	7.4	23.7	24.7	8.6	12.5	11.7	7.0

*Unpublished data, kindly provided by Dr. J. Brennan.

Appendix III
A Revised PBI

As noted in Chapter 7, several PBI items may create confusion in some respondents by their "double-negative" potential. A revised PBI was developed by removing those items (items 2, 8, 14, 18, and 24) and its properties are now examined.

Normative Data from the Second Sydney General Practice Study

Routine general practice attenders (146 females and 66 males) completed the PBI (Chapter 9) and group data for the revised scales are listed below:

Revised PBI Scale	Mean	SD	Median
Maternal care	19.1	4.5	20.3
Maternal protection	13.1	7.3	12.0
Paternal care	17.2	5.2	17.6
Paternal protection	11.3	6.3	10.7

Sociodemographic Influences

Any influences of age, sex, and social class on PBI scale scores were assessed by a series of multiple regression analyses within the same group:

Revised PBI Scale	Predictors						All Predictors Entered into the Equation	
	Age		Sex		Social Class			
	B Weight	Variance (%)	B Weight	Variance (%)	B Weight	Variance (%)	F Ratio	Variance (%)
Maternal care	−0.03	0	+0.10	1.0	0	0	0.68	1.1
Maternal protection	−0.05	0.4	0	0	−0.09	0.8	0.73	1.2
Paternal care	−0.06	0.3	+0.06	0.4	+0.04	0.2	0.54	0.9
Paternal protection	+0.05	0.4	−0.21	4.1	+0.05	0.2	3.00	4.8

The only significant association was one linking female sex of the respondent with higher paternal protection scores ($r = 0.20$).

Reliability of the Revised PBI

Test–retest reliability of the revised PBI was assessed in two clinical groups, depressed patients (described in Chapter 7) and schizophrenic patients (Chapter 8), first when clinically disturbed and subsequently when improved.

Revised PBI Scale	Depressed Patients		Schizophrenic Patients	
	25-Item PBI	20-Item PBI	25-Item PBI	20-Item PBI
Maternal care	0.87	0.86	0.77	0.75
Maternal protection	0.90	0.91	0.73	0.72
Paternal care	0.92	0.88	0.58	0.59
Paternal protection	0.87	0.88	0.69	0.67
Mean test–retest period	9 weeks		3.4 weeks	

Reduction of items in a questionnaire will tend to lower the reliability coefficient. That this has not occurred suggests that (1) the items deleted from the 25-item PBI do have lower reliability than those remaining, and (2) that the revised 20-item PBI is of acceptable reliability in clinical groups.

Validity of the Revised PBI

To assess the degree to which recipients' PBI scores agree with those of the relevant parents (scoring themselves), the second study in Chapter 7 was repeated with only the relevant 20 items of the PBI being included. The comparisons are tabulated below (25-item intercorrelation coefficients are shown in parentheses):

Revised PBI Scale	Mothers Scoring Themselves		Students Scoring Mothers		Intercorrelation of Scores by Mothers and by Students
	Mean	SD	Mean	SD	
Maternal care	21.5	3.1	18.3	4.8	+0.22 (+0.44)
Maternal protection	11.1	5.5	13.8	7.6	+0.57 (+0.55)

As with the 25-item scale, the mothers rated themselves as more caring ($t = 5.26$, $p<0.001$) and as less protective ($t = 3.57$, $p<0.001$) than did their children. The correlation coefficient on the care scale has halved in comparison to the 25-item scale.

The relevant associations between revised PBI scores, assessed by both mothers and their children, and outcome variables (state and trait depression) were assessed:

		Revised (and Full 25-item) PBI Scale Scores Correlated with	
Revised PBI Scale	Scored by	State Depression Scores	Trait Depression Scores
Maternal care	Students	−0.31* (−0.44)	−0.35* (−0.45)
	Mothers	−0.25† (−0.30)	−0.16 (−0.35)
Maternal protection	Students	+0.36* (+0.30)	+0.32* (+0.39)
	Mothers	+0.25† (+0.29)	+0.24† (+0.33)

*$p<0.01$
†$p<0.05$

Again, trait and state depression scores are negatively associated with maternal care and positively associated with maternal protection, whether judged by the subjects or by the subjects' mothers, but the associations are generally somewhat weakened. It is hardly surprising that the coefficient for the care scale is affected most clearly, since four of the five items removed from the 25-item scale are care items.

Finally, in the study of schizophrenic patients (Chapter 8) the predictive validity of the PBI had been demonstrated. In one examination of patients who had contact with parents after discharge, 75 percent of those who had assigned one or more parents to the quadrant low care–high protection, and 25 percent of those who had not so scored a parent were readmitted within 9 months. Again, using PBI scores completed at the retest period, the capacity of the revised PBI to predict readmission was assessed. It was calculated that, in the same group, 78 percent of those who assigned one or both parents to the quadrant low care–high protection (for mothers a care score less than 19.0 and a protection score of 14.0 or more; for fathers a care score less than 17.0 and a protection score of 12.0 or more), compared to 44 percent of those who did not so score a parent, were readmitted. The difference is not as clear-cut as when the 25-item scale is used but remains significant ($\chi^2 = 5.02$, df 1, $p<0.05$).

Conclusion

The revised 20-item PBI would appear to be at least as reliable as the 25-item PBI, but its validity (consensual and predictive) is somewhat lower. These results suggest that the 20-item scale should not be preferred in important studies, but that it may be useful as a brief screening measure.

Appendix IV
The Parent Opinion Form and Its Scoring

Instructions: Please consider each item and place a check in one of the four brackets that best expresses your view as a parent. Thank you.

	Strongly agree	Agree	Disagree	Strongly disagree
1. Children should disagree with their parents if they feel their own ideas are better	(0)	(1)	(2)	(3)
2. A good mother chooses the style of her child's clothes	(3)	(2)	(1)	(0)
3. A child will be grateful later on for strict training	(3)	(2)	(1)	(0)
4. A good mother shelters her child from life's difficulties	(0)	(1)	(2)	(3)
5. A child should never set his will against that of his parents	(3)	(2)	(1)	(0)
6. It is alright for a child to refuse to eat certain foods	(0)	(1)	(2)	(3)
7. Clinging children need extra support from their mothers	(0)	(1)	(2)	(3)
8. Children should not keep secrets from their parents	(3)	(2)	(1)	(0)
9. Every child needs some babying	(0)	(1)	(2)	(3)
10. A child should not be permitted to talk back	(3)	(2)	(1)	(0)
11. It is alright for a mother to dress her child even if he can do it himself	(3)	(2)	(1)	(0)
12. Mothers should be careful lest their children choose the wrong friends	(3)	(2)	(1)	(0)
13. It is alright for a mother to bathe her child regularly, even though he can do it himself	(3)	(2)	(1)	(0)
14. Children who are given firm rules grow up to be the best adults	(3)	(2)	(1)	(0)
15. If you're not firm, children will try to get away with anything	(3)	(2)	(1)	(0)
16. Mothers should be prepared to sacrifice nearly everything for their children	(3)	(2)	(1)	(0)

Appendices

17. The doctor should be always called in when a child is unwell	(3)	(2)	(1)	(0)
18. Children should be allowed to select their own television programs	(0)	(1)	(2)	(3)
19. A mother should attend to a crying child immediately	(3)	(2)	(1)	(0)
20. One of the nice things about being a mother is seeing her child perform successfully in public	(3)	(2)	(1)	(0)

Control scale: items 1, 2, 5, 6, 10, 18
Watchfullness scale: items 8, 17, 19, 20
Discipline scale: items 3, 4, 7, 9, 14, 15
Dependency scale: items 11, 12, 13, 16

REFERENCES

Abraham, M. J., & Whitlock, F. A. Childhood experience and depression. *British Journal of Psychiatry,* 1969, *115,* 883–888.

Abramson, L. Y., Seligman, M. E. P., & Teasdale, J. D. Learned helplessness in humans: Critique and reformulation. *Journal of Abnormal Psychology,* 1978, *87,* 49–74.

Adams, P. C. The WASP child. In J. D. Call, J. D. Noshpitz, R. L. Cohen, & I. N. Berlin (Eds.), *Handbook of child psychiatry* (Vol. II). New York: Basic Books, 1979.

Adler, A. *The practice and theory of individual psychology.* New York: Harcourt, Brace & World, 1924.

Agle, D. Psychological factors in hemophilia—The concept of self-care. *Annals of the New York Academy of Sciences,* 1975, *240,* 221–255.

Ainsworth, M. D. S. *Infancy in Uganda: Infant care and the growth of attachment.* Baltimore: John Hopkins Press, 1967.

Ainsworth, M. D. S. Attachment and dependency: A comparison. In J. L. Gewirtz (Ed.), *Attachment and dependence.* New York: Academic Press, 1972.

Ainsworth, M. D. S. The development of infant–mother attachment. In B. Caldwell & H. Ricciuti (Eds.), *Review of child development research* (Vol. 3). Chicago: University of Chicago Press, 1973.

Ainsworth, M. D. S., Bell, S. M., & Stayton, D. J. Individual differences in strange-situation behaviour of one-year olds. In H. R. Schaffer (Ed.), *The origins of human social relations.* New York: Academic Press, 1971.

Alanen, Y. O. The mothers of schizophrenic patients. *Acta Psychiatrica Scandinavica,* 1958, *33*(124), 1–361.

Alanen, Y. O. The family in the pathogenesis of schizophrenia and neurotic disorders. *Acta Psychiatrica Scandinavica,* 1966, *42,* Supplement 189.

Allen, J. J., & Tune, G. S. The Lynfield obsessional/compulsive questionnaires. *Scottish Medical Journal,* 1975, *20,* 21–24.

Alpert, A., & Krown, S. Treatment of a child with severe ego restriction in a

therapeutic nursery: Observations in the nursery. *Psychoanalytic Study of the Child,* 1953, *8,* 340–354.
American Psychiatric Association, Committee on Nomenclature and Statistics: *DSM-III Diagnostic and statistical manual of mental disorders.* (3rd ed.). Washington, D.C.: American Psychiatric Association, 1980.
Ananthamurthy, H. S., & Parameswaran, T. M. Management of speech problems, *Child Psychiatry Quarterly* (Hyderabad), 1978, *11,* 10–13.
Andrews E. E. *The emotionally disturbed family.* New York: Aronson, 1974.
Anthony, E. J. The syndrome of the psychologically invulnerable child. In E. Anthony (Ed.), *The child in the family* (Vol. 3). New York: Wiley, 1974.
Apley, J., MacKeith, R., & Meadow, R. *The child and his symptoms.* Oxford: Blackwell, 1978.
Arajarvi, T., Keinanen, T., & Thuneberg, P. Aspects of development of small prematurely born infants. *Psychiatria Fennica,* 1973, *301 P,* 189–202.
Armitage, P. *Statistical methods in medical research.* Oxford: Blackwell, 1971.
Arya, S. C. How a mentally retarded child develops intellectually. *Social Welfare* (New Delhi), 1969, *16,* 31–32.
Baker, B. & Merskey, H. Parental representations of hypochondriacal patients from a psychiatric hospital, *British Journal of Psychiatry,* 1982, *141,* 233–238.
Ball, J. R. B. Transsexualism and transvestitism. *Australian and New Zealand Journal of Psychiatry,* 1967, *1,* 188–195.
Barker, P. *Basic child psychiatry* (2nd ed.) London: Crosby Lockwood Staples, 1976.
Barragan, M. The child-centred family. In P. J. Guerin (Ed.), *Family therapy: Therapy and practice.* New York: Gardner Press, 1976.
Baumrind, D. Effects of authoritative parental control on child behavior. *Child Development,* 1966, *37,* 887–907.
Beatson, P. *The eye in the mandala. Patrick White: A vision of man and God.* Sydney: Reed, 1977.
Beck, A. T. *Depression.* London: Staples Press, 1967.
Beck, A. T., Ward, C. H., Mendelson, M., Mock, J., & Erbaugh, J. An inventory for measuring depression. *Archives of General Psychiatry,* 1961, *4,* 561–571.
Becker, J. *Depression: Theory and research.* Washington, D.C.: Winston, 1974.
Becker, W. C. Consequences of different kinds of parental discipline. In L. W. Hoffman & M. C. Hoffman (Eds.), *Review of child development research* (Vol. I). New York: Russell Sage Foundation, 1964.
Becker, W. C., Peterson, D. R., Hellmer, L. A., Shoemaker, D. J., & Quay, M. C. Factors in parental behavior and personality as related to problem behavior in children. *Journal of Consulting Psychology,* 1959, *23,* 107–118.
Becker, W. C., Peterson, D. R., Luria, Z., Shoemaker, D. J., & Hellmer, L. A. Relations of factors derived from parent-interview ratings to behavior problems of five-year-olds. *Child Development,* 1962, *33,* 509–535.
Beit-Hallahmi, B., & Rabin, A. I. The kibbutz as a social experiment and as a child-rearing laboratory. *American Psychologist,* 1977, *32,* 532–541.
Bell, R. Q. The effect on the family of a limitation in coping ability in a child: A

research approach and a finding. *Merrill-Palmer Quarterly*, 1964, *10*, 129–142.
Bem, S. L., Martyna, W., & Watson, C. Sex typing and androgyny: Further explorations of the expressive domain. *Journal of Personality and Social Psychology*, 1976, *34*, 1016–1023.
Benedict, R. *Patterns of culture*. New York: New American Library, 1950.
Benjamin, H. *The transsexual phenomenon*. New York: Julian Press, 1966.
Bentovim, A. Emotional disturbances of handicapped pre-school children and their families: Attitudes to the child. *British Medical Journal*, 1972a, *3*, 579–581.
Bentovim, A. Handicapped pre-school children and their families: Effects on child's early emotional development. *British Medical Journal*, 1972b, *3*, 634–637.
Bergman, G. F. J. *Judaism and its Australian history*. Address given at the Great Synagogue, Sydney, July 29, 1978.
Bianchi, G. N. Origins of disease phobia. *Australian and New Zealand Journal of Psychiatry*, 1971, *5*, 241–257.
Bibring, E. The mechanism of depression. In P. Greenacre (Ed.), *Affective disorders*. New York: International Universities Press, 1953.
Blatt, S. J., D'Afflitti, J. P., & Quinlan, D. M. *Depressive experiences questionnaire*. Obtainable from the authors, Yale University, 1975.
Blatt, S. J., Wein, S. J., Chevron, E., & Quinlan, D. M. Parental representations and depression in normal young adults. *Journal of Abnormal Psychology*, 1979, *88*, 388–397.
Block, J., Jennings, P., Harvey, E., & Simpson, E. Interaction between allergic potential and psychopathology in childhood. *Psychosomatic Medicine*, 1964, *26*, 307–320.
Block, J., Harvey, E., Jennings, P. H., & Simpson, E. Clinicians' conceptions of the asthmatogenic mother. *Archives of General Psychiatry*, 1966, *15*, 610–618.
Blos, P. The second individuation process of adolescence. *Psychoanalytic Study of the Child*, 1967, *22*, 162–186.
Bottomley, G. *After the odyssey*. Brisbane: University of Queensland Press, 1979.
Bowen, M. Family therapy and family group therapy. In H. Kaplan & B. Sadock (Eds.), *Comprehensive group psychotherapy*. Baltimore: Williams & Wilkins, 1971.
Bowen, M. Theory in the practice of psychotherapy. In P. Guerin (Ed.), *Family therapy*. New York: Gardner Press, 1976a.
Bowen, M. An interview with Murray Bowen. In M. Bowen (Ed.), *Family therapy in clinical practice*. New York: Aronson, 1976b.
Bowlby, J. *Maternal care and mental health*. Geneva: World Health Organization, 1951.
Bowlby, J. *Attachment and loss* (Vol. I): *Attachment*. London: Hogarth Press, 1969.
Bowlby, J. *Attachment and loss* (Vol. II): *Separation, anxiety and anger*. London: Hogarth Press, 1973.

Bowlby, J. The making and breaking of affectional bonds. *British Journal of Psychiatry,* 1977, *130,* 201–210.
Bowlby, J. *Attachment and loss* (Vol. III): *Loss.* London: Hogarth Press, 1980.
Brazelton, T. B., & Young, G. C. An example of imitative behavior in a nine-week-old infant. *Journal of Child Psychiatry,* 1964, *3,* 53–67.
Breger, E. Parental overprotection and rejection: Implications for the epileptic child. *Maryland State Medical Journal,* 1977, *26,* 63–67.
Brown, G. W., & Harris, T. *Social origins of depression: A study of psychiatric disorder in women.* London: Tavistock, 1978.
Brown, G. W., & Rutter, M. The measurement of family activities and relationships: A methodological study. *Human Relations,* 1966, *19,* 241–263.
Brown, G. W., Carstairs, G. M., & Topping, G. Post hospital adjustment of chronic mental patients. *Lancet,* 1958, *2,* 685–689.
Brown, G. W., Monck, E. M., Carstairs, G. M., & Wing, J. K. Influences of family life on the course of schizophrenic illness. *British Journal of Preventive and Social Medicine,* 1962, *16,* 55–68.
Brown, G. W., Birley, J. L. T., & Wing, J. K. Influence of family life on the course of schizophrenic disorders: A replication. *British Journal of Psychiatry,* 1972, *121,* 241–258.
Buglass, D., Clarke, J., Henderson, A. S., & Kreitman, N. A study of agoraphobic housewives. *Psychological Medicine,* 1977, *7,* 73–86.
Buros, O. K. *Personality tests and reviews.* New York: Gryphon Press, 1970.
Byrne, D. G., & Murrell, T. G. C. Self descriptions of mothers of asthmatic children. *Australian and New Zealand Journal of Psychiatry,* 1977, *11,* 179–183.
Cairns, R. Attachment and dependency: A psychological and social learning synthesis. In J. Gewirtz (Ed.), *Attachment and dependency.* New York: Winston, 1972.
Call, J. D. Introduction. In J. D. Noshpitz (Ed.), *Basic handbook of child psychiatry.* New York: Basic Books, 1979.
Call, J. D. Attachment disorders of infancy. In H. I. Kaplan, A. M. Freedman, B. J. Sadock (Eds.), *Comprehensive textbook of psychiatry.* Baltimore: Williams & Wilkins, 1980.
Campbell, D. T., & Fiske, D. W. Convergent and discriminant validation by the multitrait–multimethod matrix. *Psychological Bulletin,* 1959, *56,* 81–105.
Cantwell, D. P., & Tarjan, G. Constitutional-organic factors in etiology. In J. D. Noshpitz (Ed.), *Basic handbook of child psychiatry,* (Vol. II). New York: Basic Books, 1979.
Carpenter, G. Mother's face and the newborn. *New Scientist,* 1974, *61,* 742–744.
Carter, M. The management of our baby born with the Down's syndrome. *Australian Children Limited,* 1973, *4,* 210–216.
Champney, H. The measurement of parent behavior. *Child Development,* 1941, *12,* 131–166.
Chodoff, P. The depressive personality. *Archives of General Psychiatry,* 1972, *27,* 666–673.
Christodoulou, G. N., Gargoulas, A., Papaloukas, A., Marinopoulou, A., &

Sideris, E. Primary petic ulcer in childhood. Psychosocial, psychological and psychiatric aspects. *Acta Psychiatrica Scandinavica,* 1977, *56,* 215–222.

Clardy, E. R. A. A study of the development and course of schizophrenic children. *Psychiatric Quarterly,* 1951, *25,* 81–90.

Clarke, A. H. The dominant matriarch syndrome. *British Journal of Psychiatry,* 1967, *113,* 1069–1071.

Cohen, M. B., Baker, G., Cohen, R. A., Fromm-Reichman, F., & Weigert, E. B. An intensive study of twelve cases of manic-depressive psychosis. *Psychiatry,* 1954, *17,* 103–137.

Congalton, A. *Status ranking list of occupation in Australia.* Melbourne: Cheshire, 1969.

Coolidge, J. C., & Brodie, R. D. Observations of mothers of 49 school phobic children. *Journal of the American Academy of Child Psychiatry,* 1974, *13,* 275–285.

Coopersmith, S. *The antecedents of self-esteem.* San Francisco: Freeman, 1967.

Corrigan, E. G. The significance and purpose of family organization in families whose children have inflammatory bowel disease (Doctoral dissertation). *Dissertation Abstracts International,* 1977, *38,* 2851-B.

Costello, C. G., & Comrey, A. L Scales for measuring depression and anxiety. *The Journal of Psychology,* 1967 *66,* 303–313.

Costello, A. J., Gunn, J. C., & Dominian, J. Aetiological factors in young schizophrenic men. *British Journal of Psychiatry,* 1968, *114,* 433–441.

Cox, A., & Rutter, M. Diagnostic appraisal and interviewing. M. Rutter & L. Hersov (Eds.), *Child psychiatry: Modern approaches.* Oxford: Blackwell, 1976.

Crandall, R. Validation of self-report measures using ratings by others. *Sociological Methods and Research,* 1976, *4,* 380–400.

Crumley, F. E. A school phobia in a three-generation family conflict. *Journal of the American Academy of Child Psychiatry,* 1974, *13,* 536–550.

Despert, L. J. Schizophrenia in children. *Psychiatric Quarterly,* 1938, *12,* 366–371.

Dimond, S. J. *Neuropsychology.* London: Butterworth, 1980.

Douvan, E., & Gold, M. Model patterns in adolescence. In M. L. Hoffman & L. W. Hoffman (Eds.) *Review of child development research* (Vol. 2). New York: Russell Sage Foundation, 1966.

Droppleman, L. F., & Schaefer, E. S. Boys' and girls' reports of maternal and paternal behavior. *Journal of Abnormal and Social Psychology,* 1963, *67,* 648–654.

Dutton, G. *Patrick White.* Melbourne: Oxford University press, 1971.

Easterbrooks, M. A., & Lamb, M. E. The relationship between quality of infant–mother attachment and infant competence in initial encounter with peers. *Child Development,* 1979, *50,* 380–387.

Edington, G., & Wilson, B. Children of different ordinal positions. In J. D. Call, J. D. Noshpitz, R. L. Cohen, & I. N. Berlin (Eds.), *Basic handbook of child psychiatry* (Vol. II). New York: Basic Books, 1979.

Edwards, C. P., & Whiting, B. Sex differences in children's social interaction. In

Sex differences and the effects of modernization on family life cross-culturally. Report to Ford Foundation, 1978.

Encel, S., & Buckley, B. *The New South Wales Jewish community: A survey* (2nd ed.). Sydney: N. S. W. University Press, 1972.

Epstein, E. *Children of the holocaust.* New York: Putnam, 1979.

Erikson, E. *Childhood and society.* Harmondsworth, England: Penguin, 1965.

Erikson, E. *Identity: youth and crisis.* New York: Morton, 1968.

Eysenck, H. J. *The biological basis of personality.* New York: Thomas, 1967.

Eysenck, H. J. The classification of depressive illness. *British Journal of Psychiatry, 1970, 117,* 241–271.

Eysenck, H. J., & Eysenck, S. B. G. *Manual of the Eysenck Personality Inventory.* London: University of London Press, 1964.

Falloon, I. R. H., Boyd, J. L., McGill, C. W., Razani, J., Moss, H. B. & Gilderman A. M., Family management in the prevention of exacerbations of schizophrenia, *New England Journal of Medicine, 1982, 306,* 1438–1440.

Feldman, S., & Ingham, M. Attachment behavior: A validation study in two age groups. *Child Development, 1975, 46,* 319–330.

Fernando, S. J. M. A cross-cultural study of some familial and social factors in depressive illness. *British Journal of Psychiatry, 1975, 127,* 46–53.

Field, T. Interaction patterns of primary versus secondary caretaker patterns. *Developmental Psychology, 1978, 14,* 183–185.

Fife, B. L. Reducing parental overprotection of the leukemic child. *Social Science and Medicine, 1978, 12,* 117–122.

Finlay-Jones, R. A. Notions of neurosis: A comparison of community cases with declared patients. *Australian and New Zealand Journal of Psychiatry, 1980, 14,* 97–100.

Finlay-Jones, R. A., & Burvill, P. W. The prevalence of minor psychiatric morbidity in the community. *Psychological medicine, 1977, 7,* 475–489.

Finlay-Jones, R. A., & Burvill, P. W. Contrasting demographic patterns of minor psychiatric morbidity in general practice and the community. *Psychological Medicine, 1978, 8,* 455–466.

Fisher, S., Boyd, I., Walker, D., & Sheer, D. Parents of schizophrenics, neurotics and normals. *Archives of General Psychiatry, 1959, 1,* 149–166.

Fitzelle, G. T. Personality factors and certain attitudes toward child rearing among parents of asthmatic children. *Psychosomatic Medicine, 1959, 21,* 208–217.

Fleck, S. The family and psychiatry. In A. M. Freedman, H. I. Kaplan, & B. J. Sadock (Eds.), *Comprehensive textbook of psychiatry* (Vol. II). Baltimore: Williams & Wilkins, 1975.

Fox, A. M. Psychological problems of physically handicapped children. *British Journal of Hospital Medicine* (London), 1977, 17, 479–490.

Frank, G. H. The role of the family in the development of psychopathology. *Psychological Bulletin, 1965, 64,* 191–205.

Freedman, A. M., Kaplan, H. I., & Sadock, B. J. *Comprehensive textbook of psychiatry,* (2nd ed.). Baltimore: Williams & Wilkins, 1975.

Friedman, M., & Rosenman, R. H. Overt behavior pattern in coronary disease.

Detection of overt behavior pattern A in patients with coronary disease by a new psychophysiological procedure. *Journal of the American Medical Association*, 1960, *173*, 1320–1325.
Fromm-Reichmann, F. Notes on the development of treatment of schizophrenics by psychoanalytic psychotherapy. *Psychiatry*, 1948, *2*, 263–273.
Galazan, M. M. Vocational rehabilitation and mental retardation. In I. Philips (Ed.), *Prevention and treatment of mental retardation*. New York: Basic Books, 1966.
Gardner, G. G. The role of maternal psycho-pathology in male and female schizophrenics. *Journal of Consulting Psychology*, 1967, *31*, 411–413.
Gardner, R. A. Psychogenic learning disabilities. *Acta Paedopsychiatrica*, 1977, *42*, 188–209.
Garmezy, N., Clarke, A. R., & Stockner, C. Child rearing attitudes of mothers and fathers as reported by schizophrenics and normal patients. *Journal of Abnormal and Social Psychology*, 1961, *63*, 176–182.
Gerard, D. L., & Siegel, J. The family background of schizophrenia. *Psychiatric Quarterly*, 1950, *24*, 47–73.
Gibson, R. W. The family background and early life experience of the manic-depressive patient. *Psychiatry*, 1958, *21*, 71–90.
Goodman, N. Adolescent norms and behavior organization and conformity. *Merrill-Palmer Quarterly*, 1969, *15*, 199–211.
Gordon, N. Intractable epilepsy in childhood. *Development Medicine and Child Neurology*, 1980, *22*(1), 97–100.
Gordon, S. Guidance for parents. *Digest of the Mentally Retarded*, 1969, *5*, 205–208.
Green, C. M. Matricide by sons. *Medicine, Science and the Law*, 1981, *21*, 207–214.
Green, R. Childhood cross-gender identification. In R. Green & J. Money (Eds.). *Transsexualism and sex reassignment*. Baltimore: Johns Hopkins Press, 1969.
Green, R. *Sexual identity conflict in children and adults*. London: Duckworth, 1974.
Greenacre, P. The childhood of the artist: Libidinal phase development and giftedness. *Psychoanalytic Study of the Child*, 1957, *12*, 27–72.
Greenberg, N. H. A. A comparison of infant–mother behavior in infants with atypical behavior and normal infants. In J. Hellmuth (Ed.), *Exceptional infant* (Vol. 2): *Studies in abnormalities*. New York: Brunner/Mazel, 1971.
Greenburg, D. *How to be a Jewish mother*. London: Wolfe, 1964.
Grigson, G. *The concise encyclopaedia of modern world literature*. London: Hutchinson, 1963.
Hackett, J. M. *Preoperative psychological preparation for children undergoing cardiac surgery*. (Doctoral dissertation). *Dissertation Abstracts International*, 1976. (University Microfilms No. 7732477).
Hagenauer, F. & Tucker, H. The only child. In J. D. Call, J. D. Noshpitz, R. L. Cohen, & I. N. Berlin (Eds.) *Basic handbook of child psychiatry* (Vol. II). New York: Basic Books, 1979.

Hajdu-Gaines, L. Contributions to the aetiology of schizophrenia. *Psychoanalytical Review,* 1940, *27,* 421–438.
Haley, J. Family therapy: A radical change. In J. Haley (Ed.), *Changing families.* New York: Grune & Stratton, 1971.
Hall, C. S. *A primer of Freudian psychology.* New York: Octagon Books, 1978.
Harlow, H. F. Age-mate or peer affectional system. In D. S. Lehrman, R. A. Hinde, & E. Shaw (Eds.), *Advances in the study of behavior* (Vol. II). New York: Academic Press, 1969.
Harlow, H. F., & Harlow M. K. The affectional systems. In A. M. Schrier, H. F. Harlow, & F. Stollnitz (Eds.), *Behavior of nonhuman primates: Modern research trends* (Vol. II). New York: Academic Press, 1965.
Harlow, H. F., & Harlow, M. Learning to love. *American Scientist,* 1966, *54,* 244–272.
Harlow, H. F., & Harlow, M. K. Effects of various mother–infant relationships on rhesus monkey behaviors. In B. M. Foss (Ed.), *Determinants of infant behavior* (Vol. IV). London: Methuen, 1969.
Hartup, W. W. Peer relations and family relations: Two social worlds. In M. Rutter (Ed.), *Scientific foundations of developmental psychiatry.* London: Heinemann, 1980.
Heckscher, B. J. Household structure and achievement orientation in lower class Barbadian families. *Journal of Marriage and the Family,* 1967, *29,* 521–526.
Heilbrun, A. B. Perception of maternal child rearing attitudes in schizophrenics. *Journal of Consulting Psychology,* 1960, *24,* 169–173.
Henderson, S. Care-eliciting behavior in man. *Journal of Nervous and Mental Disease,* 1974, *159,* 172–181.
Henderson, S. A development in social psychiatry: The systematic study of social bonds. *The Journal of Nervous and Mental Disease,* 1980, *168,* 63–69.
Henderson, S., with Byrne, D. G., & Duncan-Jones, P. *Neurosis and the social environment.* Sydney: Academic Press, 1981.
Herbert, M. *Emotional problems of development in children.* New York: Academic Press, 1974.
Hersov, L. A. Persistent nonattendance at school/refusal to go to school. *Journal of Clinical Psychology and Psychiatry,* 1960, *1,* 130–136.
Hewson, D., & Bird, K. *PSY packaged programme.* Typescript from the School of Psychology, University of New South Wales, 1977.
Hickey, K. M. Impact of kidney disease on patient, family, and society. *Social Casework,* 1972, *53*(7), 391–398.
Hinde, R. A. Development of social behavior. In A. M. Schrier & F. Stollnitz (Eds.) *Behavior of nonhuman primates* (Vol. III). New York: Academic Press, 1971.
Hinde, R. A. *Biological bases of human social behavior.* New York: McGraw-Hill, 1974.
Hinde, R. A. Family influences. In M. Rutter (Ed.), *Scientific foundations of developmental psychology.* London: Heinemann, 1980.
Hippler, A. E. *Hunter's Point: A black ghetto.* New York: Basic Books, 1974.

Hirsch, S. R., & Leff, J. P. *Abnormalities in parents of schizophrenics.* London: Oxford University Press, 1975.
Hoenig, J. Kenna, J., & Youd, A. Social and economic aspects of transsexualism. *British Journal of Psychiatry,* 1970, *117,* 163–172.
Howe, M. G., & Madgett, M. E. Mental health problems associated with the only child. *Canadian Psychiatric Association Journal,* 1975, *20,* 189–194.
Jacob, T. Family interaction in disturbed and normal families: A methodological and substantive review. *Psychological Bulletin,* 1975, *82,* 33–65.
Jacobson, E. *The self and the object world.* New York: International Universities Press, 1964.
Jacobson, S., Sasman, J., & DiMascio, A. Deprivation in the childhood of depressed women. *Journal of Nervous and Mental Disease,* 1975, *160,* 5–14.
James, N. McI. Recent advances in the genetics of affective illness. *Australian and New Zealand Journal of Psychiatry,* 1981, *15,* 239–242.
Jenkins, R. L. *Behavior disorders of childhood and adolescence.* Springfield, Ill.: Thomas, 1973.
Jillings, C. R., Adamson, C. A., & Russell, T. An application of Roth's mother–child relationship evaluation to some mothers of handicapped children. *Psychological Reports,* 1976, *38,* 807–810.
Kagan, J., & Moss, H. A. *Birth to maturity: A study in psychological development.* New York: Wiley, 1962.
Kanner, L. Child psychiatry (4th ed.). Springfield, Ill.: Thomas, 1972.
Kantor, O., Seff, W., & Kantor, M. S. Request for residential placement: An exploration of some underlying conflicts. *Journal for Special Educators,* 1979, *15,* 252–261.
Kaplan, H. I., Sadock, B. J., & Freedman, A. M. Erik Erikson. In A. M. Freedman, H. I. Kaplan, & B. J. Sadock (Eds.), *Comprehensive textbook of psychiatry,* Vol. II. Baltimore: Williams & Wilkins, 1975.
Kaplan, H. I., Freedman, A. M., & Sadock, B. J. (Eds.), *Comprehensive textbook of psychiatry* (Vol. III). Baltimore: Williams & Wilkins, 1980.
Kardiner, A., & Ovesey, L. *The mark of oppression.* New York: Norton, 1951.
Kasanin, J., Knight, E., & Sage, P. The parent–child relationship in schizophrenia. *Journal of Nervous and Mental Disease,* 1934, *79,* 249–263.
Kasper, R. Importance of parental support to the disabled child: Let them try their wings. *Exceptional Parent,* 1978, *8,* 23–24.
Katchadourian, H. A. Development to adulthood. In P. B. Beeson, W. McDermott, & J. B. Wyngaarden (Eds.), *Cecil's textbook of medicine.* Philadelphia: Saunders, 1979.
Kaufman, I. C., & Rosenblum, L. A. Depression in infant monkeys separated from their mothers. *Science,* 1969, *155,* 1030–1031.
Kaufman, I. C., & Rosenblum, L. A. The waning of the mother–infant bond in two species of macaque. In B. M. Foss (Ed.), *Determinants of infant behavior* (Vol. IV). London: Methuen, 1969.
Kendell, R. E. The classification of depressions: A review of contemporary confusion. *British Journal of Psychiatry,* 1976, *129,* 15–28.
Kendell, R. E., Cooper, J. E., Gourlay, A. J. & Copeland, J. R. M. The

diagnostic criteria of American and British psychiatrists. *Archives of General Psychiatry,* 1971, *25,* 123–130.

Kendell, R. E., Brockington, I. F., & Leff, J. P. Prognostic implications of six alternative definitions of schizophrenia. *Archives of General Psychiatry,* 1979, *36,* 25–31.

Kennell, J. H., Voos, D. K., & Klaus, M. H. Parent–infant bonding. In J. D. Osofsky (Ed.), *Handbook of infant development.* New York: Wiley, 1979.

Kerr, M. E. Family systems theory and therapy. In A. S. Gurman & D. P. Kniskern (Eds.), *Handbook of family therapy.* New York: Brunner/Mazel, 1981.

Kessler, E. S. *Women: An anthropological view.* New York: Holt, Rinehart & Winston, 176.

Kiloh, L. G. Depressive illness. *British Medical Journal,* 1968, *4,* 813–815.

Kiloh, L. G., Andrews, G., Neilson, M., & Bianchi, G. N. The relationship of the syndromes called endogenous and neurotic depression. *British Journal of Psychiatry,* 1972, *121,* 183–196.

Klaus, M. H., & Kennell, J. H. *Maternal–infant bonding.* St. Louis: Mosby, 1976.

Klein, S. J. D. Chronic kidney disease: Impact on the child and family and strategies for coping. (Doctoral dissertation). *Dissertation Abstracts International,* 1976. University Microfilms No. 76-4055.

Kohn, M., & Clausen, J. A. Parental authority behavior and schizophrenia. *American Journal of Orthopsychiatry,* 1956, *26,* 297–313.

Kolb, L. C. *Modern clinical psychiatry.* Philadelphia: Saunders, 1973.

Koupernik, C. The roots of hypochondriasis in the child. In E. J. Anthony (Ed.), *The child in his family: The impact of disease and death.* New York: Wiley, 1973.

Krynski, S. Mental deficiency and behavioral disorders. *Acta Paedophsychiatrica* (Basel), 1975, *41*(4/5), 138–161.

Kuipers, L. Expressed emotion: A review. *British Journal of Social and Clinical Psychology,* 1979, *18,* 237–243.

Laing, R. D. *The politics of experience.* Harmondsworth, England: Penguin, 1967.

Lamb, M. E. The role of the father: An overview. M. E. Lamb (Ed.), *The role of the father in child development.* New York: Wiley, 1980.

Lane, R. C., & Singer, J. L. Familial attitudes in paranoid schizophrenics and normals from two socioeconomic classes. *Journal of Abnormal and Social Psychology,* 1957, *59,* 328–339.

Lawrence, D. H. *Sons and lovers.* Harmondsworth, England: Penguin, 1948.

Lefcourt, H. M. *Locus of control: Current trends in theory and research.* New York: Halsted Press, 1976.

Leff, J., Kuipers, L., Berkowitz, R., Eberlein-Vries and Sturgeon, D. A controlled trial of social intervention in the families of schizophrenic patients, *British Journal of Psychiatry,* 1982, 141, 121–134.

Leff, J., & Vaughn, C. The role of maintenance therapy and relatives' expressed emotion in relapse of schizophrenia: A two-year follow-up. *British Journal of Psychiatry,* 1981, *139,* 102–104.

Leiderman, P. H., Tulkin, S. R., & Rosenfeld, A. *Culture and infancy.* New York: Academic Press, 1977.
Leonhard, K. *Aufteilung der endogenen psychosen* (2nd ed.). Berlin: Akademie, 1959.
Levine, S., & Scotch, N. Cited in S. G. Haynes, M. Feinleib, & W. B. Kannel. *Psychological factors and CHD incidence in Framingham: Results from an 8 year follow-up study.* Paper presented at American Heart Association meeting, Orlando, Fl., 1978.
Levy, D. M. Maternal overprotection and rejection. *Archives of Neurology and Psychiatry,* 1931, *25,* 886–889.
Levy, D. M. *Maternal overprotection.* New York: Columbia University Press, 1943.
Lewinsohn, P. M., Mischel, W., Chaplin, W., & Barton, R. Social competence and depression: The role of illusory self-perception. *Journal of Abnormal Psychology,* 1980, *89,* 203–212.
Lewis, J. M. The family of the patient. In G. Usdin & J. M. Lewis (Eds.), *Psychiatry in general medical practice.* New York: McGraw-Hill, 1979.
Lewis, J. M., Beavers, W. R., Gossett, J. T., & Phillips, U. A. *No single thread: Psychological health in family systems.* New York: Brunner/Mazel, 1976.
Lewis, M. State as an infant–environment interaction: An analysis of mother–infant behavior as a function of sex. *Merrill-Palmer Quarterly,* 1972, *18,* 95–121.
Lewis, O. *Five families.* New York: Basic Books, 1959.
Lidz, T., Cornelison, A. R., Fleck, S., & Terry, D. The intrafamilial environment of the schizophrenic patient. II. Marital schism and marital skew. *American Journal of Psychiatry,* 1957, *114,* 241–248.
Lidz, T., Cornelison, A. R., Schafer, S. Singer, M. T., & Fleck, S. The mothers of schizophrenic patients. In T. Lidz, S. Fleck, & A. R. Cornelison (Eds.), *Schizophrenia and the family.* New York: International Universities Press, 1964.
Lieberman, A. F. Preschoolers' competence with a peer: Relations with attachment and peer experience. *Child Development,* 1977, *48,* 1277–1287.
Liem, J. M. Family studies of schizophrenia: An update and commentary. *Schizophrenia Bulletin,* 1980, *6,* 429–455.
Lozoff, B. Comment. In M. H. Klaus & J. K. Kennell (Eds.), *Maternal–infant bonding.* St. Louis: Mosby, 1976.
Lu, Y-C. Mother–child role relations in schizophrenia. *Psychiatry,* 1961, *24,* 133–142.
Maccoby, E. E., & Jacklin, C. N. *The psychology of sex differences.* Stanford, Calif.: Stanford University Press, 1974.
Maccoby, E. E., & Jacklin, C. N. Psychological sex differences. In M. Rutter (Ed.), *Scientific foundations of developmental psychiatry.* London: Heinemann, 1980.
Mack, J. E., Scherl, D. J., & Macht, L. B. Children who kill their mothers. In E. J. Anthony (Ed.), *The child in his family. The impact of disease and death.* New York: Wiley, 1973.

Mahler, M. S., & Gosliner, B. J. On symbiotic child psychosis: Genetic, dynamic and restitutive aspects. In *The psychoanalytic study of the child* (Vol. 10). In R. S. Eissler, A. Freud, H. Hartmann & E. Kris (Eds.) New York: International Universities Press, 1955.

Mahler, M. S., Pine, F., & Bergman, A. *The psychological birth of the human infant.* New York: Basic Books, 1975.

Marcia, J. E. Ego identity states: Relationship to change in self-esteem, "general maladjustment", and authoritarianism. *Journal of Personality,* 1967, *35,* 118–133.

Marcia, J. E. Identity in adolescence. In J. Adelson (Ed.), *Handbook of adolescent psychiatry.* New York: Wiley, 1980.

Mark, J. C. The attitudes of the mothers of male schizophrenics towards child behavior. *Journal of Abnormal and Social Psychology,* 1953, *48,* 185–189.

Markova, I. Rearing the child with hemophilia. *Developmental Medicine and Child Neurology,* 1979, *21,* 812–815.

Marks, I. *Fears and phobias.* London: Heinemann, 1969.

Marks, I. & Mathews, A. Brief standard self-rating for phobic patients. *Behaviour Research and Therapy,* 1979, *17,* 263–267.

Masters, J., & Wellman, H. Human infant attachment: A procedural critique. *Psychological Bulletin,* 1974, *81,* 218–237.

Mattson, A. K. E. Long-term physical illness in childhood: A challenge to psychosocial adaption. *Pediatrics,* 1972, *50,* 801–811.

McCord, J., McCord, W., & Thurber, E. Some effect of paternal absence on male children. *Journal of Abnormal and Social Psychology,* 1962, *64,* 361–369.

McFadden, E. R., & Austin, K. F. Asthma. In G. W. Thorn, R. D. Adams, E. Braunwald, K. J. Isselbacher, & R. G. Petersdorf (Eds.), *Principles of internal medicine* (8th ed.). New York: McGraw-Hill, 1977.

McGhie, A. A comparative study of the mother–child relationship in schizophrenia. *British Journal of Medical Psychology,* 1961a, *34,* 195–208.

McGhie, A. A comparative study of the mother–child relationship in schizophrenia. II. Psychological testing. *British Journal of Medical Psychology,* 1961b, *34,* 209–221.

McKeown, J. E. The behavior of parents of schizophrenic, neurotic, and normal children. *American Journal of Sociology,* 1950, *56,* 175–179.

Mead, M. Theoretical setting. In M. Mead & M. Wofenstein (Eds.), *Childhood in contemporary cultures.* Chicago: University of Chicago Press, 1955.

Medding, P. Y. *From assimilation to group survival: A political and sociological study of an Australian Jewish community.* Melbourne: Cheshire, 1968.

Mendelson, M. *Psychoanalytic concepts of depression.* New York: Spectrum, 1974.

Middleton, R. Alienation, race and education. *American Sociological Review,* 1963, *28,* 973–977.

Minuchin, S., Baker, L., Rosman, B. L., Leibman, R., Milman, L., & Todd, T. C. A conceptual model of psychosomatic illness in children. *Archives of General Psychiatry,* 1975, *32,* 1031–1038.

Minuchin, S., Rosman, B. L., & Baker, L. *Psychosomatic families: Anorexia nervosa in context.* Cambridge: Harvard University Press, 1978.
Mitchell, G., & Brandt, E. M. Paternal behavior. In F. E. Poirier (Ed.), *Primate socialization.* New York: Random House, 1972.
Molony, H. Parental reactions to mental retardation. *Medical Journal of Australia,* 1971, *1,* 914–917.
Mulder, H. C., & Suurmeijer, T. P. B. M. Families with a child with epilepsy: A sociological contribution. *Journal of Biosocial Science,* 1977, *9,* 13–24.
Munro, A Parental deprivation in depressive patients. *British Journal of Psychiatry,* 1966, *112,* 443–457.
Muus, R. E. *Theories of adolescence* (3rd ed.), New York: Random House, 1975.
Newman, B. M., & Newman, P. R. *Development through life. A psychosocial approach.* Homewood, N. J.: Rosey Press, 1975.
Nie, N. H., Hull, C. H., Jenkins, J. G., Steinbrenner, K., & Bent, D. H. *Statistical package for the social sciences* (2nd ed.). New York: McGraw-Hill, 1975.
Noshpitz, J. D. The Jewish child. in J. D. Call, J. D. Noshpitz, R. L. Cohen, & I. N. Berlin (Eds.), *Basic handbook of child psychiatry.* New York: Basic Books, 1979.
O'Neal, P. & Robins, L. N. Childhood patterns predictive of adult schizophrenia: A 30-year follow-up study. *American Journal of Psychiatry,* 1958, *115,* 385–391.
Osofsky, J. D., & Connors, K. Mother–infant interaction: An integrative view of a complex system. In J. D. Osofsky (Ed.), *Handbook of infant development.* New York: Wiley, 1979.
Overall, J. E., & Gorham, D. R. The Brief Psychiatric Rating Scale. *Psychological Reports,* 1962, *10,* 799–812.
Parke, R. D. Perspectives on father–infant interaction. In J. D. Osofsky (Ed.), *Handbook of infant development.* New York: Wiley, 1979.
Parker, G. Parental "affectionless control" as an antecedent to adult depression, *Archives of General Psychiatry,* 1983, in press.
Parker, G. *Parental antecedents to depression.* Unpublished M. D. thesis, University of New South Wales, 1977.
Parker, G. *The bonds of depression.* Sydney: Angus & Robertson, 1978.
Parker, G. Parental characteristics in relation to depressive disorders. *British Journal of Psychiatry,* 1979a, *134,* 138–147.
Parker, G. Parental deprivation and depression in a non-clinical group, *Australian and New Zealand Journal of Psychiatry,* 1979b, *13,* 51–56.
Parker, G. Reported parental characteristics in relation to trait depression and anxiety levels in a non-clinical group. *Australian and New Zealand Journal of Psychiatry,* 1979c, *13,* 260–264.
Parker, G. Reported parental characteristics of agoraphobics and social phobics. *British Journal of Psychiatry,* 1979d, *135,* 555–560.
Parker. G. Vulnerability factors to normal depression. *Journal of Psychosomatic Research,* 1980, *24,* 67–74.
Parker, G. Parental reports of depressives: An investigation of several explanations. *Journal of Affective Disorders,* 1981a, *3,* 131–140.

Parker, G. Parental representations of patients with anxiety neurosis. *Acta Psychiatrica Scandinavica*, 1981b, *63*, 33–36.
Parker, G. Parental representations and affective disorders: Examination for an hereditary link. *British Journal of Medical Psychology*, 1982a, *55*, 57–61.
Parker, G. Re-searching the schizophrenogenic mother. *Journal of Nervous and Mental Disease*, 1982b, *170*, 452–462.
Parker, G., & Barr, R. Parental representations of transsexuals. *Archives of Sexual Behavior*, 1982, *11*, 221–230.
Parker, G., & Lipscombe, P. Parental characteristics of Jews and Greeks in Australia *Australian and New Zealand Journal of Psychiatry*, 1979a, *13*, 225–230.
Parker, G., & Lipscombe, P. Parental overprotection and asthma. *Journal of Psychosomatic Research*, 1979b, *23*, 295–299.
Parker, G., & Lipscombe, P. Early parental characteristics as influences on adult dependency, hypochondriasis and utilization of primary physicians. *British Journal of Medical Psychology*, 1980, *53*, 355–363.
Parker, G. & Lipscombe, P. Influences on maternal overprotection. *British Journal of Psychiatry*, 1981, *138*, 303–311.
Parker, G., Tupling, H., & Brown, L. B. A Parental Bonding Instrument. *British Journal of Medical Psychology*, 1979, *52*, 1–10.
Parker, G., Fairley, M., Greenwood, J., Jurd, S., & Silove, D. Parental representations of schizophrenics and their association with onset and course of schizophrenia. *British Journal of Psychiatry*, 1982, *141*, 573–581.
Pauly, I. B. Female transsexualism. Part I. *Archives of Sexual Behavior*, 1974, *3*, 487–526.
Paykel, E. S. Classification of depressed patients: A cluster analysis derived grouping. *British Journal of Psychiatry*, 1971, *118*, 275–288.
Paykel, E. S. Contribution of life events to causation of psychiatric illness. *Psychological Medicine*, 1978, *8*, 245–253.
Paykel, E. S., Myers, J. K., Dienelt, M. N., Klerman, G. L., Lindenthal, J. J. & Pepper, M. P. Life events and depression. *Archives of General Psychiatry*, 1969, *21*, 753–760.
Paykel, E. S., Klerman, G. L., & Prusoff, B. A. Personality and symptom pattern in depression. *British Journal of Psychiatry*, 1976, *129*, 327–334.
Perris, C., Jacobsson, L., Lindström, H., von Knorring & Perris, H. Development of a new inventory for assessing memories of parental rearing behavior. *Acta Psychiatrica Scandinavica*, 1980, *61*, 265–274.
Peterson, A. C., & Taylor, B. The biological approach to adolescence: Biological change and psychological adaptation. In J. Adelson (Ed.), *Handbook of adolescent psychiatry*. New York: Wiley, 1980.
Piaget, J. *The construction of reality in a child*. New York: Basic Books, 1954.
Pilowsky, I., & Spencer, N. D. Patterns of illness behaviour in patients with intractable pain. *Journal of Psychosomatic Research*, 1976, *19*, 279–287.
Pinkerton, P. Parental acceptance of the handicapped child. *Developmental Medicine and Child Neurology*, 1970, *12*, 207–212.
Pitfield, M., & Oppenheim, A. N. Child rearing attitudes of mothers of psychotic children. *Journal of Child Psychology and Psychiatry*, 1964, *5*, 51–57.

Platt, S. On establishing the validity of "objective" data: Can we rely on cross-interview agreement? *Psychological Medicine*, 1980, *10*, 573–581.

Porter, H. *The right thing*. Adelaide: Rigby, 1971.

Prince, V., & Bentler, P.M. A survey of 504 cases of transvestism. *Psychological Reports*, 1972, *31*, 903–917.

Prout, C. T., & White, M. A. A controlled study of personality relationships in mothers of schizophrenic male patients. *American Journal of Psychiatry*, 1950, *107*, 251–256.

Purcell, K., & Metz, J. Distinctions between subgroups of asthmatic children: Some parent attitude variables related to age of onset of asthma. *Journal of Psychosomatic Research*, 1962, *6*, 251–158.

Purcell, K., & Weiss, J. H. Asthma. In C. G. Costello (Ed.), *Symptoms of Psychopathology*. New York: Wiley, 1971.

Purcell, K., Brady, K., Chai, H., Muser, J., Molk, L., Gordon, N. & Means, J. The effect on asthma in children of experimental separation from the family. *Psychosomatic Medicine*, 1969, *31*, 144–164.

Queen, S. A., & Habenstein, R. W. *The family in various cultures*. Philadelphia: Lippincott, 1974.

Quinton, D. Cultural and community influences. In M. Rutter (Ed.), *Scientific foundations of developmental psychiatry*. London: Heinemann, 1980.

Raskin, A., Boothe, H. H., Reatig, N. A., Schulterbrandt, J. G. & Odle, D. Factor analyses of normal and depressed patients' memories of parental behavior. *Psychological Report*, 1971, *29*, 871–879.

Redican, W. K. Adult male–infant interactions in nonhuman primates. In M. Lamb (Ed.), *The role of the father in child development*. New York: Wiley, 1976.

Reichard, S., & Tillman, C. Patterns of parent–child relationships in schizophrenia. *Psychiatry*, 1950, *13*, 247–257.

Renson, G. J., Schaefer, E. S., & Levy, B. I. Cross-national validity of a spherical conceptual model for parent behavior. *Child Development*, 1968, *39*, 1229–1235.

Rheingold, H. L., & Eckerman, C. O. Departures from the mother. In H. R. Schaffer (Ed.), *The origins of human social relations*. New York: Academic Press, 1971.

Richards, M. P. M. A comment on the social content of mother–infant interaction. In H. R. Schaffer (Ed.), *The origins of human social relations*. New York: Academic Press, 1971.

Roe, A., & Siegelman, M. A parent–child relations questionnaire. *Child Development*, 1963, *34*, 355–369.

Roff, M. A factorial study of the FELS parent behavior scales. *Child Development*, 1949, *20*, 29–44.

Rosenberg, M. *Society and the adolescent self-image*. Princeton, N. J.: Princeton University Press, 1965.

Rosenblum, L. A. Mother–infant interaction in macaques. In H. Moltz (Ed.), *The ontogeny of vertebrate behavior*. New York: Academic Press, 1971.

Rosenblum, L. A., & Harlow, H. F. Approach–avoidance conflict in the mother surrogate situation. *Psychological Reports*, 1963, *12*, 83–85.

Ross, E. Epileptic children. *Health and Social Service Journal*, 1977, *87*, 1600.
Roth, M. The phobic–anxiety–depersonalization syndrome. *Proceedings of the Royal Society of Medicine*, 1959, *52*, 587–595.
Roth P. *Portnoy's complaint*. London: Cape, 1969.
Roth, P. *My life as a man*. London: Cape, 1974.
Roth, R. M. *The Mother–Child Relationship Evaluation*. Beverley Hills, Calif.: Western Psychological Services, 1961.
Roth, M. & Kerr, T. Diagnosis of the reactive depressive illness. In J. Harding Price (Ed.), *Modern Trends in Psychological Medicine-2*. London: Butterworths, 1970.
Rotter, J. B. Generalized expectancies for internal versus external control of reinforcement. *Psychological Monographs*, 1966, *80*, 1–28.
Rutter, M. *Maternal deprivation reassessed*. Harmondsworth, England: Penguin, 1972.
Rutter, M. *Helping troubled children*. Harmondsworth, England: Penguin, 1975.
Rutter, M. Other family influences. In M. Rutter & L. Hersov (Eds.), *Child psychiatry. Modern approaches*. Oxford: Blackwell, 1977.
Rutter, M. Introduction. In M. Rutter (Ed.), *Scientific foundation of developmental psychiatry*. London: Heinemann, 1980a.
Rutter, M. Attachment and the development of social relationships. In M. Rutter (Ed.), *Scientific foundation of developmental psychiatry*. London: Heinemann, 1980b.
Rutter, M. Maternal deprivation, 1972–1978. In S. Chess & A. Thomas (Eds.), *Annual progress in child psychiatry and child development 1980*. New York: Brunner/Mazel, 1980c.
Rutter, M., Tizard, J., & Hersov, V. *Education, health and behaviour*. London: Longman, 1970.
Sameroff, A. J., & Chandler, M. J. Reproductive risk and the continuum of caretaking casualty. In F. D. Horowitz, M. Hetherington, S. Scarr-Salapatek, & G. Siegel (Eds.), *Review of child development research* (Vol. IV). Chicago: University of Chicago Press, 1975.
Sander, L. W. The longitudinal course of early mother–child interaction: Cross-case comparisons in a sample of mother–child pairs. In B. M. Foss (Ed.), *Determinants of infant behavior* (Vol. IV). London: Methuen, 1969.
Sander, L. W. Infant and caretaking environment: Investigation and conceptualization of adaptive behavior in a system of increasing complexity. In E. J. Anthony (Ed.), *The child psychiatrist as investigator*. New York: Plenum Press, 1974.
Sander, L. W. Issues in early mother–child interaction. In E. N. Rexford, L. W. Sander, & T. Shapiro (Eds.), *Infant psychiatry: A new synthesis*. New Haven, Conn.: Yale University, 1976.
Sandler, J., & Joffe, W. G. Notes on childhood depression. *International Journal of Psychoanalysis*, 1965, *46*, 88–96.
Sarpong, P. *Girls' nubility rites in Ashanti*. Accra-Tema, Ghana: Ghana Publishing, 1977.

Schaefer, E. S. A circumplex model for maternal behavior. *Journal of Abnormal and Social Psychology,* 1959, *59,* 226–235.
Schaefer, E. S. A configurational analysis of children's reports of parent behavior. *Journal of Consulting Psychology,* 1965, *29,* 552–557.
Schaefer, E. S., & Bell, R. Q. Development of a Parental Attitude Research Instrument. *Child Development,* 1958, *29,* 339–361.
Schaffer, H. R. The too-cohesive family: A form of group pathology. *International Journal of Social Psychiatry,* 1964, *10,* 266–275.
Schaffer, H. R. *The growth of sociability.* Harmondsworth, England: Penguin, 1971.
Schaffer, H. R., & Emerson, P. E. The development of social attachments in infancy. *Monographs in Social Research and Child Development,* 1964, *29,* No. 94.
Schless, A. P., Schwartz, L., Goetz, C., & Mendels, J. How depressives view the significance of life events. *British Journal of Psychiatry,* 1974, *125,* 406–410.
Schvaneveldt, J. D. Development of film test for the measurement of perceptions toward maternal overprotection. *Journal of Genetic Psychology,* 1968a, *112*(2), 255–266.
Schvaneveldt, J. D. Correlates of perceptions towards maternal overprotection. *Journal of Genetic Psychology,* 1968b, *112,* 267–273.
Sears, W. H., Mussen, P. H., & Harris, C. W. Relationships among child-training practices. *American Sociological Review,* 1955, *20,* 137–148.
Sebald, H. *Momism: The silent disease of America.* Chicago: Nelson Hall, 1976.
Seligman, M. E. P. *Helplessness.* San Francisco: Freeman, 1975.
Sharma, K. C., & Koshy, S. Psychological impact of cerebral palsy on patients and on their parents. *Journal of Rehabilitation in Asia,* 1972, *13,* 27–32.
Shaw, C. R., & Lucas, A. R. *The psychiatric disorders of childhood* (2nd ed.). New York: Appleton-Century-Crofts, 1970.
Shaw, P. M. *The nature of social phobia.* Paper presented at the annual conference of the British Psychological Society, York, 1976.
Shere, M. O. Twin studies. In W. M. Cruikshank & G. M. Raus (Eds.), *Cerebral palsy. Its individual and community problems.* Syracuse, N.Y.: Syracuse University Press, 1955.
Sigal, J. J., Chagoya, L., Villenueve, C., & Mayerovitch, J. Later psychological consequences of near-fatal illness (nephrosis) in early childhood: Some preliminary findings. *Laval Medical,* 1971, *42,* 103–108.
Skynner, A. C. R. An open-systems, group analytic approach to family therapy. In A. S. Gurman & D. P. Kniskern (Eds.), *Handbook of family therapy.* New York: Brunner/Mazel, 1981.
Slater, E., & Roth, M. *Clinical psychiatry.* London: Bailliére, Tindall and Cassell, 1969.
Snaith, R. P. A clinical investigation of phobias. *British Journal of Psychiatry,* 1968, *114,* 673–698.
Solyom, L. Beck, P., Solyom, & Hugel, R. Some etiological factors in phobic neurosis. *Canadian Psychiatric Association Journal,* 1974, *19,* 69–78.
Solyom, L., Silberfeld, M., & Solyom, C. Maternal overprotection in the aetiol-

ogy of agoraphobia. *Canadian Psychiatric Association Journal*, 1976, *21*, 109–113.
Spitzer, R. L., & Endicott, J. *Schedule for Affective Disorders and Schizophrenia. SADS* (3rd ed.). Typescript from New York State Psychiatric Institute, 1979.
Spitzer. R. L., Endicott, J., & Robins, E. *Research diagnostic criteria for a selected group of functional disorders.* Instrument No. 58. New York: New York State Psychiatric Institute, 1975.
Sroufe, L. A. Socioemotional development. In J. D. Osofsky (Ed.), *Handbook of infant development.* New York: Wiley, 1979.
Staten, R. D. Comparison and evaluation of selected attitude of mothers and fathers of mentally retarded children. *Dissertation Abstracts International*, 1972. (University Microfilms No. 72–18623)
Stechler, G., & Carpenter, G. A viewpoint on early affective development. In J. Hellmuth (Ed.), *Exceptional infant* (Vol. I): *Normal infant.* New York: Brunner/Mazel, 1967.
Steinhausen, H. C. Hemophilia: A psychological study in chronic disease in juveniles. *Journal of Psychosomatic Research*, 1976, *20*, 461–467.
Stendler, C. B. Possible causes of overdependency in young children. *Child Development*, 1954, *25*, 125–146.
Stierlin, H. Family theory: An introduction. In A. Burton (Ed.), *Operational theories of personality.* New York: Brunner/Mazel, 1974.
Stoller, R. J. Parental influences in male transsexualism. In R. Green, & J. Money (Ed.), *Transsexualism and sex reassignment.* Baltimore: Johns Hopkins Press, 1969.
Strecker, E. A. *Their mothers' sons: The psychiatrist examines an American problem.* Philadelphia: Lippincott, 1946.
Sturgeon, D., Kuipers, L., Berkowitz, R., Turpin, G., & Leff, J. Psychophysiological responses of schizophrenic patients to high and low expressed emotion relatives. *British Journal of Psychiatry*, 1981, *138*, 40–45.
Susser, M. *Causal thinking in the health sciences: Concepts and strategies of epidemiology.* New York: Oxford University Press, 1973.
Susser, M. The epidemiology of life stress. *Psychological Medicine*, 1981, *11*, 1–8.
Tarrier, N., Vaughn, C., Lader, M. H., & Leff, J. P. Bodily reactions to people and events in schizophrenics. *Archives of General Psychiatry*, 1979, *36*, 311–315.
Terhune, W. B. The phobic syndrome. *Archives of General Psychiatry*, 1949, *62*, 162–172.
Tietze, T. A study of mothers of schizophrenic patients. *Psychiatry*, 1949, *12*, 55–65.
Trause, M. A., Klaus, M. H., & Kennell, J. H. Maternal behavior in mammals. In M. H. Klaus & J. H. Kennell (Eds.): *Maternal–infant bonding.* St. Louis: Mosby, 1976.
Tucker, W. I. Diagnosis and treatment of phobic reaction, American Journal of Psychiatry, 1956, 112, 825–830.
Uddenberg, N., Wålinder, J., & Höjerback, T. Parental contact in male and female transsexuals. *Acta Psychiatrica Scandinavica*, 1979, *60*, 113–120.

Van Lawick-Goodall, J. Mother–offspring relationships in free-ranging chimpanzees. In D. Morris (Ed.), *Primate ethology*. London: Weidenfeld & Nicolson, 1967.
Van Lawick-Goodall, J. *In the shadow of man*. London: Collins, 1971.
Vaughn, C. E., & Leff, J. P. The influence of family and social factors on the course of psychiatric illness. *British Journal of Psychiatry*, 1976, *129*, 125–137.
Wahl, C. W. Some antecedent factors in the family histories of 392 schizophrenics. *American Journal of Psychiatry*, 1954, *110*, 668–676.
Wahl, C. W. Some antecedent factors in the family histories of 568 male schizophrenics of the U.S. Navy. *American Journal of Psychiatry*, 1956, *113*, 201–210.
Wålinder, J. Transsexualism: Definition, prevalence and sex distribution. *Acta Psychiatrica Scandinavica*, 1968, *203*, 255–258.
Waring, M. & Ricks, D. Family patterns of children who become adult schizophrenics. *Journal of Nervous and Mental Disease*, 1965, *140*, 351–364.
Waters, E., Wippman, J., & Sroufe, L. A. Attachment, positive affect, and competence in the peer group: Two studies in construct validation. *Child Development*, 1979, *50*, 821–829.
Webster, A. S. The development of phobias in married women. *Psychological Monographs*, 1953, *67*, No. 367.
Weissman, M. M., & Klerman, G. L. Sex differences and the epidemiology of depression. *Archives of General Psychiatry*, 1977, *34*, 98–111.
Weller, L., Eytan, R., & Sollel, M. Birth order and risk taking among kibbutz and city youth. *British Journal of Social and Clinical Psychology*, 1976, *15*, 103–104.
Wender, P., Rosenthal, D., Zahn, T., & Kety, S. The psychiatric adjustment of the adopting parents of schizophrenics. *American Journal of Psychiatry*, 1971, *127*, 1013–1018.
Wergeland, H. Elective mutism. *Acta Psychiatrica Scandinavica*, 1979, *59*, 218–228.
Werry, J. S. Psychosomatic disorders, psychogenic symptoms and hospitalization. In H. C. Quay & J. S. Werry (Eds.), *Psychopathological disorders of childhood*. New York: Wiley, 1979.
Wertham, F. Matricidal impulse: Critique of Freud's interpretation of Hamlet. *Journal of Criminal Psychopathology*, 1941, *2*, 455–464.
Wertheim, E. S. Person–environment interaction: The epigenesis of autonomy and competence. II Review of developmental literature (normal development). *British Journal of Medical Psychology*, 1975a, *48*, 95–111.
Wertheim, E. S. Person–environment interaction: The epigenesis of autonomy and competence. III Autonomy and para-liguistic and bilinguistic action systems: Review of developmental literature (normal development). *British Journal of Medical Psychology*, 1975b, *48*, 237–256.
Wertheim, E. S. Person–environment interaction: The epigenesis of autonomy and competence. IV Their interrelationship. Theoretical considerations and review of developmental literature (normal development). *British Journal of Medical Psychology*, 1975c, *48*, 391–402.

Wetter, J. The relation of parent attitude to learning disorder. Dissertation Abstracts International, 1971 (University Microfilms, No. 71-10653).
White, P. *The eye of the storm.* London: Cape, 1973.
Whiting, J. W. M. *Becoming a Kwoma: Teaching and learning in a New Guinea tribe.* New Haven: Yale University Press, 1941.
Wilson, D. C. Families of manic-depressives. *Diseases of the Nervous System,* 1951, *12,* 363–369.
Wilson, E. O. *On human nature.* Cambridge, Mass.: Harvard University Press, 1978.
Wilson, P., & Lovibond, S. *Self-Analysis Questionnaire.* Typescript from the School of Psychology, University of New South Wales, 1979.
Wing, J. K. Clinical concepts of schizophrenia. In J. Wing (Ed.), *Schizophrenia: Towards a new synthesis.* London: Academic Press, 1978.
Wolpe, J. *Psychotherapy by reciprocal inhibition.* Stanford, Calif.: Stanford University Press, 1958.
World Health Organization. *Mental disorders: Glossary and guide to their classification in accordance with the Ninth Revision of the International Classification of Diseases.* Geneva: W. H. O., 1978.
Wright, D. S. *The psychology of moral behaviour.* Harmondsworth, England: Penguin, 1971.
Wylie, P. *Generation of vipers* (Annotated version). London: Muller, 1955.
Wylie, R. C. *The self concept.* Lincoln, Neb.: University of Nebraska Press, 1961.
Wynne, L. C. Current concepts about schizophrenics and family relationships. *Journal of Nervous and Mental Disease,* 1981, *169,* 82–89.
Yarrow, L. J. Separation from parents in early childhood. In M. L. Hoffman & L. W. Hoffman (Eds.), *Review of child development research* (Vol. I). New York: Russell Sage Foundation, 1964.
Zborowski, M. Cultural components in responses to pain. *Journal of Social Issues,* 1952, *8,* 16–30.
Zuckerman, M., Oltean, M., & Monashkin, I. The parental attitudes of mothers of schizophrenics. *Journal of Consulting Psychology,* 1958a, *22,* 307–310.
Zuckerman, M., Ribback, B. B., Monashkin, I., & Norton, J. A. Normative data and factor analysis of the Parental Attitudes Research Instrument. *Journal of Consulting Psychology,* 1958b, *22,* 165–171.

Index

Adolescence
  individuation process in, 48
  psychosocial development in, 49–53
Adolescent(s)
  foreclosed, 51
  identity achieved, 52
Adult heterosexual system in macaques, 79
Adulthood, disorders in, overprotection and, 39–40
Affect hunger, maternal overprotection and, 22, 263
Affectionate constraint
  care-eliciting behavior and, 213, 216, 219–220, 275
  defined by the PBI, 121
  in Greek families, 229, 232, 274–275
  in parental overprotection, 269, 273–275
Affectionless control, see Control, affectionless
Aggressive play in peer affectional system in macaques, 78–79
Agoraphobia, 185. See also Phobic states
Alloplastic regulation of parent-infant interaction, 60
Ambivalence stage in maternal affectional system in macaques, 77
Anal phase of personality development, 43
Anorexia nervosa, parental overprotection and, 34

Anxiety
  attachment and, 56
  in child, parental overprotection and, 32, 33
  maternal
    attachment and, 283–284
    maternal overprotection and, 265, 266–267, 280–282
    parental overprotection and, 27–29
  studies of, 174–184
    on adopted group, 181–182
    on nonclinical group, 177–181
    on patients with anxiety neurosis, 175–177
Anxiety neurosis
  features of, 174
  study of patients with, 175–177
Anxious attachment, pathogenic parenting and, 278
Asthma
  parental overprotection and, 34
  study on, 195–202
Asthmatogenic mother, 195–197
Attachment. See also Mother and child, tie between
  anxiety and, 56
  and dependency, comparison of, 56
  development of, variables influencing, 57
  disorders of, symbiotic, parental overprotection and, 32

317

Attachment (*continued*)
  human, sensitive period for, 59
  maternal, in maternal affectional system in macaques, 77
  parental overprotection and, 283–284
  pathogenic parenting and anxious, 278
  processes of, ethological-evolutionary views of, 53–61
Attachment behavior(s)
  of infant, development phases of, 54–55
  of mother, 58–59
Attachment-exploration in infant development, 62
Attachment stage in infant-mother attachment in macaques, 76
Attributable risk, 127
Autonomy, development of, in early childhood, 62–65
Authoritarian mother, 24
Authoritative mother, 24
Autistic phase, normal, in separation-individuation process in childhood, 45
Autoplastic regulation of parent-infant interaction, 60

Behavior(s)
  attachment
    of infant, developmental phases of, 34–55
    of mother, 58–59
  care-eliciting, study on, 210–211. *See also* Care-eliciting behavior
  independent, prevention of
    in maternal overprotection, 21
    parental overprotection and, 269
  instinctive, characteristics of, 54
  parental, depression and, 154–155
Binding, parental overprotection and, 26
Bipolar depression, 152–153
Bipolar regulation in development of autonomy in infant, 63
Bonding, *see* Attachment; Mother and child, tie between

Care
  excessive, parental overprotection and, 269
  father deficient in, transsexualism and, 204–206, 208–209
  Jewish student group, 230
  mother deficient in, maternal overprotection and, 258

  parents deficient in
    anxiety and, 175–176, 179–184
    depression and, 154–158, 160–161, 166, 169–170, 172–173
    phobic states and, 189–190, 193–194
    schizophrenia and, 145, 150
  parents excessive in
    dependency and, 220
    hypochondriasis and, 219–220
Care-eliciting behavior
  definition of, 210
  study on, 211–221
Child(ren)
  characteristics of, maternal overprotection and, 264
  development of
    cultural influences on, 72–75
    family and, 69–72
    fathers and, 65–67
    peers and, 67–69
  index, developmental history of, 246–247
  in maternal overprotection study, 241–242
  Jewish, development of, 73–74
  and mother, tie between, 41–83. *See also* Mother and child, tie between
  of mothers in maternal overprotection study, 241
  of overprotective versus other mothers, 246
  WASP, development of, 74–75
Child-centeredness, parental overprotection and, 29–30
Chidhood
  disorders in, 33–35
  early, development of autonomy in, 62–65
Children's Reports of Parental Behavior Inventory for measuring parental behaviors, 90–92
Chronically ill children, overprotection of, 35–39
Clinical examples of parental overprotection, 3–8
Comfort stage in infant-mother attachment in macaques, 76
Confusion, identity, in adolescence, 52
Consequences of parental overprotection, 31–40
Consolidation of individuality in separation-individuation process in childhood, 47

Constancy, object
  in separation-individuation process in childhood, 47
  stage of, in ego development, 44
Constraint, affectionate
  care-eleciting behavior and, 213, 216, 219–220, 275
  defined by the PBI, 121
  in Greek families, 229, 232, 274–275
  in parental overprotection, 269, 273
Contact, excessive, in maternal overprotection, 20
Control
  affectionless
    anxiety and, 175–176, 179–184
    depression and, 156–158, 160–161, 166, 169–170, 172–173
    disorders associated with, 275–276
    phobic states and, 189–190, 193–194
    possible effects of, 277–279
    schizophrenia and, 150–151
  locus of, depression and, 163–164
  in parental overprotection, 9–10, 268–269, 273, 275–279
Controlling personality, issue of, 24
Cross-cultural studies of parental overprotection, 222–232. *See also* Greek families in Australia; Jewish families in Australia
Cultural influences on mother-child tie, 72–75

Delegating, parental overprotection and, 26
Delinquency, parental overprotection and, 34
Dependency
  and attachment, comparison of, 56
  parental overprotection and, 33
  study on, 210–221. *See also* Care-eliciting behavior
Depressed mood, 152
Depression
  affectionless control and, 156–158, 160–161, 166, 169–170, 172–173, 275
  bipolar, 152–153
  endogenous, 152–153
  level of, 110–111
    PBI validity and, 114–115
  locus of control and, 163–164
  major, 153
  neurotic, 153

parental behavior and, 154–155
parental overprotection and, 32–33
PBI scores and, neuroticism and, 171–172
psychotic, 152–153
reactive, 153
self-esteem and, 161, 163
studies of, 152–173
  on adopted group, 166–169
  on nonclinical group, 159–166
  on patients with clinical depressive disorders, 156–158
  replication, on neurotic depressive patients, 158–159
unipolar, 153
Depressive patients
  clinical, patients with, studies on, 156–158
  neurotic, replication study on, 158–159
Detachment process, ethological-evolutionary views of, 61–65
Developmental history of index child
  in maternal overprotection study, 241–242
  of overprotective versus other mothers, 246–247
Diabetes, parental overprotection and, 34
Differentiation
  of family members, failure of, parental overprotection and, 25
  in separation-individuation process in childhood, 45–46
Diffusion, identity, in adolescence, 52
Direct effects model of pubertal maturation and psychological development in adolescence, 51
Disabilities, learning, parental overprotection and, 34
Disorders in adulthood, overprotection and, 39–40
Dominant matriarch syndrome
  clinical example of, 4–5
  school phobia and, 33–34
Dual-process theories of socialization, 68

Education
  of mothers in maternal overprotection study, 240
  of overprotective versus other mothers, 244
Ego psychologists, theories of, on parent-child tie, 43
Elective mutism, parental overprotection and, 34

EMBU for measuring parental behaviors, 92–93
Emotion, expressed, in relatives, schizophrenic relapse and, 138–142
Employment
  of mothers in maternal overprotection study, 240
  of overprotective versus other mothers, 244
Ethological-evolutionary views
  of parent-child attachment, 53–61
  of parent-child detachment, 61–65
Expelling, parental overprotection and, 26
Exploratory stage in peer affectional system in macaques, 78
Expressed emotion in relatives, schizophrenic relapse and, 138–142

Factor analyses of determinants or correlates of maternal overprotection, 252, (Table) 253
Family, influences of, on mother-child tie, 69–72
Family background
  of mothers in maternal overprotection study, 239–240
  of overprotective versus other mothers, 244
Family projection process, parental overprotection and, 28–29
Family systems theories of parental overprotection, 24–30
Father(s)
  relevance of, to child development, 65–67
  of schizophrenic patients, 133, 134
  of transsexuals, 204–206, 208–209
Fels Scales for measuring parental behaviors, 87–88
Fictional descriptions of parental overprotection, 9–13. See also Parental overprotection, fictional descriptions of
Focalization in development of autonomy in infant, 63
Foreclosed adolescents, 51

Genital phase of personality development, 43
Greek families in Australia
  circumstances of, 222–223
  study of parental overprotection in, 225–232

Handicapped children, overprotection of, 35–39
Heterosexual affectional system in macaques, 79
Hunger, affect, maternal overprotection and, 22, 263
Husbands of overprotective mothers, 23, 263–264
Hypochondriasis
  parental overprotection and, 34
  study on, 210–221. See also Care-eliciting behavior

Identity
  formation of, in adolescence, 51
  in separation-individuation process in childhood, 45
Identity achieved adolescent, 52
Identity confusion in adolescence, 52
Identity diffusion in adolescence, 52
Illness
  chronic, in children, overprotection and, 35–39
  parental response to, PBI scores and, 217–219
Indepedent behavior, prevention of
  in maternal overprotection, 21
  parental overprotection and, 269
Individuality, consolidation of, in separation-individuation process in childhood, 47
Individuation process in adolescence, 48
Infant(s)
  attachment behavior of, developmental phases of, 54–55
  development of, fathers and, 65–67
  and parent, interaction between
    sex differences in, 66–67
    synchrony in, 60–61, 80–81
  symbiotic attachment disorders of, parental overprotection and, 32
Infant affectional system in macaques, 75–77
Infant heterosexual stage in macaques, 79
Infant initiative in development of autonomy in infant, 63
Infantilization
  maternal overprotection and, 21
  parental overprotection and, 269
Initiative, infant, in development of autonomy in infant, 63
Instinctive behavior, characteristics of, 54

Index

Interactive play in peer affectional system in macaques, 78
Isolation, parental overprotection and, 269

Jewish child, development of, 73–74
Jewish families in Australia
  circumstances of, 224
  study of parental overprotection, 225–232

Latency stage of psychosocial development, 49
Learning disabilities, parental overprotection and, 34
Locomotor stage of psychosocial development, 49

Marital relationships
  of mothers in maternal overprotection study, 242–243
  of overprotective versus other mothers, 247
Marital skew, schizophrenia and, 134
Marital skism, schizophrenia and, 134
Marriage
  of mothers in maternal overprotection study, 240
  of overprotective versus other mothers, 246
Maternal affectional system in macaques, 77–78
Maternal drive, maternal overprotection and, 264–265
Maternal overprotection, 14–24. *See also* Momism
  characteristics of, 19–24
  controlling personality in, 24
  determinants or correlates of, 252–259
  husbands and, 23
  influences on, 233–267
    study of, 235–267
  origins of, 22
  PBI as appropriate measure of, assessment of, 243
  sources and mechanisms of, 280–285
  theory of, 23
Maternal Overprotection Questionnaire for measuring parental behaviors, 92
Maternal self-report measure of overprotection, Parental Opinion Form as, 122–125, 270
Maternal separation stage in maternal affectional system in macaques, 77–78

Matricide, parental overprotection and, 35
Mature interaction stage in peer affectional system in macaques, 79
Measurement of parental overprotection, 85–125, 270–273
Mediated effects model of pubertal maturation and psychological development in adolescence, 51
Melancholia, 153
Momism. *See also* Maternal overprotection
  characteristics of, 19–24
  commentary on, 14–19
  consequences of, 18
  factors promoting, 16–17
  prevention of, 18
  varieties of, 15, 17–18
Moms, varieties of, 15, 17–18
Mood, depressed, 152
Moratorium phase in adolescence, 52
Mother(s)
  asthmatogenic, 195–197
  authoritarian, 24
  authoritative, 24
  and child, tie between. *See also* Attachment
    cultural influences in, 72–75
    ethological-evolutionary views in, 53–65
    family influences on, 69–72
    nature and factors influencing evolution of, 41–83
    overview of, 80–83
    peer influences on, 67–69, 72
    psychoanalytic views of, 43–48
    psychosocial views of, 48–53
    relevance of fathers in, 65–67
    subhuman primate studies in, 75–79
  overprotective and other, distinctions between 243–251
  permissive, 24
  personality of, maternal overprotection and, 265
  schizophrenogenic, 132–137
Mother-Child Relationship Evaluation for measuring parental behaviors, 89
Musculo-anal stage of psychosocial development, 49
Mutism, elective, parental overprotection and, 34
Mutual synchronization in development of autonomy in infant, 63

Neurosis
  affectionless control and, 275–277
  anxiety
    features of, 174
    patients with, study of, 175–177
Neurotic depression, 153
Neurotic depressive patient, replication study on, 158–159
Neuroticism, depression and PBI scores and, 171–172

Obesity, parental overprotection and, 34
Object constancy in separation-individuation process in childhood, 47
Object constancy stage in ego development, 44
Object permanence in separation-individuation process in childhood, 47
Obstetric history
  of mothers in maternal overprotection study, 241
  of overprotective versus other mothers, 246
Oral phase of personality development, 43
Oral-sensory stage of psychosocial development, 49
Orestes complex, parental overprotection and, 35
Overinhibited personality structure, parental overprotection and, 34
Overpossessiveness in parental overprotection, 268
Overprotection
  of chronically ill or handicapped children, 35–39
  maternal, 14–24, 233–267. See also Maternal overprotection; Momism
  self-report measure of, Parental Opinion Form as, 122–124
  parental, see Parental overprotection
Overprotective mothers and other mothers, distinctions between, 243–251

Parent(s)
  behavior of, depression and, 154–155
  characteristics of
    and onset of schizophrenia, studies relating, 133–137
    and schizophrenic relapse, studies relating, 137–142
  and child, attachment and detachment processes between, theories of 43–83. See also Mother and child, tie between
  expressed emotion in, schizophrenic relapse and, 138–142
  and infant, interaction between
    sex differences in, 66–67
    synchrony in, 60–61, 80–81
  liking of
    PBI scores and, 110, 272
    PBI validity and, 114
  schizophrenia in, PBI scores for, 146–147
Parent-Child Relations Questionnaire for measuring parental behaviors, 89
Parent Opinion Form, 122–125, 294–295
  in measurement of parental overprotection, 270
Parental Attitude Research Instrument for measuring parental behaviors, 90
Parental Bonding Instrument (PBI), (Table) 288–289
  assessment of, as appropriate measure of maternal overprotection, 243
  data collection for
    in Oxford, England, 100–102, 290
    in Sydney, Australia, 97–100, 290
  development of, 95–97
  discussion of, 111–120
  in measurement
    of parental behaviors, 92
    of parental overprotection, 270–273
    social desirability and, 110, 272–273
    validity of, 103–111, 271–272
  normative data from, in nonclinical studies (Table) 290
  reliability of, 112–113
  in study of schizophrenia, 144–145
  revised
    normative data from (Table) 291
    reliability of, 292
    sociodemographic influences on, (Table) 291
    validity of, 292–293
  scores on
    and age initial hospitalization for schizophrenia, 147–148
    in anxiety
      in adopted children, 181–184
      clinical, 175–177, 182–184
      nonclinical, 177–184
    in asthma, 199–202

capacity of, to predict readmission for schizophrenia, 148, (Table) 149
in care-eliciting behavior, 212–221
in depression
  in adopted children, 168–169
  clinical, 156–158, 170–172
  neurotic, 158–159, 170–172
  nonclinical, 160–164, 166, 170–172
extraneous influences on, 110–111
in Greek families, 226–230, 232
in Jewish families, 230–232
maternal overprotection and, 243, 252–262, 265–267
ordinal position and, 119–120
in phobic states, 189–194
for schizophrenic parents, 146–147
sex of recipient and, 118–119
social class and, 119
in transsexualism, 205–209
in schizophrenia, 142–151. *See also* Schizophrenia, PBI study on
uses of, 120–122
validity of, 114–118, 271–273
studies on, 103–110
Parent Opinion Form, 122–125, 270
development of, 122–124
Parental overprotection
anxiety and, 174–184. *See also* Anxiety
association of, with specific disorders and personality characteristics, 274–277
asthma and, 195–202. *See also* Asthma
care-eliciting behavior and, 210–221. *See also* Care-eliciting behavior
clinical examples of, 3–8
  depression in, 5–8
  dominant matriarch syndrome in, 4–5
  histrionic personality traits in, 5
components of, 3, 268–269
consequences of, 31–40
cross-cultural studies of, 222–232. *See also* Greek families in Australia; Jewish families in Australia
definition and calibration of, studies on, 87–94
  ad hoc questionnaires in, 87
  attitude inventory in, 90
  Children's Reports of Parental Behavior Inventory (CRPBI) in, 90–92
  EMBU in, 92–93
  Fels Scales in, 87–88
  Maternal Overprotection Questionnaire (MOQ) in, 92
  Mother-Child Relationship Evaluation in, 89
  Parent-Child Relations Questionnaire (PCR) in, 89
  Parental Attitude Research Instrument (PARI) in, 90
  Parental Bonding Instrument (PBI) in, 92
  standardized rating scales in, 87
  validity of, 94
depression and, 152–173. *See also* Depression
family systems theories of, 24–30
fictional descriptions of
  American, 9–10
  Australian, 10–12
  British, 12–13
  common themes in, 13
measurement of, 85–125, 270–273
over two generations, 265–266
phobic states and, 185–194. *See also* Phobic states
possible effects of affectionless control in, 277–279
research studies on, 127–285
schizophrenia and, 131–151. *See also* Schizophrenia
transsexualism and, 203–209. *See also* Transsexualism
Peer affectional system in macaques, 78–79
Peer influences on mother-child tie, 67–69, 72
Peptic ulcer, parental overprotection and, 34
Permanence, object, in separation-individuation process in childhood, 47
Permissive mother, 24
Personality
  controlling, issue of, 24
  of mother, maternal overprotection and, 265
Phallic phase of personality development, 43
Phobia, school, parental overprotection and, 33
Phobic states, study on, 105–194
Physicians, primary, utilization of, study on, 210–221. *See also* Care-eliciting behavior

Plaintive set, 114, 158–159, 171–173, 272
Possessiveness in parental overprotection, 268
Practicing subphase in separation-individuation process in childhood, 46
Preadolescent heterosexual stage in macaques, 79
Protection, maternal, in maternal affectional system in macaques, 77
Psychoanalytic views of parent-child attachment and detachment processes, 43–48
Psychosocial views in parent-child attachment and detachment processes, 48–53
Psychotic depression, 152
Puberty and psychosocial development, 49–53
Puberty rites, cultural differences in, 52–53

Rapprochement subphase in separation-individuation process in childhood, 46–47
Reactive depression, 153
Reciprocal exchange in development of autonomy in infant, 63
Reciprocity, practice of, in development of autonomy in infant, 63
Reflex stage
 in macaques, 76–79
Regulation
 bipolar, in development of autonomy in infant, 63
 initial, in development of autonomy in infant, 63
 interpersonal, shared, in development of autonomy in infant, 63
Regulatory role reversal in development of autonomy in infant, 63
Rejection
 of handicapped child, overprotection and, 37–38
 maternal, in maternal affectional system in macaques, 77–78
Relative risk, 127–128, 274–275
Reliability
 of Parental Bonding Instrument, 112–113
 in study of schizophrenia, 144–145
 of Parent Opinion Form, assessment of, 123–124
Risk
 attributable, 127
 relative, 127–128, 274–275

Schizophrenia, 131–151
 historical discussion of, 131–142
 onset of, studies relating parental characteristics to, 133–137
 PBI study on, 142–151
 PBI scores
  and age at initial hospitalization, 147–148
  capacity of, to predict readmission, 148, (Table) 149
  for "schizophrenic" parents in, 146–147
 reliability of PBI in, 144–145
 relapse of, studies relating parental characteristics to, 137–142
School phobia, parental overprotection and, 33–34
School refusal, parental overprotection and, 33–34
Secondary drive theory of parent-child attachment and detachment processes, 43
Security stage in infant-mother attachment in macaques, 76
Self-assertion in development of autonomy in infant, 63
Self-esteem, depression and, 161, 163
Self-integration, parental overprotection and, 26–27
Self-reliance, prevention of, in maternal overprotection, 21
Sensitive period for maternal attachment, 59
Sensitivity, maternal, in mother-infant interaction, 61, 80–81
Separation
 maternal, in maternal affectional system in macaques, 77–78
 in separation-individuation process in childhood, 45
Separation-individuation process in childhood, 44–47
Separation stage in infant mother attachment in macaques, 76–77
Sex differences
 in maternal overprotection, 262–263
 in parent-child interaction, 66–67
Shared interpersonal regulation in development of autonomy in infant, 63
Single-process theories of socialization, 68
Skew, marital, schizophrenia and, 134
Skism, marital, schizophrenia and, 134

Social desirability bias of PBI scores, 110, 272
Social phobias, 185–186. *See also* Phobic states
Social relationships
  of mothers in maternal overprotection study, 242–243
  of overprotective versus other mothers, 247
Socialization
  impaired, parental overprotection and, 282–283
  of mothers in maternal overprotection study, 240
  of overprotective versus other mothers, 244
  theories of, 68
Sociodemographic details of overprotective versus other mothers, 244, (Table) 245
Speech, delayed, parental overprotection and, 34
Stress, massive, parental response to, overprotection as, 35
Stuttering, parental overprotection and, 34
Subhuman primate studies on mother-child tie, 75–79
Symbiotic attachment disorders, parental overprotection and, 32

Symbiotic phase in separation-individuation process in childhood, 45–46
Synchronization, mutual, in development of autonomy in infant, 63
Synchrony
  maternal anxiety and, 283–284
  in parent-infant interaction, 60–61, 80–81

Transitional stage in maternal affectional system in macaques, 77
Transsexualism, study on, 203–209
Triangulation, parental overprotection and, 28–29

Ulcer, peptic, parental overprotection and, 34
Unipolar depression, 153

Validity
  of Parental Bonding Instrument, 114–118, 270–273
  of Parent Opinion Form, assessment of, 124, 270

White Anglo-Saxon Protestant (WASP) child, development of, 74–75

a
b
3 c
4 d
5 e
6 f
7 g
8 h
9 i
8 0 j